Aquinata Böckmann, O.S.B.

Perspectives on the Rule of St. Benedict

Expanding Our Hearts in Christ

Translated by

Matilda Handl, O.S.B., and Marianne Burkhard, O.S.B.
Edited by Marianne Burkhard, O.S.B.

LITURGICAL PRESS

Collegeville, Minnesota

www.litpress.org

Cover design by Joachim Rhoades, O.S.B.

In 1986 this book was published in German under the title *Perspektiven der Regula Bendicti: Ein Kommentar zum Prolog und den Kapiteln 53, 58, 72, 73* by Vier-Türme GmbH, © by Vier-Türme GmbH, D-97359 Münsterschwarzach Abtei, Germany.

The editor of this volume is especially indebted to the following reference works:

John Cassian, *The Conferences.* Trans. B. Ramsey, O.P. New York: Paulist, 1997; *The Institutes.* Trans. B. Ramsey, O.P. New York: Newman, 2000.

The Sayings of the Desert Fathers: The Alphabetical Collection. Trans. B. Ward. New York: MacMillan, 1975.

The Rule of the Master. Trans. L. Eberle, O.S.B. Kalamazoo: Cistercian, 1977.

John E. Rotelle, O.S.A., ed., *The Works of Saint Augustine: A Translation for the 21st Century.* Part III, *Sermons,* trans. E. Hill, O.P., 11 vols.; Part III, *Expositions on the Psalms,* trans. Marian Boulding, O.S.B., vols. 15–19. Hyde Park, NY: New City Press, November 2001.

| 1 | 2 | 3 | 4 | 5 | 6 | 7 | 8 |

Library of Congress Cataloging-in-Publication Data

Böckmann, Aquinata.
    [Perspektiven der Regula Benedicti. English]
    Perspectives on the Rule of St. Benedict : expanding our hearts in Christ / Aquinata Böckmann ; translated by Matilda Handl and Marianne Burkhard ; edited by Marianne Burkhard.
        p. cm.
    Cover title: Perspectives on the Rule of Saint Benedict.
    Summary: "A commentary on parts of the Rule of St. Benedict (prologue and chapters 53, 58, 72, and 73)"—Provided by publisher.
    Includes bibliographical references (p.   ) and index.
    ISBN 13: 978-0-8146-3041-9 (pbk. : alk. paper)
    ISBN 10: 0-8146-3041-3 (pbk. : alk. paper)
    1. Benedict, Saint, Abbot of Monte Cassino. Regula. 2. Monasticism and religious orders—Rules. I. Burkhard, Marianne. II. Title. III. Title: Perspectives on the Rule of Saint Benedict.

BX3004.Z5B6313   2005
255'.106—dc22   2004026754

Contents

Preface

This commentary has developed from practical work with the Rule of Benedict and especially from collaboration with others: from lectures and seminars at Sant'Anselmo in Rome on aspects of monastic life and the Rule of Benedict, from meetings of formators in Brazil and Germany, from seminars, talks, and group work on chapters and topics of the Rule of Benedict in Benedictine communities, and also from retreats about the spirituality of Benedict. Therefore, this book is a living dialogue with all those who posed questions, made suggestions or contributions. In addition there is my personal experience, the adventure of being engaged with a saint who took me in hand, corrected and educated me, and kept leading me to Sacred Scripture.

This commentary aims at developing a perspective of the Rule of Benedict (RB), patiently feeling our way to the concerns of Benedict so that his message may become clearer for today and tomorrow. It dares to build a bridge, attempting to unite the fruits of historical-critical research with impulses for our spirituality and the practical interpretation.

In the manner of biblical commentary, and building on the results of research, the chapters of the Rule will be explained in their historical context as a help for interpretation in our communities. The book's primary purpose is not an introduction to scholarly problems or yielding new results in research. Aware of pertinent controversies, I will try to do my work based on certain or more trustworthy positions. To avoid excessive scientific weight, questions concerning text variations in manuscripts or which source is applicable to a certain verse will be treated only when they are significant for the interpretation and might result in a different meaning.

As in biblical exegesis, the literal meaning will be determined by using possible sources, ancient texts (before or even after Benedict), and especially Sacred Scripture. It seems important to me to enter the world of Benedict, his horizon, what he dealt with day by day, what he heard and saw, so as to facilitate a well-grounded understanding of the Rule in our communities. I will try especially to illuminate the biblical background. The monks of

Benedict's time breathed Sacred Scripture like air—at the liturgy, during *lectio divina*, at meals, at work, interacting with the abbot, with each other, and with persons from outside the monastery. Breathing in this same air is really a prerequisite for a true understanding of the RB. Sacred Scripture is practically omnipresent for Benedict. Since this is no longer true to the same degree for us today, the biblical dimension will be made especially clear.

The book is addressed particularly to persons who work intimately with the RB, desiring to deepen their understanding of it and explaining it to others. The work with the text is intended to give inspiration for living it.

For easy use, the verses of the chapters are treated in sequence. This entails some repetition in order to save excessive cross-references. Several excursuses of a more systematic type are intended to complete the exegesis.

Being a Missionary Benedictine Sister with all my heart, I read the Rule from this perspective. This means I will be perhaps less perceptive regarding some values and more so regarding others. Every interpretation is subjective to some extent. This commentary is a beginning and requires rounding out by others. Ultimately, each community must write its own commentary to the Rule, its own members being a living commentary. The diversity of interpretation in our monasteries is a great enrichment as long as no interpretation is absolutized and we all remain aware of the need to have our own interpretation complemented.

I am especially grateful for four gifts related to the study of the Rule:
1. Experiencing the living tradition of the Rule, more precisely in my congregation of the Missionary Benedictine Sisters of Tutzing.
2. Giving lectures and seminars for more than thirty years at the monastic institute of the papal University of Sant'Anselmo in Rome, which meant being in lively contact with students from all over the world.
3. Getting to know many monasteries of my own congregation, but also monasteries of Benedictine men and women with different lifestyles, in Europe and on the other continents.
4. Personal conversation or at least correspondence with most current scholars on the Rule. Thus, the bibliography is for me a living gathering of many persons I know. I am especially grateful for collaboration and dialogue with Adalbert de Vogüé at Sant' Anselmo in Rome and also in Brazil and at international congresses on the RB. He has greatly assisted my investigations; I generally accept his conclusions in my exegesis of the text, even though I do not always follow him in interpreting the text for our time. I have known Terrence Kardong from our student days and keep in contact with him, greatly appreciating his commentary (which, however, was published after the original version of this book was completed).

This book is meant to provide only a perspective, a key for reading RB. One may assume that an author normally expresses his main intentions clearly at the beginning and end of his work. Regarding the RB, Benedict's own hand is clearly discernible at the beginning and closing of the Prologue and then again at the end of the entire Rule, in RB 72 and 73. Therefore, these four texts are treated first in the hope of letting the person of Benedict and his message shine out more clearly. This is not to devalue what Benedict says in the rest of the chapters or what he copies directly from his source. As the exegesis for most verses shows, we are always referred to the Rule as a whole.

Then two chapters from the practical section of the Rule follow. They can serve to test whether the perspective resulting from my work is correct and to show how spirituality is concretized. RB 58 was chosen because in a chapter on admission of members we can see something of the nature of monastic life to be lived here. RB 53 is important because of the question how the monastery will relate to the world; it also is related to RB 58 in content. May the choice of these texts help us to grow in our love for the Rule of Benedict and its author and to strengthen our identity as a monastic community, as well as our witness in today's world.

Here, I would like sincerely to thank my superiors and sisters for their encouragement, support, and patient concern. A special thank you to all who worked for the English edition, Sr. Kathryn Huber, Sr. Judith Ann Heble, Sr. Colleen Haggerty, and particularly to the capable translators, Sr. Matilda Handl in Norfolk, Nebraska, and Sr. Marianne Burkhard in Rock Island, Illinois.

Rome, March 21, 2003
Sr. Aquinata Böckmann, O.S.B.

Translators' Acknowledgments
As translators we want to thank our communities for supporting our involvement in the translating and editing of this book and to the Conference of the American Benedictine Prioresses for providing some funds for reimbursing our communities for this work. As editor I owe a special debt of gratitude to Sr. Helen Carey from my community who spent many hours in proofreading the manuscript and discussing it with me before it was submitted to Liturgical Press. Her loving care for the project and for language helped to refine our translation. In addition, I want to thank Sr. Stephanie Weisgram, O.S.B., librarian at St. John's University Library, for her generous help in locating books and English translations while I was working on the bibliography.

Peoria, December 8, 2004
Sr. Matilda Handl, O.S.B.
Sr. Marianne Burkhard, O.S.B.

Bibliography

I. ABBREVIATIONS

1. Periodicals, Encyclopedias, Series, Documents, Editions. Series of English translations are added. English translations of encyclopedias are given in parentheses.

ABR	*The American Benedictine Review*
ACW	Ancient Christian Writers
ANF	Anti-Nicene Fathers; ANF 10 [1994] contains useful indices to ANF and NPNF (both 1st and 2nd series, given as NPNF^1 and NPNF^2)
AugR	*Augustinianum*, Rome
Augustinus	*Augustinus*, Madrid
Bibl	*Biblica*, Rome
BM	*Benediktinische Monatsschrift* (later: EA)
Boon	A. Boon: *Pachominiana latina*. Louvain, 1932
BullAIM	*Bulletin de l'AIM* (Aide Inter Monastères; Alliance for International Monasticism)
CC	Corpus Christianorum, Series Latina
CCM	*Corpus Consuetudinum monasticarum.* Hallinger, K. ed. Siegburg, 1973ff.
CollCist	*Collectanea Cisterciensia.* Forges
CPG	Clavis Patrum Graecorum. Ed. M. Geerard. 4 vols. Turnhout, 1974–1983
CPL	Clavis Patrum Latinorum; Dekkers, Ed. E. Steenbrugge, ^{2}1961
CS	*Cistercian Studies*
CSCO	Corpus Scriptorum Christianorum Orientalium. Paris, Louvain, 1903ff.
CSEL	Corpus Scriptorum Ecclesiasticorum Latinorum. Vienna, 1866ff.
Cuad Mon	*Cuadernos Monasticos.* Cordoba, Argentina
DIP	Dizionario degli Istituti di Perfezione. Rome, 1973ff.
DizPat	Dizionario patristico e di antichità cristiana. 2 vols. Rome, 1983–1984. (*Encyclopedia of the Early Church.* Trans. A. Walford. New York: Oxford University Press, 1992)
DR	*The Downside Review*
DS	Dictionnaire de Spiritualité. Paris, 1937ff.
DV	*Dei Verbum* (II Vatican Council. Dogmatic Constitution on Divine Revelation)

EA	*Erbe und Auftrag* (previously BM). Beuron
EThL	*Ephemerides Theologicae Lovanienses*. Louvain
FC	Fathers of the Church
GS	*Gaudium et Spes* (II Vatican Council. Pastoral Constitution on the Church in the Modern World)
GuL	*Geist und Leben*. Würzburg
JAC	*Jahrbuch für Antike und Christentum*. Münster
JBL	*Journal of Biblical Literature*. Philadelphia
LexMA	Lexikon des Mittelalters. 2 vols. Munich/Zurich, 1980–1983
LG	*Lumen Gentium* (II Vatican Council. Dogmatic Constitution on the Church)
LL	*Lettre de Ligugé*, Ligugé
LMD	*La Maison Dieu*. Paris
LThK	Lexikon für Theologie und Kirche. Freiburg, [2]1957ff.
LthKVat	Lexikon für Theologie und Kirche: Das Zweite Vatikanische Konzil. 3 vols. Freiburg, 1966–1968
LuM	*Liturgie und Mönchtum*. Maria Laach
MonInf	*Monastische Informationen*. Eibingen
Mst	*Monastic Studies*. Mount Saviour
NCE	New Catholic Encyclopedia. 16 vols. Washington, 1967–1974
NPNF[1,2]	Nicene and Post-Nicene Fathers, series 1 and 2
NRTh	*Nouvelle Revue théologique*. Tournai
OK	*Ordenskorrespondenz*. Cologne
OrChrP	*Orientalia Christiana Periodica*. Rome
OrLab	*Ora et Labora*. Milan
PC	*Perfectae Caritatis* (II Vatican Council. Decree on the Up-to-Date Renewal of Religious Life)
PG	Patrologia Graeca. Ed. J. P. Migne. Paris, 1857ff.
PL	Patrologia Latina. Ed. J. P. Migne. Paris, 1878ff.
PW	Paulys Realenzyklopädie der klassischen Alterumswissenschaften. Stuttgart, 1983ff.
RAC	Reallexikon für Antike und Christentum. Stuttgart, 1941ff.
RAM	*Revue d'ascétique et de mystique* (Later: RHSp). Toulouse
RB (Hanslik)	*Benedicti Regula*. Ed. Hanslik, R. (CSEL 75) Vienna [2]1977
RB (Steidle)	*Die Benediktusregel lateinisch-deutsch*. Ed. Steidle, B. Beuron, [2]1975
RB (Vogüé)	*La Règle de S. Benoît*. Eds. Vogüé, A.de and J. Neufville, 2 vols. (SC 181–182). Paris, 1972
RB 80	*The Rule of St. Benedict in Latin and English with Notes*. Eds. Fry, T. and others. Collegeville, MN: Liturgical Press, 1981
RBén	*Revue bénédictine*. Maredsous
RBS	*Regula Benedicti Studia*. Hildesheim
RHSp	*Revue d'histoire et de philosophie religieuses* (previously RAM). Toulouse
RiAsc	*Rivista di Ascetica e Mistica*. Florence
RiBi	*Rivista Biblica*. Brescia

RiLi   *Rivista Liturgica.* Finalpia
RM   *Regula Magistri.* Ed. Vogüé, A. de. 2 vols., SC 105–106 (*The Rule of the Master.* Trans. L. Eberle. Kalamazoo, MI: Cistercian, 1977)
SC   Sources chrétiennes. Paris, 1941ff.
SMGBO   *Studien und Mitteilungen zur Geschichte des Benediktinerordens und seiner Zweige.* Ottobeuren–Augsburg
StA   *Studia Anselmiana.* Rome
StMon   *Studia Monastica.* Barcelona
StSil   *Studia Silensia.* Silos
SupplRBS   Supplementa, Regulae Benedicti Studia. Hildesheim, 1974ff.
ThWNT   Theologisches Wörterbuch zum Neuen Testament. Ed. Kittel, G. and G. Friedrich. Theological Dictionary of the New Testament. This is a translation of the German work, edited by G. W. Bromiley. Grand Rapids, MI/London, 1954ff.
Tj   *Tjurunga.* Tarrawarra [Australia]
TLL   Thesaurus Linguae Latinae. Leipzig, 1900ff.
TRE   Theologische Realenzyklopädie. Berlin, 1976ff.
TU   *Texte und Untersuchungen zur Geschichte der altchristlichen Literatur,* Berlin, 1882ff.
UR   *Unitatis Redintegratio.* (II Vatican Council, Decree on Ecumenism)
Vig Chr   *Vigiliae Christianae.* Amsterdam
VitCons   *Vita consacrata.* Milan
VitaMon   *Vita Monastica*
Vg   Vulgata; quoted according Bibliorum Sacrorum iuxta Vulgatam Clementinam nova editio. Gramatica, A., ed. Typis Polyglottis Vaticanis, 1951
VL   Vetus Latina: Die Reste der altlateinischen Bibel. Beuron, 1949ff.
Vogüé *IV–VII* Vogüé, de A. *La Règle de S. Benoît* (cf. Secondary Sources); Roman numerals indicate the volume of this work/edition. Vol. VII is translated into English: *The Rule of Saint Benedict: Doctrinal and Spiritual Commentary.* Kalamazoo, MI: Cistercian, 1983; cited as *RB-DSC*
VS   *La Vie spirituelle.* Paris
VSSuppl   *La Vie spirituelle, Supplément.* Paris
WSp   *Word and Spirit.* Still River

2. Other abbreviations

Art.   Article (in encyclopedias)
Cod   Codex
c.   canon
dub.   *dubia* (doubts)
Ed.   Edited by
Ep.   Epistle
fasc.   fascicle
H.   Homily
ibid.   *ibidem* (in the same place)

Lib.	*Liber* (book)
n.	Note
n.d.	no date
Praec.	*Praeceptum, Praecepta* (Precept(s))
Praef.	*Praefatio* (Preface)
Prol	Prologue
Ps	before a name: Pseudo ...
s.	*sermo* (sermon)
Th	*thema* (theme in the sense of a brief explanation)
Thp	theme/explanation on the *Pater Noster* (Our Father) in RM
Ths	theme/explanation on the psalm in RM
T	title (of a chapter, e.g., in RB)
V(v.)	Verse(s)
Vit.	*Vita* (Life of a Saint)

The numbering of the psalms follows the Vulgate in the context of Latin texts; otherwise it follows the NAB translation. In ambiguous cases both numbers are given.

The translation of RB in the German original is the author's own; the English translation is based on the author's German translation and on the Latin.

II. OTHER SCHOLARLY TOOLS

Bibliographia internationalis spiritualitatis. Ed. Teresianum. Rome, 1966ff.

Bibliographia patristica. Ed. W. Schneemelcher. Berlin, 1964ff.

Blaise, A. *Dictionnaire latin-français des auteurs chrétiens.* Turnhout, 1954

Clement, J. M. *Lexique des anciennes règles monastiques occidentales.* I and II. Steenbrugge, 1978

Concordantiarum universae Scripturae Sacrae Thesaurus. Eds. Paultier, Etienne, Gantois. Paris, 1897

Forcellini, A. *Lexicon totius latinitatis.* 7 vols. Patavia, 1940

Hamman, A. "Les instruments de travail en théologie patristique et historique." In: *Lo Studio dei Padri della Chiesa oggi* (Ist Patr. Aug.) 155–170. Rome, 1977

Jaspert, B. "*Regula Magistri—Regula Benedicti.* Bibliographie ihrer historisch-kritischen Erforschung 1938–1970. StMon 13 (1971) 129–167

Kapsner, O. L. *A Benedictine Bibliography,* III. Collegeville: Liturgical Press, 1982

Lienhard, J. "Index of Reported Patristic and Classical Citations, Allusions and Parallels in the *Regula Benedicti.* RBén 89 (1979) 230–270

Medioevo latina. Bolletino bibliografico della cultura europea dal sec. VI al. XIII, V. Spoleto, 1984

The Oxford Dictionary of the Christian Church. Eds. F. L. Cross, and E. Livingstone. Oxford, ²1983

La Règle du Maître, III. *Concordance verbale du texte critique conforme à l'orthographe du Manuscrit* Par. Lat. 12205, Eds. J. M. Clement and others. (SC 107). Paris, 1965

Sieben, H. J. *Voces: Eine Bibliographie zu Worten und Begriffen aus der Patristik.*
(Bibliographia Patristica, Suppl. 1). Berlin, 1980
Siegmund, A. *Die Überlieferung der griechischen christlichen Literatur in der lateinischen Kirche bis zum 12. Jahrhundert.* Munich, 1949

III. SOURCES AND PATRISTIC TEXTS

Latin titles according to CPG and CPL, English translations in parentheses.
ANF 10 (1994) contains indices for ANF, NPNF 1st and 2nd series;
T. C. Kardong, *Benedict's Rule: A Translation and Commentary* (Collegeville: Liturgical Press, 1996) also has a list of patristic works and English translations.

Ambrose of Milan

De Abr.	*De Abraham:* CSEL 32.1.
De Cain	*De Cain et Abel:* CSEL 32.1 (FC 42.359).
De inst.virg.	*De institutis virginum:* PL 16.
De offic.	*De officiis ministrorum:* PL 16.23; G. Banterle. Milan: Biblioteca Ambrosiana, 1977. (NPNF[2] 10.1).
De sacr.	*De sacramentis:* CSEL 73; SC 25 (dub.) (*On the Sacraments.* Trans. H. Chadwick. Chicago: Loyola University Press, 1960).
De Tob.	*De Tobia:* CSEL 32.2.
De virg.	*De virginitate:* PL 16.187; E. Cazzaniga. Turin: I. B. Paravia, 1948 (*On Virginity.* Trans. D. Callam. Saskatoon: Peregrina Publications, 1987).
In Ps.	*Explanatio super psalmos:* CSEL 64.
In PS. 118	*Expositio de psalmo cxviii:* CSEL 62 (*Homilies of Saint Ambrose on Psalm 118.* Trans. I. N. Riain. Dublin: Halcyon, 1998).

Apophthegmata Patrum

Apoph.	*Collectio alphabetica:* PG 65 (*The Sayings of the Desert Fathers: The Alphabetical Collection.* Trans. B. Ward. New York: MacMillan, 1975).

Aristides of Athens

Ap.	*Die Apologie des Aristides,* Ed. E. Raabe. TU 9:2 (1892). (*Apology.* ANF 9.263)

Augustine

A new English translation of Augustine's works is being published: *The Works of Saint Augustine: A Translation for the 21st Century.* 1990ff.; so far 24 volumes have appeared done by various translators. This translation is cited as *AW* followed by the specific title, translator, etc.; if available, this translation has been used.

Ad cath.	*Epistula ad catholicos de secta donatistarum*: CSEL 52 (dub.).
De civ.Dei	*De civitate Dei*: PL 41.13; CCL 47–48 (innumerable English editions, useful are those by Dutton Co., in the Everyman series; Doubleday, in Image Books, Penguin).
De cons Evgl.	*De consensu Evangelistarum*: CSEL 43 (NPNF[1] 6.77).
De disc. christ.	*sermo de disciplina christiana*: PL 40.
De doctr. christ.	*De doctrina christiana*: CC 31 (NPNF[1] 2.519; *AW: Teaching Christianity*. Trans. E Hill, O.P. Part I: vol. 11, 1996).
De Gen ad litt.	*De Genesi ad litteram*: CSEL 28.1 (*AW: On Genesis*. Trans. E. Hill, O.P. Part I: Vol. 13, 2002).
De mor. Eccl.	*De moribus Ecclesiae catholicae et de moribus Manichaeorum*: PL 32.1309 (FC 56; NPNF[1] 4.41).
De nat. et grat.	*De natura et gratia*: CSEL 60 (NPNF[1] 5.121).
De op. mon.	*De opere monachorum*: CSEL 41; PL 40.547 (FC 16; NPNF[1] 3.503).
Contra Ep. Parm.	*Contra Epistulam Parmesiani*: CSEL 51; PL 43.33.
Ep.	*Epistulae*: PL 38–39; PLS 2.742 (selected letters and sermons in NPNF[1] 1.219; 5.260, 281.437-40; FC 11.38; ACW 5.15; *AW: Letters*. Trans. R. Teske, S.J., 2 vols. so far, 2001ff.).
In Ep. Joh.	*In Joannis epistulam at Parthos tractatus*: PL 35.1379; CCL 36 (NPNF[1] 7.459).
In Joh.	*In Ioannis Evangelium tractatus*: PL 35.1379; CCL 36 (NPNF[1] 7.7).
In Ps.	*Enarrationes in psalmos*: PL 36.67; CCL 38-40 (NPNF[1] 8.1; ACW 29–30; *AW: Expositions on the Psalms*. Trans. M. Boulding, O.S.B. Part III., vols. 15–19 [Ps 1-120] 2000ff.).
Praec.	*Praeceptum*: Verheijen, *Règle*.
Quaest. Evgl.	*Quaestiones Evangeliorum*: CCL 44b.
s.	*Sermones*: CC 41 (1–50); PL 38–39. (*AW: Sermons*. Trans. E. Hill, O.P. Part III.: 11 vols., 1990ff.).
Ps Aug. ad fratres	*Ad fratres in eremo*: PL 40.
De visit. inf.	*De visitatione infirmorum*: PL 40.
Vit. Aug.	Possidius, *Vita Augustini*: PL 32.

Basil the Great of Caesarea

Ep.	*Epistulae*: PG 32 (NPNF[2] 8.109).
In Ps.	*Homiliae super psalmos*: PG 29.209.
Reg.	*Regula (Asceticum parvum)*: PG 31, trans. into Latin by Rufinus: PL 103.483 (*The Ascetical Works of St. Basil*. Trans. W. K. L. Clarke. London: SPCK, 1925); also FC 9.33 *Discourse on Ascetical Discipline*)
Reg. brev.	*Regulae brevius tractatae*: PG 31 [cf. Clarke above].
Reg. fus.	*Regulae fusius tractatae*: PG 31 [cf. Clarke above; also FC 9.223].
Ps Basilius, Adm.	*Admonitio ad filium spiritualem*: PL 103.683-700 (Trans. R. Rivers and H. Hagan, ABR 53:2 [June 2002] 121–146).

Benedict of Nursia, cf. RB

Benedict of Aniane

Cod. Reg.	*Codex Regularum*: PL 103; L. Holstenius, M. Brookie, 2 vols. Augsburg, 1759; reprint Graz, 1957.
Concord.Reg.	*Concordia Regularum*: PL 103.393-1440.

Bernard of Clairvaux

s.	*Sermones*: PL 183

Caesarius of Arles

Reg. mon.	*Regula ad monachos or Regula monachorum*: PL 67.1099, Ed. G. Morin. *S. Caesarii opera omnia*, vol. 2. Maredsous, 1942.
Reg. vg.	*Statuta sanctarum virginum or Regula ad virgines*: PL 67.1105; (*The Rule for Nuns of St. Caesarius of Arles*. Trans. M. C. McCarthy. Studies in Medieval History, new series, vol. 16. Washington, D.C.: The Catholic University of America, 1960).
s.	*Sermones*: CCL 103-104; PL 39, 47. Ed. G. Morin (above). (FC 31, 47, 66).
Test.	*Testamentum*: cf. Morin above.

Cassian, John

Conf.	*Conlationes*: PL 49.477; CSEL 13, SC 42, 54.64 (NPNF^2 11.293 [omits Conf. 12, 22]; and ACW 57; *The Conferences*. Trans. B. Ramsey, O.P. New York: Paulist, 1997).
Inst.	*De institutis coenobiorum et de octo principalium vitiorum remediis libri xii*: PL 49.53; CSEL 17; SC 109 (NPNF^2 11.199 [omits Inst. 6]; ACW 58; *The Institutes*. Trans. B. Ramsey, O.P. New York: Newman, 2000).

Cassiodorus, Senator

In Ps.	*Expositio psalmorum*: CCL 97-98; PL 70 (ACW 51–53).
Inst.	*Institutiones*: PL 70.1106-1110.
Var.	*Variarum libri*: CCL 96; PL 69.

Chrysostom, John

Ecl. elem. hosp.	*Ecloga de eleemosyna et hospitalitate*: PG 63.
In Act. H.	*In Acta apostolorum homiliae*: PG 60 (NPNF^1 11.1).
In 1 Cor. H.	*In epistulam I ad Corinthios argumentumn et homiliae*: PG 61 (NPNF^1 12.3).
In Gen. H.	*Homiliae in Genesim*: PG 53 (FC 74, 82, 87).
In illud. vid.	*In illud: Vidua eligatur*: PG 51.

In Mt. H.	*In Matthaeum homiliae*: PG 57 (NPNF[1] 10.1).
In illud, ne tim.	*In illud, Ne timueris*: [Ps. 48.17]: PG 55.
In Rom. H.	*In epistulam ad Romanos homiliae*: PG 60 (NPNF[1] 11.335).
In Thess. H.	*In epistulam Thessalonicenses homiliae*: PG 62 (NPNF[1] 13.323).

Clement of Rome

Ep. ad Cor.   *Epistula ad Corinthios*: PG 5.661; Latin version: Ed. M. Morin. *Anecdota Maredsolana* II. Maredsous, 1894. (ANF 9.229).

Councils of Gaul (*Concilia Gallica*)

An. 314-510;
511-695   CC 148, 148A.

Cyprian of Carthage

De dom. or.   *De dominica oratione*: PL 4.520; 47.1113; CSEL 3, 1 (ACW 20; ANF 5.447).
De hab. vg.   *De habitu virginum*: PL 4.440; CSEL 3, 1 (ANF 5.430; FC 36.25).
De op. et. el.   *De opere et eleemosynis*: CSEL 3, 1 (ANF 5.476).
De zel. et liv.   *De zelo et livore*: CSEL 3, 1 (ANF 5.491).
Ep.   *Epistulae*: PL 4.224; CSEL 3, 2 (ANF 5.275; with different numbering; FC 51).

Cyril of Alexandria

De ador. et cult   *De adoratione et cultu in spiritu et veritate*: PG 68.
In Ps.   *Expositio in psalmos*: PG 69.

Cyril of Jerusalem

Myst. Kat.   *Mystagogiae*: PG 33; SC 126 (NPNF[2] 7.1).

Decretum Gelasianum

Decr. Gelas.   *De libris recipiendis et non recipiendis*, Ed. E. von Dobschütz. TU 38:4, Berlin, 1912; PL 59.

Didache

Doctrina Apostolorum: PG 5.661 (*Didache* ACW 1; FC 5; ANF 7.465; A. Milavec. *The Didache*. Text, Translation, Analysis, and Commentary. Collegeville: Liturgical Press, 2003].

Dorotheus of Gaza

Doctr.   *Doctrinae diversae*: PG 88, SC 92 (*Discourses and Sayings*. Trans. E. Wheeler. Cistercian Studies Series 33. Kalamazoo: Cistercian, 1977).

Egeria (Etheria)

Per. Peregrinatio at loca sancta or Itineraria Hierosolymitana: PLS 1.1047; CSEL 39; CCL 175; (ACW 38).

Eucherius/Eucher of Lyons

H. Homiliae quaedam (ad monachos): PL 50 (dub.).
De laud. her. De laude heremi: PL 50.70; CSEL 31.

Eugippius

Reg. Cf. Rules.
Vit. Sev. Vita Severini: CSEL 9.2.

Evagrius

Sent. Sententiae ad monachos: PG 40 (*The Mind's Long Journey to the Holy Trinity: The Ad monachos of Evagrius Ponticus.* Trans. Jeremy Driscoll. Collegeville: Liturgical Press, 1993; also Evagrius Ponticus. *Ad monachos.* Translation and Commentary. New York: Newman, 2003 ACW 59).

Faustus of Riez

Ep. Epistulae: CSEL 21.
Ps Faustus Sermones ad monachos: PL 50 = Eusebius Gallicanus.

Ferrandus of Carthage

Ep. Epistulae: PL 65.
Vit. Fulg. Vita Fulgentii Ruspensis: PL 65.

Fructuosus of Braga

Pact. Pactum: PL 87 (dub.).
Reg. compl. Regula complutensis: PL 87; Holstenius.
Reg. com. Regula communis: PL 87; Holstenius (dub.).

Gelasius I (Pope)

Ep. Epistulae: PL 67.308; Ed. Mohlberg. Rome, 1968.
Decr. Gelasianum cf. Decretum Gelasianum.
Sacram. Cf. Sacramentarium Gelasianum.

Gennadius of Marseille

De script. eccl. De scriptoribus ecclesiasticis or De viris inlustribus: PL 58 (NPNF[2] 3.386).

Gregory the Great (Pope)

Dial.   *Dialogi; dialogorum libri iv*: PL 77.149; SC 251; 260, 265 (FC 39).
Ep.   *Epistulae*: PL 77.441; 84.831(NPNF², 12.73; 13.1).

Gregory of Nyssa

De Inst. christ.   *De instituto christiano:* PG 46.
Vita. Mos.   *De vita Moysis*: SC 1bis (*The Life of Moses*. Classics of Western Spirituality. New York: Paulist, 1978).

Hermas (Shepherd Hermas)

simil.   *Similitudines*: SC 53 (ANF 2.9).

Hilary of Arles

Ep.   *Epistulae at Eucherium*: CSEL 31.
Vit. Hon.   *Sermo de vita S. Honorati Arelatensis episcopi*: PL 50.1249; SC 235 (*The Western Fathers*. Trans. F. R. Hoare, 247–282. New York, 1954; FC 15).

Hilary of Poitiers

in Ps.   *Tractatus super psalmos*: PL 9.231; CSEL 22 (Bk. I NPNF² 9.236; includes only a few psalms).

Hildemar

Expositio Regulae ab Hildemaro tradita: R. Mittermüller. In: *Vita et regula SS. P. Benedicti una cum expositione regulae a Hildemaro tradita*, vol. 3. Ratisbon: Pustet, 1880. [xx in parentheses indicates the page in this edition.]

Hippolytus of Rome

Trad. ap.   *Traditio apostolica*: SC 11 (ANF 5.257).

Historia Lausiaca (Palladius)

Hist. Laus.   *Palladii historiae monachorum Lauso dedicatae versio*; PG 34.995; (ACW 34).

Historia monachorum

Hist. mon.   *Historia monachorum in Aegypto;* trans. Rufinus: PL.21.387 (*The Lives of the Desert Fathers*. Trans. N. Russell. Cistercian Studies Series 34. Kalamazoo: Cistercian, 1981).

Numbering of paragraphs in the English translation differs from the Latin in PL; thus, usually both references are given.

Isaia of Gaza

or.	*Orationes*: PL 40.
PsIsaias, Reg.	cf. *Rules*.

Isidor of Seville

De diff.	*De differentia verborum*: PL 83.
Reg. mon.	*Regula monachorum*: PL 83; 103.

Julian (Emperor)

Ep.	*Epistulae*; Eds. J. Bidez, F. Cumont. Paris, 1922.

Justinian (Emperor)

Corp. Nov.	*Corpus iuris civilis Novellae*; Eds. R. Schöll, W. Kroll. Berlin, 1895.

Jerome

Adv. Ruf.	*Apologia adversus libros Rufini*: CCL 70; PL 23; CCL 79 (NPNF[2] 3.482).
Ep.	*Epistulae*: PL.22.325; CSEL 54, 55, 56 (ACW 33, letters 1–22; NPNF[2] 6.1).
In Ez.	*Commentarii in Ezechielem*: PL.25.25; CCL 75 (NPNF[2] 6.499).
In Is.	*Commentarii in Isaiam*: CCL 73, 73A.
In Mc.	*Tractatus in Marci Evangelium*: CCL 78.
Reg. Pach.	cf. Pachomius.

Leander of Seville

De Inst. vg.	*De institutione virginum et de contemptu mundi*: PL 72.

Leo the Great (Pope)

Ep.	*Epistulae*: PL 54.593-1218 (FC 34; NPNF[2] 12.1 [Bk. 1]).
S.	*Sermones seu* Tractatus: CCL 138, 138A; SC 22, 49, 74 (NPNF[2] 12.115 [Bk. 1]; FC 34).

Liber diurnus

Lib. dirun.	*Liber diurnus Romanorum pontificum*: PL 105.

Lives of the Saints, cf. *Vitae*

Orsiesius

Lib.	*Orsiesii liber* (versio Latina, trans. Jerome): PL 103.453 (cf. *Pachomian Koinonia*, III. Ed. and trans. A. Veilleux. Kalamazoo: Cistercian, 1982).

Pachomius

Ep.	*Epistulae*; Ed. A. Boon.
Praec.	*Praecepta*; Ed. A. Boon.
Praec. et Inst.	*Praecepta et Instituta*; Ed. A. Boon.
Praec. atque Iud.	*Praecepta atque Iudicia*; Ed. A. Boon.
Preac. ac Leg.	*Praecepta ac Leges*; Ed. A. Boon.

(For all these texts cf. *Pachomian Koinonia I–III*. Ed. and trans. A. Veilleux. Kalamazoo: Cistercian, 1980–1982.

	Vol. I: *The Life of Pachomius and His Disciples* (Sbo);
	Vol. II: *Pachomian Chronicles and Rules* [Includes *Praecepta; Praecepta et Instituta; Praecepta et Iudicia; Praecepta ac Leges*];
	Vol. III: *Instructions, Letters and Other Writings of Saint Pachomius and His Disciples*).
Vit. bohar.	*Vita bohar. scripta*; Ed. L. Th. Lefort, *Les vies coptes de S. Pachôme et de ses premiers successeurs*. Louvain, 1942.
Vit. Pach.	cf. *Vitae*.
Cat.	*Catéchèse*: CSCO 160.

Palladius, cf. *Historia Lausiaca*.

Pelagius

Ep. ad Demetr.	*Epistula ad Demetriadem*: PL 30.15-45.
Ep. ad vg.	*Epistula ad virginem devotam*: PL 17 (for both: *The Letters of Pelagius*. Trans. B. R. Rees. Woodbridge: Boydell, 1991).

Paulinus of Nola

Carm.	*Carmina*: CSEL 30 (ACW 40).
Ep.	*Epistulae*: CSEL 29 (ACW 35–36).

Rule of St. Benedict, RB

RB (Hanslik)	*Benedicti Regula*, Ed. R. Hanslik. Wien, ²1977; CSEL 75.
RB (Steidle)	*Die Benediktusregel lateinisch-deutsch*. Beuron, ²1975.
RB (Vogüé)	*La règle de S. Benoît*; Paris, 1972, SC 182–183.
RB 80	*The Rule of St. Benedict in Latin and English with Notes*, Eds. T. Fry and others. Collegeville: Liturgical Press, 1981..

Rules

Reg. Ant.	Ps Antonius, *Regula*: PL 103.
Reg. cuisd. Patr.vg.	*Regula cuiusdam Patris ad virgines* (Waldebert): PL 88.
Reg. eug.	*Eugippii Regula*: CSEL 88.
Reg. Griml.	*Regula Grimlaici (solitariorum)*: PL 103.
Reg. Is.	*Regula PsIsaiae*: PL 103.

Reg. Mac.	*Regula Macharii*: SC 297; PL 103; (*Early Monastic Rules*. Trans. Franklin, Havener, Francis. Collegeville: Liturgical Press, 1982).
Reg. or.	*Regula orientalis*; ed. A. de Vogüé. *Benedictina* 23 (1976) 241–271; PL 103; (cf. *Early Monastic Rules* above).
Reg. Pl. St.	*Regula Pauli et Stephani*; Ed. J.E.M. Villanova. Montserrat, 1959; PL 66.
Reg 4 Patr.	*Regula quattuor Patrum*: SC 297; PL 103; (cf. *Early Monastic Rules* above).
Reg. Tarn.	*Regula Tarnatensis*: PL 66; Ed. L. Holstenius, *Codex Regularum*. 1749; reprinted Graz, 1957.
RM	*Regula Magistri*: SC 105–106; (*The Rule of the Master*. Trans. L. Eberle, o.s.b. Kalamazoo: Cistercian, 1977).
Reg. 2 Patr.	*Alia Regula Patrum or Statuta Patrum*: SC 297; PL 103.441 (cf. *Early Monastic Rules* above).

Rufinus

	cf. Basil, *Regula, Historia monachorum*.
PS Rufinus	*In Ps. Commentarius in LXXV psalmos*: PL 21.

Sacramentarium Gelasianum

Sacram. Gelas.	*Liber Sacramentorum Romanae Aeclesiae ordinis anni circuli*; Ed. L. C. Mohlberg, Rome, ²1968.

Sacramentarium Veronese

Sacram. Veron.	*Sacramentarium Veronese, I and II*, Ed. L. C. Mohlberg, Rome, 1955f.

Smaragdus

	Expositio in Regulam S. Benedicti: CCM 8 (quoted as Smaragdus on this passage), Siegburg: Schmitt, 1974.

Sulpicius Severus

Dial.	*Dialogorum libri II*: PL 20.175; CSEL 1 (FC 7; NPNF² 11.24).
Vit. Mart.	*Vita Martini Turonensis*: PL 20.159; CSEL 1; SC 133–135 (FC 7; NPNF² 11.3).
	The above texts are also found in *The Western Fathers*. Ed. and trans. F. R. Hoare. New York: Sheed and Ward, 1954.

Tertullian

De or.	*De oratione*: PL 1.1149; CSEL 20; CCL 1 (FC 40; ANF 3.681).

Theodoret

Hist. Rel.	*Historia religiosa*: PG 82 (NPNF² 3.33).

Vitae (Lives of the Saints)

Vit. Ant.	*Vita Antonii*: PG 26.835; PL 73.127 (ACW 10; NPNF² 4.195).
Vit. Bas.	*Vita Basilii, Vitae Patrum.* I: PL 73, cf. *Verba Seniorum*: PL 73.855 (O. Chadwick. *Western Asceticism.* Library of Christian Classics. Philadelphia: Westminster, 1958).
Vit. Mac.	*Vita Macharii*, cf. above *Vitae Patrum.*
Vit. Mel.	*Vita S. Melaniae Iunioris*: SC 90.
Vit. Pach.	*Vita Pachomii* (Ps Dionysius), *Vitae Patrum.* I (cf. above).
Vit. Patr. III–IV	*Vitae Patrum*: PL 73.
Vit. Patr. Jur.	*Vitae Patrum Iurensium*: SC 142; (*The Lives of the Jura Fathers.* Trans. J. B. Russell, K. Vivian, T. Vivian. Cistercian Studies Series 178. Kalamazoo: Cistercian, 1999).

Introduction

The renewal movements of religious life after the Second Vatican Council aim at a return to the sources of Christian life and the original spirit of the individual institutes with adaptations to the changed conditions of our time, but also at openness to the future (cf. PC 2b). The two dimensions are interrelated: A person who is deeply rooted in a healthy tradition is able to stretch and grow and has the courage to change. Or using another image: A person who really feels at home can open the door wide. H. Nouwen said:

> It seems that progress is always connected with a refreshing of our collective memory. Practically all reforms in the Church and the Orders of the Church have been marked by a new appreciation of the intentions of the early Church and a renewed study of the past, not to repeat it but to find there the inspiration for real renewal.[1]

During the nineteenth century nearly all Benedictine communities experienced a renewal and a fresh impetus to connect with older traditions (usually the Middle Ages). This met a need of that time. The abbey of Beuron strongly influenced monasticism in German-speaking regions.[2]

For a future-oriented renewal today, it is helpful to reach back to a tradition even more ancient than the Middle Ages, to the Rule of Benedict and to the early church. On the one hand, we feel Benedict to be closer to us in many respects than the nineteenth century.[3] On the other hand, we also realize the distance of 1500 years of history. We need to enter into St. Benedict's world in order to understand better what he intended and what the Gospel demands of us. The Rule of Benedict in its historical context is directing us again and again to Sacred Scripture, moving us also to a deeper biblical spirituality.

The introduction to this commentary will first try to sketch the historical and intellectual background of Benedict, then his personal life story and the development of his Rule. In conclusion, some principles of an objective interpretation will be stated.

1. Benedict's Context

Benedict was born in 480, soon after the decisive year of 476, which practically meant the end of the Roman Empire of the West. The rule of the Ostrogoth Theodoric (493–526) brought an initially peaceful coexistence of Ostrogoths and Romans. Toward the end of his life, Theodoric became suspicious and persecuted the church. Between 535 and 553 the wars of the Ostrogoths devastated the countryside of the Italian peninsula. The Byzantine emperor Justinian and his general Belisarius wanted to reconquer Italy for Byzantium. After his initial victory, the Ostrogoth Totila resisted with some occasional gains, but in the end Justinian prevailed. The wars brought cruelty, injustice, plundering, material and moral chaos. Rome was under siege several times during this time. Soon after Benedict's death, the Lombards invaded, destroyed Monte Cassino and established their rule in Italy (568–774).

In studying the sources, we note a colorful mixture of peoples and races:[4] Romans, barbarians, Ostrogoths, Greeks. Under Theodoric a last attempt was made to save antique culture (also in monastic circles like that of Cassiodorus). The Ostrogoth nobles largely imitated the Roman nobles in exploiting their subjects and in their lifestyle; the wealthy and the influential merchants did likewise. Craftsmen, laborers, servants, slaves and also the Jews constituted the lower class; below them still was an entire group of the *egentes*, the needy. The Gothic wars increased their misery.

The *church*[5] was not at its apex of power. A contested papal election (schism between Symmachus and Laurentius) called the Ostrogoth king Theodoric to Rome for settling the problem (500). The church suffered further interference in its affairs. The Gothic wars were also religious wars. Arianism, though officially condemned a long time before (Council of Nicaea, 325), was a real danger to the Catholic Church because of the rule of the Ostrogoths. The Catholics fought on the side of Byzantium.

Another danger was semi-Pelagianism, less in Rome and its surroundings than in Gaul (cf. notes on Prol 4 (fn. 42) and RB 73 (vv. 5ff.).

Paganism was still alive or flared up again. Texts of that time often complain about the low moral level of Christians and their indifference as compared to the heroic times of persecution. The growing monastic centers provided a contrast.

What kinds of people were attracted by the monastic ideal? In fifth-century Rome the nobility was open to it, which also is true of the sixth century and of other regions. The monasteries, however, also attracted people of the lower classes, rural laborers, illiterates, soldiers, Goths, as well as the educated, priests, Romans, Greeks. The monasteries were a true mirror of the time's mixed society, but without distinctions of race or class[6] (cf. introduction to RB 72, p. 50).

Italian monasticism at Benedict's time was open to the most diverse monastic movements and writings:[7] Eastern (Basil, Pachomius, the Desert Fathers),[8] Southern (Augustine)[9] and Gallic (Lérins, Martin of Tours, the Jura Fathers, Caesarius, Cassian, etc.).[10] Since people traveled often, monastic texts passed quickly from one center to another.

Monte Cassino is situated near an important south-north road. Fontaine calls this region a kind of crossroads between north and south, east and west (because of ports such as Naples, with access to Greek culture).[11] This also explains the list of RB 73. From the Rule we can sense the nearness of Rome, especially in regard to liturgy. Benedict used many texts of patristic and monastic literature, which in his time were translated into Latin, especially texts which he was able to use in the liturgy (cf. RB 9, 8). Probably he also had many personal contacts,[12] and the oral tradition of monastic stories and the *Apophthegmata* must have been important to him. He had an open eye for legislation in his time (between the Eastern Roman Empire and the Ostrogoths). Above all, the spiritual atmosphere in which he lived was marked by efforts to understand Sacred Scripture and good law codes.[13]

Reading the Rule on this background (political, sociocultural, ecclesiastical, literary), Benedict appears to have been a man living in his world with open ears and an attentive heart, taking ideas and norms from wherever he perceived something good.[14] He was not so much a gifted inventor as a good selector and editor. We see clearly that he had a feeling for everything in his world that was needed and promising for the future, especially for whatever was in harmony with the Gospel and in the most profound sense addressed the questions of his time.

2. The Life of Benedict

The main stages of Benedict's life are clear, even though the traditional dates (480–547) and the historical value of Gregory's dialogs are not recognized by everyone.[15]

Benedict was born in Nursia, probably in a well-off, middle-class family. The area around Nursia was evangelized by monks (cf. *Dial.* III.15.2 of Gregory the Great). Thus he may have had contact with monks already in his youth. During his studies in Rome he got to know not only decadence, but also monastic circles. Judging from the language used in the Rule and from its rhetoric, Benedict probably was not as "ignorant" as Gregory described him.[16]

Enfide (Affile) was an early step in his "withdrawal from the world." Was it there that he became familiar with community life according to Augustine?

The narrow valley of the Anio River at Subiaco was the next step. Under the spiritual guidance of the monk Romanus, he lived for three years as a hermit in a small cave. There he probably had profound experiences of the depths of the human heart. He meditated on Sacred Scripture and let it permeate his life. He had to learn how to overcome *acedia* (boredom) and to persevere in difficulties. After Benedict's victory over temptation, Gregory portrays him as a monk now capable of guiding others (*Dial.* II.2.3). Following the period with the monks at Vicovaro, which ended with their attempt to poison him, Benedict returned to Subiaco. There he founded the first monastery in the old *Villa Neronis* near the dam and the location of the earlier settlement. Here he spent most of his time at Subiaco.[17]

According to which rule did they live? Ideas differ greatly. Certainly Sacred Scripture was the primary rule. As abbot, Benedict helped the monks by his instruction, by his personal word and by his living example to have Scripture shape the life of the community. There probably were other normative texts that furthered this aim (see below).

Benedict changed at Subiaco. He relived in his own person, as it were, the development of monasticism from the hermits to the cenobites. While personal salvation may initially have been the primary aim, now his main concern was communion in Christ. If during the first stage the emphasis had presumably been on asceticism in the sense of *agere contra*, going against the grain, we now see, in the instructions of the Rule, a person who despises neither the body nor the world and who integrates and subordinates asceticism to the striving for love. Whereas he had previously turned away from the world in a radical way, he began at Subiaco, and even more at Monte Cassino, to turn to the world, to be open to its needs. The three years as a hermit certainly helped him to integrate important goals and values of the eremitical life into the cenobitical life for which he wrote his Rule. He stresses the value of silence, of humility, of interior prayer; he recognizes the value of the individual person before God, knows the importance of spiritual guidance and realistically appraises what is evil in and around a human being.

Already at Subiaco, Benedict founded several monastic communities, traces of which can be seen even today. A kind of monastic federation evolved.

Around the year 529 Benedict moved to Monte Cassino. This could be called a kind of "return to the world."[18] The property probably was acquired through connections with nobles in Rome. It offered sufficient safety for the monastery, yet was near enough to a busy road. This was an area rich in culture, marked by a great openness to diverse movements; paganism still was alive. Gregory describes Benedict here as a mediator for peace with Totila (*Dial.* II.15.1-2), as the defender of the oppressed (*Dial.*

II.27.1; 31.2f.), as the helper to the poor (*Dial.* II.26; 28; 32.3f.) and as one
who kept preaching the Gospel (*Dial.* II.8.11).

3. The Rule of Benedict in the Light of Tradition

(a) A monastic rule chiefly aims at helping a community to live according to the Gospel. As long as the community's founder is alive, there is no
great need for normative texts besides the Bible. Monks live in a vibrant
tradition of interpreting the Scriptures; the community has developed customs and a lifestyle. For reading there are other normative texts, such as
the lives of monks and commentaries on Sacred Scripture. Perhaps after
the founder's death, the community might collect texts which had been
found helpful. Such a collection could be supplemented according to need;
it might not necessarily have a logical arrangement (cf. the Rules of Eugip-
ius, Caesarius, *Regula Orientalis*). There were many diverse rules,[19] which
were adapted to the concrete situation by omission or additions. They did
not need to be complete, for they were supplemented by a living tradition.

The basic structure of early monastic rules can be seen, for example, in
the instructions of the Desert Fathers or in the Rules of Basil. The disciple
asks how he might be saved, what he must do in order to make progress, or
what a Bible text means to him. The father then answers, usually with a
word from Sacred Scripture or from his own or another's experience with
Sacred Scripture.

The Rule of Benedict could perhaps be considered as such a collection
of rules, for it also contains various parts, such as a spiritual section, a
liturgical code, a penal code, the order of community life, added chapters,
a Prologue and an epilogue; yet we sense, throughout the entire Rule, *one*
creative hand, *one* spiritual stance, in all its diversity. The words of Sacred
Scripture, of the Fathers and his own life experience have grown into a
whole within Benedict's heart.

The Rule certainly was not written in one sitting but took shape in the
course of many years, was corrected, revised, and supplemented. We can
trace Benedict's development in large measure from his Rule. In the spiritual part the great virtues of the eremitical life are emphasized. In the
schedule of the monastery he gives ever greater importance to life in community while keeping largely to the sequence of his models. In the additional chapters, especially in RB 72–73, he becomes quite autonomous, he
is himself.

(b) The *Regula Magistri* (RM) was not just discovered recently; it was
known throughout the centuries. Benedict of Aniane called it the Rule of
the *"Magister."* It is about three times as long as RB and was written for a

fairly small community that lived in stricter separation from the world. Formerly the Rule of Benedict was thought to have been written earlier than the Rule of the Master, that the Master had used the RB and expanded it. Benedict was considered a creative genius.

When A. Genestout in 1938 first voiced the opinion that Benedict had copied most of his Rule from RM,[20] his thesis was dismissed as simply absurd. But the discussion continued, especially in the French- and Italian-speaking regions. In the meantime, Adalbert de Vogüé has proved conclusively that Benedict knew and used RM. He copied the first seven chapters and the Prologue almost verbatim or with some extensions and omissions. In Chapters 8–66 he follows its general structure and takes issue with it, but as his chapters go on, he diverges more and more from RM.

After it had become clear that RM existed prior to RB, discussions continued regarding which manuscript of RM Benedict might have used. Though Manning still contests it, Vogüé's thesis rightly is prevailing: RM in its long form of ninety-five chapters was available to Benedict (perhaps Manuscript P), and this version arose in central Italy shortly before the RB.[21]

It is precisely against the background of the RM that we can recognize Benedict's uniqueness more clearly. We can see what he accepted, what he omitted, what he corrected and what he added from other traditions or from his own experience.

In this introduction, only a brief sketch of RM's characteristics will be given.

School is the central concept of the Master for the monastery. The monk does not go there to live in fraternal community, but in order to learn, under the abbot as teacher, the art of spiritual warfare, of fighting self-will and the devil. The relationship between abbot and disciple is of primary importance; the relationships among the brothers less so. As in schools of an earlier style, there is a pedagogy of ambition. The diligent students should always shame the negligent by their good conduct (cf. 53.9; 92.2, 41f.). The Master does not trust the monks to assume much personal responsibility but always has them watched (cf. 11.23-29). The Master's view of human beings and of the world is rather negative and dualistic. RM ends by saying that the gates are tightly barred to show separation from the world (95.23f.). The body is but dust (8.5); earthly things should be alien to the monk (82.9-11); he is a stranger in this world (Th 4; 8.14; 82.4) and he should despise earthly things (15.34; 90.21; 91.24, 64). RM recommends unhesitating blind obedience (7.55ff.). The monks' striving is mostly a battle of warding off the devil who lies in wait everywhere. Thus the deans keep asking the brothers whether they think bad thoughts (11. 91). What a brother does not want is assigned to him; what he desires is forbidden to him (90.6, 9); what he finds pleasing is taken away from him; what he does not like is given to him (90.62f.; cf. 81.15-19). The basic pattern is that here on earth we must suffer torment (martyrdom, imprisonment) so that we will have a higher place in heaven (joy, reward, happiness). Added to these traits is a love for minute detail, ceremonies and pompous speeches.[22]

A comparison with some books of the nineteenth and early twentieth centuries would reveal many similarities. Sometimes one might think that we formerly lived in some respects more according to the Rule of the Master rather than that of Benedict.

If we read the RB anew after this description of the RM, we are surprised and glad to see how Benedict differs from the source he used. Instead of individualistic salvation he puts more and more emphasis on fraternal love. He only has *one* class of monks who all are imperfect and in need of healing. Starting with chapter 6, Benedict substitutes the word "monk" for "student." The abbot is not only the teacher, but also the good shepherd and loving father who can be loved by the monks (64.15; 72.10).

Instead of negative asceticism, Benedict emphasizes the dignity of the human person and consideration for the weak and the sick (cf. 27; 36). He trusts the individual monk more (32; 68). He decreases the requirements of external penitential exercises, such as fasting or the length of the Divine Office, but he is very strict regarding essential points and basic attitudes. There are no nonsensical commands or deliberate torments in his rule. He takes care that the brothers are not saddened (cf. 34.3; 48.7; 31). There is joy already here on earth (49), there is the wide open heart and the inexpressible sweetness of love (Prol 49). Benedict shows a greater openness to the world (53) and genuine concern for the poor.

But sometimes he is stricter, for example in regard to the vice of private ownership and where murmuring and a questioning of authority are concerned. He had probably made bad experiences in all three areas.

In RM Benedict encountered the great monastic virtues of obedience, silence, humility, asceticism, patience and perseverance, the art of spiritual warfare, the primacy of prayer, the importance of the abbot as teacher and spiritual father, and he accepted these virtues. From the cenobitic tradition and from his own experience he added, or gave more emphasis, to the community of fraternal love, mutual service, respect for each person, an understanding of differing needs, a greater trust in the monks, more openness to the world, and a more positive view of monasticism.[23]

This shows his balance between strictness and kindness, solitude and community, openness to the world and the internal structure of the community, rising to the heights and consideration for the weak.

(c) The Rule of Benedict also is incomplete and in need of supplementation. During the early time (the era of mixed rules) it was used together with other rules (entirely or in segments), copied, and thus adapted to the monasteries (often together with the Rule of Columban). Finally the RB was officially prescribed through the reforms of Benedict of Aniane (+821) and became more and more dominant. There were also political motives involved. Benedict of Aniane still thought that the RB was not comprehensible without the other rules. Therefore he compiled a *Codex Regularum* and the *Concordia Regularum*. To explain individual chapters of RB, he added pertinent chapters of the other rules. He himself responded to objections such as, "What's the purpose of these other rules which I have not promised to keep? Why should I read them?"—"This is the talk of those who do not know Saint Benedict and who do not know that he compiled his rule from other rules, as if joining different bouquets of flowers into one" (PL 103.715).

Ever since the Rule has been considered as fixed, it has existed together with explanations (cf. already Hildemar, Smaragdus), declarations, and customaries. We sense that the RB gives no detailed practical regulations for direct application to later communities, and people have tried through the centuries to unite both fidelity and liberty of spirit.

Trying to implement the Rule literally, without using the oral and written tradition, especially of the Bible, and without receiving the instruction of the abbot, actually contradicts the Rule itself. History shows that the Rule was not meant to be a book of traffic regulations, but as a guide along the way. Benedict himself says that "in this Rule not everything is laid down" (title of RB 73). He considers it as a minimum which should help to stop monks on the way of decadence and to be a basis for a new upswing. It is not even enough to live the Rule literally. Traditionally, living by the Rule has always meant: to live the Rule as it is understood in the tradition of our monastery as an aid to living the Gospel and as it is interpreted today by the respective declarations and the persons in authority.[24] Interpretation also requires a good understanding of the literal meaning. What did Benedict want to say in his time?

4. Principles for a Maximally Objective Interpretation of the RB

(a) There is no totally objective interpretation. It is important to live within the influence and history of the Rule and to place oneself deliberately within it. A person becoming a Benedictine has an affinity with the charism of Benedict. A "relationship" between the author and the interpreter is one condition for real understanding.[25] Others speak of a union of horizons or a "monastic instinct."[26]

(b) But it is equally important to read the RB in its historical context and against the background of the known texts, especially of Sacred Scripture, in order that the essential intent of Benedict may become clear. One must know which questions the text seeks to answer in order to dialogue with it. It is of no use to ask questions which the text cannot and will not answer. The "proportional manner of reading" leads to phantasy: "What would Benedict do today?" This is interesting, but it differs from real interpretation.

(c) Which texts and sources are used to interpret the RB? Some specialists interpret it primarily in light of RM and Cassian,[27] others wish to rely chiefly on Augustine, Basil and Pachomius.[28] It is important to recognize our own biases and question them by the facts, which might have personal consequences for our own life.

(d) Certainly we cannot interpret the RB properly today without consulting the Rule of the Master. Benedict evidently considered that which he copied as important. But his special concern is shown when he adds and changes something in the text he took over. This is especially significant when changes are made in various places and always in the same sense. It is equally significant when Benedict often omits certain concepts of the Master in a context he takes over. We can also assume special importance when he uses expressions such as "above all," "in no way" in the texts proper to him.

(e) Each interpreter must be aware of his or her previous decision, of his or her own context, and the a priori attitudes with which he or she approaches the text. This also shows clearly the distance from the ancient text, and we will not readily project our favorite ideas or our own situation into the text. Otherwise Benedict might be made into a modern prophet of peace, a protector of the environment, a super-hermit or a community promoter.

(f) Since the ninth century, there has been a diversity of interpretations, both theoretical and practical ones.[29] The diversity arises from the history of a person's own monastery, the charism of the monastery's founder and also the monastery's declarations (constitutions) which were approved by the church. No interpretation is complete or absolute; the various interpretations complement and enrich each other.

(g) Finally, RB itself keeps referring to Sacred Scripture, taking us by the hand, as it were, leading us away from itself and towards the Bible and to Christ, who is acknowledged as its core. Absolutizing the Rule is not the aim of RB. As one certain way of living the Gospel, the Benedictine way of life is complemented by other forms of life in the church. When each community has the courage for its proper manner of life, the rich abundance of Sacred Scripture will become evident in the church.

Notes

1. H. Nouwen, *Genesee* Diary (New York: Doubleday, 1976) 166.

2. Cf. Fiala, "Ausprägung"; Misonne, "Restauration"; Aubert, "Restauration"; F. Renner, *Der fünfarmige Leuchter*, vol. I: *Grundlegung der Kongregation von St. Ottilien* (St. Ottilien, 1971); Doppelfeld, *Mönchtum*.

3. Cf. Goritschewa, *Die Rettung der Verlorenen* (Wuppertal, 1983) 58f. (writing about Russia): "What did we talk about at that time, in the beginning? About the Church Fathers, about the history of the early church. We read and commented on Basil the Great, Gregory of Nyssa and Gregory Nazianzen, Tertullian, Origen, Athanasius the Great. The holy Fathers seem like our contemporaries, as if living in our neighborhood." Ibid., 87: "The works of the Fathers and of the ancient ascetics are read with enthusiasm, they are studied and copied by hand, whereas recent ideologies only produce a smile or a sense of boredom."

4. Cf. Luiselli, "Società"; Bonamente, "Ambiente"; Penco, "Composizione."

5. Cf. Penco, *Storia della Chiesa*, 77–90.

6. Cf. Penco, "Composizione"; Luiselli, "Società," 109–116; Brechter, "Soziologische Gestalt."

7. Cf. Penco, "Monachesimo"; Fontaine, "Monachisme," 41–44.

8. Some literature he may have known: *Vit. Ant.*; Latin translations of Jerome (Pachomius, *Vita Pauli*); *Hist. mon.; Hist. Laus; Vit. Patr.* V–VI; Basil, *Reg.; Admonitio* (attributed to Basil).

9. Not only his Rule, but his other works as well. Vogüé, *Autour de S. Benoît*, 26, speaks of his "vague augustinienne," yet there is also the influence of Cyprian; cf. Borias, "Influence."

10. *Reg. 4 Patr.; 2 Reg. Patr.*.; Sulpicius Severus, *Vit. Mart.; Vit. Patr. Jur.*; Cassian, *Conf., Inst.*; Caesarius, *Reg. Vg.*, etc.

11. Fontaine, "Monachisme," 44, and "Romanité," 427.

12. Cf. Parys, "Accès."

13. Cf. Vaccari, "Bibbia."

14. Fontaine, "Monachisme," 38, speaks of an "interior pilgrimage of Benedict to all the monastic sources which were accessible to someone speaking Latin;" cf. concordance of Latin translations in Siegmund, *Überlieferung*. One must keep in mind the nearness of Lucullanum (*Reg. Eug.*), Vivarium (Cassiodorus), and the influence of Roman popes such as Leo the Great.

15. Cf. Rochais, *Règle*, Introduction, XXVII. Regarding the *Dialogs*: cf. Hallinger, "Gregor"; for another view, cf. Vogüé in "Introduction to Gregory," *Dial.* SC 251, 155–160.

16. Cf. Lentini, *Ritmo*; Widhalm, *Die rhetorischen Elemente*.

17. Cf. Carosi, "Primo monastero."

18. Cf. Lecisotti, "Venuta"; Fontaine, "Monachisme," 41f.

19. Cf. Vogüé, "Ducatum Evangelii" and "Sub regula vel abbate: The Theological Significance," 35: The rules "were born out of a desire to make the Word of God penetrate into the very existence of such or such a group of men and they drew their authority before all else from their conformity to this Word. . . . If all monastic rules have the same origin and the same foundation, their multiplicity is not opposed to the unity of monasticism but is rather at its service. . . . Besides the multiple connections

of literary dependence which unite the texts . . . , it is evident that their common reference to Scripture binds them very closely together. The particular elements which distinguish them are less striking than the strong homogeneity of their doctrines and their respective observances, all of them being derived from the same divine source."

20. Genestout, "Unité."

21. This seems evident to German readers since Roth's article "Ursprung der Regula Magistri" summarizes the entire controversy.

22. Cf. for example excommunication and reconciliation, RM 12–14; details regarding the bread basket, 21.13f.; food on Saturdays, 25; service at table 19–23; how the abbot is to be awakened, 32.5, etc.

23. Steidle (*Die Regel Benedikts*, 28) writes: "Benedict took over a complete house from RM, but he perfected and altered it, practically making it into a new building according to his own new insights and experiences."

24. Cf. Leclercq, *Moines*, 131–141; Vogüé, "Sub regula vel abbate [Engl.]," 53–63ff.

25. Cf. Bultmann, R.: "Das Problem der Hermeneutik," in *Glauben und Verstehen*, vol. 2 (Tübingen, 1961) 226f. Cf. Frank, "Erforschung"; Zegveld, "Que veut dire," 164–167.

26. Casey, "Hermeneutics," 43–46 and "RB: Damals und heute," 20–24; Frei, "Bedeutung."

27. A. de Vogüé; earlier Stebler and most commentators (in the light of Cassian).

28. Cf. Wathen, "Methodological," and his other articles.

29. Cf. Zegveld, "Que veut dire," 175; Calati, "Pluralismo."

Listen

If we want to find out an author's purpose, we usually look at the introduction and the closing of a book. The introduction will indicate the content as a whole, state the purpose and significance of the writing, and invite us to read. It is no different for the Rule of Benedict. However, he calls his introduction a "Prologue," which already points to the spoken word.

The first four verses of the Prologue show similarities to the last chapter (73). For example: monastic life is a way to God, to the eternal homeland (our final goal); Sacred Scripture, the teachings of the Fathers, the Rule, are aids on this way; obedience seems to be the core of monastic life. There are also verbal parallels.[1] Also, in the last sentence of his Rule, Benedict resumes directly addressing an individual person as he had done at the beginning ("to you—whoever you are" 73.8; Prol 3) and uses imperatives (only in Prol 1 and 73.8!).

The first and last words of the Rule are especially significant: *obsculta—pervenies*. Between these words stands the entire Rule. *Obsculta*, listen, which in its full sense includes obeying, and *pervenies*, you will reach it, you will arrive there. It is a promise offered personally to each monastic and expresses the optimistic tone in RB.

Similarities between the beginning and the end of the Rule show that Benedict envisioned it as a whole even though the individual chapters were written at various times.

Like the Rule as a whole, the Prologue shows the author's personal hand at the beginning and at the end, in verses 1-4 and 46-49. The rest of the Prologue is found almost verbatim in the Rule of the Master, whose introduction was certainly known to Benedict and which forms a kind of backdrop to his first sentences.

The Master's Prologue has two phases: listening—doing. The author wants to draw the listener's attention to the Rule through which God is speaking. The person who has a choice of the narrow or the wide way ought to choose the narrow way. One who does not faces judgment. The main introduction (theme) of the Master consists of three sections: The parable of the source comments on Matthew 11:28-30. In these verses he repeatedly speaks of baptism. The second part is an explanation of the Our Father in which the Master stresses moral demands and the account we must give.

The third section is a commentary on Psalms 33 (34) and 14 (15). Benedict incorporated only this part. A person should listen to the Rule which, when presented, leads us to the Gospel, which leads to the Our Father, which leads to the Psalms. The message of the Rule does not claim to be anything original, much less anything autonomous. Listening to the Rule means first of all listening to Sacred Scripture.[2]

The Master probably used an ancient baptismal catechesis as his model. In his introduction, he speaks about Christian life in general and mentions monastic life only toward the end. A person turns from sin, finds the source of living water, is born anew; takes on the yoke of Christ, walks the way under the guidance of Christ, shares in his sufferings, and thus attains to glory. The new way contains obstacles and difficulties, but our very God has invited us and helps us with God's grace. There are traces of baptismal symbolism also in Benedict's Prologue, but they are less noticeable than in the Master's.

Not many of the ancient rules have such a Prologue. It resembles an exhortation[3] similar to those found in the Wisdom literature of the Old Testament. The exhortation of the master and father addresses all who are starting monastic life and then all monastics. We can imagine that similar exhortations were used at the reception of a candidate in the presence of the community.[4]

The first verse wants to tune the listener in, preparing him to give his whole attention to the speaker and get ready to practice the teaching. Then the goal is stated: return to God. It is a serious matter; total engagement is demanded. But the demand is not too difficult, since God will bring everything to completion. The idea of baptism is not excluded, for the aim is new life, intense Christian life, conversion, rejection of sin and of all obstacles to the service of Christ. The goal is a full response to a delightful call, to the way pointed out by the Gospel.[5]

OVERVIEW

Benedict placed the first four verses before the text that he took over from the Master. There is a break between verses 4 and 5. In verse 5, he begins to quote the Master literally (note also the change to "we"). Benedict must have had special reasons for not simply starting with the words of the

Master. We can assume that Benedict's own intent becomes very clear in these four verses and that we come especially close to his mind and spirit.

These four verses are very carefully crafted[6] and constitute a coherent unit by themselves. Though they contain a high proportion of words that are used only here and nowhere else (fourteen out of sixty-six occur only here and thus are *hapaxlegomena*), we should not hastily conclude that they are the work of an author other than the rest of the Rule, for these verses, as will be shown, are in accord with the Rule as a whole.

The verb forms also give insights: The newcomer is confronted with four imperatives: "Listen— incline—receive—fulfill." He is at that moment preparing to take up arms, which negatively means giving up his own will; he begins the good work. Behind him, in the past, lies the negative part; the departing from God; ahead of him is the return home and service for Christ. Finally, there is the exhortation to intensive prayer.

The author seems to put his very heart into the text: *o fili* (my son) stresses feeling; it is the "loving father" who is speaking; who speaks to the ear of the heart; the son should receive the word willingly, gladly. The Latin in verse 3 *ad te. . . mihi sermo dirigitur*, also expresses feeling. The weapons of obedience are termed "most strong and splendid." This is a dialog between two committed persons. The author wants to arouse enthusiasm for Christ, and he does it with personal kindness and cordiality, a tone that is characteristic of the entire Rule.

In the opening verses the two partners are presented: on one side is the master, who is also the loving father, who imparts to the other a word (*sermo*), an admonition as well as commands and teachings. On the other side is anyone who has made a decision for Christ, described as a son who has a heart, but whose self-will is opposed to his basic intent. Finally, there seems to be a divine Other who at first is only alluded to, possibly in the master and loving father, and more clearly in verse 2 as the one "from whom you departed . . . to whom you are returning," and who is finally named in verse 3: the Lord Christ, the true King. It is he who brings everything to completion (v. 4).

The means for arriving at the final goal are also presented in these verses, at first in general: listening, receiving, doing (v. 1). Then the key word of obedience appears (v. 2), and in verse 3 the means are described negatively as rejection of self-will, positively as military service with the weapons of obedience, and finally above all fervent prayer (v. 4).[7]

These first verses have a nearly literal parallel in the *Admonitio S. Basilii ad filium spiritualem*. We may assume that Benedict knew the Latin text.

> My son, listen, son, to your father's instruction, and incline your ear to my words. Readily devote your attention to me, and with a faithful heart give

heed to all that is said. For I want to teach you about the spiritual battle and to instruct you in the ways that you should fight for your king.[8]

Just as Benedict specifically names the "Rule of our holy father Basil" (73.5) as an aid for obedient monks, so he places himself right from the start under the patronage of this orthodox, Catholic, oriental father of the church and father of monastics.

In regard to the Prologue as a whole, verses 1-4 are a kind of overture whose themes are repeated several times.[9] There is concern about listening to the voice of the Lord (Sacred Scripture, *praecepta, monita*), about doing or walking on the way, about obedience and acknowledging that the good things come from the Lord. These introductory verses also resemble RB 5 in a special way and should be read together with RB 58.

V. l: Listen, my son, to the precepts of your master
    and incline the ear of your heart;
    willingly receive the admonition of the loving father
    and put it into practice.

1. *Listen.* Benedict deliberately chose this word as the beginning of his Rule. It also is the first word that strikes us when the Rule is read on January 1; and it stands as a kind of theme for every year. In contrast to the verbose beginning of the Rule of the Master, Benedict starts without preliminaries and addresses the person directly. The last word of this sentence (*comple*) forms an inclusion together with the first word: "Listen— fulfill!" The entire verse describes this listening in its fullest sense.

Benedict here is influenced not only by monastic models (cf. Ps Basil, *Adm. Prol: Audi . . . ausculta*), but especially by the Bible, presumably by the admonitions of the Wisdom books. "My son, to my words pay attention, to my sayings incline your ear" (Prov 4:20).[10] Or Psalm 44 (45):11: "Listen daughter, . . . incline your ear, forget. . . . The king desires your beauty." The word "listen" must be understood in the full biblical sense. It denotes an integral attitude, including obedience. One listens with the heart, from the core of the person, as is also indicated by Psalm 94 (95):8 that Benedict adds in the Prologue to the Master's text later on: "Today, when you hear his voice, do not harden your hearts" (Prol 10). God's great admonition to Israel was: "Listen, O Israel!" "Listen to my call. I will be your God and you shall be my people. Walk in the way which I enjoin on you so that you may prosper" (Jer 7:23). Not listening is *the* sin: "But they obeyed not nor did they pay heed. They walked in the hardness of their evil hearts and turned their backs, not their faces to me" (Jer 7:24). The promises of life are linked to listening in Isaiah 55:2-3 and also in Psalm 33 (34):12-23 that Benedict explains in the course of the Prologue. However, a full vessel cannot receive life; emptiness is needed. Thus a person must remove or silence certain things (cf. Ps 44 [45]:11; RM, Prol 1) in order to be open.

At the very beginning of the Rule, the person is confronted by a call, ultimately by the word of God. All human life begins like this: It is a response to the word of God. "God spoke, and it came into being" (Gen 1, cf. John 1:1). The word of God addresses us. The life of every person is a special realization of a personal divine call. The person is shown as someone whose essence it is to be called. This is our dignity and also our obligation.

Obsculta. The word "listen" characterizes the spirituality of the entire Rule; it indicates that receiving comes before acting (cf. also RB 53; *lectio divina*), the priority of the word over the image, of listening before seeing. Words concerned with listening predominate in the Rule as in Sacred Scripture.[11] (Seeing is for eternal life, cf. Prol 21; 4.77)

Benedict himself seems to have been such a listening person, and he wants to lead his monastics to such an integral attitude of listening, be it to God and the divine Word, be it to persons and the situation of the times, be it to the written word or the spoken word, even to the unarticulated, not yet formulated word.

2. *O son.* The address shows the warm tone of a loving father. The "O," used only here in the Rule, shows a fully convinced speaker who wants to win the heart of the other person. The address also refers once again to the Wisdom literature of the Old Testament. That which follows is tested life experience, nourished by biblical sources. By listening—and faith comes from listening, cf. Romans 10:17—the person becomes a child of God. The Master points to the biblical word that we become God's children when we keep the commandments (John 15:17; RM Thp 9). By baptism we already have become God's children; we are members of the new family of God, born anew by the word. To be a child means dignity and also responsibility to become like the father in our conduct (cf. RM Thp 12-14).[12] When Benedict uses the term *filius* in the Rule, he never designates the monk as a son of the abbot (except in 2.29), but rather as a son of God or a son of Christ the Lord.

3. *The master, the loving father.* The speaker first introduces himself as master (perhaps influenced by the RM?). The master teaches (cf. *praecepta*), but as Benedict says later on, his is a double teaching, that is by deeds and by words (2.11-12). According to the RB, the abbot ought to have integrated all of Sacred Scripture into himself (64.9) and may not teach anything that is contrary to the Lord's command (2.4). He himself has become a master by listening to the word of God, by obedience, and by fulfilling what he heard. By his instruction a master also becomes a spirit-

ual father. Paul says something similar: ". . . for I became your father in Christ Jesus through the gospel" (1 Cor 4:15). The abbot of the RB should show the "strictness of the master and the kindness of the father" (2.24). He is the loving father, in Latin *pius* means not devout or pious, but benevolent, good, full of love and mercy (cf. also comments on 53.14).

Who is this master and father? It certainly could be the abbot, but also Benedict himself, the author of the Rule; we can recognize him from the image of the abbot that he sketches. But behind him there shines, already here, even though faintly, the image of Christ, who is clearly mentioned in verse 3 (cf. v. 5: father). Jesus tells the disciples that they should not call anyone on earth their master or father, for one is our father, God in heaven, one is our master, Christ (Matt 23:10). Smaragdus, commenting on this verse, cites this Scripture text. Christ and God the Father are speaking through human mediators, but especially through the Word of Sacred Scripture, as becomes clearer in the course of the Prologue.

4. *Teaching, admonition, word (praecepta, admonitio, sermo)*. Three words express what is promised to the newcomer by the speaker. *Praecepta*, teaching or instruction, may already point to the Rule and the *disciplina*, while *admonitio* pertains to the father and certainly is a spoken word. *Praecepta* also are not read, but heard. In verse 3, Benedict uses "word" (*sermo*). These are never theoretical words and instructions, but guides to right living, showing the way. Benedict uses all three words for Sacred Scripture as well as for the teachings of the abbot and the Rule. He probably is deliberately vague, trying to suggest that human words are to transmit God's Word. Thus also *Ps Basil* had said, "For these words are not mine but have come from inspired sources. I am not going to instruct you with a new teaching but with one that I have learned from my fathers."[13] As Smaragdus says, the main content of the *praecepta* is the love of God and of neighbor. We certainly may also think of RB 72.

5. *Incline the ear of your heart*. Benedict is not content with the first call to listen. He reinforces it by the biblical metaphor of inclining the ear of the heart. Incline or bend always occurs in the Rule in the context of humility. The old commentaries also explain it as a humble lowering of self and being open to what is above, doing so from our core. Many might open their physical ears and hear sounds, but if they don't bend their hearts, they will never experience truth.[14] Most biblical texts speak of the inclining of the ear (including Basil); but they also add that it is the heart to which the Word of God speaks.

The heart, for Benedict as well as in Sacred Scripture, not only designates the core of a person with its power of loving, but also the ability to think. Benedict mentions the heart especially when envisioning the monk in his relationship to God and when confronting Sacred Scripture.[15] The monk even speaks in his heart (four times, always in words of Scripture). However, temptations also want to enter the heart, and he must drive them away from the gaze of the heart (Prol 28; 4.50; 7.44). The heart is the field into which the seed of the Word of God falls. The ear should be connected to it. The heart that receives the Word of God also receives the life of God and so can expand to become God's dwelling (cf. comment to Prol 49).

6. *Willingly receive (libenter excipe).*[16] The kindness of the father is accepted with good will, readily. We should open from the inside. Someone might harden the heart (Prol 10).[17] The heart is like the good soil that needs to open up for the seed. The word *libenter* occurs only one more time in the Rule: "to listen willingly to holy reading" (4.55). Again, the human person is confronted by the word of God! It is typical of Benedict to emphasize openness three times before mentioning action.[18] But opening oneself requires an effort, for God's voice is not always heard in thunder (Prol 8), nor is it obtrusive like advertising, but it is often very soft and unobtrusive and needs to be listened to with love and in recollection.

The Rule of Benedict begins with a dialogue between the newcomer and the human mediator of the Word of God. This reminds us of the process so often described in the *Apophthegmata*. The question of a young person is answered by the elder or father with a word, an admonition; and this word comes from Sacred Scripture or from his own experience with Scripture.

7. *And put it into practice (efficaciter comple).* There are few parallels to these two words in the Bible and in patristic literature. We can consider them characteristic of the author. What good is the opening of ourselves if it does not lead to deeds? Before the deed comes listening, but listening fully should include acting. *Efficaciter* implies a certain energy; the word should be translated "put it into action—not half-heartedly, not sluggishly, but quickly, perseveringly, with strength." Benedict does not want to draft a theory, but practically to spur us on to action.[19] We may recall the Letter of James admonishing us to be not only hearers, but doers of the word (Jas 1:19-25). We could compare this first verse with Luke 11:28, the Word of Jesus about Mary, "Blessed are those who hear the word of God and observe it." She is the listener who willingly bent her ear and received God's Word into herself. This first verse also expresses the spirituality of the *lectio divina*. According to the old monastics it means just this: making room for the Word, bending the ear to the Scriptures, taking the Word into the heart, treasuring it there and letting it bear fruit, so that it may permeate all the veins and become flesh in daily life. The Rule of Benedict wants to teach us this attitude toward the Word of God.

**V. 2: So that by the labor of obedience
you may return to him
from whom you had wandered by the laziness of disobedience.**

In this second verse Benedict now indicates the goal and motive for listening and acting (Latin *ut*).

1. *So that you may . . . return to him from whom you . . . had wandered.* Here is the first reference in the Rule to the theme of the way. Life on earth is a return, a going home to God. The going away, the falling away from God, lies in the past. The person is not confronted by the choice of two ways, the narrow and the broad way, as in the case of the Master (cf. Prol 9–14), but only by the one positive way to the goal. Who is "he?" Evidently, he is so naturally near and present to the author that he does not need to be named. From the immediate context we could conclude that "he" means Christ, who in the following verse is specifically named, but also concealed in the "pray to him" of verse 4 (cf. vv. 5ff.) as father of his sons, and who seems already alluded to in the master and loving father of verse 1. However, we will think more of God the Father when we consider the probable biblical background of Romans 5:12-19. There Christ is described as the second Adam who by his obedience reopens the way to the Father after all of humanity had withdrawn from God by Adam's disobedience. This also is suggested by a parallel text in Augustine that is probably nearer to Benedict than a text of Cyprian who speaks of a return to Christ.[20] According to the Master, the human family may by grace return to Paradise, from which it had fallen by freely choosing sin (Thp 6).[21]

Probably "he" simply refers to God. The Rule uses the Latin word *ad* regarding the personal goal several times in texts proper to Benedict: we go to God through hardships and difficulties (*itur ad Deum*—58.8), and by obedience (*se ituros ad Deum*—71.2); and finally the last chapter says: we go to the creator (*ad creatorem*—73.4). The beginning of RB 72 most nearly approximates Prologue 2: Wicked zeal separates from God (*a Deo*); the good zeal leads to God (*ad Deum*—72.1-2). This way toward God is basically obedience, in RB 72 the good zeal, that is, the most ardent love. God is called the origin and the goal of our way in both 72.1-2 and in Prol 2 (cf. comments on RB 58).

2. *Obedience (oboedientia).* Like Paul and Augustine, Benedict sees the return by obedience as the opposite of the Fall. By the way of obedience the monastics go to God (71.2). In 73.6 the "monks living rightly" are simply called "obedient" monks. Here already RB seems to point to the chief virtue of cenobites. For the cenobite does not follow Christ by difficult individual asceticism and hard external penances, but by obedience. Synkletika

said, "When you live in a cenobitic community, you must prefer obedience to asceticism. The latter teaches pride, the former humility."[22]

A saying of the Fathers probably known to Benedict was, "God expects every Christian to obey the Sacred Scriptures, for in them one finds guidelines for speaking and acting, and that he should agree with all authorities and orthodox Fathers."[23] Another saying in the same collection praises obedience as the highest among the virtues, as the salvation of the believer, mother of all the virtues, and the way to heaven.[24] Smaragdus comments on this text by listing the chief maxims of RB 4. *Oboedientia* according to the Rule is obedience to Christ, obedience to the Word of God, the Rule and the brothers. It means listening in all directions.

3. *The laziness of disobedience.* After reading the first verse, we might get the impression that openness is much more important than action. But being receptive does not mean letting everything be. On the contrary, laziness and negligence can prevent openness. Laziness shuts the ear of the heart, is Smaragdus's comment on this verse. In this sense, laziness and disobedience are the same. In chapter 73 monastics living badly are called "negligent and lazy" (73.7), while the good monks are called "obedient" (73.6). One more time Benedict speaks of negligent or lazy monks (48.23); there it means that they do not want to be open for *lectio divina*. Laziness may be related to *acedia*, for the *frater acediosus* also does not want to engage in *lectio divina* (48.18).[25] Presumably, Benedict sees human beings on a downward slope. When we let ourselves go, we slide down. Sin is not only doing something evil, but also doing nothing. Benedict does not have an ideal vision of persons as naturally good. He knows the reality of evil inclinations, in this case unwillingness to listen, to obey.

4. *The labor of obedience.* The opposite of laziness is effort. One might translate: "Effort and obedience, obedient effort, or laborious obedience, or still better, the effort which is proper to obedience, which is proved by obedience."[26] Benedict may have known the term "labor of obedience" from the *Vitae Patrum* or from Cassian. "God demands from beginners in the spiritual life above all the effort of obedience."[27] But as the Fathers also show, not all of life is effort, only its beginning. Benedict seems to say the same, first calling obedience a "labor" and at the end a "good" (71.1). Whereas life on earth for the Master is effort, martyrdom, torment from beginning to end, Benedict's thinking is more positive. At first the way is narrow (cf. Prol 48), but already in chapter 5 obedience is for those "who hold nothing dearer than Christ" (5.2), and in the third degree of humility Benedict adds the motive of love for Christ to the text of the Master (RB 7.34). In progressing, the heart is expanded. Toward the end the monastic does everything "without effort . . . out of love for Christ . . . out of joy in virtue" (7.68f.).

If Benedict's model is the text of the Rule of the Master, we may here re-call Matthew 11:28f.: "Come to me, all you who labor and are burdened, and I will give you rest. Learn from me . . . my yoke is easy." Listening and obeying, the monk is attracted by the Lord's invitation. The Lord's yoke is easy because it is his yoke. On the other hand, the monastic's way is the same way Jesus walked in obedience, the way that cost him everything, even his life.

Let us think of the great plan of salvation that shines out from this verse: the return of humanity fallen from God by disobedience, home to God the Father under the guidance of the obedient Christ. This also shows clearly that our obedience, in this perspective, helps to lead the world home again.

V. 3: **To you, therefore, my word is now directed.**
> **whoever you are, renouncing self-will,**
> **who in order to serve the Lord Christ,**
> **the true King,**
> **are taking up**
> **the very strong and splendid weapons of obedience.**

This verse can be considered a kind of dedication to the newcomer.[28] It is addressed to "whoever" (cf. 73.8; 58.1). Benedict opens his monastery not just to the elite. He sets no prerequisites as to race, class, level of education, and so on. In the context of his time, this is remarkable. The only prerequisite is seeking God (58.7), the desire to renounce the selfish ego and so surrender to Christ.

1. *To you, therefore, my word is now directed.* Before Benedict says "whoever you are," he puts special emphasis on "to you" (sg.). It is "you" I am addressing here and now. (This is the only time he uses a "you" in the singular, except in Prol 16 and in quotations from other authors.) The author of the Rule also reveals himself. It is the only time he speaks directly in the first person singular (in Latin, *mihi*).

Ergo, therefore—this little word always calls for attention when it is used in the Rule: it signals that something important is coming (cf. 19.6; 49.10; 72.3). What may have been vague and general now becomes concrete (cf. also 73.8). The "you" is more clearly described as you also wish to renounce and begin serving Christ. The concrete demand comes only in verse 4 and initially requires prayer (good deeds are mentioned only in v. 6). "Word" (*sermo*) means the spoken word, which is directly addressed to the individual. The word is not the author's own, but comes from the fountain of Sacred Scripture, nourished by experience (cf. 73.3-5). We may think of Jesus saying : "The word you hear is not from me, but from my Father" (John 14:24).

2. *Renouncing.* Renouncing could also be translated as "rejecting." The word comes from the liturgy of baptism. Those to be baptized renounce Satan, his works, and his pomp. The Master speaks of the burden of the sins that "we have renounced on the way to the baptismal font" (Th 18). Cassian used this word for the entrance into monastic life. One must renounce worldly possessions, sins, and every remembrance of the world.[29] In entering monastic life, we must renounce not only bad things, but as Basil specifies, anything that hinders our following of Christ (*Reg.* 4).

3. *Self-will (propriae voluntates).* This is foreign vocabulary to us. Benedict took it over from monastic literature, especially from the Master, who often speaks of renouncing one's own will in connection with obedience. The word of John's Gospel, "I came down from heaven not to do my own will, but the will of the one who sent me" (John 6:38) was interpreted by him to mean that in following Christ the monastic may not do his own will. "Self-will" is usually negative for the Master, and also for Benedict until the end of chapter 7, that is, in the texts he took from RM. But in his later chapters, "will" is either negative or positive, depending on circumstances, but mostly positive. The case is similar for the adjective "own" (*proprius*). This accords with the usage of the Bible, where one's own will is not inherently negative. We do, however, find one verse that gives a negative value to "will," and this verse was frequently used by the Master:[30] Sirach 18:30, "Go not after your lusts (Vulgata: *concupiscentiae*), but keep your desires (Vulgata: *voluntas*) in check." Benedict also quotes this sentence (7.19, 25; cf. 4.60) and uses the expression "self-will" negatively a number of times, aware that the human person is not quite healed, not yet completely turned toward God. There is resistance to God's plan of salvation (cf. Rom 7). The cenobite should not be like the gyrovagues who are slaves of "self-will and their appetites" (1.11). Smaragdus, in speaking of this text, describes thus a person living according to self-will: "He goes wherever he wants and with whom he wants, he sleeps as much and when he wants, he talks when and how long he wants, he eats and drinks how much and when he wants, he laughs when and how much he wants." We can understand that such a person is not fit to live in community. Benedict does not teach that we should do what we do not want (as does the Master), but we must renounce what is opposed to our relationship with God and people. The person who renounces self-will wishes to please God with all his energies and to obey God in the community of brothers. Self-will, as Hildemar says (12), may also be fixed on good things, such as vigils, prayers, fasts. But we must renounce it if our desire is against obedience and the common life (cf. RB 49.8-10).

4. *The Lord Christ, the true King.* At the beginning of the Prologue stands the dominant, sublime image of Christ as we know him from the

apses of ancient Christian basilicas. It reappears at the end of the Prologue (Prol 50). The image of the king is alien to our times. Benedict knew the king of the Ostrogoths. He also knew other mighty rulers who struggled for dominance. It was important to follow the right one. The expression "the true King" also may relativize all human kings. Christ is the King of all kings, the only king, whom we want to serve everywhere (61.10). We are reminded of the core meditation in Ignatius's *Spiritual Exercises*, in which he portrays the temporal and the eternal king, Christ our Lord, as appealing to the newcomer to follow him.[31] He is "Lord;" he rules and is Lord over all. All creatures must serve him. He is "Christ," because he is anointed with the fullness of the Spirit.[32]

5. *Want to serve.* The renouncing of hindrances is followed by the commitment to serving Christ. RB 4.10 shows a similar structure: "To renounce oneself in order to follow Christ," echoes the biblical words, "They left all and followed him" (Luke 5:11). The service for Christ, the life of following him, is described as a military service. We read, "everywhere we serve the same Lord as slaves, the same King as soldiers" (61.10). This implies both the reality of the struggle against whatever opposes the good, against evil and the evil one, and implies also a personal relationship to the king, the loyalty of a follower, the willingness to risk one's life for the king. As will be demonstrated in the following, in using the words *militare, militia*, and so on, Benedict means especially the personal relationship with Christ.

Excursus: *Militia*

In older editions of the Rule we often find *militia* translated as "military service" and *militare* as "to fight." Formerly, people saw military service in a more positive light. Benedict's community was considered a "castle" in which a Roman camp was continued in a spiritual form, a "spiritual barracks." It was said that the Rule resounded with a "clang of invisible weapons," and there was talk of "military discipline." The Rule was called a manual for spiritual warfare. Herwegen compared the "*meditare*" of the novices with the exercise of fighting troops and the promise of profession with the Roman oath of allegiance to the flag.[33]

In the ancient church the word *militia* was generally used to describe the task of the Christian. Martyrdom was a special form of this *militia Christi*. Christ, in contrast to the emperor, was represented as the true king of Christians. After the persecutions, baptism was viewed as entering Christ's *militia*.[34] The Christian "soldier's" weapons are prayer, fasting, and good works. After the fourth century, the word lost its connotation of fighting. It was even used for people employed in the king's service. Christian life generally was seen as *militia Christi*, the struggle against powers opposed to Christ, a battle for acquiring virtue, but still more, service of the true King.[35]

Thus it is also used for monastics.[36] In the beginning the emphasis was on fighting demons, later the acquiring of virtue was stressed more, and then the idea of Christ the King was central. The *Admonitio ad filium spiritualem* of Ps Basil has a first chapter on the spiritual militia. The true Christian is compared to a soldier. These main elements were stressed: obedience, preparedness, struggle against the devil with spiritual weapons, acceptance of the Lord's yoke by a prompt decision, and focusing on Christ, the Lord. In Benedict's time the word *militia* meant service.[37]

Benedict probably takes his orientation from the Bible rather than from military models. In biblical lands the image of spiritual warfare arose as counteracting the military duty of the time.[38] The Sermon on the Mount demands renunciation of force, nonviolence. Christians found themselves marginalized in their society. Wars were interpreted as apocalyptical signs or as punishment from God (cf. Mark 13:14-20). In using the image of military service, Paul seems to say, "Our military service is not there, but on an entirely different field." He used the image of the "breastplate of faith," of the "helmet that is hope for salvation" (cf. 1 Thess 5:8-9), of being girded with truth, of the breastplate of justice, and the sword of the Spirit that is the Word of God. One concrete form of this service is to be always alert and vigilant in prayer (Eph 6:10-20). Like a soldier standing guard, Christians share in military duty by being sober and vigilant in awaiting the coming of the Lord. Monastic life was greatly influenced by the word of Paul in 2 Timothy 2:3-5: "Bear your hardship along with me like a good soldier of Christ Jesus. To satisfy the one who recruited him, a soldier does not become entangled in the business affairs of life. Similarly, an athlete cannot receive the winner's crown except by competing according to the rules." Paul often speaks of weapons: Weapons of justice (Rom 6:13), weapons of light (Rom 13:13), weapons that are not of the flesh (2 Cor 10:4). Christians living during the times of persecution and messengers of the Gospel needed to be clear and decisive, ready to commit themselves fully.

By comparing RB with RM and other monastic texts, we note that the military vocabulary diminishes in RB.[39] The Master says more about the battle against the devil and about struggle in the cenobitic community (cf. 82.2; 92.72). Benedict is more concerned about the positive goal. Like the Master, he uses three texts: Prol 40, preparing heart and body for the service of obedience (*oboedientiae militanda*); 1.2, cenobites serve (*militant*) under a rule and an abbot; and 2.20, all render the same military service (*aequalem servitutis militiam baiulamus*). Here already the militant accent is weak. Benedict used the word three more times in the texts proper to him: Prol 3, serving Christ the true King with the weapons of obedience; 58.10, beholding "the law under which you want to serve" (Rule); 61.10, all serving the same king. In all these texts it is not the fighting against external foes, the devil, or vices that is primary, but rather the personal relationship with the king, Christ, who unites the monastics as a community and makes them one (2.20), without class distinctions (61.10). Obedience is usually indicated as the content of the service. Cenobites serve under a rule and an abbot. Obedience, community, Christ, these are the three accents of Benedict in using military terms.

By contrast, it is interesting that he uses fighting terms in describing the hermits. In 1.4-5: "trained by the help of many others, they learned to fight (*pugnare*) the devil, and now, well instructed in the community, they are able to fight in single combat, without the help of others, with their own hand and arm against the evils of the flesh and of thought."

For Benedict, *militare* comes to mean "serving in community, in obedience." The engagement for Christ is emphasized rather than the battle against negative forces. This applies also today in the various forms of struggling for justice and solidarity.

6. *You take up the very strong and splendid weapons of obedience* (*oboedientiae fortissima atque praeclara arma sumis*). Obedience is definitely first. This is the fight of the cenobite, not a one-sided asceticism, silence, bodily mortification, battle against evil spirits. Therefore the cenobites are the strongest kind of monks (1.13). The cenobites serve under a rule and an abbot (1.2). This verse of the Prologue contains the three elements from Matthew 16:24: leaving everything (*abrenuntiare*), taking up the Cross (*arma sumere*), and following Christ (*militaturus Christo*). The weapons are very strong (superlative in Latin). They must be still stronger than the strong one who invades the house of the strongly armed one (Luke 11:21). The weapons are also splendid, glorious (*praeclara*). The psalmist similarly says that his portion, his cup is splendid (Ps 15 [16]:6). They are splendid, as

Smaragdus says of this text, because they already reflect the glory that Christ received from his Father and gave to his disciples (John 17:22). In the adjectives *fortissima* (very strong) and *praeclara* (splendid), Benedict shows the two aspects of serving Christ, expressed in negative and positive form. The strong weapons are what is done with effort: for example, denying oneself, turning from evil, not despising the sinner, not harboring hatred in the heart, fasting, bearing illness, and so on. By contrast, the splendid weapons are the positive element: following Christ, doing what is good, repaying evil with good, loving neighbor and enemy, relieving the lot of the poor, visiting the sick.

Prayer also is part of the battle (cf. Eph 6:11-18), as Benedict states in the next verse. The first three verses sketch in large lines the attitude necessary for joining a monastic community. It is something great and splendid, but it also entails effort and sacrifice. It means essentially listening, then obeying. Obedience is presented as listening, as return, as military service. As is clear by the end of the Prologue, all this is done in the school of the Lord's service.

These three verses remind us of the vocation stories in the New Testament. The master's call, which reaches the disciple's ear, is succeeded by the obedient following on the way, through hardship and the Cross. Following Christ cannot be conceived apart from service in the community of the disciples and service to the kingdom (cf. Matt 23:8-12; Mark 1:16-20; 10:41-45).

V. 4:   First of all, whenever you begin a good work,
**   you are to pray most earnestly**
**   that he will complete it.**

1. *First of all, whenever you begin a good work.* Prior to entering service, there is prayer, but it is also an essential, integrating part of this service. Benedict wants the newcomer, perhaps eager to plunge into action, to recognize this priority. This is a community in which nothing is preferred to the *opus Dei*, the work of God (43.3). We are not doing the main work, but the Lord. Without the Lord we are unable to act (cf. Prol 6,29f.). This is true not only of the beginning of monastic life, but for any good work. From Cassian Benedict took over the formula for constant prayer, "O God, come to my assistance . . ." (*Conf.* X.10). He has every liturgical Hour begin with it, but also the weekly service in the kitchen that involved all the practical services in the community, and thus he shows that without God's help we can do nothing at all (cf. 35.17).

2. *Pray most earnestly (instantissima). Oratio* in RB denotes both communal and private prayer. The root of this word means petition, but in

Benedict's time it also included praise and thanksgiving. Together with "earnestly" the meaning probably is an urgent petition.[40]

The word *instantissima* is derived from *instare*, to invade, to press hard, to push someone. We should storm God by our prayer. *Instare* also means to keep someone in view, to follow closely. Thus we must pursue God by our instant or earnest prayer.[41]

We are reminded of the biblical parable of the persistent widow in Luke 18:1-8. The Master in his introduction also had pointed out the importance of prayer and had admonished us to plead with the Lord unceasingly (Thp 71). The Rule of Benedict wants to lead us to this incessant prayer (4.56; 7, first degree).

3. *That he will complete it.* The personal pronoun refers grammatically to him who graciously counts us as his sons (v. 5). He is Christ, the father of monks. In 73.8 we read that the monastic should observe this little Rule with the help of Christ. Christ completing our deeds is not an idea foreign to Benedict's thinking. In this case, our earnest prayer would also be directed to Christ. Jesus tells his disciples that without him they can do nothing (John 15:5). He completes the work the Father gave him to do (John 5:36; 4:34). The closest parallel is in Philippians 1:6: "The one who began a good work in you will continue to complete it." It is God who creates both the desire and the completion (Phil 2:13). Paul certainly is referring to God the Father who completes everything in the end, which Benedict does not exclude. He is dealing with practical, not with theoretical matters here.

The newcomer is confronted with the law under which he or she will serve. But he or she can only walk this way trusting in the Lord's help. During the solemn receiving of the Rule, we answered the question whether we would be able to keep this law by saying: "Not trusting in our own strength, but in the mercy of God, I hope to fulfill everything."

From this verse we cannot deduce the heresy of semi-Pelagianism,[42] as though Benedict wanted to say, "You are beginning a good work without grace, but it is only completed by grace." Benedict addresses the person taking the first step and states: "Now you are taking up arms. Consider that it is God who carries on and completes it." The Master had said something similar: "God desires to do this in us before we ask him, for he is powerful and nothing is difficult for him" (Thp 76). There is no denying that God's prevenient grace already has touched the person by the call of grace. It is presupposed. An ancient oration says, "O God, precede our action by your inspiration and accompany it by your help, so that all our prayer and work may always begin in you and also be completed by you."[43]

Benedict knows the great power of prayer (cf. also 28.4). The monastic is totally dependent on God. All he or she does is fragmentary. He or she never can accomplish anything that is perfect. But God does wonders with all our fragments we offer to God, and God makes them into a whole.

This is prayer that is directed toward action and leads to action. It helps us to see all our work in the light of God and therefore assign the proper value to it.

Listing all the ancient texts Benedict might have used, one discovers that, contrary to expectations, they show not Benedict's dependence on them, but his uniqueness and self-reliance. He is a man who is firmly rooted in the tradition and who seeks out good items wherever he can find them. However, his is not just a small collection of stones for a mosaic. He not only shaped the mosaic, but added much that is his own. He seems to have had an open ear during all the readings of the liturgy and in his own *lectio divina*. The bits and pieces have grown in his heart, becoming a whole, his own. It might be interesting to collect all the elements that existed prior to Benedict as in a mosaic: "Listen, son, to the precepts of your master / incline your ear / gladly listen and with a believing heart receive the admonitions of the father and fulfill them by deeds. / Let us return to God, from whom we have fallen away by disobedience. / The way leads through the effort of obedience. / To you my words are addressed, as you begin military service for Christ, the King. / You give up self-will. / Pray without ceasing. / Whatever you begin to do, pray. / All that is good will be completed by God."[44]

Onto this common foundation, Benedict places his special coloring: *O* son, and *loving* father, *effectively* put into practice, *so that* you may return. Disobedience is *laziness. Therefore . . .* you are taking up the *very strong and splendid weapons of obedience* for the Lord Christ, the *true* King. *First of all*, ask by *most earnest prayer.*

In these words proper to Benedict we recognize a person of great empathy, human warmth, and capacity for enthusiasm, goal-oriented in his thinking and of energetic will. He is a man of prayer: at the very beginning he points to earnest prayer! The image of Christ shines out more clearly than in all of Benedict's sources. It is preeminent at the beginning and throughout the Rule because Christ has taken hold of the man Benedict.

Notes

1. Cf. for example *sermo, pater, quisquis, perficere, oboedientes (oboedientia), desidiosi (desidia* only in 73 and Prol 2), *inchoatio (inchoare* only in 73 and Prol 4).

2. Cf. Vogüé, *Règle*, IV, 42.

3. The following, for example, have no Prologue: Pachomius, *Praec.; Reg. Or.;* Augustine, *Praec.* Others, such as Isidore, Basil, and Fructuosus, begin with love of God; still others with the reception of new members, for example *Reg. Tarn.;* Caesarius, *Reg.*

Mon. Cf. also the beginning of *Reg. Ant.* and *Reg. Is.* Cf. further admonitions, for example Orsiesius, *Lib.* 1: "Listen, Israel." Pachomius, *Cat.* 1: "My son, listen." Pelagius, *Ep. ad vg.* 1: "Listen, my daughter."

4. This could also account for the change from "you" to "we," and from the singular to the plural. The individual should listen first, then the whole community will be able to listen.

5. Cf. Reetz, "Wort zur Regel," 224; Augrain, "Sources," 6.

6. Cf. The corresponding sounds in vv. 1-2:

Obscul*ta*	o fil*i*
praecep*ta*	magister*i*
et inclina *aurem*	cord*is* tu*i*
et admonitione*m*	p*ii* patr*is*
libent*er* excip*e*	et efficacit*er* compl*e*
ut ad eum *per oboedientiae*	labor*em* red*eas*
a quo *per inoboedientiae*	desidi*am* recesser*as.*

Cf. Lentini, *Ritmo*, 73; Borias, "Nouveaux cas," 318; the following words occur only here: *obsculta, o, inclina, excipe, efficaciter, inoboedientiae, desidia, recedere, abrenuntians, praeclara, arma, inchoare, instantissima, deposcas.*

7. Note also that all key words of the first four verses begin with the letter "O": *obsculta, oboedientia, oratio.*

8. The Latin text says: "*Audi, fili, admonitionem Patris tui et inclina aurem tuam ad verba mea, adcommoda mihi libenter auditum tuum et corde credulo cuncta quae dicuntur ausculta. Cupio enim te instruere, quae sit spiritalis militia et quibus modis regi tuo militare debeas*" (*Prooemium*). Note the verbal parallels: *ausculta, fili, praecepta, inclina aurem, cor, pater, libenter.* Add from chapter 1: *Oboedire, labor, Regi militare, arma.* Cf. Manning, "*Admonitio.*" Regarding authorship, cf. Vogüé, "Entre Basile," 20 f.

9. Cf. Prol 8–13: Listening, heart, action;

Prol 14–21: Hear, do good, way of life;

Prol 23–34: Hear, dash the evil against Christ, the Lord accomplishes the good deeds, hear, act;

Prol 35–41: Hear the precepts, answer the admonition by deeds, prepare heart and body, service of obedience to the commandments, help of grace.

10. Cf. also Prov 1:8; 2:2; Sir 51:21; Prov 6:20; cf. Sir 2:1f.; 6:33f.

11. Fattorini, "Ascolto," 101–109 points out the importance of listening in the Acts of the Apostles for salvation and in reference to baptism. Miquel, "Oeil," gathered many ancient texts about hearing and seeing. Philo of Alexandria, *De Abraham* 150 (ed. Cohn, L.: *Die Werke Philos von Alexandrien*, vol. I [Breslau, 1909]): "The ear, being slower and more feminine, ought to take second place."

12. "So when saying 'Our Father who art in heaven,' brothers, let us now show that we are sons such as God wants to have, and may the Divinity rightly grant us the title of sons, seeing our will conformable to his own. For he who resembles his father not only in appearance but also in conduct is a true son." Cf. also Hildemar, 4.

13. *Admonitio,* "Prooemium"; cf. also RM Prol 2, 5, 17.

14. Hildemar, 5; cf. Augustine, *In Ps.* 33.II.16 (12).

15. According to Gewehr, "Zu den Begriffen," 54, this would correspond to Augustine's usage. One can distinguish two movements in ancient spiritual literature. First, there is a more intellectual trend, influenced by Platonic ideas where the heart is not

important, even in reference to Sacred Scripture. Benedict is part of the second trend, where the heart plays an important role and where authors are not speaking from intellectual speculation, but from their experience, e.g., Origen, John Climacus, Anthony, Diadochus of Photice, and others. Cf. the article "Cor et cordis affectus" in DS 2 (1953) 2278; Guillaumont, "Sens."

16. In the third element of the sentence, the accusative precedes (*admonitionem pii patris*). *Libenter excipe* is parallel to *efficaciter comple*. In the Vulgate, the word *libenter* usually occurs together with receiving and hearing, e.g., Prov 19:12; Mark 12:37.

17. Cf. Mark 4:20; Luke 8:15.

18. This also places the more feminine aspect ahead of the masculine; cf. Torre, "Hapax," 77.

19. The Prologue of the Master is constructed in a similar manner. Each section begins with a verb of listening or paying attention, followed by the admonition to act, cf. vv. 1, 3, 5, 7, 8, 14, 16, 19, 22. A drastic apophthegma of Anthony gives a good illustration of Prol 1 (cf. Régnault, *Les sentences des Pères du désert*, vol. III [Solesmes, 1976] 148f.): "The camel needs only little food. It carries the food within until it reaches its stable. Then it regurgitates and chews its cud anew until it permeates its bones and flesh. But the horse needs much food; it eats at any hour and immediately loses what it has eaten. Therefore: Let's not be like the horse! I mean: We recite the word of God every hour, but we don't put it into practice. Let's follow the camel's example by reciting each word of Sacred Scripture, keeping it within us until we have put it into practice." (Translation from French, mb.)

20. Cyprian, *Ep.* 65.5; Augustine, *De Civ. Dei* XI.28; *De nat. et grat.* XX.22. Cf. Borias, "Christ," 114; Widhalm, *Die rhetorischen Elemente,* 172f. Benedict's borrowing a sentence from an ancient author does not imply that he also makes its ideological context his own.

21. According to the Master, we are born of Adam and Eve and have descended into this world (Th 3; cf. Thp 4), but now we should recognize the Lord who is inviting us as our father and mother (Th 24), throwing off the weight of sin (Th 19–23); cf. the connection between the return to paradise and baptism.

22. *Vit. Patr.* V. 14.9; cf. also V. 1.9, 19.

23. *Vit. Patr.* V. 14.13.

24. *Vit. Patr.* V. 14.19. Then he lists four levels: first, the people who thank God in illness; then, those who practice hospitality; then, those who live in solitude. The highest level is reserved for those who obey. In conclusion, he says that obedience is the salvation of all the faithful, the mother of all virtues, . . . that it opens the heavens, elevates all people from the earth, and is the food of all the saints . . . through which they reached perfection.

25. Compare the two lists:

bene viventes et obedientes—73.6	*male viventes . . . desidiosi . . . neglegentes*—73.7
lectioni vacent—48.22	*neglegens et desidiosus ut non velit aut not possit meditare aut legere*—48.23
vacant lectioni—48.17	*frater acediosus qui vacat otio aut fabulis*—48.18 *non est intentus lectioni*—48.18
Cf. *labor oboedientiae*	*desidia inoboedientiae*

26. Steidle, "*Oboedientiae,*" 433.

27. *Vit. Patr.* V. 14.15; cf. *Vit. Patr.* V. 7.14; *Apoph.* John the Dwarf, 37; *Vit. Patr.* V. 3.16; Cassian, *Conf.* XX.1.2; Faustus v. Riez, *Ep.* 1.

28. Cf. Jerome, *Ep.* 22.15; and *Ep.* 130.7.11; Cyprian, *De hab. vg.* 3. Cf. Borias, "Influence de S. Cyprien," 56; Mohrmann, "Latinité," 134: *Dativus sympatheticus.*

29. *Conf.* III.6; cf. also III.10; *Inst.* IV.34.

30. Cf. RM 7.46 (the entire quotation, especially the second part, *a voluntatibus tuis avertere*); 10.30, 36; cf. 3.66. The Scripture text is not found in Pachomius, Basil (*Reg.*) and Cassian (*Conf.; Inst.*).

31. *Spiritual Exercises*, Nos. 91–98; cf. No. 95, where Christ, the Lord, says: "It is my will to conquer the entire world and all enemies and thus to enter into the glory of my Father. Therefore, whoever wishes to join me in this enterprise must be willing to labor with me, that by following me in suffering, he may follow me in glory" (*Spiritual Exercises of St. Ignatius.* Ed. L. J. Puhl, S.J. [Chicago: Loyola University Press, 1951] 44). Cf. RB Prol 50.

32. Cf. Hildemar, 13; Smaragdus's comment to this text.

33. Cf. Herwegen, *Sinn*, 329, 337; Steidle, "Versprechen," 121f. and "*Oboedientiae*," 429. With regard to the entire concept, cf. "Militia," in DIP, especially 1319–1321.

34. Cf. Auer, "Militia Christi," 343f.; Fontaine, "Chrétiens," 99; "Militia," in TTL, 967f.; Cyprian, *Ep.* 58.2; 56.2.

35. Cf. Auer, "Militia," 344; "Militia," TTL, 969; Campenhausen, "Kriegsdienst," 205; Caesarius, *s.* 80.3; Cyprian, *Ep.* 74.9.

36. Cf. Colombas, "Concepto," 283–285; Penco, "Concetto," 22–23; Ps Fausstus v. Lérins, *s.* 1 (*ad monachos*); Jerome, *Ep.* 14.2.3; Caesarius, *s.* 238.2 speaks of the psalms as *arma* against the devil; cf. Orsiesius, *Lib.* 34; Augustine, *De op.mon.* 25.32; 28.36; Cassian, *Inst.* I.1.1 and V.18.2: "*athleta Christi.*"

37. Cf. Mohrmann, "Langue," 335–339; cf. 2 Tim 2:4 (Vg); RM 82.16 and 91.11 use *serviens Deo.*

38. Cf. J. Blank, "Ziehet die Waffenrüstung Gottes an," in *Orientierung* 46 (1982) 213–216.

39. Cf. Manning, "Signification," 135–138; cf. also for example, how Eph 6:14 is used in Prol 21 in a nonmilitary sense: "girded with faith and the doing of good works."

40. The word *deposcere* for "to pray" occurs only once in RB (*hapax*); it is not used in RM or the Vulgate.

41. Reetz, "Das Wort zur Regel," 481. The superlative form of the adjective is rare in patristic literature and does not occur in the Vulgate.

42. According to semi-Pelagianism, faith and the will to do what is good originate from the human person. The person begins the good work, even though it cannot be completed without the help of grace (*nostrum est velle, Dei autem perficere*). This teaching was prevalent in Benedict's time, also in monastic circles. It was condemned at the Second Council of Orange in 529 (cf. Hefele, II, 1097). Presumably, Benedict did not want to make an explicit statement about it. He is not concerned about theological speculations, but rather deals with the practical. In the text of his Rule, however, he puts more emphasis on grace than the Master does. Cf. 4.42 f.: "To attribute whatever good you notice in yourself to God, not to oneself (RM: more to God than to oneself). But to be certain that the evil we commit is our own and ours to acknowledge" (RM: to self and to the devil). Cf. also RM together with Prol 29: "Who are convinced that our good deeds do not come from ourselves, but from the Lord . . . , 30: they praise the Lord

working in them." If Benedict here is referring to *Adm.* XI (Ps Basil), which does not seem certain to me, it would still be clearer that he speaks radically for the need of grace. The *Admonitio* says: "Whenever you begin some work, first call upon God, and do not cease to give thanks once you have completed it." Thus the changes made by Benedict would indicate his awareness that it is not we, but only God, who completes the work.

43. In the old Missal, it was the oration after the fourth lesson on Ember Saturday in Lent. *Sacram. Veron.* XXII.542: *"cum omne opus bonum a te incoari constet et perfici."*

44. Looking at the Latin texts, we see that most of the material comes from Basil, but also from Augustine, RM, *Vit. Patr.*, the liturgy, and Sacred Scripture.

School of the Lord's Service

Only here, in the final paragraph of the Prologue, does Benedict speak specifically about the monastic life to which he wants to introduce us.[1] The first and last verses (45, 50) are taken almost verbatim from the Master, but as a correction to his concept of "school," verses 46-49 are inserted. This addition is strikingly similar to chapter 72.[2]

V. 45: Therefore we wish to establish a school of the Lord's service.

1. *Therefore we wish . . . to establish. Ergo,* "therefore" leads us to expect the summing up of the entire Prologue. The Prologue treated Christian life in general. Now everything is concretized in view of monastic life. The word *constituere,* to found, set up, establish is repeated in the next verse. It sets a legal tone and refers to an institution with regulations and laws. However, the inserted verses show that good order has only an auxiliary function.

Excursus: *Scola*[3]

Many of us do not like this term for a monastery, and not because it might evoke old, lingering, unpleasant memories of former times. For us, school was not primarily a community, but a place where learning mattered, perhaps even the teacher. Students strove for the best grades. School seemed only a preparation for life. Real life started after school was finished.

This corresponds quite closely to the concept of school in RM. For the Master, learning under a reliable teacher is important. Christ is this teacher, and after him the abbot as his representative. The individual monastic is learning the spiritual art, how to fight the devil and the self, how to attain salvation. The monastics are treated as in a school of the old style. The school is oriented to the future of each pupil-monk. The whole student body, governed by the abbot, does not aim at fostering brotherly community. The biblical statements about the first Christian community, the band of disciples or Psalm 132 (133) about the joy of living together in harmony are less important for RM.[4]

Background of the Times:

a. School signifies a place where one spends leisure time (*scola* in its original meaning), where one practices, learns or does a specific service. Thus the ancient Roman churches have a *scola cantorum*, a space reserved for the singers.

b. School means a group of people pursuing similar goals. Since the fourth century, the term was applied to the associations and corporations of the emperor's service. There was a military *scola*, whose head was a master and whose members called each other brothers. The church also is called a *scola*. Augustine says that all Christians are students of Christ, that in him we have gathered in his *scola* and that we are fellow pupils.[5]

c. *Scola* designates the practice, the work, the zeal and the effort one applies in order to reach a desired goal.[6]

Monasticism:

a. In monastic literature, *scola* also designates the place of the monastery, the monastic compound which is separated from the world outside.[7]

b. It is the community of those who serve and fight. According to the concept of monastic life, the communal aspect is emphasized or the aspect of exercise.[8] For Cassian, the school of cenobites is a preparation for eremitical life. After the monk has learned to practice virtue in the monastic enclosure of the community, he is able to leave the school in order to strive for the summit of perfection as a hermit.[9] But no real community can exist in this situation. The Master, and Benedict after him, adds that the monk perseveres in this school until death (Ths 46; RB Prol 50).

c. In the Prologue of the Master, the theological background is more clearly noticeable. By the Lord's word, "Come to me, I will refresh you" (Matt 11:28), he alludes to baptism (Th 11). With the second call of Jesus, "Take my yoke upon you and learn from me" (Matt 11:29) he points to the school of the Lord's service (Th 16–18). The yoke of Jesus is monastic living. The old, oppressive yoke is sin. The main purpose of the school is letting oneself be imbued wholeheartedly by Christ the teacher, by his word, the Gospel. This builds upon baptism and leads by sharing in Christ's passion to a sharing in his reign (Ths 46). The monastery is a *scola* within the *scola* of the church, through the church, and for the church.[10]

Benedict uses the word *scola* only here, in verse 45, which he took over from RM. In the next verses he adds a corrective. He certainly does mean the place, the monastic compound, in which the monk perseveres. *Scola* includes exercises and learning doctrine, Sacred Scripture, the teaching of Christ (Prol 50; cf. 2.4; 64.9). The abbot also is a teacher (cf. RB 2) who teaches the spiritual art (RB 4), so that the monk can be healed and can attain to true life. The concept of school shows that the monk is always on the way, has never finished learning. But Benedict differs essentially from the school concept of the RM. He does not want to impose harsh and difficult things. He is rather concerned about love (Prol 47, 49; especially RB 72), about service done with love (35.6), about real fraternal relations. Also, joy does not come only after one is done with school. It shines out here and now in daily life (cf. Prol 49). Benedict is not concerned about competing in virtue, in humility and asceticism, but about outdoing one another in love, in mutual obedience (71; 72); all together we want to be guided and led by Christ (72.12). *Discretio* (discretion) requires consideration for the weak and good use of strengths. Benedict is rather cautious regarding the term "school" and words like student, teacher, teaching, master, and so on. Most of these occur only in the first chapters of the Rule, in which he depends on the Master.[11] So we can say with fair certainty that the concept of "school" is not, as sometimes assumed, his ideal for a community.

3. *Of the Lord's service.*[12] This is service due to the Lord, belonging to him. Already Prol 3 was a call to serve Christ the Lord as loyal followers. The subject matter and purpose of this school are here indicated briefly and strikingly as "service of the Lord." Profession is also described simply as "holy service" (*servitium sanctum*, 5.2); liturgical life is *devotionis servitium* (18.24). Serving and service (*servitium, servitus, servire*) are used by Benedict to denote liturgical prayer, obedience, all practical work for the common good, service to brothers, the sick and the guests. In all these activities, the service of the Lord is realized. Considering the meaning of *scola*, we also might translate, "We want to establish a community which does a specific service for Christ."[13]

The circle of disciples around Jesus is such a school, a community of service to the Lord. Unlike the rabbis whom the disciples choose (cf. John 15:16), Jesus himself calls his disciples. In a similar way the Lord, by the word of Sacred Scripture, calls the laborers to the monastery (cf. Prol 14). The disciple of Jesus never becomes a master like a rabbi (Luke 6:40). The Torah unites the disciples of the rabbis, but for Jesus' disciples it is the person of Christ. Benedict also stresses the person of Christ rather than objective doctrine. The disciple of Christ never stops learning. He remains a person who listens and obeys until death (Prol 1; 72). The disciples also realize the service of the Lord in mutual service and service for the kingdom; they share in Jesus' tasks by deeds and by proclaiming the word (cf. missioning discourses). Every monastery is given such a task of witnessing to the kingdom, whether by direct service to people, by the radiant witness of life, or by prayer. In our time, the element of learning is particularly important. We keep learning throughout life, we are never finished learning. Thus we always stand before God and people as receiving persons.

The adjective *dominicus* throughout the Rule designates what belongs to the Lord, for example the Lord's sheepfold (*dominicis. . . ovilibus*, 1.8), but it also refers to the words which the Lord himself spoke (*Genitivus subjectivus*: for example, *dominicum praeceptum*, 4.61; *oratio dominica*, 13.12). Thus, from a grammatical vantage point, one may interpret "the Lord's service" as service which the Lord renders to us, even though Benedict may not have intended it directly. It is the function of a rule to show how we are to respond, by our service, to the service which the Lord renders to us. Jesus called himself a servant who came not to be served but to serve and to give up his life (Mark 10:45; cf. John 13:1-15). This service of the Lord to us takes place in the celebration of the liturgy, for example, but throughout the day he also lovingly works and helps us. In this community we become joined to his service, we are healed and redeemed by him, we share in his service and we pass it on.

V. 46: In this foundation we hope
to set down nothing harsh, nothing burdensome.

Here begins the corrective insertion of Benedict. For the Master the school involved much that was "harsh and difficult," like an imposed martyrdom: suppression of self-will, penitential exercises, humiliations.[14]

1. *In this foundation we hope . . . to set down.* Benedict knows that hard and difficult things will come; they are part of human reality. But he does not seek them out as means for perfection; they are not intended by him.

2. *Nothing harsh, nothing burdensome.* This seems to contradict RB 58.8: The novice "is to be told at the start about all the hardships and difficulties

by which we go to God." If we infer from the Rule for what kind of community it was written, some terrible things occurred there, such as slander, difficulties of all kinds, hatred, jealousy, even persecutions, and so on. The community consisted of robust and also of very weak persons, of very different characters living together. Add to this the hard times during which Benedict wrote his Rule. The monks had to work hard and suffer various privations. Today we might also think of an overburdening with work.

If a brother is commanded something difficult or impossible (RB 68.1), he may start an open dialog with his superior. The Rule should not make it too difficult to keep the fast (38.10) or to perform the needed services (35.13). Hard things are not deliberately imposed on the monks. Benedict tries to avoid harsh things or to deal with them in the spirit of the Gospel (cf. RB 48).

Patristic literature contains many similar kinds of encouragement. Pelagius writes that full justice is not harsh, not unapproachable.[15] Augustine in his homily on Matthew 11:28-30 mentions that some things seem hard and difficult, but that the Lord took them upon himself.[16] And Honoratus is said to have tried to make the yoke of Christ easy for the brothers.[17] It should not be hard and burdensome, for the Lord himself said that his yoke is easy and light.

V. 47: However, if there is occasionally a little strictness
  when sufficient reason requires it
  (when reason and justice call for it),
  for wiping out faults and preserving love,
V. 48: do not flee immediately, daunted by fear,
  from the way of salvation,
  which is bound to be narrow at the beginning.

1. *However, if there is . . . a little strictness.* Although Benedict does not want to command anything harsh or burdensome, there comes this "however." Sometimes strictness is necessary. This and the following verse provide an insight into the person of Benedict. Though certainly far advanced in the spiritual life himself, he can feel with a newcomer and comfort and encourage him.

The Latin word *paululum*, a very little, does not occur again in the RB. It is also not found in the Master's text nor in the sources from the Fathers. Benedict does not want to impose anything on the newcomer which he is not yet able to bear. The 'if' indicates that it is not inevitable that life becomes difficult. Besides, there is only "a little" strictness. Benedict seems to be a man of balance, standing in the middle between strictness and laxity, a person of discretion, open to both sides and listening to the circumstances.

For things that may seem difficult, he gives reasons. If one can accept these reasons, one will also be prepared to accept the difficulties that arise.

2. *When there is sufficient reason (when reason and justice [aequitas] require it).* *Ratio* can mean both "reason/cause" or "sense." The Rule uses it in both senses.[18] *Ratio* with the meaning of common sense is assigned an important role.

Benedict uses a similar expression in 2.19. He is explaining that the abbot may make exceptions in the normal monastic rank for reasons of justice or good sense (2.18-19). *Aequitas* is what is proper, just, giving each one what he is entitled to or needs, not a simple rigid application of the law to persons, but consideration of the personal situation.[19] This marks the entire Rule of Benedict, though the actual word is not used again. Thus, everything should be so ordered that "the strong will find what they seek and the weak will not be turned back by fear" (64.19). Each one is to receive what he needs (cf. 34). This means for the others that they should back off, forgive, understand. In this sense *aequitas*, which makes community life possible, may also be hard for the individual.

3. *For wiping out faults.* For this purpose, as Prol 36 states, the days of our life are lengthened. The abbot also stands in need of this purification; it is accomplished while he is serving the others (2.40). Benedict is writing his Rule for sinful human beings who all need conversion and purification. RB 7 describes this way of purification for the individual monk, until he at last is "cleansed of vices and sins" (7.70). Purification of faults for Cassian is the first degree of the practical life.[20] Life in community purifies the individual; it helps to rub off the rough edges (cf. comments on RB 73.1).

4. *For preserving love.* Purification from faults only makes sense if it creates space for love. What kind of love is meant here? In RB 65 Benedict sets down a regulation "for preserving peace and love" (65.11). There he means brotherly love, the love for the community, without excluding the vertical dimension, love of God (cf. comments on RB 72). In chapter 72 we see what this kind of love requires; also in RB 35–36 and 53. One is reminded of the "apostolic love" in Cassian. Chapter 7 is intended to lead to love, the "bond of perfection" (Col 3:14). Love determines everything. Paul says, "If I give away all my possessions and surrender my body to fire, yet have no love, it profits me nothing" (1 Cor 13:3). Love should not pass like a fire of straw, but must be preserved and safeguarded (*conversatio*).[21]

5. *Do not flee immediately, daunted by fear.* In this verse Benedict resumes the use of "you" (sg.), addressing the individual (cf. Prol 1–4). He will use it again at the very end, in the last two verses of the Rule (73.8-9). The encouragement is meant very personally, for the individual. The ex-

pression "daunted/seized by fear" (*pavore perterritus*) does not recur in RB, and it does not occur in RM, in Basil (*Reg.* and *Adm*) or Cassian.[22] In the Latin Bible this expression shows the reaction to God's manifestation and action in situations of human crises (cf. Gen 41:8; 1 Kings 31:4; Mark 16:8, etc.). Benedict can imagine that someone, especially a newcomer, might be totally gripped by fear. He also names this feeling, so that one can deal with it. Do not flee! Presumably it has happened that someone ran away from the monastery in fright. Similarly he says "to arrange everything so that the strong find what they desire and the weak will not run away" (64.19), "without overwhelming them with work or driving them away" (48.24). Throughout his Rule, Benedict is concerned about not overtaxing or discouraging the weak. Not to run away, but to have perseverance and trust in the way is demanded. Only then will the monastic experience the guidance and beauty of the way.

6. *The way of salvation*. Here and in the next verse Benedict uses the image of the way to describe monastic life (*via*, Prol 48 and 49; cf. excursus: dynamism, pp. 95–96). He always uses the word "way" in the general Christian sense as "way of life" (Prol 20), as the "way to the tent" (Prol 24), as the "way to God" (71.2), as the narrow way leading to life (5.11). The Bible also calls Christianity the way (cf. Acts 9:2; 19:2, 23, etc). The monastery as a school and as the way—both metaphors convey a dynamism, implying movement towards a goal. Here the goal is not called perfection, but "salvation." Benedict is concerned about the final goal of Christian life. We reach it by the way of the commandments or by obedience (Prol 49; Prol 2). We may be surprised by two facts: first, that monastic life is not termed a special way, but simply as the Christian way; and second, that for someone called, this way of life as a monastic apparently is the way to salvation, a concretization of the way of God's commandments. Already the beginning of the Prologue was concerned simply about the return to God through obedience. One might be shocked that here for a beginner, monastic life is called the "way of salvation." A similar shock must have been felt by the rich man when he asked Jesus what he had to do to attain eternal life (Mark 10:17-21). After Jesus becomes fond of him, it is clear he can win eternal life only by following Christ. One becomes aware in the course of the Rule that Benedict deals with sinful people. He is not talking about greater or lesser degrees of perfection, but about death and life, perdition and salvation (cf. 28.5).[23]

7. *It is bound to be narrow at the beginning*. The beginning is difficult. This resembles the biblical text: "The gate leading to life is narrow, and the way leading there is narrow" (Matt 7:14). Both the gate and the way are narrow. In this sense Benedict once mentions the narrow way as the way of

obedience (5.11). The Gospel takes a more objective view. A narrow way means one must walk carefully, as Hilary and Basil put it, there is danger to the right and to the left; one needs a good guide.[24] It is the way of the center, the way of virtue. The Rule does not promise that the way becomes wider; it will probably remain narrow. Benedict goes to a subjective level in telling how the way is experienced. Thus he can give hope to the discouraged. The way is hard only at the beginning. Benedict is emboldened to make this interpretation by another Gospel text which forms a background (and Ps 118 [119]:32): "Take my yoke upon you and learn from me . . . my yoke is easy and my burden is light" (Matt 11:29-30).

The tight beginning, the narrow gate means leaving everything behind, setting out on the way with determination, without undue attachment, without hesitation, not looking back (cf. Luke 9:62). Cassian explains that even this beginning of conversion and of faith is God's gift of grace (*Conf.* III.15.2). Hilary of Poitiers describes the narrow way as a passage to freedom.[25] Caesarius of Arles admits that the way seems arduous and sometimes even impossible, but only as long as we think we must run with our human strength.[26] Augustine explains that the narrowness arises from human limitations and a lack of love.[27] All point to later progress in love and liberty.

V. 49: But as we progress
           in the monastic life and in faith
           our hearts expand
           and with unspeakable sweetness of love
           we run the way of God's commandments.

This verse stresses going ahead, whereas verse 50 expresses persevering. The two complement each other: On the way (v. 49) we should persevere (v. 50). The same progression of beginning, progress, immediate and final goal is found in RB 73 and 7.

1. *As we progress in monastic life and in faith. Conversatio* is the monastic way of the virtues, the life in community, a steady advancing together with all its members (72.12). It comprises the monastic life as interpreted in a particular community and also includes the specific task of the community. *Conversatio* is based on faith and shown in good works. As Prologue 21–22 says, "Let us gird our loins with faith and the doing of good works and walk his ways under the guidance of the Gospel, that we may deserve to see him who has called us to his kingdom . . . we must hasten forward with good works if we wish to arrive at all."

Fides, faith, can mean the living faith as distinct from vision,[28] but it can also denote faithfulness to one's vocation, faithfulness to our monastic profession. In this sense, the two terms *conversatio, fides* are similar.[29] Monastic life is a life by faith, a life of faithfulness to our given word.

2. *The heart expands (dilatato corde)*.[30] This term, together with "running the way of God's commandments," certainly is influenced by Psalm 118 (119):32: "I will run the way of your commands, for you open my docile heart." This verse also talks of the way of God's commandments; it was a verse which was very dear to monastics. They prayed it to Christ and with Christ, in a "Christian mode."[31] Benedict uses one verse of this psalm for profession (*Suscipe me*) and bases the liturgical Hours on it (RB 16).

Benedict probably felt that this psalm verse expressed his own experience. Therefore he did not have to create new terms. While maturing in the spiritual life, he penetrated ever more into Sacred Scripture. At the same time, it was probably Sacred Scripture guiding him. Spaciousness is the core of liberation. "In danger I called on the Lord; the Lord answered me and set me free" (Ps 117 [118]:5). Hildemar says that the heart expands when someone reaches out beyond himself, fixing his eyes on God, seeing joy and goodness.

3. *With unspeakable sweetness of love*. The expanded heart is filled with love, with joy, with the sweetness of love.[32] Benedict's personal experience of God seems to shine out here, and perhaps this is the reason he emphasizes that it cannot be expressed in words. We are reminded of 1 Peter 1:8: ". . . even though you do not see him now, yet believe in him, you rejoice with an indescribable and glorious joy." Paul calls God's gift to us unspeakable (2 Cor 9:5). As in RB 4.77, the background might be Paul's words, "what eye has not seen and ear has not heard, and what has not entered the human heart, what God has prepared for those who love him" (1 Cor 2:9).

It is also because of love that the hard things become easy. "Nothing is hard for those who love."[33] At the beginning the monastic must make a great effort (*labor*), as Benedict indicates (cf. also Prol 2), but as love is given greater scope within, the burden becomes easier. The monastic does not think of self, but of the Lord, of the community, of the whole world, forgetting self. Benedict himself seems to have been such a big-hearted person, full of "good zeal." Love prefers nothing whatsoever to Christ and is shown clearly in fraternal service. Isn't it a sign of our genuine prayer life when our heart opens up in compassion for all people? This can happen in prayer, in our daily service and our tasks done for people. "The love of Christ impels us" (2 Cor 5:4).

In the parallel monastic and patristic texts we frequently find reflections on this expanded heart and on love, but rarely such a precise summary, with the glow of personal experience shining through. Cassian says that hearts are narrowed by impatience and lack of courage, that they are expanded by long-suffering, patience, and love (*Conf.* XVI.27). Like Augustine, Benedict seems to have consciously chosen two similar expressions: *dilatato corde . . . dilectionis dulcedine*. The expanse is love, and with it comes joy. Augustine says, "Expanse of heart is joy in justice. . . . We should not be constricted by fear of punishment, but expanded by love and joy in justice."[34] The Church Fathers trace the expanded heart to the indwelling of God or the Holy Spirit or the whole Blessed Trinity. The Holy Spirit is love in person. Once space has been created in a person, the heart can become God's dwelling.[35]

This goal can be reached already here on earth. Benedict also describes it in RB 72. Good zeal for him is ultimately the person of Christ who guides us from within (cf. also 7.67-70). Love, joy, and freedom belong together. Gregory describes a similar relationship in the *Dialogs*. After Benedict had overcome temptations, working hard on himself and maturing spiritually, he sees the whole world as in a single ray of sunlight (II.35.5-7). He realizes the smallness and narrowness of all earthly things. The inmost soul expands and extends into God. Progress from the laborious beginning to love and joy while advancing is a frequent topic. Synkletika says, "Sinners who turn to God are laboring and struggling, but afterwards they experience unspeakable joy" (*Vit. Patr.* V.3, 16). A piece of wood held in the fire first turns black and starts to smoke—this means tears of compunction—only then does it begin to glow (ibid.).

4. *We run the way of God's commandments.* As has become clear, this is no special way, but the way shown to us by Sacred Scripture. The commandments of God include not only the Ten Commandments, but also wholehearted love of God and neighbor (cf. Mark 12:30). Like the Master, Benedict seems to believe that walking, just moving ahead, is not enough. Rather one should hasten, run (cf. RB 73). This seems to be a sign of intense love and zeal, as well as of longing for God and the magnetism of God who comes to meet us.

In the next verse, "hastening" and "persevering" are connected. Gregory of Nyssa says that by being grounded in the rock and persevering in doing good, one makes rapid progress.[36] We must never settle down comfortably, but keep hastening onward.

Here we come very close to the heart of Benedict and to his experience of God. He seems to forget himself. His usually sober speech becomes almost exuberant. Already in the next verse he takes hold of himself again.

V. 50: Never swerving from his instructions,
we want to persevere in the monastery until death,
faithfully observing his teaching

**and sharing by patience in the sufferings of Christ,
so that we may also deserve to share in his glory.**

The beginning of this sentence shows that the verse follows most naturally after verse 45.[37]

1. Instruction, teaching (magisterium, doctrina). These two terms fit with the word "school" in verse 45. Whereas the Master loves these expressions, Benedict uses them chiefly in the first chapters of his Rule. Whose instruction and teaching is this? Following verse 49, it refers to God (*Deus*); following verse 45, it would pertain to the Lord (Christ). It is the latter meaning which Benedict probably intended. Here in the monastery, Christ is the instructor. He teaches through Sacred Scripture and through the abbot, who is to convey his instruction (cf. 2.4).

2. Never swerving, . . . persevering in the monastery until death. Before being handed the Rule, the candidate is told that he is free to leave (58.10). However, once he has committed himself, he is forbidden to depart (58.15). He must persevere despite difficulties and not withdraw (7.36).[38]

In the Acts of the Apostles the first Christian community is twice described as "devoting themselves to the teaching of the apostles" (2:42; cf. also 1:14). This instruction is mentioned first, before community (*koinonia*) and the breaking of the bread. The Acts of the Apostles speak of the instruction by the apostles, which of course handed on the words of the Lord. RB calls it "his instruction." One may recall 2 John 9: "Whoever does not remain in Christ's instruction does not stay with God. But whoever remains in the instruction is in communion with the Father and the Son." Christ and his word is highlighted right at the beginning as the unifying core of this community. At the same time the nature of the community is emphasized, modeled on the original Christian community. The monastery is to be a real Christian community formed by the Word of God. The Prologue begins with "listen." When all are open and obedient to the Word of God, such a community can arise and grow.

We are to persevere not only in the instruction, but also in the monastery. This means that the cenobitic community is not just a preparation for eremitical life. This school can lead monastics to love. "Never departing," this does not mean never leaving the monastic compound (cf. RB 50,67), but that remaining in the monastery is the normal way of persevering in obedience. The monastery is both, the place and the community. It seems to indicate that the work of Benedictines normally is performed in community and as a community.

Until death reminds us of Christ who became obedient unto death (Phil 2:8). Benedict quotes this verse in 7.34. Jesus also says, "But the one who perseveres to the end will be saved" (Matt 24:13; 10:22). The martyrs had this kind of courage. The time of persecutions was over, but day-to-day perseverance also calls for heroism. Already before his profession, the new-comer had to practice perseverance as he was kept standing at the door: "If he keeps knocking at the door and patiently bears the harsh treatment and difficulties of entry, persisting in his request" (58.3). This was the first proof of his fitness for the life of a monk.[39]

Persevering and staying are not something static, but taking root as does a tree, which then can extend its branches far out. It is perseverance in has-tening toward God. Eucherius says, "We must win our race by perseverance and persistence, standing in this place of our calling and advancing"[40] (cf. excursus on stability, pp. 134–136). Being aware of our roots is particularly important in our mobile and dynamic society. A person with a certain "place," a firm position, having an identity, can be flexible and open to the whole world with an inner security. Was not Benedict's firm grounding in the monastic tradition, especially in the church and in the Word of God, the reason why he could be so open and ready to listen? This gave him the courage to take risks. Without such roots we easily give way to anxiety, be-coming rigid and immobile. This is true of our own person and our life story, but also for a community and its history. We can only advance into the future when we acknowledge our roots.

Blocking the ways of escape and persevering makes the individual con-front his or her own depths and the darkness of self. In this sense the wis-dom of the Desert Fathers still applies today: "Stay in your cell. Persevering in the cell keeps the monk true to himself" (*Apoph.* Arsenius, 11). One of the ancient Fathers said, "The cell of a monk is the fiery furnace of Babylon in which the three young men found God" (*Vit. Patr.* V.7.38).

3. *Sharing by patience*[41] *in the sufferings of Christ.* Patience is a powerful virtue, joined to the determination to remain under the load and bear it; this virtue is proved by living with other people. Although the Master may have had in mind imposed tests of obedience here, this verse in the Prologue surely may be read in light of RB 72: We are to bear one another's weaknesses with the utmost patience, just as Christ bore our weaknesses. Patience does not shrink from suffering while engaged in something good. It is our response to God's patience (cf. Prol 37). Patience is to be practiced by the newcomer from the very start. Patience is tested not only by obedience in difficulties (7.34, 42; 68.2), but also in serving the sick (36.5) and in fraternal community (72.5). By patience we run toward the goal, as the letter to the Hebrews put it (12:1). By patience the heart is expanded, says Cassian (*Conf.* XVI.27.2).

Benedict here links patience with the passion of Christ. It is even a par-ticipation in his sufferings (plural here, not singular as in RM). While this is almost the only view of monastic life for the Master, Benedict adds the expanded heart, the unspeakable sweetness, the joy of the Holy Spirit already for the here and now (cf. v. 49). The Master speaks far more frequently of Christ's passion (Thp 5.35; 53.51; 55f.; 62). The First Letter of Peter exhorts us to rejoice in the measure of our share in Christ's sufferings (4:13). He even sees it as a grace to suffer innocently, thus following in the footsteps of our suffering Lord (1 Pet 2:19-21). Beyond the direct sources, we also might think of Paul's words: "Now I rejoice in my sufferings for your sake, and in my flesh I am filling up what is lacking in the afflictions of Christ on behalf of his body, which is the Church" (Col 1:24). In Benedict's time there are no more persecutions of Christians, but there still are the daily difficulties, the demands of service, by which one may be united to Christ, a realization of our baptism and profession. However, Benedict does not create contrived situations.

Here the Master says, "so that we may *merit* to share in the suffering of Christ." Benedict says it more realistically. Suffering in itself is difficult, but it can become fruitful for the church and the world by union with Christ.

In our society, which tends to avoid pain as far as possible, to withdraw from mourning, to evade suffering and death, this courageous and sober accepting of reality and making sense of suffering as a Christian seems particularly important. Every community can recall certain members who persevered through suffering and darkness and to whom it owes blessings, growth, and a fruitful apostolate. "Unless the grain falls to the ground and dies, it remains just a grain of wheat; but if it dies, it produces much fruit" (John 12:24).

In Benedict the statement in verse 50 follows immediately after unspeakable love and joy have been mentioned. It is in the very fact of sharing in the sufferings of Christ that we experience the paradox of the Beatitudes: ". . . when people hate you and . . . exclude and insult you . . . , rejoice" (Luke 6:23). It is not the sufferings that distinguish Christians (and monastics) from the non-Christians, but their attitude towards these sufferings.

4. *That we may deserve also to share in his glory.* This last portion is colored by Romans 8:17: "We are heirs of God and co-heirs with Christ when we suffer with him in order to be glorified with him." In the two parts of the sentence, Benedict uses different words to translate the Greek word *koinonia: partecipare, consors.*[42] This created the first Christian community, this made them into one body, that they shared the Body of Christ, the Lord himself, and that they shared themselves and shared with each other (cf. 1 Cor 10:16; Acts 2:44; 4:32). The community is established, built up, and held together by Christ.

The Prologue ends with the eschatological view of the reign, the kingdom. This refers back to the beginning, to Christ the Lord and true King. To obey and serve him now by patience means union with him and gives a share in his glory. This is the final goal of monastic and Christian life. This sentence hearkens back literally to Prol 21f.: "Let us walk his ways under the guidance of the Gospel so that we may deserve to see him who has called us to his kingdom. If we live in his tent and his kingdom. . ." We may also call to mind the very end of the entire Rule : "Under God's protection you will arrive" (73.9). The closing of the Prologue is probably influenced by the liturgy, especially the orations.[43] The entire Prologue describes this way to the final goal. As is clear here at the end, the way becomes concrete in the school of the Lord's service, whose first requirement is listening and obeying. Listen, and you will reach the goal. This is the optimistic tone of both the Prologue and the entire Rule. It is underscored by the solemn "Amen."

Taking one more look at these verses and their likely sources or parallels (the Fathers, Sacred Scripture), we can see clearly that all the main terms such as "school, narrow beginning, expanded heart, teaching of Christ, joy, in patience" are taken from Sacred Scripture. We also see clearly that Sacred Scripture was handed on by the explanations of the Fathers (in parts even verbatim). Benedict stands before us as a person who can share his very personal experiences in biblical terms. His own hand can be seen in the following formulations: "we hope . . . a little strictness . . . for reasons of justice . . . for fostering love . . . do not flee, daunted by fear . . . in sweetness of love." He adds the characteristic Roman virtue of justice, *aequitas*, and emphasizes love in its positive aspects. Above all Benedict is seen in his warm humanity and empathy. His spiritual experiences have also enabled him to become a mature human being.

Notes

1. All this applies if the long Prologue, including vv. 40-50, really is Benedict's work. The oldest preserved manuscript (O) ends with v. 39 and a conclusion ("we become heirs of the kingdom of heaven"). The uncertainty also pertains to RM. Only manuscript P has the long Prologue mentioning the school of the Lord's service and the admonition to persevere in this school until death (Ths 45–46). In manuscript E these verses were placed after the chapter on the kinds of monks, and they introduce the chapter on the abbot. According to Vogüé, this arrangement is secondary; the author of ms E made many similar changes. He thinks that the long Prologue (in RM and RB) is the original, is well crafted as climax of the entire Prologue, and is in harmony with entire Rules. According to Manning and Masai, the long Prologue in RB is a later addition, to which still later someone added vv. 46-49 at the same time as RB 73 (also the work of a later author, not Benedict's; cf. comments on RB 73). For this discussion see, for ex-

ample, Manning, "A propos de la tradition manuscrite," 47–49; Masai, "Les états du chapitre premier," 400–404; Hanslik, "Sprache," 207, 205; Vogüé, "Règle d'Eugippe" and *IV*, 65–69, as well as his criticism of Masai in "Les recherches de F. Masai," 29f.; 300–304; Roth, "Ursprung der RM," 124–127. On the basis of the entire discussion, I concluded that the long Prologue is authentic.

2. Cf. the motive of the way mentioning the final goal (*telos*) and the immediate goal (*skopos*), the difference between the beginning and progress in monastic life, the direct address (*tu*) as well as *currere, cursus, conversatio, initium*, and in v. 50, *doctrina, monasterium, Amen*. Cf. Manning, "Le chapitre 73," 136–139.

3. For the concept of "school," cf. Steidle, "Dominici schola servitii"; Mohrmann, "Langue," 339f.; Reetz, "Das Wort zur Regel," 454f.; Frank, "Vom Kloster als *scola*," 81–84; Penco, "Il concetto di monaco," 23–25; Vogüé, "L'école du Christ," 1–12.

4. Cf. RM (Vogüé), 92, 118, also *VII*, 52f. (*RB-DSC*, 24f.).

5. Augustine, *s*. 177.2; 292.1 and *De disc. Christ*. 11.12; further examples from Augustine in Vogüé, "L'école du Christ," 6f. We might also recall the title of the church in Rome, "Sta Maria in scola greca," in which *scola* designated the Greek settlement. In the larger sense today we also speak of schools of art, theology, etc.

6. Cf. Pelagius, *Ep. ad Demeter*. 12 where *scola* means effort (*studium*).

7. Cf. Steidle, "Dominici scola servitii," 401–403; for Lérins, Faustus, *Ep*. 8; Smaragdus in commenting on this term refers to Ps 45:11: *Vacate et videte quondam ego sum Deus*. The first word was used for the Greek term *scholazete*. In this sense it also alludes to the ancient concept of "a place of being free for." The concept is also used by Caesarius, *Reg. Mon*. 1 and *Reg. vg*. 4 to denote a common living room.

8. Cf. Mohrmann, "Langue," 340; Penco, "Il concetto di monaco," 23–25. The Master uses the word nine more times, three of them in reference to the teacher, the abbot, and his teaching (1.83; 92.26, 29). Thus the monastery is also a school he directs within the church of the Lord. Five times the emphasis is on what is learned: to fight against self-will, to serve or to fight, doing the will of God.

9. *Conf*. III.1.2; XVIII.11; cf. *Conf*. XVIII.16.15; XIX.2.4; XIX.11.1.

10. Cf. Vogüé, *VII*, 48 (*RB-DSC*, 22f.), "L'école du Christ," 8f. where he distinguishes school as school of perfection according to the example of Jesus' disciples from church (*ecclesia*).

11. Cf. Masai, "Les états du chapitre I," 402. *Magister* is used by Benedict only in the first six chapters, whereas in RM it occurs sixty-six times. Checking the use of *doctrina, doctor, docere* yields similar results.

12. According to Mohrmann, "Langue," 340, it should not read "school for the purpose of serving the Lord," but "school that teaches how to serve the Lord."

13. With regard to Prol 45, Rev. Amrhein, O.S.B., states in the first Constitutions for the Congregation of St. Ottilien and the Missionary Benedictine Sisters of 1887 that we must not only learn how to serve the Lord, but that the same love that leads us to God also urges us to be concerned about others who are still far from him.

14. Cf. Butler, *Benedictine Monasticism*, 45: Adjusting to the situation in Italy and Gaul, Benedict "did not gather up what remained still in exercise of the primitive austerities and attempt a restoration of the old ascetic life, but struck out a new line. . . . In place of rivalry in ascetical achievement, he established a common mode of life . . ." Cf., for example, RM 90; 43; 12–14.

15. *Ad Demeter*. 8.

16. *s.* 70.2; cf. also *s.* 69 and 70 on Matt 11:28-30; Cassian, *Conf.* XXIV.25.2f. emphasizes that the royal way is sweet and easy even though it seems hard and difficult, the rough ways should be made smooth. When we come to the Lord, the yoke becomes easy; then follows the reference to Matt 11:28-30.

17. Hilary, *Vit. Hon.* 4.18; also 5.24.

18. In the sense of reason, good sense, it is used five times in the texts proper to Benedict, and the adjective *rationalis* occurs five times also in Benedict's own texts (cf. RB 8.1; 70.5; 2.18; 7.60; 31.7; 71.4; 65.14). Therefore, *aequitatis* could be considered a *genetivus epex*egeticus; cf. Steidle, "Genititvius,"197; Fontaine, "Romanité," 422.

19. Cf. "Aequitas" in TLL 1 (1900) 1015; Herwegen, *Sinn*, 43; "Aequitas" in RAC 1 (1950) 141–144.

20. *Conf.* XV.2; XVIII.1; also *Inst.* IX.9. Regarding his teaching on stages, cf. Art. "Cassien," in DS 2 (1953) 236.

21. Cf. Smaragdus's comment on this text which refers to 1 Pet 4:8.

22. At least not in the *Conferences*. It is noteworthy that expressions of feelings such *paululum restrictius, non . . . refugias, pavore perterritus, inenarrabili . . . dulcedine* rarely are found in the parallel texts of the Fathers. Such expressions also do not recur later on in the Rule.

23. In 28.5 all remedies have been tried on an obstinate brother; the ultimate one is the prayer of the abbot and all the brothers so that "the Lord, who can do all things, may save the ailing brother." In 2.33 Benedict adds that the abbot may not neglect the salvation of the brothers' souls. It is a matter of life or death, cf. 6.5; 7.21; cf. also comments on 72.1-2. The expression *via salutis* also occurs in *Hist. Mon.* 9.422 (*Lives of the Desert Fathers* 10.1) regarding monastic life; cf. also Cassian, *Conf.* III.19.1.

24. Cf. Basil, *Reg.* 139, 140; Hilary of Poitiers, *In Ps.* 118.11.

25. *In Ps.* 118.12.

26. *s.* 236.5.

27. *s.* 69.1: "Why after all, do we all labor? Isn't it because we are mortal human beings, . . . which don't leave each other much room here. But if the vessels of flesh are all squashed together, the space made by charity can always expand." Cf. also *s.* 70.3.

28. Cf. Borias, "La foi," 254.

29. Cf. Vogüé, *IV*, 93; Steidle, "Genitivus," 197f.; Pachomius, *Praec et leges* 14; 53; Ambrose, *De virginitate* 10.59.

30. This word occurs only here (*hapax*) and is not used by the Master.

31. Cf. Harl, "La chaîne," 128–131. Commandments, word, teaching, lamp—all were interpreted as referring to Christ, *the* Word of God.

32. All three words are *hapax* and occur in no other part of the rule. They are also rare in RM. According to Steidle, "Genitivus," 199, *dulcedo* and *dilectio* also mean the same; thus we could translate, "with unspeakable, sweet love," or "with unspeakable sweetness and love." Cf. G. Schultz; "The Sweetness of God," in GuL 57 (1984) 420–424.

33. Jerome, *Ep.* 22.40; Augustine, *In Joh.* 48.1; Gregory of Nyssa, *De Inst. Christ* (PG 46.302); cf. also Diadochus Photicus, *Cent.* 93 (SC 5bis, 154f.); Vogüé, "Cassien," 232–234.

34. *In Ps.* 118; *s.* 10.6; Cassiodorus, *In Ps.* 118.32: "Though it is said that the way of his commandments is narrow, it cannot be run without a large heart."

35. Cf. Ambrose, *In Ps.* 118.4. 27: "Notice the distinction: let the way be narrower, let the heart be wider, so that it can support the habitation of God the Father, the Son and

the Holy Sprit." Augustine, *In Ps.* 118; *S.* 10.6: "How spacious must be the place where God walks! In this breadth of heart there is poured out in us that charity which comes from the Holy Spirit who has been given to us." Hilary of Poitiers, *In Ps* 118.12: "Our heart becomes large, the mystery of the Father and the Son dwells in it; in it the Holy Spirit delights as in a dwelling befitting him"; Gregory of Nyssa, *De Inst. Christ.* (PG 46.305): "And the grace of the Holy Spirit grants eternal life and unspeakable joy in heaven" (this is said in the context of labor and the easy yoke).

36. Gregory of Nyssa, *Life of Moses* II.246; cf. also 243f.

37. Cf. the consecutive *ut* at its beginning; note also the stylistic structuring of the four parts of v. 50: (1a) negative, (1b) positive—(2a) negative, (2b) positive. In Latin there are many alliterations: *Magisterio, mortem, monasterio; passionibus, patientiam participemur*; cf. Lentini, *Il ritmo prosaico* , 75. There is also a connection to *scola,* cf. Marrou, *"Doctrina* et *disciplina,"* 12–15.

38. Cyprian uses similar formulations in *Ep.* 63.18: "Therefore, if we wish to walk in Christ's light, let us not depart from his precepts and admonitions" and in *Ep.* 63.10: ". . . we must not depart at all from the evangelical teachings, the disciples ought also to observe and do those same things which the Master taught and did." Cf. Vogüé, "Persévérer," 342–344.

39. Cf. the alliteration *magisterio, mortem, monasterio,* cf. also RM 79.28, and Caesarius, *Reg. Mon.* 1: "When someone comes to the monastery, he is received only on condition that he remain there until his death."

40. Cf. Steidle, "Versprechen," 111; Eucherius, *H. ad mon.* 5 (PL 50.846); Steidle (ibid.), 109, attributes these homilies to Faustus.

41. On *patientia,* cf. Borias, "S. Benoît, maître en patience"; *patientia* occurs mostly in the New Testament of the Latin Bible.

42. Cf. *participatio, participamus* in 1 Cor 10:16-17; 2 Cor 1:7; cf. also Smaragdus's comment on this text.

43. *Sacram. Veron.* 1487.

Of the Good Zeal
Which Monks Ought to Have

When we hear the title of chapter 72 of the Rule of Benedict, "Of the good zeal . . ." and compare it with our feelings about our world, perhaps we first think of its opposite: evil zeal. Hatred, mistrust, lies, fanaticism, terrorism, and its concrete manifestations: the arms race, violations of human rights, injustice, the loneliness of people— all these seem closer to us. On the other hand, we know of movements for peace, for human rights and dignity, for more effective dialog, for new forms of community in our world as well as in the church.

In this situation of ours, it is not a bourgeois, well-functioning monastic life that can give answers to the profound longings of human beings, but a life that is marked by "the most ardent zeal" (72.3), by radical living of the Gospel, by love of God and neighbor.

Benedict's time was not unlike our own. It was a period of decline and transition. RB 72 probably was written during the Gothic wars. In this context, we can surmise what kind of people composed Benedict's community. Some newcomers may have been motivated to flee from rural areas, or from service in the army; others may have been fleeing the poverty of the peasants and craftsmen, or the rigors of public penance in the church. The monastery offered security and for sinners a way of making atonement. In reading the *Dialogs* of Gregory the Great and the Rule itself, we note a colorful mixture in Benedict's community: nobles, rich people, highly educated persons (*Dial.* II.3.14; 11.1; 20.1; IV.9; RB 48.7-9; 59.1-6), poor, destitute, illiterate people (RB 58.20; 59.7-8; 48.23), soldiers, government functionaries, administrative officials (*Dial.* II.11), craftsmen (57), Romans, Goths (*Dial.* II.6.1f.), priests, visiting monks (RB 60–61), former slaves and free men (RB 2.18), the old and the young (*Dial.* II.11; 24.1; RB 37), and finally, sinners who wished to do penance for grave sins (cf. comments on RB 27–28). Benedict speaks of the strong and the weak (64.19), of the undisciplined, the restless, the obedient, the gentle, the patient, and the negligent (2.25).[1]

How could such diverse people become a community in Christ? In chapter 72, Benedict shows how. Putting this chapter into practice can also be a guideline for today's world, just as it was in Benedict's time.

OVERVIEW

1. Chapter 72 is crafted very carefully. In verses 1-2, Benedict starts with a general principle. First he presents the negative reality, then the positive one (parallelism and antitheses). Verse 12 refers back to it and, together with verse 2, forms an inclusion, as some words are repeated with notable changes.[2] Verse 3 is the first concrete picture of good zeal and a kind of title for the following sentences. Verses 4-8 are crafted like a poem, each verse beginning with a key word and ending with the verb (v. 7 differs and seems to be the core sentence). These five verses describe the daily realization of good zeal in fraternal love. Verses 9-11 are similar in style; their content points to the foundation (God, abbot, Christ).

2. The sentences are skillfully interrelated and show the connection of mutual obedience and fraternal love (*inpendant*—vv. 6 and 8), of ardent love of brothers and of God (*amor*—vv. 3 and 9), of love for the brothers and love for the abbot (*caritas*—vv. 8 and 10), of mutual respect and love for Christ (vv. 4 and 11), of most ardent love and greatest patience (superlatives—vv. 3 and 5). According to its structure, verse 7 belongs to verses 1-2 (v. 7a: evil zeal—v. 1; v. 7b: good zeal—v. 2) or, because of its radicality (*nullus—nihil*) to verse 11 as a concretization of love for Christ.

3. Nearly every sentence stresses "how" one is to act (adverbs or adverbial clauses). At the end, Benedict does not give any further external regulations of conduct but appeals to the heart with these goals of observance. These cannot simply be "fulfilled," but they challenge the entire person and we are never finished doing them. However, Benedict does not want them to remain a matter of attitude. They are to be practiced in daily life (v. 3). This is one of the most intense chapters of the entire Rule (cf., for example, "most ardent love" [*zelus ferventissimo amore*], "with utmost patience" [*patientissime*], "no one" [*nullus*], "nothing whatsoever" [*omnino nihil*]).[3] All three Latin words for love are used in this chapter (*caritas, amor, diligere*) as well as expressions of mutuality of behavior (for example, "with each other" [*se invicem*], "vie with one another" [*sibi certatim*], "brotherly love" [*fraternitas*], "all together" [*pariter*]).

4. In verses 1-2, the evil or good zeal acts. Beginning in verse 3, the monks act (in v. 7 no one), and finally Christ takes over and acts in verse 12. The monastics are to let him lead. In verses 1-2, the vertical dimension is stressed; starting with verse 3 the horizontal dimension; and in verse 12

the entire community is included in the vertical dimension with the person of Christ ("lead us all together to everlasting life").

5. By its structure, this chapter is a collection of Christian sayings to which Benedict has added two monastic aspects: obedience (v. 6) and the relationship with the abbot (v. 10). These pregnant sayings are easily memorized and readily quoted.[4]

6. RB 72 is the apex of the last chapters of the Rule. In the preceding chapter Benedict had already spoken of mutual obedience, still emphasizing obedience to elders. RB 63–72 might be called "the way from good order to love."[5] By the law, by order and discipline, the monk is to be trained in love. Once the law has been internalized in the heart, detailed regulations are no longer needed. Some manuscripts have the word "Amen" at the end of this chapter. It is indeed a beautiful ending for the Rule (cf. comments on RB 73 below).

7. Comparing RB 72 with RB 4 (which is also a collection of Christian sayings with some monastic additions), we can see clearly how Benedict in RB 72 briefly summarizes the basics and how he is in fact orientating himself on 4.1-2: "To love the Lord God with our whole heart, our whole soul and our whole strength and the neighbor as ourselves." Comparing RB 72 with RB 7, we can see that RB 72 begins where RB 7 ends. Humility leads the monastic to perfect love of God and Christ (7.67, 69). In RB 72 the ladder begins with the most fervent love, and the steps include respect, patience, obedience, selflessness, loving fear of God, love for the abbot and for Christ.

8. The abbot, having been formed in community by the Rule, reflects the qualities of RB 72, which Benedict here requires of every monk (compare especially RB 64 with 72). There is also a special connection between RB 72 and RB 27, 28, and 36, where good zeal is proved by the treatment of failing and sick brothers, or RB 35, where it is concretized in the daily service in the kitchen and in the house. We also find a clear parallel in the first sections of chapters 53 and 66. Good zeal is to be practiced not only within the community, but also in dealing with people outside the monastery.[6]

9. Benedict certainly did not write chapter 72 first. After his experiences of community life he was convinced that love is the most important dimension. "The fundamental concern of the Rule of Benedict is a truly Christian community, a community in Christ."[7]

10. Thus one can truly say that this chapter is the climax of Benedict's Rule (see comments on individual verses), his testament as it were, that opens to us the depths of his Rule and lets us see his innermost concern. There are doubts

about the authorship of many chapters, but no one, to my knowledge, has doubted that this chapter is Benedict's very own. We might compare it to the hymn to love in 1 Corinthians 13. It gives us the perspective for reading the entire Rule, in order to interpret it according to Benedict's heart.

Title—Of the good zeal which monks ought to have.

V. 1: Just as there is an evil zeal of bitterness
   which separates from God and leads to hell,
V. 2: there is also a good zeal
   which separates from sins
   and leads to God and everlasting life.

In the first two verses, Benedict presents two kinds of zeal and two different ways. He inserts the contrasting elements into a parallel pattern. The first and last parts are expanded. Thus the following phrases are contrasted: 1. evil and good zeal; 2. separates from God, separates from sins; 3. leads to hell, leads to God and life everlasting. The second and third pair are not quite logical. Strictly speaking, it should be: separates from the devil (or separates from virtue, in the case of evil zeal). Benedict probably wants to say that this separation occurs within the human person. In the last phrase Benedict deliberately places "God" before "leads to life everlasting." He is not only concerned about our eternal happiness, but about God as the goal of all our ways. As in the preceding phrase ("separates from sins"), Benedict might logically have written "leads to the heights of virtue" (cf. RB 73.9). But here he is concerned with the final goal of Christian and monastic life. We may wonder why Benedict names first the evil and then the good zeal, for verse 1 differs from the title of the chapter. It seems that Benedict wants to start from reality as he has lived and experienced it. We also may have experienced more of the evil zeal in our world.[8]

1. *Two kinds of zeal.* The Letter of James (3:14-18) speaks of a bitter zeal that denotes argumentation and boasting (*zelus amarus*, the word *amarus* with this meaning is rare in the Vulgate). He contrasts it with wisdom from above, described as chaste, peaceable, merciful, and without pretense. Paul admonishes the Galatians (Gal 4:17-18) to be zealous not in evil but in good (but there the Vulgate uses the word *aemulari*). One may see a further link in Galatians 5:13-26. We are called to freedom, not bound by the Law. Paul contrasts the works of the flesh with the fruits of the spirit: "Love, joy, peace, patience, kindness, generosity, faithfulness, gentleness and self-control" (5:22). The Law ought to train us toward love and freedom. This process can be seen in Benedict's Rule. A person who loves does not need regulations anymore, fulfilling the Law naturally as it were, from within (cf. RB 7.67-70).

The theme of good and evil zeal was common in the patristic and monastic literature of the time. The *Letter of Clement* of Rome to the Corinthians (of which an ancient Latin translation has been found that Benedict might have known) lists these contrasts: jealousy and strife lead to death; holy zeal, justice, and peace build up the community.[9] Augustine speaks of a twofold love: One is holy, the other is impure; one is looking out for the community, the other for self; one is concerned about the well-being of all . . . the other subjects the common good to itself and usurps and dominates; one is subject to God, the other is jealous of God; one is calm, the other restless; one is peaceable, the other rebellious; one prefers the truth to adulation, the other always and everywhere seeks praise; one is friendly, the other envious; one wishes for the neighbor what it wishes for itself, the other oppresses the neighbor; one guides the neighbor for his benefit, the other does so to gain advantages for self.[10]

The struggle of the powers of good and evil takes place within the small community of monastics. The listing of opposites should motivate us to stand on the side of good zeal. Our experience of bitter and destructive zeal in the world calls all the more for its opposite, the good zeal. One might be frightened by this radical choice. There is no "holy indifference" here. Jesus calls his followers to decide for or against him, to wholehearted engagement (cf. Matt 12:30; 6:24).

2. *Two ways.* One way leads to God and life everlasting, the other to hell. This theme also is quite common. Benedict alludes to it in his Rule, although he makes no theoretical reflection about the two ways. The narrow way to life is obedience (5.10-11). We want to avoid hell and reach eternal life (cf. Prol 42). Some ways may seem right, but lead to the depths of hell (7.21). The Master describes the two ways at length, already at the beginning of his Prologue (10–14, cf. also 7.22-24).[11] Compared to the Master's lengthy description of the way to perdition, Benedict speaks more about the positive goal of the way (cf. Prol 2).

The Sermon of the Mount admonishes us to walk not on the broad, but on the narrow way that leads to life (Matt 7:13-14; cf. Prol 46–49). The theme of the two ways also occurs frequently in the Old Testament. One text: "Here, then, I have today set before you life and prosperity, death and doom. If you obey the commandments of the Lord, your God . . . loving him, and walking in his ways . . . you will live. . . . If, however, you turn away your hearts and will not listen . . . you will certainly perish. . . . I have set before you life and death. . . . Choose life, then, that you may live . . . by loving the Lord, your God, heeding his voice and holding fast to him" (Deut 30:15-20).

The *Didache* speaks of the two ways in its very first chapters (1–5). Love of God and neighbor, mercy, justice, truth, and humility lead to life, but passion, jealousy, anger, greed, lies, and pride lead to death.

3. *Zeal* as a key word occurs four times in this chapter alone. "Zeal" denotes intensive striving, referring to the power of motivation in a person. If zeal is directed to virtue, to what is good, it is good. If directed to evil, succumbing to envy and jealousy, it is destructive and evil. The Latin word *zelus* occurs in RB in both senses. If the people in the vicinity of an abbey show concern for a good abbatial election, they are to do so selflessly and with zeal for God (64.6). Three times the word zeal denotes envy and jealousy that ought to be avoided (jealousy: 4.66; cf. 65.22; 64.16).

In the Latin Bible the word *zelus* occurs in three ways. "Zeal" denotes jealousy, anger, and strife, and injures people (cf. Sir 40:4; Prov 6:34; 1 Cor 3:3). But God also has zeal. God is a jealous, sometimes an angry God, for God is holy and has a heart full of love (cf. Ps 79:5; Ezek 5:13; 39:25, etc.). Finally, zeal is used to describe persons who have zeal for God, for example Elijah. "Zeal for your house devours me," the psalmist says (Ps 69:10; cf. Ps 119:139), and this psalm verse is applied to Jesus (John 2:17). Looking back at RB 72 from this point, we see that zeal is a radical passion in people. It is exclusive, permeates everything, and knows no half-measures. It is a dynamic reality,[12] the direct opposite of weak, tired, timid, or hesitant movement.

4. *The evil zeal of bitterness separates from God.* This word "bitterness" occurs only here in the Rule, whereas the Master often speaks of this life as "bitter-tasting," promising heaven as bliss without bitterness. Here it means a corroding, injurious bitterness that in turn causes bitterness in others. It is simply a description of evil zeal: evil zeal, that is, bitterness, malice (as a *genitivus epexegeticus*). In other passages of the Rule, this bitterness is jealousy (cf. 65.22; 64.6), a sinister force that pushes a person into ever stronger dynamics. The individual, seeing oneself as the center, can survive only when others are put down and made small. An evil, intensive force, this zeal destroys the community. We find two descriptions in the Rule. "This leads to envy, quarrels, slander, rivalry, factions and disorders of every kind" (65.7); and there is the admonition: "Harbor no hatred nor jealousy of anyone, and do nothing out of envy. Do not love quarreling; shun arrogance" (4.65-69).

Cyprian of Carthage describes the effects of evil zeal in a separate work. Manifested as hunger for power and hatred of the brother, it leads to the brother's death.[13] Because this zeal destroys love in the person and in the brother, it leads not only to divisions in the community but also to separation from God.

5. *Leads to hell.* In preceding chapters, Benedict had described disobedience as the way to hell (7.21; cf. Prol 2). Now hatred and jealousy lead to hell. Benedict realizes that this dreadful end is possible; he wants to remind

the monastic to choose the good way. However, he has no drastic descriptions of hell, as given by the Master among others (cf. RM 90.14f., 45). On the whole, unlike the Master, Benedict does not accentuate the broad way.[14]

6. *Good zeal.* Good zeal is the opposite. According to the Rule, good zeal is zeal for God's affairs. Comparing RB 72 with 4.64-73, one could explain good zeal as honoring the elders, loving the younger, praying for one's enemies in the love of Christ, making peace, loving chastity, or—as the beginning of the chapter says—"loving the Lord God with one's whole heart, with one's whole soul, with all our strength, then our neighbor as ourselves" (4.1-2; cf. *Didache* 2). The intensity of effort now is directed to what is good and to the Good One. In the next verse we see clearly that zeal is most ardent love.

For Benedict, good zeal is quite different from the "good zeal" the Master wanted to see in his monastery. There the brothers were to compete in humility, in good deeds, in monastic observance. With "good zeal and the desire for honor," they should "vie with each other in striving to get ahead" (95.21). There is the zeal for becoming the abbot's successor, and the Master assumes that each one might like to hold this office![15] We can see clearly how far Benedict has progressed from his source.

7. *It separates from sins.*[16] Benedict knows that the monastic has to deal with sins all through life, that they are rooted deep within us, and that uprooting them is becoming ever more difficult. Toward the end of chapter 7, he writes that the monastic is purified of sins (7.70), and spends a long time on the way of purgation. It is for such monastics that Benedict is writing his Rule. To be purified of sins and to preserve love, strictness is needed at times (Prol 47). Love can enter a monastic who acknowledges being a sinner, for then the Holy Spirit can work in him or her. In RB 72 Benedict begins where RB 7 ended and looks at the situation from another angle: Let's practice good zeal, and it will drive out what is evil.

8. *It leads to God and life everlasting.* "To God" occurs three times in the Rule: we go to God through hard and difficult things (58.8), by obedience (71.2), and here it is the power of good zeal, of love that moves us toward God.

And to life everlasting. The Master gives a broad description of eternal life (cf. 3.84-94; 70.94-117; 90.16-27); Benedict lets God determine it. Eternal life had been put before the new monastic: "If you desire true and eternal life" (Prol 17), and "In his goodness the Lord shows us the way of life" (Prol 20).

In preceding chapters, Benedict had named obedience (5.11; 71.2), good works (Prol 17), and humility (7.5) as ways to life eternal. In chapter

72 there is just one way, all-embracing love. We are reminded of John the apostle, in whose old age the individual commandments made room for this single commandment of love (see, for example, 1 John 2:10; 3:14, 23; 4:7-16).

V. 3: This zeal the monks are to practice with the most fervent love.

Now it is quite clear that zeal and ardent love belong together. Earlier, one might have been unsure whether this zeal concerned humility, good order, faithful observance of the Rule, or asceticism.

1. *Therefore (ergo)*. This is the beginning of the verse in the original version. It is just a small word, but very characteristic of Benedict, appearing in many important passages (e.g., Prol 3; 19.6; 49.10). It is like a signal that makes us pay attention. After stating a general truth probably recognized by everyone (indicative form of the verbs), Benedict goes to the first important consequence for the monastics (in the Latin original "monks" is actually the last word of the verse).

2. *Love (amor)*. *Amor* as distinct from *caritas* connotes a vital love that takes hold of a person's entire being and implies passionate love.[17] Benedict repeatedly adds the motive of love (*amor*) for Christ or God to a text he has taken over from the Master. The monastic is to pray for enemies out of love for Christ (4.72), and for love of God to be subject to the superior (7.34). It is this motive that prompts him to call the superior *abbas* (63.13), and at the end of the way of humility "the monastic does everything . . . out of love for Christ" (the word "Christ" was added by Benedict in 7.69). *Amor* is positive for Benedict, whereas the Master also speaks of the negative love of the world or love for one's family as an obstacle to the monastic life (RM 86.3; 91.48).

3. *Practice with the most fervent love*. It is striking that Benedict uses the superlative of "ardent/fervent." He seems to put his heart into the text, desiring to evoke all the spiritual energies and the deepest powers of his monastics. It is no longer the initial zeal (1.3), but a proven, mature, and therefore more ardent zeal. *Fervor* is never used negatively in the RB (as for example *fervor malitiae* in RM 15.11). The porter is to give a prompt answer "in the fervor of love" (66.4) when a poor person calls. Fervor and love are congruent. They are to be practiced not only within the community, but also in our conduct toward all people who need us. Good zeal thus is ardent enthusiasm, the total engagement of our power of loving. It urges us to hasten, not just to walk (RB 73), with the whole community (72.12), and it marks all our actions. Romans 12:11 admonishes us to "be

fervent in the spirit." In Prol 49 Benedict promises an expanded heart to the monastic who is striving. When we think of the texts from the Fathers that emphasize that the Holy Spirit makes our hearts wide, that the Spirit is love in person, dwelling within us, then we also can say here (especially since Benedict himself by his inclusion in verse 12 points in this direction): zeal is not just a good force within people and flowing from people, but it is the active presence of Christ himself who urges us on. Zeal is the ardor, the fire of the Holy Spirit, and the dynamic power of community life and of the apostolate. "For the love of Christ impels us" (2 Cor 5:14).[18]

4. *Practice*. After this soaring to the heights comes a very practical word: We should practice the good zeal, activate it, exercise it. There is effort involved as well. What good is the most fervent enthusiasm if it is not realized in daily life? This verse shows a characteristic of Benedict: uniting ardent idealism with sober realism. This verse also shows the mutuality of divine and human acts. Divine action has priority; the monastic is to give scope to the good zeal, but we also must completely engage ourselves.

V. 4: That is, they are to vie with each other in mutual respect.

Verses 4-8 are tightly woven. The monks are acting, except in verse 7 that admonishes the individual. The sentences follow one another without conjunctions. The verb is at the end, except in verse 7 that is framed by verses 6 and 8, both of which end with the verb *inpendant*.

1. *That is*. The structure of the sentence shows again how goal-oriented Benedict is (cf. for example 49.7). Additional practical consequences are listed in memorable sayings. Having heard the word of the most ardent love, we might expect exalted matters or heroic deeds, but the word "practice" has prepared us. Benedict lists attitudes that can be actualized every day. Zeal does not consist in correctness and order, not even in acts of love, but in attitudes that can be shown by various ways. Almost every sentence (except v. 7) says *how* things should be done (adverb or adverbial phrase). Thus this chapter can be practiced everywhere, no matter how varied the expressions and forms might be in different countries.

2. Benedict deliberately places a Scripture text ahead of the various "instruments." The entire chapter 72 is in tune with Scripture, so that no *scriptum est* is necessary. The text on which this and other verses are based says, "Let love be sincere . . . love another with mutual affection, anticipate one another in showing honor. Do not grow slack in zeal, be fervent in spirit, serve the Lord" (Rom 12:9-11).[19] In the Letter of Peter we read, "Give honor to all, love the community, fear God" (1 Pet 2: 17) that has the same

sequence as RB 72. It is characteristic of Benedict that he begins with mutual respect. It is the basic prerequisite for fraternal love (cf. also 53.2).

3. *Honor, respect* (Latin, *honor*). In earlier chapters, Benedict stressed reverence (*honor*) for God, the abbot, the elders, and all people (cf. 36.4; 4.8; 63.10, 13). In 63.17 he cites the same Scripture text, but the practical application is chiefly concerned with reverence for the seniors. In RB 72 the admonition applies to everyone, even the younger members, the little ones. It is respect for the other as a brother, as a person, not because of age, rank, or position. Benedict already had adapted the text of the Master from "honoring father and mother" (RM 3.8) to "honoring all persons" (4.8). The Master uses the word *honor* in the context of striving for honor. It occurs nineteen times in this sense just in chapter 92.[20]

Christians of the first centuries avoided gestures of honor and emphasized a fraternal spirit. Although the New Testament speaks of "honor to whom honor is due" (Rom 13:7), it is opposed to different treatment within the community based on race, social rank, position, and so on (cf. James 2:1-6). This follows from our essential equality before God and from the new brotherhood established by Christ. "You all are one in Christ" (Gal 3:28; RB 2.20). The ordinary conduct of that period and monastic rank are superseded by love that shows itself in basic mutual respect (cf. Rom 12:10; 1 Pet 2:17). The dignity of the human person is central. Each one is created by God, loved, and redeemed by Christ. For Benedict, mutual respect is not just a human virtue, but it is rooted in our faith in the presence of Christ in people, especially in the least of them (cf. RB 36.2; 53.15).

Cassian (*Conf.* XVI.11) interprets this Scripture text to mean that each one values the other above self (in his beautiful chapter on friendship). In honoring others, we place ourselves below them, look up to them. We also realize that we can learn much from others. The practice of observing RB 7 is presupposed: if we realize we are the least and believe it in our hearts (7.51), we will truly give honor to others.

4. *Vying in mutual respect.* The word *invicem* is typical for Benedict and occurs more frequently in RB than in RM; for example, as mutual service (35.1, 6), as mutual obedience (71), as mutual respect (63.17 and here). To vie with another means not waiting to see whether the other is first to show proper respect, as he or she should, but that honor is shown to the other in advance. There is vying from ambition which, for example, the Master mentions; there is also vying to be the first at the Divine Office (22.6); but when each vies with the others in showing respect, all are reaching the goal together (72.12).

If we recall the mixed society of Benedict's time, we see clearly how important this respect for others is, for those who think differently, behave differently, possess different qualities and abilities. In spite of many negative experiences, or because of them, Benedict emphasizes this respect. It implies that we do not try to change the others to fit our criteria, but have respect for their uniqueness, their mystery, even if the other person does wrong.[21] For today, the meaning of respect might be outlined as: "a sense for honor and dignity, respect for the person and personal matters, fostering what is valuable, knowing rights and duties, putting persons ahead of things and causes, respecting the convictions of others, awakening and fostering freedom and devotion, sensitivity to any minimizing or marginalizing of persons."[22]

Concerning the expressions of reverence, the last decades have brought change. In this chapter Benedict prescribes no external forms. These can become a façade unless they are enlivened by a profound reverence for the mystery of the others, especially of the lowly ones, ultimately by reverence for the presence of Christ in the others.

Important questions for every community: How is mutual respect expressed today? What forms can we find? We have learned that forms can be a great support. Benedict wants reverence to be practiced by each one vying with the others. It is especially important when we live close together day after day or when we work with people of a different mentality, cultural, or social background. The documents of the Second Vatican Council name this respect as a basic requirement for true dialog (cf. GS 92; 23).

V. 5: They are to bear each other's weaknesses of body and character with utmost patience.

When we reflect on what makes mutual reverence so difficult, we find various weaknesses that Benedict names very realistically. He knows that in a cenobitic community one can practice the same heroism demanded of a hermit. The entire person with all the powers of loving should be engaged.

1. *Weaknesses of body and character.* There are, first of all, the physical illnesses (e.g., 36), but the concept is larger: someone easily gets excited or confused (42.4); someone is depressed by the amount of work and wants to run away (48; cf. 64.19); another cannot even perform the kitchen service without assistance (35.4); and another cannot live as simply and poorly as the rest (34.4; 55.21), but needs more things or different food (39.1; 40.3). There also may be faults. The sinful brother is called "sick" (28.5). The abbot has taken on the care for the weak and the sick, that is, also for sinful persons (27.6; cf. 27.1-9). Some may even suffer injustice, and in this case, Benedict says we should bear false brethren and even persecution (4.30-33; 7.35-43). In RB 72 Benedict includes all human weaknesses in two words (physical and moral).

In this context, the Master usually talks of pretended weakness or laziness (cf. for example RM 1.67; 7.10; the same is true of illness). Benedict, in his entire Rule, shows a compassionate attitude toward moral and physical weakness. This is in accord with Sacred Scripture. First Thessalonians 5:14 admonishes us "to care for the weak and to be patient with everyone." Early monastic communities were strongly influenced by Galatians 6:2: "Bear one another's burdens, and you will fulfill the law of Christ." As Smaragdus comments on this text: the law of Christ is love, just as RB 72 teaches.

2. *Their weaknesses.* Benedict seems to imply that everyone has weaknesses, and that a community cannot simply be divided into the weak and the strong. Each one in some respects is a weak person, in other respects a strong person. We all depend on one another for patience and mutual understanding. We also can reflect on bearing our own weaknesses. If we do not accept them, they act like a magnifying glass as we look at the weaknesses and faults of others.

3. *With utmost patience.* Benedict surely knows from experience why he uses the superlative form of patient. Patience is related to the "most ardent" love (v. 3) and is an expression of this love. Cassian, in his *Conferences*, describes a different experience: Having lived as a hermit for a long time, a monk returned to the community because there he found more chances for self-denial and perfection, for example in "bearing the weaknesses of the brothers with equanimity and generosity" (*Conf.* XIX.9.1). The Master similarly sees patience mainly in relation to God and in obedience; it is one rung of the ladder of virtues on the way to God. Benedict expands the concept of patience. True, he also speaks of practicing patience in the fourth degree of humility and of monastic life as a sharing in the sufferings of Christ by patience (Prol 50); but he also sees patience in the service of love; for example, in chapter 36 by serving the sick, even those who are difficult to serve. Patience does not mean simply accepting, resigning oneself to a situation, but firmness, strength, and courage to bear something and to persevere actively. "Love is patient" (Vulgate: 1 Cor 13:4, 7). Cassian admonishes that we all should "be enlarged in [our] hearts, receiving the adverse waves of wrath in the broad harbor of love which 'suffers all things, endures all things'" (*Conf.* XVI.27). Patience is the day-to-day expression of love.

4. *To bear.* This word is used only here in the Rule (the Master does not use it).[23] Asked how the stronger ones should bear the weaknesses of the weaker members, Basil referred to the word of Scripture: "Yet it was our infirmities that he bore, our sufferings that he endured" (Isa 53:4). By bearing our weaknesses, Christ healed us. He bore our loads and thus took them

from us (Basil, *Reg.* 177f.). We also think of the various translations of the *Agnus Dei*. The Lamb of God bears the sins of the world and thus takes them away. Christ bore our sins on the wood of the cross (1 Pet 2:24).[24] This was the expression of his love.

Thus to bear one another's weaknesses with the utmost patience means to take them upon ourselves, to help carry them, to walk the way with the others, and to help them to overcome what is negative. This is a sign of the most ardent love (72.3 and 1 Cor 13:7) and a form of following Christ.

V. 6: They are to vie with one another in rendering obedience.

1. *Obedience* is linked with patience (cf. fourth degree of humility). In earlier chapters, Benedict had stressed obedience to Christ, to the superior, and to the senior members, and in chapter 71 he also mentioned mutual obedience. In chapter 72 obedience is due to everyone. The Master says, "To obey all good persons wholeheartedly" (3.76), but Benedict wants us to practice obedience to all, regardless of their moral qualities. Similarly, in 4.61 Benedict had added to the Master's text, "to obey the abbot's commands in everything, even if he himself, which God forbid, should act otherwise, mindful of the Lord's command 'What they say, do; but what they do, do not.'" Benedict knows how easily we excuse ourselves from obeying by pointing out the vices and weaknesses of others.

Why did Benedict broaden the scope of obedience in this manner? Obedience is the way to God, as Benedict emphasizes several times (Prol 2; 71.1-2; cf. 58.8). Human self-will is our greatest enemy (Prol 2–3), so obedience is a help for the individual in letting love prevail. The last word about obedience in difficulties is: "Out of love and trusting in God's help, let him obey" (68.5). In 5.2 Benedict gave the same reason for obeying without delay as the Master: "It comes naturally to those who "hold nothing dearer than Christ." Benedict sees obedience as a form of love. Thus he adds the motive of love for the Lord twice in this context (7.34; 63.13). Here he sees obedience together with selfless fraternal love (vv. 6 and 8; both verses use *inpendant* and serve as a frame for v. 7; cf. also Eph 4:2-3).[25]

All of us can be mediators of God's will for one another. And God often uses rather fragile instruments to do it. God doesn't always use the most virtuous people in manifesting God's will. The monastic's entire life should be one of ceaseless listening and obeying God, to whom all obedience is ultimately rendered. In this sense, Benedict can speak of the good of obedience (71.1).

2. *To vie with one another.* The brothers are to outdo one another in obeying. Pachomius had recommended a competition in humility (*Praec. et leges* 3). The Master speaks of a competition for honor (22.11);[26] one

wishes to stand higher than another on the ladder of virtue. In contrast, the competition in obedience unifies the community.

3. Concretely, a competing in mutual obedience might look like this: feeling with another, "walking in his shoes," adjusting to his pace, adapting oneself; being open to correction from the other, to a critical word, to a different opinion; considering a correction in God's light and asking what message from God every member of the community has for each one personally, asking what we can learn from each individual. . . The will of God also comes to us from outside by the needs of the time, the people we encounter (cf. RB 61.4). Benedict himself is our instructor in this listening to all sides and in this way of obeying.

V. 7: No one
    is to follow what he judges useful to himself,
    but what seems more useful to the other.

This is the only sentence which has no direct parallel statement in the RB. However, the Rule as a whole wants to train us toward this goal. Verse 7 is a practical description of good zeal (cf. its central placement in this chapter). We should not start from ourselves in thinking, as if making concentric circles: "how can I perform many acts of love?" This might be a refined way of seeking our own benefit, for example, our own role as a helpful or virtuous person. The real question should start from the other person: "Who needs my help?" This is an inversion. My own self no longer stands in the center. In this sense, the sentence has a parallel in RB 4.10: "To deny oneself to follow Christ." Placing the other person in the center as Christ did, is the concrete fulfillment of the key sentence of preferring nothing to Christ. It is a way of following him.

1. *To follow what he judges is useful for himself.* In Benedict's community, it is possible to "judge," to decide, and then to "follow" what is beneficial to the other person. RM does not allow such freedom. Everything is regulated by detailed prescriptions. The Master does not think highly of the individual's judgment.

2. *What is more useful to the other.* Whereas the Master very often speaks about the monastery's usefulness and also seems quite concerned about increasing its material goods, Benedict wants us to consider what is truly good or useful for the other person. He does not say we should consider what pleases the other person, or what might be good for him or her at the moment or what would satisfy him or her, but what is truly useful to the other person. We may add: useful in view of one seeking God. Benedict does not mean the wrong kind of indulgence.

Pursuing what suits me (or what I consider useful), seeking fulfillment of my inauthentic needs, leads into a vicious circle. With each fulfillment, desires increase and new ones keep arising.[27] Benedict points in the opposite direction. It is in extending ourselves toward others that we also achieve true self-actualization, a happy life (Prol 15). When we strive only for ourselves, we go astray; when we aim at the true benefit of the others, we attain happiness also for ourselves. Here Benedict shows a concrete way of making the other, and ultimately Christ, the center of our own life. "Father John the Dwarf said: 'A house is not built by beginning at the top and working down. You must begin with the foundations in order to reach the top.' They said to him, 'What does this saying mean?' He said, 'The foundation is our neighbor whom we must win, and that is the place to begin. For all the commandments of Christ depend on this one'" (Matt 22:39f.) (*Apoph.* John the Dwarf, 39).

Cassian combines into one sentence three texts from the letters of Paul on the topic of love and truth: "Love does not seek its own interests" (1 Cor 13:5); "no one should seek his own advantage, but that of his neighbor" (1 Cor 10:24); and "I do not seek my own benefit, but that of the many others" (1 Cor 10:33).[28] Philippians 2:4 illumines and explains RB 72.7: "Each looking out not for his own interests, but everyone for those of others." The Philippians were to have the attitude of Christ who humbled himself in order to benefit them and became obedient unto death. Monastics are following this Jesus. Paul was also aware that he was following Jesus, seeking to benefit everyone in order to save everyone (cf. 1 Cor 9:19-23). This is the actualization of apostolic love, the most ardent love for Christ and all the others.

Everything is at stake here. We can understand why Benedict emphasizes this sentence and highlights it by a different structure, placing it in the center of the chapter. And only here does he say that "no one" is to seek his own advantage. In other words, all, without exception, are to follow the maxim of Sacred Scripture, the law of Christ.

V. 8: They are to show pure brotherly love to one another.[29]

1. *Caritas* is the second word for love used here. In RB it often describes the type and manner or the motive for action: for obedience (68.5; 71.4), for service to the community (35.6), for service to those outside the community (53.3). Sometimes more strictness is needed to preserve love (Prol 47). The doorkeeper should respond to people's call "in the fervor of love" (66.4). Considering all texts in which Benedict uses *caritas*, we can see that it is directed to community and manifests itself in the way we relate to the weakest members (27.4). The climax of the chapter on humility is the monk's arrival at the "love of God, *caritas Dei*" (7.67).

In the Latin literature of early Christianity, *caritas* is generally used to translate the biblical term *agape*. It is the highest Christian virtue and includes love of God as well as love of neighbor. It is expressed by service to the neighbor. While *amor* can also be directed toward evil, *caritas* is only used in the positive sense.[30] *Caritas* is poured into our hearts by the Holy Spirit (Rom 5:5). In verses 8 and 10 it characterizes the conduct toward the brothers and the abbot.

2. *Brotherhood.* This is the love characteristic of the brotherhood (*genetivus epexegeticus*), brotherly love as distinct from the love of family, of friends, of enemies, of humanity in general. All monastics are brothers to each other, no matter how different they may be. The Latin word *fraternitas* occurs only once in the Rule, but Benedict (together with the Master) had spoken of the "brotherhood in arms" (*fraterna acies*) in RB 1.5. He decrees that "brother" is to be used as an honorary address before the brother's name (63.12). This points out a fresh discovery of the meaning of Christian brotherhood at a time when the church had outgrown the scope of a brotherhood. The monks want to try to realize this general Christian ideal. This seems to be one of Benedict's basic concerns. This title of brother is not even omitted when a monk has proven unworthy of it (RB 27 and 28). Sacred Scripture admonishes Christians to love one another in fraternal love (Rom 12:10).[31]

Excursus: *Brotherhood*

In chapter 72, the word "brotherhood" is used, raising the question whether the monastic community is a brotherhood or a family.

We are acquainted with the family model. We speak of family spirit, of a family atmosphere. Points of comparison are the abbot as father of the family, the monks as his sons. The stable abbey creates something like a physical bond among the monks. The community is self-reliant, being not only a community of prayer and work, but also of common life. The intimacy of the community also recalls that of a family. This goes sometimes hand in hand with the idea that Benedict had modeled his community on the idea of the ancient Roman family. Accordingly, the abbot in his function as educator resembles the *pater familias*, having authority in temporal and spiritual matters.[32] The Abbots' Congress of 1967 made the following statement: "Because of the stability and the vital intimacy of the bond among its members, a Benedictine community is rightly compared to a family, a term which is also used by tradition. Like a family, it possesses an original uniqueness, its own manner of life, its own problems, and a unique destiny."[33]

How does this accord with the RB? The Rule of the Master in 2.31 emphasizes that the abbot is to model equal love for all and by his kindness show himself a father to the monks. Benedict omits this sentence as well as the comparison of the community with the extended family (RM 11.6-7). Where the Master says that one should "honor father and mother" (3.8), Benedict says "honor all persons" (4.8). In chapter 64, he alludes to a biblical text, saying that a good steward should be appointed, but he omits "for the family" and uses the term "fellow servants" instead. He seems to be avoiding the analogy to the family. RB never uses the word "mother" to describe a person in the monastery. "Father" is used for Christ, for the Church Fathers, for the abbot, and also for the cellarer. RM often speaks of the abbot as "father." It is worthy of note that the counterpart of the abbot is not the "sons," but the brothers, except in a biblical quotation ("Discipline your son with the rod," 2.29). The Master calls the monks sons of the abbot four more times (2.30; 90.74; 92.8, 77).

What seems more important is the fact that Benedict does not want the brothers to address each other by their mere name (63.11) as would be proper in a family, but rather use the honorary title "brother" or *nonnus*. He emphasizes reverence and rank as opposed to undue familiarity. Even if brothers from the same family are living in the community, they may not defend each other; The bonds of blood are not to weaken the community (RB 69). When Benedict speaks of children, he means real children. He does not use the term for his adult monks. For the community, Benedict prefers biblical imagery, such as community, house of God, body, and so on.

The image of family for a community was historically applicable to a preconciliar monastery and the preindustrial extended family with its several generations under one roof, greater autonomy, unity of life and production, and patriarchal leadership. It does not fit so well for a two-generation family, the nuclear family, where life is separated from work in an industrial society.

The family image also has its dangers. We might draw a harmonizing picture and thereby cover up conflicts. One might foster infantile attitudes by comparing the supervisors to parents and the monastics to children, and this, in turn, might place too great a burden on the superiors. In using the image of a family for the community, we need, at least, to be aware of its limitations.

3. *Show the pure love.* The word "pure" (*castus*) often made us think of "chaste," and we saw in this verse a prohibition of private friendships. In the patristic texts the word often signifies being selfless, sincere, without seeking one's own advantage. In 64.6 Benedict also said that the people in the vicinity who worked for a good abbatial election should do so selflessly (*caste*) and out of zeal for God. Dekkers translates: "In total self-forgetfulness the brothers should fulfill the duties of love of neighbor."[34] Augustine writes: If anyone "were looking for God, they would be chaste (*castus*). . . . Anybody who is seeking from God anything besides God is not seeking God chastely. Consider, brothers and sisters: if a wife loves her husband because he is rich, she is not chaste. I mean, she does not love her husband, but her husband's gold." (*s.* 137.8.9). Caesarius of Arles admonishes the priest to love the nuns selflessly. The context shows the meaning clearly: he is to take good care of them.[35]

This verse is a continuation of verse 7. All are brothers to one another, no matter how much they differ: there is no respect of persons. They want to implement the biblical exhortations for a Christian community life, loving and serving each other in selfless charity, without looking out for their own advantage, without secondary motives, without expecting a reward from the other. Selfless fraternal love gives of itself to those who are in special need. This love, considered by the Fathers as the high goal of monastic life, is seen by Benedict as the absolute requirement for life in the community. This love is also the guideline for all external activity.

The following verses show clearly that all this is impossible without being grounded in the vertical dimension. But the love of brothers is put first since it is the measure of our love of God. "If anyone says, 'I love God,' but hates his brother, he is a liar; for whoever does not love a brother whom he sees, cannot love God whom he has not seen" (1 John 4:20).

For the next three verses, there exists a striking parallel in the ancient preface for virgins: "May they be fervent in love and love nothing beside you. . . . May they fear you and serve you in love. May you be their honor, their joy, their desire. . . . May they possess everything in you whom they have placed above everything."[36] Cyprian writes as follows in his commentary on the Our Father about the petition "Your will be done":

> The will of God is what Christ did and taught. Humility in conversation, steadfastness in faith, modesty in words, justice in deeds, mercy in works, discipline in morals, not to know how to do an injury and to be able to bear one done, to keep peace with the brothers, to love the Lord with a whole heart, to love Him in that he is Father, to fear Him in that He is God, to place nothing at all before Christ, because he placed nothing before us, to cling inseparably to His love, to stand bravely and faithfully at His cross . . . (*De dom. or.* 15).

Cyprian also describes first brotherly love and then moves on to the love of God and Christ until martyrdom.

V. 9: They are to fear God in love.

On the surface, this contradicts 7.67. There we read that the monk arrives at the perfect love of God which casts out fear. He no longer acts from fear of hell, but from love for Christ (7.69). RB 7 describes the way from servile fear, fear of hell (which in the first chapters 5–7 is taken seriously as a motive), to a love without this fear. But the fear of God, the childlike fear coupled with love, has grown in the monastic (cf. the small differences between RB 7.67 and RM 10.87-91).

The fear of God is learned in the monastery (Prol 12). It is a basic attitude, embracing trust in God (2.36) and including that we give glory to God in everything (Prol 29), obeying him (5.9), serving him in the others and in worship (19.3; 36.7); it includes justice in dealing with other people (65.15). Benedict requires the fear of God as the basic attitude for all who hold an office in the monastery (abbot, cellarer, infirmarian, porter). Whereas in RM it is fear of hell, judgment, and of the superior that predominates, in Benedict fear is already united with love. The porter is to "give a response in the gentleness of fear of God, promptly and with the fervor of love" (66.4).

In Sacred Scripture, fear of God is the initial response to the holiness of God. It comprises reverence and adoration, and in it fullest sense it also includes love. "What does the Lord your God ask of you, but to fear the Lord, your God, and follow his ways exactly, to love and serve the Lord, your God, with all your heart and all your soul" (Deut 10:12). "The Lord, your God, shall you fear and him shall you serve; hold fast to him" (Deut 10:20). The New Testament opposes only servile fear, not fear of God. "Be subordinate to one another out of reverence for Christ" (Eph 5:21; cf. Col 3:22; 1 Pet 2:17).

Christian tradition, with which Benedict must have been familiar, is even more explicit. Cassian and Dorotheus of Gaza after him describe a way from a servile fear to the fear of love. Servile fear is that of the slaves. Its motive is fear of punishment. Fear of God is a quality of lovers. It is the fear of perfect love. Augustine calls it fear of love, or chaste fear.[37]

While Cassian concedes this loving reverence only to hermits, Benedict requires it of the cenobites. In this regard, verse 9 is the climax of the Rule and describes the right relationship to God as the *mysterium fascinosum et tremendum*. Without fear, God is demoted to a benign grandfather or comrade; without love, God becomes a terrifying tyrant. Love always has priority, but how can one love God if we do not need to fear God? In the oration for the Twelfth Sunday of Ordinary Time we pray, "Holy God, grant that we may always fear and love your holy name, for you withdraw your fatherly hand from no one who is firmly rooted in your love."

V. 10: They are to love their abbot
with a sincere and humble love.

1. *Their abbot.* This chapter talks first of the *community* and of fraternal love, and only then is the *abbot* mentioned. This sequence might have been influenced by Augustine (*Praec*, cf. RB 64) and would indicate that it is one of the abbot's chief tasks to foster and strengthen the community. He is called "their abbot," that is, the abbot of the brothers. He belongs to the community, is part of it. The word "love" is repeated here. When "brotherly love" is mentioned in verse 8, the abbot is included. Whatever was said earlier about the relationship with the brothers also applies to the relationship with the abbot/superior: We are to outdo each other in showing him or her respect, also bear his or her weaknesses with the utmost patience, vie in obeying him or her, consider what is useful to him or her and show him or her brotherly love. Yet the superior not only stands in this horizontal relationship, but—in a manner almost shocking to us—is included in the *vertical dimension*. Love for the abbot is grounded in the foundation of the love and fear of God and is a concretization of preferring nothing to the love of Christ (v. 11). "The abbot is to be addressed as 'Lord' and 'abbot' because faith sees in him the representative of Christ. It is not a prerogative which he claims for himself. Rather, we honor and love him for Christ's sake" (63.13). Like the love for the brothers and sisters, the love for the superior must even more be rooted in faith if it is to last.

2. *They are to love with love (caritate diligent).* Again, this verse is the climax of all that is said in the Rule about the relationship with the abbot. It was less striking in the first chapters that this abbot can, and should, be loved. In the RM the abbot is not loved, only feared (7.64; 11.6; 89.20). Benedict desires, especially in the final chapters, a personal, warm relationship among the brothers/sisters and with the abbot/superior, marked not only by respect and obedience, but also by a love rooted in faith. This presupposes effort on both sides. Thus Benedict had required that the abbot "hate what is evil, love the brothers . . . striving to be loved rather than feared" (64.11, 15; both verses being based on Augustine). We may ask whether love can be commanded. But here the word is not *amor* but *caritas* (cf. p. 64), which is a gift of God, and *diligere* (not *amare*) that presumably emphasizes the aspect of the will. Love is the fruit of a decision.[38]

3. *Sincere and humble love.* These two adjectives characterize the love for the abbot. The word "sincere" occurs only here in the Rule and signifies

straightforward, transparent, without secondary motives, not flattering, not striving for a good impression. It also implies the courage, when necessary, to express an uncomfortable truth. This adjective is followed by "humble" which provides a balance for "sincere" and "love." It provides a boundary to a false familiarity, to a crude, too familiar comradeship. The monastics' behavior ought to be marked by reverence, respect, humility, and truthfulness. We could compare it with RB 68: "in all gentleness and obedience . . . with patience and in an appropriate manner . . . without pride or resistance or contradicting . . . in love, trusting in God's help."

V. 11: They are to prefer nothing whatsoever to Christ,
V. 12: and may he lead us all to everlasting life.

Now we have arrived at the foundation and climax of this chapter and presumably also of the RB. It seems that Benedict one last time wants to stress what is dearest to his heart before he closes. Without Christ, nothing of what has been written makes sense, nor can it be put into practice. Here, as in Prol 49, the fire of his own love for Christ seems to break through.

1. *Preferring nothing whatsoever to Christ.* Cyprian had said, "to place nothing at all before Christ, because He placed nothing before us" (*De dom. or.* 15). Preferring nothing to Christ is simply our response to Christ's love for us. Of course, this fact of Christ's love for us is not expressed as strongly in the Rule as in Sacred Scripture. The Rule is only trying to draw the practical consequences for a community from Sacred Scripture. Still, Benedict repeatedly appeals to this prevenient love when he says that the Lord is seeking laborers (Prol 14), that Christ is going after the lost sheep, that it is the sick, not the healthy who need the physician (27; cf. Prol 20, 28). Preferring nothing whatsoever to Christ is the response of a person who has met the Lord (cf. Phil 3:8). Thus, the young person had set out to serve Christ the King (Prol 3). Enthusiasm, ardent love for Christ, stands at the beginning of the Rule and at its end. In 4.21 we read "preferring nothing to the love of Christ." Now the Rule says, "preferring nothing whatsoever to Christ." May we draw the conclusion that the love of Christ should become ever more radical, more ardent? Initial enthusiasm must grow deeper, become stronger through difficulties and discouragement (Prol 48), become more radical and permeate the entire person. The monastic is ever in danger of preferring something else to Christ: persons, his own honor, comfort, self-interest. But there is also the grace of a second or third conversion, chances for a fresh decision.

For Benedict the love of Christ is closely linked to the community. These diverse human beings are "all one in Christ" (2.20). The more one prefers nothing to Christ, growing in love of Christ, the more closely he is united with his brother. If he distances himself from Christ, he also distances himself from the brother, and vice versa.[39] It is through Christ that all these persons are united; he is their common center. This ardent relationship to Christ expresses itself not only in obedience, as the Master says, but just as much in brotherly love and in love for all persons whom we encounter. This Christ-centered love is like a red thread in Benedict's Rule. Whenever Benedict differs from the Master in his teaching, he refers to Christ, for example, Christ in the sick (36). The concern for excommunicated brothers is motivated by reference to the Good Shepherd (27). The loving reception of the poor and of strangers is founded on the reference that in them it is Christ who comes (53.1, 7, 15), Christ, the incarnate mercy of God (53.14). Monastic life means following Christ, serving Christ, the true King. Christ is present through the abbot; he is the unifying center of the community, leading us on the way to the Gospel.

2. *May he lead (perducat) us.* Benedict reinforces the *ducit* of verses 1 and 2 by using the prefix *per-* (see below p. 83). It is Christ who brings it to completion. In this word the theme of the way shines out again. We are not only gathered around Christ in community as on an island, but we are on the way with Christ, as the church, God's pilgrim people.

This word *perducat* (lead) expresses a request, or even a prayer of Benedict, asking Christ to do it. "Us" includes himself, for he realizes that he also is still on the way (cf. the following chapter RB 73). Whereas the monastics had been the persons acting, now it is Christ who takes over. It becomes clear that Christ in his person is the good zeal.

From here we can look back at the entire chapter and interpret nearly every verse with this "key." The monks were accustomed to such interpretations from the Bible. Evil zeal can be shattered by dashing it against Christ. Christ himself is the most ardent zeal. He has loved us without measure till the end, to perfection (cf. John 13.1). Since Christ is present in every person, especially in every brother or sister, we should vie with one another in showing respect. Because Christ bore our weaknesses, we should also bear each others' burdens, aware that he is especially present in the weakest and the least of our brothers/sisters (RB 36). Because Christ was obedient, we ought to vie with one another in obedience since he can manifest his will through any human person. Since Christ did not live to please himself, humbling himself for our benefit (salvation), we should think of the benefit of the other. Because Christ became our brother and is living in every brother/sister, we can practice brotherly love. It is Christ who takes us into this relationship to God the Father. And Christ is the ultimate reason for our loving and humble obedience toward superiors.

3. *All together (pariter).* Christ does not lead each person individually to eternal life. This view would apply to the Master, but not to Benedict.

Christ is leading us all together, and this means that no one may be lost as RB 27 and 28 clearly show. If there is danger, the abbot should, like the Good Shepherd, go after the lost one and bring him back to the fold (27.8-9). We are not in a race, each one trying to get there first; rather, we are running together so that one shall become the crown of the other, as Augustine said.[40]

This running together begins at profession. The monastic was initiated not only into the service of Christ, but also into the community. Since then, he or she is responsible for the others, and the others are responsible for him or her. The monastic should no longer strive to arrive at the goal alone, without concern for the others. And when there is danger of one falling behind or quitting, "love for him should be reaffirmed" in a special manner (27.4).

It is striking that this word *pariter* occurs so seldom in the Vulgate, only two times in the Acts of the Apostles (2:1, 2:44). Was Benedict thinking of *koinonia*? Of the fact that the monastic community, like the early church, is being made one by the Holy Spirit?

The word "together" in a deeper sense refers to solidarity with all humanity. Every person whom Christ calls to follow him is helping to bring the world home to the Father.

4. *To everlasting life.* Here Benedict no longer says, "to God and life everlasting" (v. 2), for in Christ we are already with God. The goal mentioned in verse 2 is restated, eternal life that is the goal of all Christian and human life (*telos* in Greek).

A comparison with RM, from which Benedict distances himself more and more in his Rule, shows clearly that in chapter 72 he has become fully himself. If we recall the biblical and literary context, various elements from other authors are scattered here and there: bitter and good zeal, two ways, ardent love, vying with one another in respect, bearing weaknesses with the utmost patience, love not seeking its own advantage, but what will benefit the other, loving one another with brotherly love, loving God in fear, preferring nothing to Christ who is leading us to the Father. Yet there are no parallels for mutual obedience and for the humble, loving, and sincere relationship with the abbot.

Probably Benedict was not working like an artist, gathering little stones here and there and putting them together to make a picture. Though he is in line with tradition, he is chiefly an autonomous author who knows what he wants to say and who knows how to use the available means well. The entire chapter seems to have been meditated in his heart, growing out of his experience, in harmony with the spirit of Sacred Scripture. Recalling liturgical readings from the Fathers, from his own *lectio*, and oral accounts may have helped him formulate his thoughts succinctly. Benedict can truly be called the author and creator of this chapter.

The entire Rule is a preparation for chapter 72, and in various regards this chapter can be seen as its climax or deepest dimension. It reflects the basic themes of the Rule: reverence, obedience, patience, bearing of weaknesses, love of the brothers, *discretio*. In a masterful way, verses 11 and 12 seem to be the core of the Rule. Here we find the ardent and radical love of Christ and the brothers, the importance of community and fraternity, Christ as the center, the dynamism of our way to God, the interdependence of grace and human cooperation, the importance of prayer, the interconnectedness of the horizontal and vertical dimensions. Thus this chapter, and in particular these two verses, provide us with the real key that will open the entire Rule in the spirit of Benedict.

If we live this chapter, we truly follow Christ in community according to the Gospel, providing service needed in our time and for our time.

Notes

1. The Rule attributed to Fructuosus, *Reg. Com.* 4, speaks of freemen and slaves, the rich and the poor, married persons, stupid and clever people, ignorant persons and craftsmen, children and older people. Concerning the members of the community, cf. Penco, "Composizione," 266–269; Brechter, "Soziologische Gestalt," 60–67; Luiselli, "Società," 113–116.

2. Cf. Borias, "Quelques exemples," 51f.

3. Cf. Russel, "Good Zeal," 44; Renner, "Stilformen," 383.

4. Cf. A. Grün, *Einreden*, Münsterschwarzach, 1983.

5. Cf. Vogüé, *Communauté*, 438ff. (*Community and Abbot*, vol. 2, 394ff.), and *VII*, 415–432 (*RB-DSC*, 301–314).

6. A later Rule, *Reg. Griml.* 53, uses the beginning of RB 72 as a guideline for conduct toward students and adds to the first sentences from RB 72 some sentences from the chapters on the abbot (RB 2 and RB 64).

7. Hagemeyer, "Gemeinschaft," 54; cf. Bamberger, "Le chapitre 72," 104, 106; Manning, "L'importance du chapitre 72," 286 and "Problèmes," 329 and "Le chapitre 73," 140.

8. After the title "*De zelo bono . . .*" *Reg. Griml.* 53 starts with the good zeal, as would be expected.

9. *Ep.* 9.1; 3.2; 6.3-4; 14.1: *zelus, invidia, contentio, contumatio, iustitia, pax, fraternitas, in timore Dei; ad mortem adducit*; cf. Wathen, "Exigencies," 58 ff. Ambrose, *In Ps.* 118.18.10 f., 17f., speaks of the good zeal for life that is love of God, and of the evil zeal that leads to death. Cassian also knows the evil zeal (*zelus, invidia*) that is related to death (*Conf.* XVIII.16.10 f.) and a good zeal (*zelus Dei*: *Conf.* II.26.4; *zelus castitatis*: *Conf.* VII. 2.1; *zelus sanctitatis*: *Conf.* XII.1.3) that he related with spirit and ardor: *Conf.* VII.31.2. John Chrysostom, *In 1 Cor H.* 31.3, admonishes to turn the evil zeal that is jealous and harms the neighbor into good zeal.

10. *De Gen. Ad litt.* 11.15.20; translated according to Steidle, "Der gute Eifer," 106 f.; cf. Augustine, *De civ. Dei* XIV.28.

11. Prol 12–14: "Let us consider upon which of these roads we can attain God. If we take the one to the left, we have reason to fear, because it is wide, that it is the one which leads to perdition. If we turn to the right, we are on the correct road because it is narrow and is the one which brings loving servants to him who is their Lord."

12. Cf. Art. "Zelos" in ThWNT 2 (1935) 879–884; Steidle, "Der gute Eifer," 109.

13. *De zel. et liv.* esp. 10–11; also John Chrysostom and Basil describe evil zeal in their sermons, cited by Steidle, "Der gute Eifer," 105; Caesarius, *s.* 238.3.

14. Cf. RM (Vogüé), "Introduction," 97; cf. RM 7.24: On the broad way, according to the translation in RM (Vogüé), "the worldly people walk, the Sarabaite and Gyrovague monks"; cf. RM 7.31, 41, and Smaragdus's comment on this text.

15. Some examples from this chapter 92, which by its location, corresponds approximately to RB 72: 92.2: ". . . by not causing anyone to become proud of the honor and by promising the honor of being his successor to someone who lives a holy life, he may make all eager to rival one another in doing what is good and in humility. . ." 71: "So while the abbot sees all the brothers thirst for this honor and each competing to evince in himself works of holiness in what is good according to the precepts of God. . . ." In these chapters, the Master twice lists good qualities whose vocabulary somewhat resembles RB 72 (*oboedientia, caritas, patientia, castitas*), yet often with a different meaning. The differences predominate. These lists are borrowed from Galatians 5:22, the fruits of the Spirit; however, for example, *gaudium, benignitas, longanimitas* are omitted.

16. The best manuscripts say "*a vitia.*" In RB the *vitia* are not clearly distinguished from the *peccata.* Cassian calls the capital sins *vitia.*

17. At Benedict's time, the two words had become practically synonymous. According to Pétré, *Caritas,* Augustine in particular "christianized the term *amor*; cf. ibid., 87, 90–95; Kuhn, *Liebe,* 80–87.

18. Cf. Smaragdus on this text; also Augustine, *In Ps.* 118, *s.* 10.6; 11.1; Ambrose, *In Ps.* 118.4. 27.

19. The entire text of Rom 12:9-11 could be a kind of basic source for RB 72. It is interesting to compare the text of the Vulgate with RB 72. *Dilectio sine simulatione, odientes malum, adhaerentes bono. Caritate fraternitatis invicem diligentes, honore invicem praevenientes, sollicitudine non pigri, spiritu ferventes, Domino servientes.*

20. Some examples: 92.39f. "Thus, if no one is raised above the rest . . . and each may look forward, in the sense of expectation, to being considered for receiving the honor if he lives a holy life . . . 42 . . . all can make progress by competing with one another, 43 if not out of fear of the judgment to come, then at least for the sake of honor in the present life." 92.71: "So while the abbot sees all the brothers panting with thirst for this honor. . . ." The quotation "to vie in showing respect to one another" is used by the Master only for contact with brothers from outside. Seeking honor is usually frowned upon in monastic literature; cf. for example Basil, *Reg.* 63.

21. Cf. Grün, "Benediktinische Gemeinschaft," 244f.

22. Schütz, "Benediktinisches Gemeinschatfsleben," 8.

23. We find it, for example, in Basil, Cyprian, and Cassian. In Cyprian, *De dom. or.* 15 (which as a whole influenced RB 72), we read that we may suffer injustice; Cassian, *Inst.* XII.33 says that we should bear everything with the utmost patience. Cf. *Conf.*

XVI.7; and Basil, *Reg.* 134 refers to Christ, who bore death for us. As RB (Hanslik) 178 shows, some manuscripts read *tollerent.*

24. The entire paragraph of 1 Pet 2:17-25 deserves to be meditated together with RB 72.

25. In the later Regula *cujusdam Patris ad vg.* chapter 5 bears the title: *De se invicem diligendo, vel sibi invicem oboediendo.* Smaragdus says on this text: *Apostolus ait: Oboedientes invicem in vinculo pacis.* Cyprian, *De dom. or.* 15 (influence on RB 72) is an explanation of "Your will be done" and begins thus: "The will of God is what Christ both did and taught." Cf. Steidle, "Der gute Eifer," 111: "Benedict wants, according to his consistent cenobitic ideal, a rivalry in selfless service of love by obedience."

26. In chapter 92, the word *certatim* occurs four times: Competition in doing good and in humility (92.2); in making progress (92.43); in fulfilling the commandments (92.49); in showing good works (92.71).

27. Cf. Rulla, *Depth Psychology and Vocation* (Rome, 1972) 49: "But this self-actualization in Christ is reached neither by a cult of personality which might entail a more or less covert egotism, not by self-gratification of needs. . . . Self-actualization is the side-effect, the by-product of self- transcendence . . . of realization of values which go beyond the 'ego-centered self' and follow the invitations of the 'ego-transcending self.'"

28. *Conf.* XVII.19.7. In all these patristic and monastic texts, the wording of Sacred Scripture is used, *quaerere*, to seek. Benedict seems to take a further step into the practical by using *sequitur*, let him follow. Cf. Ps Basil, *Adm.* 4.

29. In some editions of the text, the following sequence is used: "Let them practice fraternal charity with a chaste love; let them fear God." The first word of v. 9 (love, *amor*) is taken into v. 8. Penco, "*Amore Deum timeant*," has shown convincingly that this was not the original text. The flow of the Latin sentences is interrupted where all verses end with the verb. "They fear God" is too brief compared to the other verses. One can also refer to similarities in sources. The more difficult version is the more likely (cf. comment on v. 9).

30. Cf. Isidore, *De diff.* II.37.142; Petré, *Caritas*, 72–76, 43–61; Sainte-Marie, "Vocabulaire," 116–118.

31. Cf. 1 Pet 2:17; Heb 13:1; 1 Thess 4:9. The Master also uses the expression *caritas fraterna* (70.1-3), yet this is preceded by the long chapter 69 about preventing monks from pretending to be sick. One also wonders whether RM 70 is truly concerned with the sick or more with showing one's good works and fulfilling the law.

32. Cf. Vogüé, *Communauté*, 534 (*Community and Abbot*, 478, 137); regarding the following thoughts, cf. Doppelfeld, "Das Kloster als Familie," 4–10; Steidle, "St. Benedikts Kritik," 26; for a positive comparison with the family, cf. Schmiedeler, "Benedictine Family," 307–334; Herwegen, *Sinn*, e.g., 22, 26, 81ff.; Lentini, "Il monastero-famiglia," 278.

33. In EA 45 (1969) 37f.

34. Dekkers, "*Caritatem caste inpendant*," 666. In interpreting this verse as well as the patristic texts, I rely on his article.

35. Caesarius, *Test.* Cf. Augustine, *In Ps.* 55.17; in 1 Pet 1:22 a brotherly love with a selfless undivided heart is demanded; cf. also Leo, *Ep.* 111.3, and Eugippius, *Vit. Sev.* 28 (29).3 for a the use of *inpendere* in the weaker sense of "to render."

36. *Sacram. Veron.* XXX.1104. Cf. also a similar sequence in 1 Pet 2:17: "Love the brothers, fear God"; also Rom 12:9-11.

37. Augustine, *De civ. Dei* XIV.9. Cassian (*Conf.* XI.11-13) describes the way from fear of the slave to the fear of love: ". . . the more sublime fear of love, which is begotten not by dread of punishment or by desire for rewards but by the greatness of one's love. . . . Therefore there are two degrees of fear. The one is for beginners—that is, for those who are still under the yoke and under servile dread . . ." The fear of love is meant in Isa 11:2f.; this "spirit of the fear of the Lord . . . clings to that love which 'never fails' (1 Cor 13:8), it not only fills but also possesses everlastingly and inseparably the person whom it has seized. . . . This, then, is the perfect fear with which the Lord, in human form . . . is said to have been filled." Dorotheus of Gaza (*Doct.* 4.1-3) points out the difference between the beginner, who does the will of God for fear of the pains of hell, and the perfect person, who has the deeper fear of lacking, or even losing "the sweetness of being with God. . . . This person has the perfect and true love, and this very love leads to perfect fear." When God said to Abraham after the sacrifice of Isaac, "Now, I know that you fear God," he means this fear that arises from love.

38. Benedict added the word *diligere* to RM a number of times, e.g., 4.71: *iuniores diligere*; 63:13: *seniors suos diligent. Dilectio* is a refined expression and is used less frequently (cf. Prol 49). It can also be a translation for *agape*, cf. Petré, *Caritas*, 30–32, 69–71; Sainte-Marie, "Vocabulaire," 114. Cyprian uses the term *caritate diligere* in *Ep.* 61.4 and 78.1.

39. Dorotheus of Gaza (*Doctr.* 6) says that we should imagine a wheel with its center and spokes. The circle is the world, God is the center. "To the degree that the saints enter into the things of the spirit, they desire to come near to God; and in preparation to their progress in the things of the spirit, they do in fact come close to God and to their neighbor. The closer they are to God, the closer they are to one another, the closer they become to God. Now consider in the same context the question of separation; for when they stand away from God and turn to external things, it is clear that the more they recede and become distant from God, the more they become distant from one another. . . . The more we are turned away from and do not love God, the greater the distance that separates us from our neighbor." There is an expression similar to 72.11 in Augustine, *In Ps.* 29.2.10: "and they are to prefer nothing to Christ" (*Et nihil praeponant Christo*).

40. Augustine, *In Ps.* 39:11; cf. also Hildemar, 631.

That This Rule Does Not Contain the Full Observance of Justice

1. RB 73 is not simply the last chapter of the Rule, but rather a real epilogue explaining the purpose of the entire Rule. It is a reflection on how to observe the Rule, a kind of cover letter.[1] Together with chapter 72 it provides a view of the entire Rule, a key for interpreting it.

2. However, RB 73 seems very different from RB 72 in content, form, and vocabulary. After the beautiful concluding sentence of RB 72 with its eschatological vista, RB 73 begins very simply here on earth. RB 72 named love as the goal of monastic life. Here the goal is described in terms of justice, perfection, and virtue. Scholars have pointed out the great number of words that occur only in this chapter (nineteen *hapax*), and the string of three rhetorical questions, unusual in the Rule. Some scholars have drawn the conclusion that this chapter might not have been written by Benedict, but added by someone later on to refute objections. The Rule had not dealt with contemplative life. Therefore some persons might have considered it incomplete.[2]

3. It is evident that Benedict did not write the Rule in one sitting, chapter by chapter. There are traces of various revisions. RB 66.8 may have been the first ending of the Rule. RB 73 could have been the end after a revision. RB 67–72 might have been inserted at a later time.[3] The end of a document requires some rhetorical device; one senses a certain pathos.[4] A deepened knowledge of Eastern monasticism may have confirmed Benedict's feeling that monastics had become decadent in his time. His ongoing experience of God and of life probably helped him see his own work in context (cf. Prol 49; *Dial.* II.35.5-7) so that he could truly call his Rule a "very little rule for the beginning" (v. 8). What later writer could have passed such a judgment if not Benedict himself? Chapter 73 accords with his person and work. He probably wrote it as an epilogue, later placing it after RB 72, and thus linking the two chapters.

4. RB 73 elaborates on RB 72 as a way under the guidance of Christ (72.12), under God's protection (73.9). Already the last sentence in RB 72 begins to use the "we/us" with which RB 73 now begins. In all texts wherein Benedict uses "we," he ranks himself with his monks. These texts go beyond the Master's ideas in stressing decadence and an awareness of being just at the beginning (18.25; 40.6; 49). The epilogue is also clearly linked to the Prologue's beginning and ending. In Prol 45–50 we find the same structure:[5] beginning the way and progressing through *conversatio* until with great love one hastens to the final goal. The direct address of 73.8 occurs only two more times in the Rule, at the beginning and at the end of the Prologue, which are proper to Benedict. In Prol 1–4 there is the contrast of obedience and the laziness of disobedience, of beginning and completing. It seems important that the first and last words of the Rule are related: "Listen—and you will reach it" (*obsculta—pervenies*). At the beginning and at the end, Benedict wants to encourage those who desire to reach the final goal, in obedience to Christ and with his help, to follow the Rule as a guide. Despite all its diversity, the Rule with its seventy-three chapters and the Prologue is an impressive whole, the work of a strong personality.

OVERVIEW

1. The entire chapter is characterized by the terms for the various stages on the way. Where are the monastics standing now? They are living badly, they are negligent and half-hearted (v. 7). With the help of the little Rule for beginners they have made a start in monastic living, have achieved a somewhat appropriate conduct, but have not yet reached full justice (cf. title, vv. 1, 8). The Rule, however, points to the heights of teaching, of virtue, of perfection that is the immediate goal (vv. 2, 9). Aided by the instruction of the Fathers (vv. 2, 4), by Sacred Scripture as their "best guide" (v. 3) and by the monastic writings (v. 5), they will be able to live well and obediently (v. 6). The final goal is named "our creator" (v. 4) or "our heavenly home" (v. 8). For reaching both of these goals, the personal help of Christ and God's protection are needed (vv. 8, 9).

2. The chapter consists of two parts: Verses 7-9 restate and refer to verses 1-2 (little Rule for beginners; heights of teaching and virtue).[6] In between are the rhetorical questions concerning Sacred Scripture, the Catholic Fathers, and the monastic writings. Verses 6 and 7 are contrasting the virtue of ideal monastics and the negligence of the actual ones. Verse 9 links the heights of teaching with the heights of virtue and probably is referring to all writings previously mentioned (in vv. 2-5).

3. In verse 1, Benedict begins with monastic life, extending verses 2-5 to human life in general, and after verse 6 focusing his statements once again on monastic life. Repetitions show that the movement on the way concerns both the immediate and the final goal: one hastens to perfection (v. 2) and also to the heavenly home (v. 8); one wants to reach both the Creator (v. 4) and the heights of virtue (v. 9). The dynamic vocabulary of this chapter is impressive (beginning, hasten, lead, norm, running straight, height) as is the emphasis on "toward, to, and through" (*ad, per*).[7] We can sense a great determination to lead monastics to the goal, to motivate them to goal-oriented hastening (cf. excursus on dynamism of RB pp. 96–97).

4. At the end of his Rule, Benedict does not rest content, saying, "Here is the Rule which will make you perfect." Certainly, authors of other rules also do not think that they have found all wisdom, deferring to other works,[8] but no other author judges his own work with the severity and modesty of Benedict. The Master is rather sure of himself and often repeats that God is speaking through him; his Rule contains the Fathers' teachings and is on a par with them, thus leading his pupils to perfection.[9] Benedict is not content with just fulfilling the norms of the Rule. He does not end his Rule with a barred door as the Master does so drastically,[10] but he concludes with the door open, and with a strong incentive not to rest, but to continue striving (cf. also RB 62.4).

Title—That this Rule does not contain everything
   that pertains to the full observance of justice.

The dynamic character of this chapter and of the Rule appears already in the title: it is a guide toward full justice, but does not contain it. As almost always for Benedict, justice in regard to human beings means biblical justice.[11] It is a description of the covenant response to the saving justice of God, expressed in love of God and neighbor. Christ himself came to "fulfill all justice" (Matt 3:15). He is *the* great rule, not RB, which only wants to lead to Christ. The Rule is left incomplete on purpose (cf. introduction).

V. 1: We have, however, written this Rule
   so that by observing it in monasteries,
   we may show a somewhat appropriate way of life
   and a beginning of monastic life.

1. *We have, however, written this Rule.* "This Rule" encompasses in its final form all chapters, including chapter 72. The word "however" (*autem*) usually indicates that a chapter is to be read in close connection with the preceding one (cf. also 10.1; 13.1; 25.1, and so on). The term "we have written"

in the perfect tense is Benedict's personal signature at the end of a completed document.[12]

2. *Observing it in monasteries.* The word "observe" appears three times in this chapter and refers to justice (title), the Rule (v. 1), and the teachings of the Fathers (v. 2). All of them provide guidance and direction for life and should not only be contemplated, but carefully fulfilled. Observance of the Rule is a deep concern for Benedict (cf. 3.11; 60.9; 65.17, all proper to Benedict), even though it is just the first step. The plural form "monasteries" is not used anywhere else in the RB ("monastery" in the singular occurs about seventy-three times). Benedict is thinking primarily of his monastery at Monte Cassino. However, there are other passages (for example, 48.7; 35.4; 55.2, 7, when he speaks of different local situations), indicating that the Rule was written with a view to other monasteries as well.

3. *So that we may show to some extent . . .*[13] The weighty term "so that" at the beginning of the chapter points out the purpose of the entire Rule, "to teach only a beginning" of the way to the final goal, the Creator. It shows Benedict's goal-oriented thinking, formulated very cautiously, as often in the Rule. Using "we," Benedict clearly counts himself among his monks, one who is at the beginning. He continues the "we" of RB 72.12: "May Christ lead us altogether to everlasting life." Even at the end of his life, Benedict does not see himself as one who had already arrived or as one standing high above the other monastics.

4. *An appropriate way of life (honestas morum).* The expression *honestas morum* is difficult to translate. Benedict probably adopted it from Greek philosophy, as was done already in the New Testament. Paul admonishes the Christians to live "appropriately," as in the daytime (Rom 13:13). Everything should be done with integrity and propriety (1 Cor 14:40; cf. 1 Thess 4:12).[14] Integrity (*honestas*) includes whatever is according to "reason," to human nature; it is the mark of the wise. The term often occurs together with gravity, dignity, modesty, virtue, and in the Christian context, with order and moderation. Integrity shows good manners in external forms and interior disposition.[15] The Rule is intended to lead to a life appropriate for monastics in a monastery. This certainly includes good manners, dignity, discipline, modesty, and gravity, but also a capacity for living in community, a noble attitude, and above all love, for love never acts unseemly (1 Cor 13:5).[16]

5. *A beginning of monastic life.* We may find it sobering that observing the Rule will lead us only to a beginning of monastic life. Yet *conversatio morum* is part of the promise at profession (cf. comments to 58.17). Two experiences seem to be reflected in this statement:

(a) There are stages of organic development in the spiritual life that must be respected. Benedict himself speaks of the beginning (Prol 48), which may be narrow, and then of progress in monastic life (Prol 49). He does not need to write his Rule for this second stage. Monastic stories with which Benedict was probably familiar, tell of one who wanted to live in the desert as a recluse immediately after becoming a monk. He had to be converted and recognize that he had not even begun in earnest (*Vit. Patr.* V.10.110). The next instruction is even more drastic: "If you see a youth who wants to ascend to heaven by his own willpower, grasp his foot and bring him back to earth."[17]

(b) As a person progresses in the spiritual life, all human activity becomes relative compared to God's greatness and may seem inappropriate. At the beginning of monastic life, one might hope to accomplish something with much good will and effort. This phase is necessary. By and by such illusions vanish. God deprives a human being of all self-assurance. How many monastics recognize after many years in the monastery, perhaps toward the end of their life, that they have not even made a real beginning. Such experiences prepare us to accept *everything* from the mercy of God. When Father Pambo lay dying, he said, "I am going to God as someone who has not even begun to serve God."[18] This attitude is linked with striving to begin anew each day, even each hour, and the optimistic conviction that this is possible with the grace of God. "Abbot Moses asked Abbot Silvanus, 'Can a person make a new start in monastic life (*initium conversationis*) each day?' Abbot Silvanus replied, 'If the person is willing to work, he can start monastic life every hour' (*inchoare initium conversationis*)."[19]

V. 2: But for anyone hastening toward the perfection of monastic life, there are the teachings of the Fathers, the observance of which leads a human being to the heights of perfection.

This carefully crafted and complete sentence[20] is like a title for verses 3-6.

1. *But for anyone hastening.* With the word *ceterum* (by the way, however, but) a new train of thought is begun in contrast to the first, the Rule as a small beginning. Now the individual person is envisioned, no longer the "we" or monastics in general. The author addresses each one who wants to hasten, not just to move along. Is hastening the progress of an individual disregarding losses? Considering RB 72 and 66.4, we can say that hastening is a sign of good zeal, of love, which also helps the others to keep going with us on the way (cf. excursus on dynamism, pp. 96–97).

2. *Toward the perfection of monastic life . . . to the heights of perfection.* The word "perfection" is not used much in the religious language of today.

What did Benedict want to express, and what does he tell us today by this word? Does he mean a state of perfection, or even eremitical life, or a condition of contemplation beyond common life?

Benedict addresses any human being, "anyone," indicating that he is not referring to special perfection for a certain group. In Christian antiquity, perfection was not confined to a certain state of life, for example, in distinction from the laity. People were aware that all Christians are called to perfection. Basil wrote his Rules for everyone who wanted to lead a Christian life. Gregory of Nyssa entitled one book "For the Monk Olympus, or about Perfection, and What a Christian Should Be Like."[21]

In RB perfection is contrasted with the beginning of monastic life and denotes progress. Benedict says that "our heart expands and we run the way of the commandments with the unspeakable joy of love" (Prol 49—again, no separate perfection!). In chapter 73 this progress is called *perfectio*. Basil distinguishes between a first phase of renunciation and a phase of progress (*Reg.* 4). For him this clearly happens in community. Generally, at least two stages are described: the practical life, keeping the commandments, asceticism; and the "theoretical" life, contemplation, called *theologia* on its highest level. Cassian, often using the expression "height of perfection," sees perfection as including purity of heart, contemplation, unceasing prayer, and above all, "apostolic love" (cf. especially *Inst.* IV.43). He mentions various forms of perfection, just as there are various beatitudes (*Conf.* XI.12). Perfection for him is dynamic, meaning: always keep walking forward.[22] Leo the Great says, "This is the true justice (*iustitia*) of perfection, never to consider ourselves perfect."[23] In this sense, all weighing and comparing with others ceases. Whereas the Master speaks of disciples who are more or less perfect (about thirteen times),[24] Benedict deletes most traces of this two-stage theory in the monastery. He does not mean a perfection that distances us from others (cf. also 4.62).

Cassian once uses the term "hastening to perfection" as obeying the Law of Moses or following Saint Paul (*Conf.* XXI.5.4). Benedict tries even more to use biblical language (cf. the link with *iustitia*). We may think of the Sermon on the Mount that summarizes full justice with "Be perfect, as your heavenly Father is perfect" (Matt 5:48). Paul speaks of love as the bond of perfection (Col 3:14). Perfection of love, like full justice, includes loving God wholeheartedly and passing love on (cf. also LG 40). For Benedict it seems to lie along the line of good zeal, of the most ardent love (RB 72; cf. 4.1-2). It is a pure gift of God's grace. We cannot test it and then boast about it (cf. Prol 29–32). Rahner says in this regard:

> In accordance with Matt 5:48, perfection is that moral and religious maturity of man, made possible and bestowed by God's grace, which man freely

develops in accordance with the objective law of God and the ever various capacities of the individual: loving God and our neighbor with our whole heart and our whole strength (Matt 22:37; Rom 13:10).[25]

It is evident that Benedict does not intend to lead a person away from the community by this verse, but rather to unite the heights of love and prayer with life in community (cf. comments on v. 9).

3. *There are the teachings of the holy Fathers.* He first mentions the teachings of the holy Fathers, but in connection with observance. Here, as throughout the Rule,[26] the close link of "teaching" to Sacred Scripture becomes clear (v. 3). He means the holy Fathers, that is those who can lead others to perfection by the double teaching of their own life and of their word (cf. 2.11). As in other rules, it is also customary in RB to refer to the forefathers, the holy Fathers, "our Fathers."[27] However, Benedict does not place his Rule on a level with theirs (in contrast to the Master, cf. RM 95.24). Since the fifth century, the Fathers meant those who left us their writings, who lived a holy life and whose teaching was recognized by the church as orthodox.[28] Also, the forefathers of the Bible are called "Fathers" or "our Fathers." Thus, the term could already include Sacred Scripture[29] and our forefathers in the faith, for example, Abraham, Isaac, Jacob, the prophets, David, and so on.

It is also possible that Benedict simply wished to refer to the Fathers of the Church, such as Augustine, Ambrose, Basil, Cyprian, Jerome, and Leo the Great. If this is the case, they prompted his mention of Sacred Scripture. After that he again mentions the Catholic Fathers, framing Sacred Scripture with the Fathers as an indication that the Bible always was used together with the explanations and interpretations of the Fathers.

Whichever opinion is correct, in both cases Sacred Scripture and tradition are seen together as the pillars of orthodoxy.

4. *Whose observance leads a human being.* The Latin word *perducere* used here is in RB 72 applied to Christ, who leads us to everlasting life, whereas zeal only has *ducere*. Christ leads us from within. He leads us through Sacred Scripture and its explanation by holy persons. However, we also must do our part, following the guidelines. The holy Fathers are not the exclusive property of monks. They belong to Christianity, even to humanity as a whole. It is remarkable that Benedict in many portions of the Rule speaks simply of persons (usually in their relationship with God). He realizes his solidarity with all of humanity that ought to let the Fathers, especially through Sacred Scripture, help us on the way to the Creator (v. 4).

Verses 3-6 provide three rhetorical questions, perhaps an indication that Benedict wanted to remind the hearers of what they were familiar with in daily life. On the way to immediate and the final goals, the guides for orientation are named: Sacred Scripture, the holy and orthodox Fathers, and the monastic writings.

V. 3: For which page
   or which divinely inspired saying
   (of divine authorship)
   of the Old and New Testament
   is not a very straight norm for human life?

1. *For which page.* "For," (*enim*) is a confirmation and foundation of what precedes, showing the close connection between the Fathers and Sacred Scripture. Perhaps we imagine a page full of letters, but the Fathers also speak of the "voice" of the pages.[30] Probably no one among us would insist that every page of Sacred Scripture could be a guideline. We rather are inclined to skip some things. Benedict respects every page and believes that God thereby lights our way.

2. *Which divinely inspired saying (sermo) of the Old and New Testament.* *Sermo* is a spoken word that enters the ear. It alludes to the belief of the Fathers that one word suffices to work salvation.[31] *Sermo* can also mean a conversation, a dialogue (cf. introduction; Prologue). Through Sacred Scripture God enters into dialogue with us. Unlike human words that can be good (cf. 31.14) or useless (67.4), this word is divinely confirmed, of divine authorship. In 9.8, Benedict also says: "For the readings at Vigils one should take the divinely inspired books of the Old and New Testament." This expression could also be translated as: of divine confirmation, sponsorship, power, authority, of divine origin. In ancient Christian literature the word *auctoritas* often is applied to Sacred Scripture.[32]

In chapter 9, as in 73, the Old and New Testaments are also mentioned. In times threatened by false teachings, it was important for Benedict and his monks not to exclude any book of the Sacred Scriptures, to take the entire Bible as their norm (cf. introduction).

3. *A very straight norm for human life.* The Latin word *norma* in its concrete denotation is a square measure, a ruler, a guideline; it serves for erecting a straight building, drawing straight lines. In the moral sense, it is used for guidelines and prescriptions that also help us walk straight. Sacred Scripture here is seen in its power and normative sense as a help to a straight life, without detours. A monastic rule in this respect is normative in making Sacred Scripture penetrate the life of a particular community.

The term "very straight" refers to our way toward the goal. As Benedict says in 7.21, there are ways that *seem* straight but do not lead to God. Therefore, the help of Sacred Scripture is important (cf. Prologue 21). We human beings keep finding crooked ways, and a reorientation is needed. Cassian says, "We must fix our gaze on the final goal and set our course exactly on a straight line. If we stray from it in our thoughts, we need to take a new look. We must turn around and correct our course according to this guideline."[33] As human beings we are weak, sin has twisted us, a straight path does not come to us naturally. We need a prop, a guideline, to keep running straight. Any page and saying of the Old and New Testament can serve this purpose. Thus we walk Christ's ways under the guidance of the Gospel (Prol 21). The words of Benedict show great respect and a profound spirit of faith.

This attitude of Benedict toward Sacred Scripture can also inspire us today. We can ask ourselves whether Sacred Scripture, in every one of its parts, even in every saying, has such importance for us and our communities today. Benedict uses the resources of his time for understanding the sacred texts: the teachings of the holy Catholic Fathers. Sacred Scripture requires interpretation by persons who are guided in a special way by the Holy Spirit, the inspirer of Sacred Scripture, by persons who live at the heart of the church to whom the Bible is entrusted as a precious treasure (cf. DV 9–10). The "Catholic Fathers" were the commentaries of Benedict's time. Today we have many aids for understanding the Bible, new commentaries, exegetes, and leaders of the church. However, these have not made the Fathers of the Church superfluous. There is a veritable renaissance of the Church Fathers today. They can help us in a special way, starting from the literal meaning, delving deeper, discovering the "heart beneath the letter" (Gregory the Great). They can introduce us to a spiritual exegesis in which they excelled: how can we read the Sacred Scriptures from Christ's viewpoint and in reference to Christ, and how can we let them permeate our lives?

V. 4: Or which book of the holy Catholic Fathers
does not speak loudly
of how we can run straight to our creator?

1. *The book . . . speaks.* We are surprised. This text may be a further indication that we are concerned with readings in community, when the words enter into the ear (cf. 42.3-8; 4.55). The word *re-sonare* is used accurately; someone has put meaning into the text (the author), and now it echoes back from the pages of the book. It is a living, ongoing process!

2. *The holy Catholic Fathers.* Having spoken of the holy Fathers in verse 2 in a general way, Benedict returns to them again after mentioning Sacred Scripture. He speaks more specifically of the Catholic Church Fathers, that is, those who proclaim the true teaching. This means they are in union with the universal church and within the orthodox tradition.[34] Also in 9.8

on the readings for Vigils, Benedict lists Sacred Scripture "and its interpretation by well-known, orthodox and Catholic Fathers." The Master does not seem to have this concern; he uses neither the word "catholic" nor the word "orthodox." He also uses apocryphal writings and does not make Benedict's clear distinction between Sacred Scripture and later related works. One of the Fathers said, "This is what God desires of Christians, that everyone obeys Sacred Scripture, learning from it the norms of speaking and acting, and being in accord with the authorities and the orthodox Fathers."[35] The well-known formulation of the decree attributed to Gelasius, which carried great weight, may have influenced Benedict.[36] These were the holy Fathers who adhered to the truth until death and who in no way strayed from communion with the holy Roman Church (similar to the term "Fathers"). This shows once again Benedict's connection with the Roman Church which in his time was threatened by false teachings. By comparison with other rules we can sense Benedict's great concern to live in the heart of the Catholic Church and to make its cause his own. He names these Catholic Fathers ahead of monastic authors.

In this chapter, Benedict stresses three times that the Fathers (or Father Basil) are holy. They have allowed the Sacred Scriptures to permeate their entire lives, have reached the perfection of love and have, with the help of God's grace, remained faithful until death. So they are able to lead others, by their teaching and example, to the heights, to the ultimate goal that they themselves have reached. Sacred Scripture in its entirety, together with tradition, united with the interpretation of the Catholic Church—these are the two main pillars of orthodoxy.[37] Today the circle of the "holy Catholic Fathers" has expanded considerably. According to the Rule, we must be open to them also. It includes the teachings of the Second Vatican Council as well.

3. *How we can run straight to our Creator.* Running straight[38] and reaching the goal, that is our concern as well: not having to make detours or even straying onto the wrong ways that seem right but do not lead to the goal (7.21). The holy Fathers who already have reached it can aid us by the wisdom of their lives and their experience with Sacred Scripture.

"Our Creator" is given as the goal of all human life. RB 16.5 likewise says that "we sing praise to our Creator" (this reminds us of the natural order, the sanctification of the day). "Our" refers not only to the monks, but to all people. The holy Fathers lead all their readers to the ultimate goal, they also lead to the heights of perfection (*perducere*—v. 2; *pervenire*—v. 4). The verb both times is reinforced by an energetic prefix *per*.

V. 5: But also the Conferences of the Fathers and their Institutions and their Lives

as well as the Rule of our Holy Father Basil,
V. 6: what else are they but tools of virtue for monks
who live rightly and obediently?

Only after speaking of the official Fathers of the Church and especially of Sacred Scripture does Benedict now mention the monastic Fathers and some important works of monastic literature as concrete aids for a good monastic life. It seems to be a reading list for the monastery, also giving clues concerning the sources Benedict used for his Rule.[39] For Compline, Benedict had recommended: "One should read aloud from the dialogs or the lives of the Fathers or something which edifies the hearers."[40] 73.5 lists four important works: the *Conferences, Institutes*, the *Lives of the Fathers*, and the Rule of Basil (in the translation of Rufinus). There is a similar passage in the biographies of the Jura Fathers:

> My discourse has caused me to touch upon some of the institutions of the fathers. . . . In no way am I belittling, by a disdainful presumptuousness, the institutions of the holy and eminent Basil, bishop of the episcopal see of Cappadocia, or those of the holy fathers of Lérins and of Saint Pachomius, the ancient abbot of the Syrians, or those that the venerable Cassian formulated more recently. But while we read these daily, we strive to follow those of Condadisco: they are more conformable with our local conditions and with the demands that our work entails than are those of the East. without a doubt the Gallic nature—or weakness—follows the former more easily and efficaciously.[41]

And Gregory of Tours writes about Aredius, "He founded a community in which were observed the rules not only of Cassian, but also those of Basil and of the abbots that instituted monastic life."[42]

1 *The Conferences of the Fathers and their Institutes.* These are named first. Much discussion has taken place as to what specifically Benedict wanted to recommend. Did he wish to recommend such monastic literature in general or the works of Cassian? Did he have the courage to recommend Cassian who had been suspected of heresy? Is this the reason for not mentioning his name? Or did he presuppose his works were so well known that mentioning his name was not necessary?[43]

The listing of the two titles *Conferences* and *Institutes* points to Cassian who himself used the terms.[44] These two collections were well known in the West and were highly praised. "He wrote, taught by experience, in a noble style . . . about all things monastic." Someone was "kindled to fervor by spiritual meditation on the Institutions and Collations." "Diligently read Cassian, who wrote about the institutions of faithful monks, and gladly listen to his writings!"[45] Probably Benedict was moved less than the

Gallic monks by semi-Pelagianism that was condemned by the Synod of Orange in 529. In Rome, the popes and the liturgy had spoken clearly on this question in the fifth and sixth centuries, presumably ending the controversy.[46] Benedict must have known about the question (consider his nearness to Rome), but for his practical mind, fine theoretical distinctions and formulations were less important. He does not explicitly oppose it, but in his Rule gives more weight to grace vis-à-vis human will than the Master does. Interestingly, Benedict never used chapter 13 of the *Conferences*, which was suspected of heresy, though he otherwise used the *Conferences* frequently and freely.

One may assume that Benedict could recommend an author, even though he was aware of his orthodoxy being questioned. From the same period we have the recommendations of Cassiodorus that advise choosing what is right. We see Benedict's largeness of heart when he recommends such an author and trusts that his monks can distinguish what is good from what is dangerous.[47] His nearness to Rome may have prevented him from naming Cassian, or he did not need to mention him because his works were so well known.

Benedict does not become narrow and anxious in his concern for orthodoxy. He follows Sacred Scripture: "Test everything and retain what is good" (1 Thess 5:21).

2. *Their Lives.* Immediately after Cassian's works, the influential biographies are named. Admonitions instruct, but the example of the saints goes deeper and inspires even more to imitation. One might think of Anthony, for example, of Paul, Pachomius, monastic stories, and so on.[48] Benedict also recommends them for reading at Compline (42.3).

3. *The Rule of our holy Father Basil.* Basil is the only author mentioned by name. He is also called "our holy Father," probably as a guarantee of orthodoxy, as the Catholic and Oriental Father of monks and of the church. Besides naming him at the end, Benedict was also influenced by him in the first four verses of the Prologue.[49] His "Rule" refers to the small *Asketikon*, translated by Rufinus into Latin and known to Benedict. Although it was not meant to be a rule, Benedict calls it that. Basil only wanted to give guidelines culled from Sacred Scripture, applying them to life in community. That is precisely what RB is meant to be. Basil had emphasized the preeminence of community over the eremitical life, the importance of obedience and living in the presence of God.

RB 73.2 shows us how important it is not to isolate RB, but to read it in the context of the Fathers and Sacred Scripture. Therefore, we have tried in each monastery to consider the Church Fathers and monastic fathers in the readings of the liturgy, in personal *lectio divina*, and in the readings at table. It will be evident by now how important Oriental literature was for Benedict; nearly all titles point to it. Perhaps our monasteries have easier access to the Eastern church for this reason, as well as a task in ecumenical dialogue.

4. *Instruments of virtue.* Today we have a problem with this expression. The word "virtue" means practically nothing to people of today.[50] Formerly it attracted and inspired people. The word is derived from *vir* (man) and has an energetic quality. Power, fitness, enthusiasm, courage—all these are implied. In the Latin version of Sacred Scripture the word often denotes power, mighty deed, sign of God's power. We are to love God, as RB 4.1 states, with all our strength (cf. also RM 11.18; Thp 65). Benedict here follows biblical usage. In the remaining texts, perhaps with the exception of 49.2, he is probably influenced by Cassian, who has a preference for the word and develops a teaching on virtue and vice. According to Benedict (64.19), discretion is the mother of the virtues, and at the end of the ascent there is even joy in virtue (7.69; also in RM); there are tools of virtue, and finally the summits of teaching and of virtue (73.9). Virtue means the movement of the whole person toward God in the power of the Holy Spirit. Grace precedes, and we make room for it so that it can fill the person ever more.[51]

The word "instruments" is taken from the world of craftsmanship and was familiar to Benedict's monks. Today we might prefer the abstract term of means or help. Concretely, which means are included? Cassian mentions psalms, prayer, *lectio*, solitude, humility of the heart, and asceticism. In the early church, Sacred Scripture often is called *the* instrument.[52] Benedict here refers to the monastic writings that are designated as the readings for diligent monks. For him, Sacred Scripture and the readings from the Church Fathers and monastic fathers are inseparable. The word "instruments" also indicates that a person must do something. Instruments are not to be contemplated, but we must take them in hand and work with them. It is useless just to receive beautiful ideas or teachings into the head. We must implement them in our life. However, Benedict does not stress action to the detriment of grace, which is prior (cf. comment on Prol 4; the semi-Pelagian question, p. 27).

5. *Monks who live rightly and obediently.* Benedict probably equates "living rightly" and "obediently." These are opposed to "ill-living, lazy and negligent monks" in the following verse. Benedict had described disobedience as negligence or laziness in Prol 2. Obedience requires effort. Obedience is highlighted once again as the main element of monastic life. Since this term is mentioned in connection with Basil's Rule, we can assume that Benedict is influenced here by Basil and that obedience is used in the radical

and comprehensive sense, not only toward superiors. "Living rightly" is not goodness that results from the monastics' own efforts, but flows from divine grace. However, monastics must take hold of this grace and cooperate with it (cf. also RB 31.8; 64.21; 53.17).

V. 7: Yet we lazy and ill-living, negligent monks must blush for shame.

1. Here Benedict leaves the questions and returns to the reality of his monks and the concern of his little Rule. He deeply feels the contrast between monastics living a right life and in obedience (perhaps those of the East) and the monks of his own time. He passes a harsh judgment: they are decadent. But Benedict includes himself. He does not abandon the ill-living monks in order to seek his personal perfection. Abbot Isaac said: "I am not giving you any more directions because you would not keep them" (*Apoph.* Isaac, 7). Benedict writes his Rule precisely for the sinners without concealing his own bad experiences. In 18.25 Benedict says, in contrast to the Fathers, "we negligent monks." In 40.6: "Though we read . . . but since monks of our times cannot be convinced of it. . . ." In 49.1-2 he writes, "The life of a monk ought to be . . . but since only a few have the strength for it . . ."

2. *Lazy and negligent.* A lazy (*desidiosus*) person sits down (*de-sedere*) and simply does nothing, is idle, resting his hands in his lap (cf. *frater desidiosus* in 48.23) and omitting what is good in every respect. The word is used for disobedience in Prol 2. Simply doing nothing puts us on the wrong track, for we are inclined by sin toward what is evil. Negligence is worse: not paying attention, not caring, failing to do, or even despising.[53] Cassian says, "I think that [these things] will be considered impossible by the lazy and the negligent" (*Conf.* XII.16.3), and he exclaims in his disappointment: "What lukewarmness we see today!"[54] Benedict is firmly convinced of the decadence of his monks and his time by comparison with the heights of earlier times. This certainly is a sign of his deep experience of God. It is also an anthropological fact that people believe the earlier times were better. It may be consoling for us to know that this was the case in the sixth century, yes, even in the centuries preceding it.

> The holy Fathers were making predictions about the last generation. They said, "What have we ourselves done?" One of them, the great Abba Ischyrion replied, "We ourselves have fulfilled the commandments of God." The others replied, "and those who come after us, what will they do?" He said, "They will struggle to achieve half our works." And they said, "And to those who come after them, what will happen?" He said, "The men of that generation will not accomplish any works at all . . ." (*Apoph.* Ischyrion).

While there is a rhetorical rule of modesty that makes an author depreciate his own work, Benedict seems convinced of decadence throughout his Rule.

3. *We must blush for shame.* Both words mean nearly the same, denoting confusion, shock, blushing, feeling embarrassed and ashamed. Each term implies reddening of the face.[55] We think of the penitential songs of the Old Testament, for example Daniel 9:5-7: "We have sinned, been wicked and done evil; we have rebelled and departed from your commandments and your laws. We have not obeyed your servants. . . . Justice, O Lord, is on your side; we are shame-faced even to this day . . ." (cf. also Bar 1:15; Isa 45:6-17). In this sense the meaning of Benedict becomes clearer: A person sees himself guilty before the great God, before God's justice and love. When someone complained about another person, a Russian holy man said, "I have lived in this world for 70 years now and have met no bad person except myself."[56]

Using this emphasis rooted in the pedagogy of his time, Benedict wants to spur us on to conversion (note the *ergo* which follows). "If you can't live like the forefathers, at least keep this Rule!" Isidore of Seville later on was to say in a similar vein, "If some cannot keep all the instructions of the Fathers, let them guide their steps according to this little instruction" (*Reg. Mon.* 2nd preface).

What can motivate us today to energy and a new beginning, to individual and communal conversion? This is the question Benedict poses here. Perhaps the beginnings of our monastery, of our community? Perhaps the world situation of today, its poverty and its injustice?

**V. 8: Whoever you are, hastening to the heavenly home,
       observe with Christ's help
       this very little Rule which we have written for beginners.**

In this verse Benedict changes from "we" back to the direct address "you." He turns to the individual person just as he did at the beginning of the Prologue. There he also spoke of the return to the Father (Prol 2 and Prol 3), of beginning a good work and of prayer, so that everything might be completed by God (Prol 4).[57]

1. *Whoever you are, hastening.* The word *ergo*, usually a signal in RB, shows the concrete application for the individual person to whom Benedict now addresses himself: something needs to be done. "Whoever you are" pertains not to certain qualifications, to selection by race, class, or training, but here everyone is addressed who really is determined to hasten on the way to the heavenly home, not just to walking along (cf. comments to 58.1, 7).

2. *To the heavenly home.* The ultimate goal is thus described only in this part of the Rule. It may echo the "him," the Father (*pater*), to whom we return by obedience (Prol 2). *Patria* is one's homeland, native land, the home of our parents, implying a feeling at home.[58] The term "heavenly home" is probably biblical language, derived from the customary *pater caelestis* (cf. for example RM 11.105; 16.16; 17.20). The letter to the Hebrews points out that the patriarchs, considering themselves strangers and guests, "show that they were seeking a home. If they had meant the home they had left, they could have returned there. But they now strive for a better one, the heavenly home" (Heb 11:14). This would also mark the monastic of the RB as a pilgrim, *peregrinus*, a stranger on the way. In stressing the dynamics of the way with all its risks and uncertainties, Benedict points out our true home where our roots are and where we will find rest.

3. *This little Rule for beginners.* It is little because compared to other Rules, such as that of the Master or of Basil, it is brief. It is little because it wants to help beginners on the first stage of the way and because it seems poor by comparison with the Fathers and their teachings. This shows Benedict's humility and experience. There is also the encouragement to observe at least this little Rule. When we look at the end of the Prologue, we might paraphrase it thus: "Do not flee, for this Rule does not demand the impossible. It is modest, but it helps those who know themselves to be only beginners." Benedict truly has a lowly opinion of his Rule. This also becomes clear when we compare it with the self-assurance of the Master, who considered himself on a par with the Fathers (cf. comment on Verse 2). To begin designates the first stage of the spiritual life. It occurs only one more time, in Prol 4. We may remember Hebrews 6:1: "Therefore, let us leave behind the basic teaching about Christ and advance to maturity, without laying the foundation all over again: repentance from dead works and faith in God." Benedict does want to start at the beginning with this "little Rule for beginners." Then God will lead us on. Though the desire to hasten is good, we must not, out of great zeal, skip any steps and stages.

4. *Observe with Christ's help.* Grammatically, the formulation "with Christ's help" could also refer to "we have written" and then we could translate: "This little Rule for beginners, which we have written with Christ's help." Then this text would recall 1.13: "Let us therefore set out, with the Lord's help, to write a rule for cenobites" and would throw light on Benedict, a person who can do nothing and wants to do nothing without the help of God's grace.

However, if Benedict is referring to the beginning of the Prologue here, Christ's help concerns the "fulfilling." Benedict, seems to be very aware, contrary to semi-Pelagianism, of the necessity of grace and the help of God that he emphasizes regarding human activity. This places him entirely within orthodox teaching. "As often as you begin a good work, you must first pray most earnestly that he will complete it" (Prol 4). Benedict says here: "Observe this little Rule for beginners with Christ's help." You cannot even observe this little Rule by your own power. Every work, even the least, requires the help of Christ. Benedict here envisions grace, in the person of Christ, assisting the monastic. Similarly in the following verse he speaks of God's protection. He helps us to realize that active observance and the more passive reaching of the goal are a grace. Benedict may here be influenced by Cassian's chapter on the "O God, come to my assistance" (*Conf.* X.10). He introduces this ejaculation at the beginning of the Office during the day (cf. 17.3; 18.1) and of the weekly service (35.17). Then follows the prayer, ". . . God, you have helped me" (35.16). God's help is the foundation of all our deeds and surrounds them. Cassian believes that this verse contains humility, trust in being heard, confident hope for effective and ever-present protection. For whoever keeps calling on his protector may be sure that he is ever present. This verse also contains the ardor of tender love (*Conf.* X. 10).

**V. 9: And then you will finally, under God's protection,
    reach the greater heights of teaching and of virtue described above.**

The connecting phrase "and then . . . finally"[59] shows that there is indeed a progression. It also expresses the confidence that it is the normal result of observing the beginning of the Rule. Cassian says if someone wants to try whether these things are really possible, he should first embrace this way of life with zeal, and then he will discover that these things, which seem superhuman, are not only possible, but will even prove easy (*Conf.* I.Praef.7). Here he is not speaking of a change in one's life situation, but of a further stage of the spiritual life. Something changes in the innermost part of a person who really is fulfilling what is commanded.

1. *The greater heights of teaching and virtue.* Now we again face the question what these greater heights entail. Are they a higher kind of perfection that can only be reached by leaving the community that lives according to RB? The word *culmen* only occurs one other time in Benedict: "If we wish to reach the highest degree of humility and arrive quickly at that heavenly exaltation . . ." (7.5). Probably Benedict means a goal that monastics can reach in community on this earth and that prepares them to arrive at exaltation in heaven (remote, final goal). This exaltation is not the result of an ascent. It surpasses every human goal. When one arrives on the summit, the ultimate goal will seem even further removed, as Benedict himself must have discovered.

Cassian, in using this and similar expressions (*culmen perfectionis, culmen doctrinae, culmen virtutum*), refers to heights of virtue, of perfection, of living according to the Beatitudes in liberty of spirit.[60] Only once does he mention the eremitical life. Benedict stays with the first stage of ascetical life for his monastics: purification from faults, practicing of good habits; and for the second part refers to the classics, especially of Eastern monasticism. Still, this ideal seems attainable to him within a zealous community (cf. comments to v. 2).[61] When we look at the other texts of the Rule that Benedict added from his own experience, we could describe the heights as unspeakable sweetness of love (Prol 49), good zeal, the most ardent zeal (72.3), and love of God which drives out fear (together with Cassian and RM 7.67-70).

2. *Under God's protection you will reach.* Here the text does not say "under Christ's guidance" (72.12) or "with Christ's help" (73.8), but "under God's protection." He himself is our shelter, our roof, our safeguard on the way that may be dangerous, but leads to freedom. At first there can still be the protection of people, things, tools, but in the end it is God alone. The formula may come from the liturgy. In Compline we pray, "protect us under the shadow of your wings" (cf. RM 19.5). Benedict is saying, "You really will reach it, you will attain the goal." In other passages he uses several expressions for the final goal: Benedict also uses this word in other places to point to the final goal: "the tent of his kingdom" (Prol 22), "eternal life" (Prol 42), "heavenly exaltation" (7.5), "the Creator" (73.4), and for the Christian and monastic goal he uses "love of God" (7.67), "heights of teaching and virtues" (73.9).

Many manuscripts have added "Amen" after this text; some say, "here ends the monastic Rule," or "here ends the Rule of Saint Benedict," and a few state "heaven is open to all who observe it" (Hanslik, 181).

In this chapter, we touch on the problem of the letter and the spirit, literal observance and liberty of spirit. As Christ surpasses the Law of the Old Testament and "fulfills" it in a more profound way, so the monastic must "go beyond the Rule," not by neglecting his duty, but by internalizing it and surpassing it in the freedom of the children of God and out of love for Christ. The ancient monastics always knew the danger of legalism. A rule, no matter how good, when regarded as a law, can dampen the élan of the spiritual life. No one should stop at a literal observance of the Rule. The Rule is teaching us liberty and love. The Fathers have made the same statement concerning Sacred Scripture. The letter of the law, necessary as it is, can also prevent us from grasping its essence. We must break through the shell, accepting life with the help of the Holy Spirit, letting it permeate us and thus living in the liberty of love. This is the liberation that Benedict means here and that Gregory the Great illustrates in the story of the last dialogue of Benedict and Scholastica. It is the greater love that matters. Any divinization or cult of the Rule is excluded. The Rule is a means whose letter grows superfluous as we draw nearer to the goal.[62]

Excursus: The Dynamism of RB

Benedictines generally give an impression of stability. Here in the last chapter, however, the dynamism of the way is stressed, opening to infinite vistas, a movement that ends only when it has reached the final goal of all human life. This is different from RM that closes with stability and safety in the monastery (95.23 f.). In our time of uncertainty, we sometimes are tempted to establish ourselves, settling in, becoming defensive. The Second Vatican Council used the image of the church as God's pilgrim people; the pilgrim's way leads through constant reform (cf. UR 2, 6; GS 1). Can one say that for Benedict stability means persevering on this pilgrim road? I think so.

His Rule often uses the image of the way. This is not a stroll for pleasure, nor a "restless and unsteady wandering about" (1.11) like that of the gyrovagues, but there is a goal, return (Prol 2; 73.4, 8) to the Creator, to the heavenly home or tent (Prol 23–24). The positive goal helps us in going forward joyfully.

Benedict describes this movement as a way of life (Prol 20), of salvation (Prol 48), of "God's commandments" (Prol 49), or "his" (the Lord's) way (Prol 21). It is no special way, but the normal way of all Christians under the guidance of the commandments and of the Gospel, the way of Christ leading to the goal of all human beings. This way requires obedience ("in this way we go to God"—71.2; Prol 2) and/or good works: "Now we must run ahead and act." "If we wish to live in his royal tent, we only can reach it by hastening there with good works" (Prol 22; cf. Prol 15–20—Ps 14[15]).

Benedict also tells us something about the way. Once he takes over the image of the narrow way from the Master to describe the obedience the monk embraces (5.11). But in his own texts he only calls the beginning narrow (Prol 48). Then the heart is expanded (Prol 49). In some texts he says that the way goes upward, especially in RB 7: "Brothers, if we therefore want to reach the highest summit of humility and quickly attain heavenly exaltation . . . we must erect that ladder by our ascent . . ." (7.5-6; cf. 5.10). There is a similar image in 73: the ascent to the height of perfection or to the summits of teaching and virtue (vv. 2, 9). However, it is also clear that it is "the Lord who erects the ladder" (7.8), not we ourselves. This image recalls biblical models such as Jacob's ladder, the ascent to Mount Zion, to Mount Sinai. It shows components of the way, that we need to struggle and engage our energies. Yet we must not expect to find God on the summit. When we reach that, we will learn how infinitely far we are from our real goal.

While ascending, one cannot run and hurry. Two images are intertwined: running and ascending. Benedict uses the image of running more frequently. He and the Master change a biblical text in Prologue 13: John 12:35, "Walk while you have the light of life." Both authors say, "Run while you have the light of life." This running is characteristic of Benedict's spirituality.[63] "If we want to reach the tent of his kingdom, we must run" (Prol 22). "If we want to reach eternal life, we must run now . . . while there is still time" (Prol 42–44). He uses the word "hasten" in the same sense. One hastens to perfection and to the heavenly home (73.2, 8), wishes to reach exaltation quickly (7.5). There is an underlying awareness that the time given to us is brief (cf. Prol 42–44), possibly still expecting in faith that the Lord is coming soon.

It is important to note that hastening does not mean individual running ahead of the others, as one might understand it, for example, in the context of obedience: "As in one moment, by the speed of the fear of God, both follow each other . . . the command . . . and the deed is accomplished," obedience without delay (5.4-9). This obedience still is motivated by fear. But one likewise hastens to the Divine Office (43.1-3), to which nothing its preferred. The monks hasten and try to outdo each other, but they also encourage each other (22.5-8).

Speed is marked by mutual interaction—an indication that the hastening is done within the community. The abbot must literally "hasten" with the greatest prudence and zeal so that he may not lose any brother (27.5). The cellarer gives out goods promptly and without delay (31.16, cf. 64-18). Christ leads us all "together" to eternal life (72.12). All of us are to reach the goal together. The same speed applies in dealing with people outside! The brothers run to meet the guests (53.3) as a sign of good zeal; the doorkeeper responds to the call from outside quickly in the zeal of love (66.4). This certainly does not encourage activism, but emphasizes fervor of love and readiness to serve.

What is the motive for this hastening? In the texts taken from the Master, the fear of God is stressed (cf. 5.9).[64] Benedict speaks of longing, of the desire for life (4.46; 49.7; Prol 15). The driving force is love, an ardent heart, in which good zeal resides. As we have noted, the driving force is ultimately not a person's own, but the presence of the Lord who urges us on from within and enables us to hasten.

The source of hastening is in God. It is the Lord who invites us (Prol 19). The Lord calls us (Prol 21), shows us the way (Prol 20, 24), waits for us (Prol 35; 7.30). More yet, God not only meets us, God also goes after us (27.8) as Christ went after the lost sheep. God goes with us (72.12). God is our shelter and protector, our helper (73.8-9). He gives us wings for hastening (Prol 49), and finally, even God is expected to hurry, "Lord make haste to help me." It is God's longing for us that makes him precede us and that stimulates us and enables us to hasten. Since this hurrying is a sign of love, ours should be the same: love for him and for each other, a joint hastening forward in community, not just among ourselves, but as part of the whole people of God.

At the end of this chapter, the person of Benedict is seen more clearly. He is a man of the church, who wants to live consciously within its tradition and catholicity. He stands on the pillars of orthodoxy and stays close to the Roman Church. He thus sees his monastic life as an element of this church, being on the way with all people.

We are impressed by his humility, shown by his awareness that he is always at the beginning, a sinner, a little one before the great God. Regarding his Rule, he also refers to the heights pointed out by others. He does not make his Rule an absolute. He is a man of liberty,[65] opening himself and his monks to diverse movements within the church and in the world. He is a listener who knows how to choose the best. Above all, he is a person who always wants to advance, not alone, but rather together with his monks.

Notes

1. Cf. Holzherr, *Benediktsregel*, 284–286; Rochais, *Règle*, 195; Vogüé, *IV*, 95 and *VII*, 433 (*RB-DSC*, 315). The *Concordia Regularum* of Benedict of Aniane places chapter 73 ahead of all the others; cf. also Menardus PL 103.717.

2. One is Manning, "Le chapitre 73," 139, 131–134. He also stresses the contrast to RB 72, cf. ibid., 131 f., 140; Penco, "Ricerche," 26–28. *Hapax: describere, honestas, ceterum, perfectio, celsitudo, pagina, norma, liber, resonare, cursus, necnon, instituta, Basilius, rubor, confusio, patria, inchoatio, commemorare, protegere.*

3. Cf. Vogüé, *IV*, 95 f.; Gribomont, "*Sed et,*" 29. The difference in vocabulary is explained not only by the different time of editing, but especially by Benedict's dependence on Cassian in thought and vocabulary.

4. Cf. Widhalm, *Die rhetorischen Elemente*, 161. This also explains the great number of *hapax*.

5. When Manning, "Le chapitre 73," 139, draws from this the conclusion that both parts are not Benedict's work, he is missing the coherence of these passages with the Rule as a whole. Cf. note on Prol 45–50 (n. 1, p. ••).

6. *Regulam autem hanc descripsimus*	*nobis autem . . . regulam descriptam*
initium conversationis	*hanc minimam inchoationis regulam*
aliquatenus	*nobis . . . desidiosis . . . neglegentibus*
ad perfectionem . . . festinat	*ad patriam caelestem festinas*
doctrinae sanctorum Patrum	*doctrinae . . . culmina*
celsitudo perfectionis	*virtutum . . . culmina*
	maiora . . . culmina . . . quae supra
	commemoravimus

7. *Ad perfectionem, ad celsitudinem, ad creatorem, ad patriam, ad culmina; perfectio, perducere, perfectio, pervenire, perficere, pervenire.* Dynamic vocabulary: *initium conversationis, perfectio conversationis, festinare, perducere, celsitudo perfectionis, rectissima norma, recto cursu, pervenire, festinare, inchoationis regula, maiora culmina, pervenire.*

8. Cf. for example, *Reg. Pl. St.* 41: "We should read the rules of the Fathers with such zeal that we adjust our inner ear to their holy admonitions, acquire a great love for discipline and follow the example of their lives with the all-embracing help of God. . . .What we here present to you as a single document, we did not want to recite with bold presumption, nor meanly despise the rules of the holy and blessed Fathers. We only wanted to show you what is special in their written regulations. The entire fullness of holy conduct and the perfect teaching for the spiritual life are told to us daily in the rules of the holy Fathers. Their proven life, by God's help, has the authority to instruct us"; Isidore, *Reg. Mon.* Preface 2: "Whoever wants to learn the entire teaching of the ancients, let him stride forward as far as he wishes, walking on the lofty summit and on the precipitous heights. But whoever is not able to fulfill all the instructions of the Fathers, let him direct his steps according to this limited teaching. . . . For those instructions were intended for the best and most perfect monk, these teachings are for the least. The perfect monks have observed those, while this rule is followed by persons who have been converted after sinning." On the theme of modesty; cf. Vogüé, *IV*, 103–107; Vigolo, "*Hanc minimam inchoationis*," 166.

9. Cf. RM Prol 24: "For the Rule begins in truth and ends in justice"; 11.1: ". . . the Lord has prescribed for us the ways of holiness which, if followed to the full, procure eternal life. . . ." RM 11T: "The Lord has replied through the master" and others; 13.65 [13.64 in Engl. trans.]: ". . . provided by the abbot, under God's guidance," etc.

10. RM 95.22 f.: "Therefore, since all these things are located inside, let the gate of the monastery always be shut so that the brothers, enclosed within with the Lord, may so to say be already in heaven, separated from the world for the sake of God."

11. Benedict speaks of justice nine times, four being quotations from the psalms, and four referring to Matthew. We may therefore consider the content as "covenant conduct," as it is explained especially in the Sermon on the Mount. Justice occurs only once in the sense of weighing the various demands of human justice (perhaps as a synonym of equity, *aequitas*). The Master uses it more frequently in this latter sense. We already noted that the Master considers his rule a regulation of justice. Benedict here has a much more biblical orientation. For Ambrose, *iustitia* is the mother of all the virtues, including

duties to God and people and love of enemies. Cf. Art. "Gerechtigkeit," in TRE, 422f.; Kardong, *"Justitia,"* 43–73; regarding *iustitia* and *caritas*, cf. Hök, "Augustin," 125–128.

12. Cf. Gribomont, *"Sed et,"* 30f. Probably *describere* already had lost the classical Latin meaning of "copying" and simply designates writing or describing (late Latin, Vulgate). Therefore this term cannot be seen as a reference to Benedict's copying of texts or even of his dependence on the Master.

13. *Demonstrare*, to manifest itself, to show, here does not denote an activity of Sacred Scripture or of God (as usual in RB, RM, and the Vulgate), but of the human person. We also must show our good will.

14. Cf. in RB: "After Compline one should speak only with proper gravity and modest reserve" (42.11). A guest brother who does not seem suitable for being admitted, should be "told in an appropriate manner that he ought to depart" (61.7). In the monastery there are not only malicious people, but also honorable and sensible ones (2.27). Concerning the meaning of the word, cf. Rothenhäusler, *"Honestas morum,"* 127–156.

15. *Honestas* is dear not only to Cicero, but also to Ambrose and is used by Augustine, Cassian, and Basil, but not by the Master. Cassian once speaks of a widow who distinguished herself by *honestate morum et gravitate et disciplina* (*Conf.* XVIII.14.2), cf. also Pelagius *Ad Demeter.* 14.

16. Rufinus translates in Basil, *Reg.* 165: *Caritas non deshonestatur* and explains that love does not transgress boundaries, does not depart from the essence; he speaks of *honestas caritatis* while the Vulgate has a different translation.

17. *Vit. Patr.* V.10.111; cf. also V.10.19. Cassian moves in the same direction, but he always speaks of *initium conversionis*. For him this means: fear of God, purification of sins, preservation of virtue; only then follows perfection, see *Inst.* IV.39; *Conf.* XXI.10.1.

18. *Apoph.* Pambo, 8. Cf. *Apoph.* Arsenios, 3: "I have done nothing good in your sight, but according to your goodness let me now make a beginning of good." Cassian, *Conf.* XXIII.19.2: "The more the human mind makes greater progress and attains to a more sincere purity of contemplation, the more unclean it will see itself in the mirror of its purity. . . ."

19. *Vit. Patr.* V.11.29; cf. *Vit. Patr.* VII.43.2. *Apoph.* Poimen, 85: Of Abbot Pior it was said "that he started anew each day."

20. *Ceterum ad perfectionem conversationis*
   quis festinat,
     sunt docrtinae sanctorum patrum, quarum observatio
   perducat hominem
   ad celsitudinem perfectionis.

21. PG 46.251; cf. Art. "Perfezione," in DIP, 1433–1445. I do not think that Benedict here is saying, "If you wish to seek perfection, go somewhere else." See Wathen, "Methodological Considerations," 106.

22. Art. "Perfezione," in DIP, 1455; there are expressions similar to RB 73.2 in Cassian: *Conf.* I.Praef.5; II.4.4; II.24; III.22; IX.2.3; IX.7.4; X.8.4; XX.3; XXI.33; also *Inst.* IV.8.43; V.28.

23. *s.* 40.1.

24. The less perfect are second-rate monks; they are unable to practice abstinence and obedience like the more perfect ones. The new abbot should be "better than the rest in every perfection" (92.76).

25. *Theological Dictionary.* Trans. C. Ernst, o.p. (New York: Herder, 1965) 349f.; cf. Ranke-Heinemann, "Zum Vollkommenheitsideal," 121.

26. *Doctrina* is used twice in the Rule regarding the holy Fathers (73), once referring to Christ (Prol 50); in all other cases, it always concerns the teaching of the abbot (or of the dean). However, the abbot is admonished to proclaim the teaching of Sacred Scripture by word and example and to teach nothing that is outside the divine law, cf. 2.4-6, 12, 23; 64.9.

27. There is a reference to "our Fathers" in 18.25; in 48.8 he refers specifically to the monastic Fathers in the Orient. Cf. RM 26.12; 34.2; 63.3; 90.92; 91.48; 92.57; cf. note 8; Caesarius, *Reg. Vg.* 1; ibid. 65 he speaks of the *institutio sanctorum patrum.*

28. Cf. "Pères,"in DTC, 1190–1194. There exists a seventh-century *Florilegium* bearing the title *Doctrina Patrum.* It is a selection from diverse Fathers; cf. Art. "Florilegium," in TRE, 217.

29. Gribomont, "*Sed et,*" 31, thinks so; cf. Vogüé, *IV,* 109f.; Augustine, *Contra Ep. Parm.* 2.19.38; Ambrose, *De Cain.* I.8.31; cf. similar expressions in the Bible, e.g., in Rom 4:11, 16, 18; John 8:39; Jas 2:21.

30. Cf., for example, Augustine, *Ad cath,* 8.22. The word *pagina* or *pagina divina* is used elsewhere for all of Sacred Scripture, cf. Jerome, *Ep.* 22.17 and Cassian, *Conf.* X.10.8; however, in RB 73 the meaning is "page." Cf. J. de Ghellinck: "Pagina" et "Sacra Pagina" in: *Mélanges Aug. Pelzer* (Louvain, 1947) 23–59.

31. Cf. "But only say the word, and my soul will be healed," in the liturgy. *Vit. Patr.* V.2.4; V.2.9; V.3.25, and throughout. One word suffices. The meaning of the prayer *monologistos* (one-word prayer) also is derived from this tradition.

32. *Auctoritas divina* or *auctoritates divinae* can mean simply the Sacred Scriptures; cf. Art. "Auctoritas," in RAC 1 (1950) 904 f.; Augustine, *De cons. Evgl.* 1.1.1; Cassiodorus, *In Ps.Praef.* 16 and *Inst.* 15.

33. *Conf.* I.4.4; cf. also Isa 40:3; and Matt 3:3. The term *rectissima* or *recta norma* is also used in connection with orthodoxy.

34. Cf. also the many words in this chapter that indicate orthodoxy: *sancti patres, divina auctoritas, V. ac N.T, rectissima norma, recto cursu, sancti catholici patres, S. pater noster Basilius.* Cf. R. M. Brlek: "De vocis 'catholica' origine et notione," in *Antonianum* 38 (1963) 271–274; M. S. Sesan: "Zur Geschichte des Wortes 'orthodox'" in: *Überlieferungsgeschichtliche Untersuchungen,* ed. F. Paschke (Berlin, 1981) 526f.

35. *Vit. Patr.* V.14.13; Cassian also places himself within the Catholic tradition and distances himself from others; cf. *Conf.* I.20.6; XVIII.7.8; X.3.5; Gribomont, "*Sed et,*" 32f.

36. In the fifth or sixth century. The *Decretum Gelasianum* determined which books of Sacred Scripture and which authors could be read, being orthodox; cf. (ed. Dobschütz) 69.

37. Cf. DV 10: "Tradition and scripture make up a single sacred deposit of the Word of God, which is entrusted to the church. By adhering to it the entire holy people, united to its pastors, remains always faithful to the teaching of the apostles, to the communion of life, to the breaking of bread and the prayers. So, in maintaining, practicing and professing the faith that has been handed on there is a unique interplay between the bishops and the faithful." Also UR 15: "Therefore it is earnestly recommended that Catholics avail themselves more often of the spiritual riches of the eastern Fathers which lift up all that is human to the contemplation of divine mysteries." *Vatican Council II: Constitution, Decrees, Declarations.* Trans. A. Flannery, O.P. (New York: Costello, 1995).

38. The term *recto cursu . . . venire* occurs only here and could be a biblical expression; cf. Acts 16:11 and 21:1.

39. Cf. Goutagny, *Commentaire*, 128; Turbessi, *Ascetismo*, 46; Gribomont, "*Sed et,*" 33.

40. RB 42.3; cf. 42.5; ". . . after a brief pause, the readings of the *Conferences* should begin." All four works are linked with *et* and listed in a row in 73.5, possibly in ascending order like a *crescendo*.

41. *The Lives of the Jura Fathers*, 174.

42. *Hist. Franc.* 10.29 (PL 71.560); cf. Vogüé, "Les mentions des oeuvres," 282.

43. All these opinions have been stated. Some also tried, from 73.5, to deduce information about the time RB 73 was edited. It had to be written before 529, or else Benedict would not have mentioned Cassian; others assert it was certainly written after 529, since he did not name Cassian. Concerning semi-Pelagianism, cf. "Prol 4," n. 42, above.

44. Cassian, *Conf.* I. Preface 7; regarding the whole: Vogüé, "Les mentions des oeuvres"; by contrast cf. Wathen, "La *Regula Benedicti* c. 73." Gennadius, Cassiodorus, and Ferrandus mention both works together: *Vit. Fulg.* (Ferrandus) 23–24; Gennadius, *De script.eccl.* 61; Cassiodorus, *Inst.* 29.

45. Cassiodorus, *In Ps.* 118.28; *Vit. Fulg.* (Ferrandus) 23; Gennadius, *De script. Eccl.* 61.

46. Cf. Vagaggini, "Posizione," 53.

47. Cassiodorus, *In Ps.* 118.28: "True, he was accused . . . But you, beloved brothers, choose with God's help those parts which can be read profitably." Cf. Gregory of Tours, *Vit. Patr.* 20.3 (PL 71.1094).

48. Of course, this concerns lives which at Benedict's time had already been translated into Latin, for example, Jerome, *Vita Pauli*; Evagrius, *Vita Antonii*; Rufinus, *Historia Monachorum*, Ps Dionysius, *Vita Pachomii*, especially, however, the fifth book of the *Vitae Patrum* ("*Verba seniorum*"), translated at the beginning of the sixth century by Pelagius which apparently impressed Benedict very much. RB 40.6: "Though we read that wine is not at all suitable for monks" (from *Vit. Patr.* V); 18.25: "Though we read that our Fathers prayed the whole Psalter in one day" (also from *Vit.Patr.* V). Cf. Siegmund, *Überlieferung*.

49. Concerning the influence of Basil, cf. Tamburrino, "Incidenza," 103f., 115; Lienhard, "S. Basil's *Asceticon parvum*," 241f.; Ledoyen, "S. Basile," 30–45; Hübner, "*Rubor confusionis*," 338–343; especially Gribomont in several articles of his, for example, "*Sed et,*" 34–36 and "S. Basile," 15. Vogüé in *IV*, 147, concludes that there was no special relationship. *Pater noster* in the singular is less common than the plural, however, cf. Augustine, *Ep.* 88.10; Caesarius, *s.* 236.1; the same text also contains *virtutum culmina.*

50. Valéry as quoted in Art. "Tugend," in *Handbuch theol. Grundbegriffe* (Munich, 1963) 714.

51. Cf. Art. "Tugend" in *Sacramentum Mundi*, vol. IV (Freiburg, 1969) 1037–1042. In the sense of virtue, the expression occurs especially in biblical texts influenced by Greek philosophy. Cf. Phil 4:8: "Your thoughts should be directed to whatever is true, noble, right, pure, lovable, appealing, whatever is called virtue and is praiseworthy."

52. Augustine, *s.* 36.8: *lege evangelium instrumentum tuum*; concerning the concept of *instrumenta virtutum*, cf. Cassian, *Conf.* VI.10.3; XXIV.24.3.

53. Benedict is referring to worshiping God, to reading, or to the sick who might be neglected; cf. 43.5, 15; 36.10, 16. In the Latin Bible, "negligent" is used, for example, in the following contexts: putting God aside, not respecting God's messengers, not respecting other persons.

54. *Conf.* VII.23; cf. *Inst.* IV.33; *Lives of the Jura Fathers* 113: At that time it was not as it is today "and it provokes shame to refer to this or speak about it now that the monastic

ordinances are everywhere thwarted. . . ." *Apoph.* John the Dwarf, 14: "So it is with the present generation; if they are given wings, they are not of fire, but wings that are weak and without power." Augustine also uses the term *male viventibus* once, but in a different context, *s.* [Caillau] 7 in PL Suppl II, 440. He says there is no reason to complain about evil times; we ourselves should improve, then better times would follow, "but not for those who are ill-living." Furthermore, the times are not so bad, since Christ came precisely in order to comfort us; cf. Cawly, "4 Themes," 92–98.

55. Genitive of identity; cf. Jerome, *In Is.* 17.61.6; cf. Vogüé, "Deux réminiscences scripturaires non encore remarquées dans la Règle de S. Pachôme et de S. Benoît," in StMon 25 (1983) 9–10.

56. In T. Goritschewa, *Die Rettung der Verlorenen* (Wuppertal, 1983) 49.

57. Cf. Prol 1–4   73

ad te ergo. . . quisquis	*quisquis ergo*
ad eum . . . redeas	*ad patriam caelestem festinas*
quidquid agendum inchoas bonum	*hanc minimam inchoationis regulam*
Domino Christo vero Regi militaturus	*adiuvante Christo*
instantissima oratione	
ab eo perfici	*perfice*

58. Cassian in the *Conferences* always used the word *patria* for the actual homeland, never for heaven. *Caelestis* occurs in RB 7.5: "If we therefore, brothers, want to reach the highest summit of humility, and quickly attain that heavenly exaltation, to which in this life we ascend by humility, we must by our deeds . . . erect this ladder" (we also find the words *culmen, caelestis exaltatio, velociter, pervenire*). There we have an image of ascent; here in RB 73 that of a race. *Caelestis patria* also occurs in Cassiodorus, *Inst.* 32.

59. *Tunc demum* in Latin should indicate that something cannot happen at a different time, especially not before. In RB both words occur together in 2.10; cf. RM 2.10, 9.6, etc. The term is rare in the Vulgate. It is found in Cassian, *Conf.* Praef.7: One first should hasten to purify oneself from vices, study the Desert Fathers, then finally one can arrive at contemplation; cf. also Isidore, *Reg. mon.* Praef.2.

60. Cf. Cassian, *Inst.* IV, 23; *Conf.* XXI.34.3; XXII.7.2; XVIII.15; Caesarius also uses this expression, *s.* 236.1.

61. Cf. Vogüé, "Règle, vie contempl.," 101; Déseille, "Propos," 301; Barros Morães, "Plan," 20–23.

62. Cf. Vogüé, "Cassien," 226, 228f. and "La rencontre de Benoît et Scholastique," 272; Veilleux, "De l'interprétation," 207; Herwegen, *Sinn*, 412f.; Vigolo, "*Hanc minimam*," 166f.

63. Cf. Borias, "Le dynamisme spirituel," 18–30; Fattorini, "L'immagine biblica della corsa," 481–483, also points to Benedict's love for Paul.

64. Cf. Fattorini, "L'immagine biblica della corsa," 462f.

65. Cf. Leclercq, "La liberté bénédictine."

Chapter 58

The Procedure
for Receiving Brothers

Introduction

It is evident that this chapter is important for all those who prepare for final profession. But is it also important for most of us who made profession many years ago? In my opinion, it is, and for several reasons.

1. This chapter is a creative memory: for what have I come? What has led me here? What did I promise? Profession is not an action completed once and for all; rather, it must be appropriated, affirmed, integrated into one's life, and deepened. In times of crises or half-heartedness, remembering can be a call to conversion or can strengthen our trust in God's guidance. If God, who had plans for me, had not stood by me, I never would have been able to come through the difficulties encountered on the way. God remains faithful to God's self and will continue to help me.

2. In exemplary fashion we experience such "thresholds" again and again. We speak of a second and third conversion. The decisive profession may not happen until ten or twenty years later in a situation that seems hopeless, at the occasion of a transfer, or in a retreat. In a deeper way we are brought into Christ's sacrifice and receive the gift of a new breakthrough to God, the community, and the world.

3. In the end, our whole life is a kind of novitiate for the final profession at the hour of our death. God is leading us step by step. God accepts our efforts, but wants to gift us with what is essential.

RB 58 within the Rule

Growth and development of every community is closely connected with a proper way of introducing new members to monastic life and with their further formation. We may assume that a chapter that deals with the preparation of new members will show something about the understanding of the monastic life to be lived in the monastery. As each chapter about formation in our constitutions can only be understood within the framework of the whole and presupposes all the other chapters, so it is with chapter 58 in the Rule of Benedict.

This chapter is placed in the practical part of the Rule, indeed at the center of the part which, beginning with RB 53, considers the relations between the monastery and the world. RB 58 deals with very special "guests," that is, those who desire to join the monastic community for life. This chapter is also the foundation for the following chapters: RB 59 "About the Sons of the Noble and the Poor," and RB 61 "How Visiting Monks Are to Be Received." (Chapters 59–62 all begin with "If someone.")

Excursus:
RB 58 within Monastic Tradition and Its Biblical Foundation

When speaking about receiving and introducing new members and about their final bonding with the community, Benedict is part of a long tradition that has its roots in Sacred Scripture.

Jesus' call to the first disciples reaches them in the midst of their professional work (Mark 1:16-20). Hearing his authoritative call, they abandon their possessions, work, and family. Soon after this we hear in the same Gospel about the call of the Twelve (Mark 3:13-19) whom Jesus appoints to be with him and to be sent out by him. And after they refuse to follow him, he calls them anew after the resurrection. Discipleship is an undeserved gift (John 21:1-19).

The meaning of their discipleship is entirely determined by the person of Jesus. They live with him, follow him on his journeys, share his life, and eventually his destiny. They serve him and his kingdom. Imitation of Christ takes place in community. The disciples continue his actions and proclaim his message.

Jesus does not spare them from crises (cf. John 6:60-71); he tells them openly what is in store for him and for them (Mark 8:31-37), yet despite their reluctance he does not abandon them. Times of crisis are times for a new and deeper calling. At the end Jesus asks only one crucial question: "Peter, do you love me?" (John 21:15-17). He introduces the disciples into their life step by step depending on how much they can take. They experience his miracles and his teachings and share already in his mission; yet he also sets apart a time for their special instruction.

Already in the course of the development of the New Testament it becomes clear that all Christians are called to follow Jesus. Within this general vocation there are special vocations that call followers out of their usual area of life and make every other professional work impossible. Widows and virgins practice discipleship in their own ways while still living at home in their original community. The Third Letter of John mentions itinerant prophets, and martyrdom is a radical form of discipleship for early Christianity.

We hear from Antony how the call to follow Christ touches him in his innermost heart and how he then abandons not only family and possessions, but also the environment where he lived with his Christian community and withdraws into the desert (*Vit. Ant.* 2–3). Many follow his example, and there is yet no need to have rules for accepting individuals into monastic life that is simply a matter of radical discipleship containing two seminal elements: surrendering to Christ and rejecting the "world." In concrete terms this means: rejecting possessions, wealth, family, and marriage, but also rejecting vain fame, egotism, and striving for power. Benedict will express it thus: "to become a stranger to worldly activities; to prefer nothing to the love of Christ" (RB 4.20f.), or: "to renounce yourself in order to follow Christ" (RB 4.10). To accept monastic life means to become a stranger in the "world," to set out like Abraham.[1] Genesis 12:1 is interpreted in this manner: abandon your home, that is, your worldly goods and your carnal desires; abandon your family, that is, your sinful ways, the customs of your earlier life; abandon the house of your father, that is, all the memories of the world and of the devil.[2] We have to become a stranger to everything that prevents a true following of Christ: to the devil and his works, to earlier customs and practices, to worldly pleasures, blood relatives, and even to ourselves, our passions and vainglory (cf. Basil, *Reg.* 4). What discipleship entails becomes tangible in monastic profession ceremonies. In the oldest times acceptance of the monastic habit is regarded as the entrance into monastic life. One can take it up oneself or—as in most cases—one receives it from the monastic father. This gesture contains everything: renunciation of possessions and marriage, the will to live a monastic life as a disciple of Christ, and to persevere in it (cf. Gregory the Great, *Dial.* II.1.4).

A candidate who arrives at the monastery of Pachomius remains outside the gate for several days. He learns the Our Father and some psalms, and his previous life and his motivations are examined as well as his ability to renounce parents and possessions and to assume the monastic obligations. After this kind of novitiate, he is integrated into the community; he is divested of his worldly clothes and is clothed with the monastic habit. At the time of prayer the porter assigns him his place (*Praec.* 49).

Basil (*Reg.* 6–7) points out that human beings must not be rejected since this would be in opposition to Jesus' word "Come to me all . . ." (Matt 11:28). The scrutiny refers to examining their previous life and testing their motivation, their ability to do all kinds of difficult work (*opprobria*) with humility and "their desire for the *opus Dei.*" Basil does not talk specifically about the ritual of reception, but mentions a vow to God that must not be broken.[3] This vow includes chastity, renunciation of all dependency on the world, humility, conformity to Christ—in short, monastic life.

For Cassian (*Inst.* IV.3-7), the young individual who has renounced the world must give proof of his perseverance by waiting outside the gate for ten days and by patiently bearing insults and injustices. Removal of his clothes and receiving the monastic habit in the assembly of the brothers is the sign of dispossession and descent into the poverty and lowliness of Christ. Then he is assigned to the porter for a year. In taking care of strangers, he is supposed to learn patience and humility. Only then comes the definitive reception (cf. also *Inst.* IV.32-36).

The profession formula presumed to be the oldest goes back to the Desert Father Schenute of Atripa (+ ca. 466). The candidate makes a commitment to observe the obligations of a Christian life. From the groups around Schenute, we also have the first evidence of a written document.[4]

The rules from Gaul emphasize renouncing possessions and reading the rule.[5]

The Rule of the Master has two reception rituals, one after the other. Despite some overlapping and some contradictions, the following elements are clear: reception is not allowed at once. A long, negative speech of the abbot predicts all the difficulties: the monastery is a school of suffering, a military service, martyrdom, a prison, an imminent death, a lifelong test that is contrasted with eternal life and its joys. After the Rule has been read, the candidate promises obedience and is accepted provisionally. Much room is given to a discussion of whether or not the new brother has renounced all possessions so that his own will can no longer influence him and whether he has not concealed anything.

There is great worry that he not steal anything from the monastery's property. For two months he lives in the guest quarters and works together with the brothers. Then he makes an official promise in the oratory. The *donatio*, the donation of his properties, is placed on the altar. In doing this, the candidate gives himself with heart and soul to God through the monastery. A versicle and the kiss of peace follow after the *Suscipe*. Then the brother is received into the monastic community and assigned to the dean. Only after another year is he allowed to receive the tonsure and the monastic habit.

OVERVIEW

Pachomius *before reception*	Cassian	RM	RB
testing	testing	testing	testing
renouncing	injustice	predicting	injustice
parents, possessions	patience, humility	difficulties	predicting difficulties
teaching		reading of Rule	
ADMISSION	ADMISSION	ADMISSION	ADMISSION
	Dispossession	Dispossession	
Clothing	clothing	two months in	two months in
w/the habit	w/the habit	guest quarters	guest quarters
Assigning of place	one year in guest		Reading of Rule—
	quarters		promise
			Novitiate:
			six months, then
			four months
			Promise
		ORATORY	ORATORY
		Promise:	Promise *promissio*
		Obedience,	Petition *petitio*
		Donation	
		Suscipe, peace	*Suscipe*, prayer
		one year in deanery	[dispossession],
			receiving the habit
	Entrance into	clothing w/the	
	deanery	habit, tonsure	
storing of old	storing of old	storing of old	storing of old clothes
clothes	clothes	clothes	
		Donation remains	Petition remains

Coming from this general survey to the Rule of Benedict, it is evident that he, too, introduces the newcomer by stages: coming from the world, testing at the gate, renunciation of possessions, clothing with the habit, and entering the community as the old clothes are stored away. Common to the Master and Benedict is an explicit promise, one (or several) reading(s) of the Rule, and a probationary period in the monastery. Like Cassian, Benedict makes the days outside the gate more difficult as the candidate has to suffer some injustice. Following the Egyptian tradition, the clothing with the habit seems to be an important act that becomes an integral part of the profession ceremony.

In a slow and pedagogical manner, Benedict increases and intensifies the length of time in each phase after entering, the candidate's testing and promises.

Benedict's process of initiation is ordered more logically, is more transparent and more complete than the previous ones. He is the first to mention a separate novice master and a separate "cell" for novices. In comparison with the Rule of the Master, Benedict's sober rationality is a welcome change. He eliminates all the long speeches and the dualism between world and monastery. More than the Master, he focuses on a completely personal decision of the candidate.

OVERVIEW OF THE CHAPTER

The first part (vv. 1-16) discusses testing and preparations; the second (vv. 17-26) the profession ceremony. This is followed by an appendix regarding the storage of the old clothes and of the petition. The transition from the first to the second part is interesting (vv. 16-17): the candidate can "receive/accept" (*suscipere*) the Rule. The following verse begins with "the one to be received" (*suscipiendus*) and thus indicates a change from the novice's acting to his being received. The first part proceeds from "one who is newly arriving" to one "to be granted entrance" (v. 4), to one to be "received into the community" (v. 14). The second part concludes the ceremony with the words, "he is to be counted as one of the community" (v. 23), and "he is clothed with what belongs to the monastery" (v. 26). Thus the candidate's belonging to the monastery is described in ever more intensive ways.

When we consider the *sentence structure*, we note that the words "if," "whether" (*si*) appear ten times in the first part, in the second only four times, and in a weakened, negative sense.[6] This already shows that the first part focuses on testing and conditions and emphasizes freedom, while the ceremony in the second part is definitive and binding.

In this chapter Benedict gives free room to his predilection for *tripartite expressions*: there are three activities for novices (v. 5), three criteria (v. 7), three gates through which the candidate for profession passes (vv. 4, 11, 14), and three promises (vv. 9, 14, 17). The statement that the candidate "stays" or perseveres is emphasized three times (vv. 9, 11, 13), the Rule is read three times (vv. 9, 12, 13), and the *Suscipe* is sung three times (v. 22). Thus it is not surprising that the profession "formula" also has three parts: stability, fidelity to monastic life, and obedience.

The *specifications of time* have a dynamism of their own: four to five days (v. 3), some days (v. 4), two months (v. 9), six months (v. 12), four months (v. 13). After this Benedict says three times "from this day on" (vv. 15, 23, 25). Verse 23 in Codex A (cf. Hanslik) even reads "from this hour on." And during the profession ceremony the expression "at once" (*mox*) occurs twice (vv. 21, 26). These expressions describe a proceeding, a being led to an important day, even an important hour which designates a change in one's entire life. And for this very hour Benedict took all the elements he found in the preceding tradition and tied them together into a single ceremony (promise, petition, prayer, clothing, renunciation of possessions). The moment of this renunciation, however, is indicated only through a vague "earlier"—in contrast to RM, this point seems to be less important. Twice we find a threatening "some time" (vv. 18, 28); it is not supposed to happen that, at "some time," a brother acts against his promise and leaves the monastery.

In the same manner, the expressions designating *places* intensify, leading from the gate (in the first four verses the word "entrance" (*ingressus*) occurs three times) to the guesthouse (v. 4), then to the novitiate (vv. 5, 11), and ultimately to the oratory (v. 17), and its center, the altar (v. 20). From there the path leads to the feet of the brothers (prostration, v. 23). In the oratory, the space also opens up to the vertical dimension (vv. 18f.). From now on, leaving the monastery is prohibited (vv. 28, 15).

Three gates lead to the altar where profession is made:

- the first gate, the entrance, includes the following condition: perseverance in knocking on the door, patience, and insistence on the request for entrance;
- the second gate, from verse 9 on, is surrounded with more ritual actions: the promise to stay, reading the Rule with subsequent dialogue, assurance that the candidate remains firm, solemn entrance into the novitiate;
- the third gate leads to profession: after careful reflection, the novice promises obedience and knows that his decision is definitive.

In this chapter we find a number of *radical expressions*: the novice master looks after the novices with *great* care (v. 6). *All* the hardships and difficulties must be predicted (v. 8); the candidate is being tested in *every kind* of patience (*omni patientia*, v. 11). He promises to keep *everything* and to observe *everything* (v. 14). In the presence of *all* the brothers he makes his promise (v. 17). The *entire* community repeats the *Suscipe* (v. 22). The new brother prostrates himself at the feet of *each monk* (v. 23) and does not keep back *anything at all* of his possessions (v. 24). All these expressions indicate that this is a total act: the commitment of an entire person as well as that of the entire community, a consenting to being involved with the great God. Either—or, everything—or nothing.

It is interesting to consider the entire chapter regarding the candidate's *activity* and *passivity*:

vv. 1, 3 he comes	1 no easy entrance is granted
3 he perseveres in knocking	
patiently bears	
persists in his request	4 entrance is granted
7 he seeks God, shows eagerness for . . .	
9 he promises	
10 he wants to serve . . . if you can	
11 he stands	11 he is being led
	He is being tested
12 he knows	
13 he stands	
14 he reflects, he promises	14 he is being received
15 he knows	
16 can shake off the Rule	
[or] can take it up	17 the one to be received
17 he promises	
19 he draws up the petition	
20 writes with his own hand	
or puts his mark on it	
lays it with his own hand on the altar	
21 he begins the verse	
23 he prostrates	23 he is counted as one of the community
(he distributes his possessions earlier)	25 he is no longer his own master
(Leaving is prohibited)	26 he is stripped of his clothing and clothed.

One gets a clear sense how, on the one hand, the actions of the candidate are important requirements and are taken very seriously, and how, on the other hand, all that is essential is given to him. Especially at the end of the ceremony, he is passive, allowing things to be done to him.

Finally, it is informative to consider the *various agents* in this chapter. At the beginning the candidate is in the foreground. First he is called "the newcomer" (v. 1), then becomes a novice (*novicius*, vv. 5, 20f.), and eventually becomes a brother (*frater novicius*, v. 23) during the profession ceremony, more specifically, at the altar. The community is first mentioned in a very general manner as *conversatio* (v. 1). Benedict uses passive forms for the things done by the community (is to be allowed, v. 4; is to be appointed, v. 6; is to be read, v. 9, etc.). At the beginning, only the master of novices appears in person. Not until the profession ceremony do we hear of the presence of the abbot and of the entire community (vv. 17, 19). From verse 22 on the community begins to act by repeating the *Suscipe* (v. 22) and by praying for the new brother (v. 23). Yet, at the beginning of the second part, God is also clearly mentioned as an agent. Already in verse 2 the question is asked whether the spirits are from God, and soon it becomes clear that the candidate's journey not only leads to profession, but ultimately to God (v. 8). The profession ceremony takes place in the presence of God and the saints (v. 18). The *Suscipe* addresses the Lord (*Dominus*, v. 21), and it is followed by the *Gloria Patri*. And at the end the antagonist, the devil, also makes his appearance (v. 28).

Profession is neither a commitment to God alone nor simply a being received into the community, but rather an interplay of abandonment to the Lord and entrance into the community; beginning at the altar of profession, the new brother/sister walks toward God together with the community.

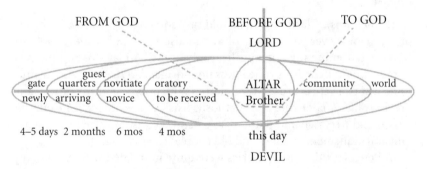

Title: About the Procedure for Receiving Brothers

The Latin word *disciplina* in the title has a meaning similar to the one in the title of RB 19 ("About the Discipline of Psalmody"): it describes the way in which something is to be done, the method or procedure, and thus has little in common with the word "discipline."[7] The word "receiving" already indicates how one proceeds: new members are not simply entered into, or added to, a register, but are accepted and received with a certain caution, just as God also receives us. This is a core word of this chapter: The brothers are being received by the community (vv. 14, 17) and by God

(v. 21), and thus they will be able to receive others (cf. RB 53). The newcomer is not to remain simply as a permanent guest or novice, but the objective here is that one becomes a brother/sister, a member of a community.

OVERVIEW OF THE FIRST PART

vv. 1-2:   a type of heading,
vv. 3-4:   initial conditions and first entrance (with an addition),
vv. 5-6:   insert about the cell of the novice and about the novice master,
vv. 7-8:   criteria and scrutinies,
vv. 9-11:   ritual for entering the novitiate,
vv. 12-13:   readings of the Rule,
vv. 14-16:   prerequisites for profession.

**V. 1: If one newly arrives to the monastic life,
          he is not to be granted entrance easily,
V. 2: but as the apostle says:
          "Test the spirits if they are from God."**

The first part of the sentence presents the two sides: the newcomer and the monastery (or monastic life, *conversatio*). The main clause establishes the principle: entrance is not to be granted easily. Thus reception is not to follow the ways of our emotions, but rather the ways prescribed by the Scriptures (v. 2).

1. *One (quis)*. Clarifying one could say "someone." This recalls the expression "whoever you are" (Prol 3) and also RB 73.8, "whoever you are who are hastening toward your heavenly home." Today this sounds very normal, but in Benedict's time it was not normal that he makes no distinctions whatsoever regarding race, national identity, class, education, and previous life. A later rule by Fructuosus lists as newcomers, for example, "slaves and free, rich and poor, married and virgins, fools and wise, ignorant and craftsmen, children and old people" (*Reg. com.* I.4).

In Benedict's time monasteries were quite inundated with candidates. Augustine (*De op. mon.* XXII. 25) and Basil (*Reg.* 6) state clearly that excluding certain groups of people would fly in the face of the Gospel. Benedict seems to be of the same opinion. He does not set any conditions at the beginning. In reading the *Dialogs* and the Rule we are confronted with a very motley monastic community, and thus can make some assumptions about those asking for admission.

2. *A newcomer (noviter veniens):* A new beginning is inspiring; it is open to the future. Actually, only God can create something new; it is God's gift. This first sentence of the chapter gives the impression that the initiative comes from the candidate. In another passage Benedict described God's

call. The Lord invited the young person, showed him the way, and the one who was called opened himself to the Sacred Scriptures, listened to the voice of the spirit and followed it, setting aside everything else (cf. Prol 1–22). Actually, the entire Prologue pertains to this verse as its introduction. Coming to the monastery is the result of being drawn to it, for no one can come to Christ unless the Father draws him or her (John 6:44).

Here Benedict does not speak of what the newly arriving candidate has left behind, as is the case in other rules.[8] He only states positively why he comes. It is simply implied that he has left his or her possessions, family, and native place, has like Abraham detached himself from his habitual life and, following the call, has gone to a "new land."

3. *To the monastery, to monastic life (ad conversationem).* This expression indicates both the place and content of the life in this place. According to RB *conversatio* also means conversion (*conversio*), and means here the beginning of a number of conversions since, in this life, God calls us again and again to conversion (Prol 38).[9] Here, he presumably means simply monastic life "under a rule and an abbot" (1.2) that corresponds to the terms used in older rules.[10] Monastic life is communal life in imitation of Christ that for each monastic is to become ever more intense.

4. *Entrance is not to be granted easily.* The expression "not easily" corresponds to the difficulties of the entrance mentioned in verse 3.[11] One is not to proceed with levity or superficially, but rather plumb the depth of a candidate's motivation and examine him or her thoroughly. In Benedict's opinion, this deeper layer is uncovered through the difficulties. "Entering" (*ingressus*) the monastery also corresponds to "leaving" (*egressus*) the "world," as the old texts say. Here the word "entrance" is used in its full meaning as a momentous entering into a new way of life. This short paragraph culminates in the expression: "Entrance be granted" (v. 4).

In his commentary on RB, Hildemar (ninth century) says that some people with little understanding encourage others to come to the monastery, yet that such a thing is against the Rule. Professional recruitment would have seemed absurd to the monastic fathers. Yet, what we consider even today as the core of vocation work always existed: the personal witness of the monastic, the radiant force of community life, of the liturgy, and especially of hospitality. We also must not underestimate the influence of ascetical literature and of the life stories of monks that became popular and encouraged others to emulate them (cf. the influence of the *Life of Antony* for Augustine, etc.).

5. *But, as the apostle says.* Deliberately, Benedict begins with a Scripture quote, while the Master uses it only among many other instructions (RM 90.17). Benedict wants to recognize the Sacred Scriptures explicitly as the highest norm (cf. RB 53.1; 36.2-3). This is one of the important principles

he announces in Prol 21: "to walk under the guidance of the Gospel." The "apostle" here is, for once, John (1 John 4:1), while otherwise it is always Benedict's favorite apostle Paul. Just as in the Prologue the voice of Christ reached the candidate through the word of Sacred Scripture, so the scrutiny of the call is also done under the guidance of Sacred Scripture.

6. *Test the spirits if they are from God.* In 1 John 4:1 we read: "Do not trust every spirit, but test the spirits to see whether they belong to God because many false prophets have gone out into the world." Benedict applies the Scripture quote in a practical way.[12] He does not speak directly about the discernment of spirits, about discerning a decision, as it was practiced so often by the Fathers and developed into an art. Yet Benedict knows the good spirit, on the one hand, and on the other, the spirit of pride or vanity (cf. 38.2; 65.2) that is an evil spirit. In discernment it is helpful to know from where the spirits come. In verse 28 we read that the monastic who agrees to leave the monastery after having made profession does so upon the insinuation of the devil. This is evil only when the monastic had first been inspired by the good spirit to commit him- or herself irrevocably to the service of the Lord. But someone could also come to the monastery upon the insinuation of the evil spirit. The old rules and sources indicate some such motivations: it can be an escape into a better life; a slave wants to be free; someone is on the run because of an evil deed; someone is being forced, or has run away from his or her master out of fear; someone wants to gain honor in the eyes of others. Furthermore, in the period of the Gothic wars, the flight from the world had become fashionable as well as the flight to the countryside or to security.[13] From where come these motivations? Someone can also come out of love for Christ, freely, so as to progress in love. The good spirit does not manifest itself right away in the first encounter, but is recognized in a person's patience and humility.

Today, as in the time Benedict, the discernment of spirits is a principal component of the formation period. As then, a candidate today cannot undertake this all by oneself, but needs the help of the community and of a spiritual director, needs prayer and vigilance as well as to experience oneself and God in the difficulties (v. 3).

V. 3: Therefore, if the newcomer perseveres in knocking
    and if it becomes evident in four or five days
    that he patiently bears the injustices done to him
    and the difficulties of entering and persists in his request,
V. 4: then entrance is to be granted,
    and he may first stay in the guest quarters
    for a few days.

With a determined "therefore" (*ergo*) Benedict begins to concretize the general principle. After a long conditional clause: "if he perseveres . . . bears . . . persists," comes the brief and terse statement: "admission is to be granted." It is followed by a stay in the guest quarters. The actions of the candidate (three verbs) lead to his being granted admission (v. 4). In the Latin text, alliteration makes this text easy to memorize: *per*severaverit . . . *p*ulsans . . . *p*atienter *p*ortare . . . *p*ersistere *p*etitioni.

1. *Four to five days.* Benedict shortened by about half the periods for this stage that were known to him,[14] yet he makes them an intensive experience. The later Rule of Fructuosus puts emphasis on "three days and three nights," probably in order to indicate the hardship (*Reg. com.* 4). Presumably the candidate remains really outside the gate as Pachomius says (*Praec.* 49). A hard test if we think of members from noble families and of the cold climate in Monte Cassino!

2. *If the newcomer perseveres in knocking.* Doing this requires not only courage and perseverance, but also the conviction of one's call. If the spirit is truly "from God," someone may do such a thing. This is probably an allusion to the persistent friend whom Jesus recommends as a model to his disciples. That friend perseveres in knocking on the locked door until it is opened. The end of this parable seems to have influenced these verses of the Rule even to the choice of words. "Ask, and you will receive, seek, and you will find, knock, and the door will be opened to you!" (Luke 11:9).[15] The action of persevering recalls the Prologue, "persevering in the monastery until death" (v. 50), and the fourth step of humility, "anyone who perseveres to the end will be saved" (7.36). Already at the beginning the candidate must prove that with the grace of God he or she is able to persevere. Thus he or she is introduced experientially into the reality of monastic life.

Yet we may also recall that the Lord himself knocks in this way on our door and remains there even if we do not open to let him in readily (cf. Rev 3:20).

3. *If it becomes evident that he patiently bears the injustices done to him and the difficulties of entering.* Following Cassian (*Inst.* IV.3), Benedict again adds inflicted injustices and difficulties although RM does not mention them.[16] What did he mean here? The candidate stays outside the gate while other guests are being received with honor (RB 53). Probably the candidate is given a description of the difficulties awaiting him, and some texts speak about casting suspicions on him.[17] Yet Benedict does not use the tests of obedience and the absurd commands of Cassian (*Inst.* IV.23-27), and thus we need not think of chicaneries here. It is certain, however, that the newcomer is not shown any affection. One who is truly called will

persevere. Yet one who comes from a climate of human affection or is seeking a secure life or a kind of happy family life, will be scared away. Making the entrance difficult counterbalances the fact that Benedict first accepts everyone without inquiring into their previous life or setting other conditions. In experiencing limits the candidate will show the actual depths of his or her personality and what ultimately motivates him or her. One may experience offenses again later (cf. fourth step of humility, esp. 7.35, 42). One must learn "not to injure anyone, but to bear injuries patiently" (4.30). Today, such injuries perhaps occur rather in a candidate's earlier life before he or she takes the decisive step. Staying power in difficulties will later provide the monastic with greater certainty in times of crisis or doubts: "It must have been God's call that urged me, otherwise I would not have been able to endure it all" (cf. Cassian, *Inst.* IV.32).

It is a matter of patient forbearance just as the nurse "patiently bears" disagreeable sick monastics (36.5) and just as the individual monastics bear with the greatest patience their mutual weaknesses (72.5). According to Benedict, another part of patience is silence that shows psychological maturity (fourth step of humility).[18] Christ, too, bore injuries patiently and silently (cf. 1 Pet 2:19-22).

It becomes evident—this not yet an infallible indication. The porter sees only the external signs; only God can look into the heart, or someone who has the special gift of knowing people's hearts; all others can judge only by appearances.

4. *And if he . . . persists in his request.* This is the request for admission. Similarly, 60.2 says of the priest: "If, however, he persists altogether in his request, he must know that he will have to keep the full discipline of the Rule." Again we are reminded of Luke 11:9, "Ask, and you will receive." Similarly, Prol 4 admonishes to ask God with earnest supplications. We are allowed to do so on the basis of Jesus' instruction, but certainly not on the basis of our human wilfulness. When experiencing rejection at the gate, the young Pachomius said: "I believe in the Lord Jesus Christ who will give strength and patience to the humble" (*Vit. Pach.* 6).

5. *Entrance is to be granted to him.* This important sentence is short and impressive. It does not yet concern the definitive entrance because after this the candidate can still leave freely (cf. v. 10), but the first gate has opened for him.

6. *And he is to stay in the guest quarters for a few days.* This follows as a sort of addition. After the candidate was at, or outside, the gate, he is now allowed to enter the guest quarters as do other guests. The guest quarters are separated from the monastery and are entrusted to a particular monastic who is "God fearing" and administers the house of God wisely and as a

wise person (cf. commentary on 53.21f.). Through life experiences he or she is suited to be a teacher and a model for the young person.

There he is "a few days." This is probably the two months mentioned later (v. 9). We know old texts that say that a candidate is not allowed to enter the monastery space proper for three years.[19] Compared to this, two months would be only "a few days." In RM the newcomer also stays in the guest quarters for two months.[20]

**V. 5: After that he is to be in the quarters of the novices
where they study, eat and sleep.**

**V. 6: For them a senior is to be appointed
who is skilled in winning souls
and who is to look after them with careful attention.**

1. *After that he is to be in the quarters of the novices.* Verses 5 and 6 seem to be an insert. Both contain innovations introduced by Benedict. As he just mentioned the guest quarters, he adds the regulations for the novice quarters composing, as it were, by headings. There is a good possibility that separate quarters for the novices as well as the separate position of novice master developed over the course of time as a response to necessities. Positions multiply, monastery buildings grow larger; there are now various areas for various purposes.[21]

The quarters of the novices are to some extent separated from the community. Perhaps they need more lenience because they still have to get used to their new life. Yet it is not a full separation for in the important monastic obligations of the *opus Dei* and work they come in contact with the entire community.

2. *Where they study (meditent), eat and sleep.* "Meditating" is mentioned as the first activity of the novices, even before eating and sleeping (both seem to be very important!). Similarly the *opus Dei* is mentioned as the first criterion in verse 7. What is meant by "meditating"? Not what we designate with the English word "to meditate." "Meditate" occurs in two other passages in RB. "Monastics need something for "meditating" on the psalms and the lessons" (8.3). And "Whoever does not want or is unable to "'meditate' or read" is to do some other work (48.23). The subject of "meditation" is, above all, Scripture, and it is furthermore connected with reading. In old texts, especially in Pachomius and RM, *meditare* means to read, learn, repeat, learn by heart, explain, study, to acquire knowledge; and translating what one has read into actual living is also part of such "meditating." The center of all this effort is Sacred Scripture.[22]

Today, too, Sacred Scripture is to be at the center of novitiate teaching; it is to be its "soul," as it were. In a similar vein, the Decree *Optatam Totius* (16) states that Sacred Scripture is to be the "soul of theology." Certainly for Benedict, Scripture is not isolated, but rather surrounded by texts from the Church Fathers who are interpreters of Sacred Scripture as well as by texts of monastic fathers that show in a concrete way how Sacred Scripture is being translated into monastic life (cf. 9.8, and commentary on 73.2-5). In this sense, the Rule of Benedict itself is for us today an object for "meditating."

The novices have their own dormitory and apparently also their own refectory. Should they have a separate table reading? Or should they still be excused from severe fasting and, for example, eat earlier?

3. *A senior is to be appointed.* Does this mean someone who is advanced in chronological age? Probably not. Benedict knows spiritual "seniors" to whom one can disclose thoughts (4.50), who know "how to heal their own wounds as well as those of others" (46.5-6), wise "seniors" who will go after an excommunicated monastic and, without being noticed, will be able to motivate him to reconcile (27.2f.). There are "seniors" who watch over the spiritual atmosphere (48.17), and they are generally required to love the younger monastics (4.71). Probably Benedict draws here from the tradition of the Desert Fathers. A "senior" is a spiritual person in whom the spirit dwells and who knows how to guide others not only through words, but also through an exemplary life. A senior has the gift of discerning the spirits (*diakrisis*) and knows how to show others the love of God.[23] Apparently Benedict wants to train many community members to become such wise persons. Since the word "senior" itself is so rich in meaning, Benedict can be brief in what follows and only needs to mention two more qualities that are spiritual and human at the same time.

4. *One skilled in winning souls.* Although this is not a biblical quotation, it is certainly based on scriptural texts. Paul becomes a Jew for the Jews in order to win over the Jews; he becomes all things to all in order to win all for salvation (1 Cor 9:19-22; cf. Matt 18:15). It is also possible that this biblical expression has been passed on by tradition as is so often the case. In the *Life of Pachomius* we read that a "director is appointed who is to help 'win souls' among the people who arrived every day" (*Vit. Pach.* 25).

The word "to win" (*lucrare*) indicates that what one desires to win has great value and that, therefore, one is willing to risk much. This can indicate a person's amiable manner expressed in their entire demeanor rather than in their words. For what purpose is the novice master to "win souls"? Certainly not for himself, but for the Lord and the "Lord's service" (cf. Prol 45). And in doing so the young persons are being led to the fullness of life and to their salvation (that concerns not only their souls, cf. 1 Cor 9:22; Prol 19–22, 49).

5. *Who is to look after them with greatest care (omnino curiose intendat).* In the Latin word *curiosus* we recognize its root *cura*, care. Benedict speaks of great or eager care that the abbot shows, for example, for the excommunicated (27.1, 5f.) and the sick (36.1, 6, 10); that the cellarer shows for the poor, the children, the guests, and the sick (31.9); and that the community is to show to the poor and strangers (53.15). Here the word is intensified by *omnino* that Benedict likes to use for emphasizing main concerns (cf. in 33.3 where it is translated as "nothing at all"; in 36.9 where it denotes the very weak brothers; in 72.11 where it is translated as "nothing whatever").

Watch, pay attention (*intendere*), be open—such an attitude is more receptive than active and indicates an ability to receive others, to let them be themselves while continuing to guide them. Yet it expresses also movement, concentration, interest, even love.[24] Similarly we beg the Lord at the beginning of the Liturgy of the Hours that he give us his attention, be open to us (*Deus, in aiutorium meam intende,* "Lord, come to my assistance"). After the test at the gate was so hard, the "senior" reveals God's goodness and benevolence to the young people (Titus 3:4). In the monastery young people are to meet such monastics in whose behavior Christ is transparent.

V. 7: One must keenly observe
         if he truly seeks God,
         if he shows eagerness for the *opus Dei*,
         for obedience and trials.
V. 8: One must inform the novice beforehand about all the hardships and
         difficulties
         through which one goes to God.

After the insertion of verses 5-6, Benedict again uses the singular for the candidate. Verses 7-8 can apply to the time in the guest quarters as well as to that in the novitiate.

1. *One must keenly observe . . . if he shows eagerness.* In the same verse, not only the word "keenness" (*sollicitudo*)[25] occurs, but also the word "eager" (*sollicitus*). There is eagerness and care, readiness coming from both sides, first from the novice master or the community, then also from the candidate. This attitude is not just a passing fancy, an initial enthusiasm (1.3), but rather the eagerness the Holy Spirit kindles in us and the motor for continued striving (*magis*—more, cf. comments on 72.1-2).

2. *Truly.* This word contains a strong emphasis; it occurs only one other time in the Rule: "One must serve the sick truly as Christ" (36.1). It may be that someone feigns pious wishes while seeking something else in the depth of his or her heart. One can pretend to seek God while, in reality,

seeking human development, a good career, secure work, tranquillity or adventure—in short: seeking oneself. Motivations are never 100 percent pure. Where is the main emphasis? "For what did you come?" (60.3). Bernard of Clairvaux says: "If we seek nothing else instead of him, nothing else besides him, nothing else after him. . . . If we do not want to seek God in vain, let us seek him truly, often and persistently."[26] Augustine calls this "being chaste" in seeking God (*castus*).[27]

We can let the Lord ask us anew as he asked John's disciples who followed him: "What are you looking for?" (John 1:38). When our motivation is not yet entirely pure, when we do not yet seek God "truly," we can offer our seeking to God that God may heal it and initiate us into the truth.

3. Excursus: Seeking God

At the outset, it is God who desires a relationship with the human being. God anticipates us. In Jesus Christ, God's seeking for us became, as it were, incarnate. Benedict describes how God seeks his workers in the multitude (Prol 14), how Christ as the Good Shepherd searches for the lost sheep and goes after it (27.8). Ambrose begs the Lord: "Seek me for I am also seeking you, seek me, find me, receive me"! (Commentary on Ps 118.22.28f.).

God is waiting for our answer; God "looks down from heaven to see if someone seeks God" (7.27). Benedict describes "seeking God" concretely with "seeking first the kingdom of God and his justice" (2.35, this is Benedict's own formulation and is not found in RM). This means concern about God's concerns, God's kingdom and values, and not getting lost in everyday concerns and the worries about ourselves. Our first concern is for God's kingdom, and then God will also take good care of us.

A person's entire activity is to be directed toward the Lord. "First of all, love the Lord with your whole heart, your whole soul and all your strength" (4.1). Seeking is a matter of love. We can think of the Song of Songs and how the lover is looking everywhere for the bridegroom (Cant 3:1-4; 5:6; 6:1). Augustine says: "May we seek what needs to be found and still seek it after we have found it; for what is to be found is hidden so that it is sought, and what is found is infinite so that it is sought without ceasing" (*In Joh.* 63.1). Basil speaks of a "burning desire to please God that is never stilled" so that one always thinks of God and loves God with one's whole heart, pointing to Psalm 42: "As the deer longs for running streams, so my soul longs for you, O God."[28]

The expression "seeking God" is certainly rooted in *Sacred Scripture* and must be understood in this context.[29] In the Hebrew Scriptures, seeking God means to desire, to strive, to devote oneself with all one's strength to this search. The expression occurs often in the context of praying. "Your face, Lord, do I seek" (Ps 27:8). Those who seek God are the pious worshipers of Yahweh who raise their hands to God in prayer. They rely on God and depend entirely on God. For the poor of Yahweh, this total orientation to God is a permanent attitude. The Lord is the only being who attracts their entire will and affectivity. Seeking God is not so much an intellectual activity, but an attitude of the entire person.

Seeking God also means: asking God's advice, begging God's guidance, discerning God's will before making a decision. When our faith is strong, we take questions to Yahweh; when our faith is weak, we often go to the soothsayer. Such questioning occurs not only in momentous decisions, but also in the many vicissitudes of daily life and includes the desire to do God's will in everything, to please God, to make God's will our own, and to follow God's commandments. "Happy are those who keep God's decrees, who seek the Lord with all their heart" (Ps 119:2).

In the Greek Scriptures, this holistic attitude still prevails, although Greek thought now adds another meaning to the word "seeking," namely, to try to perceive God and God's being through the works of creation (cf. Wis 13:6-9; Rom 1:19-20). Or in another text from Wisdom: "Love justice . . . think of the Lord in goodness and seek him with integrity of heart. Because he is to be found by those who test him not and he manifests himself to those who do not disbelieve him" (Wis 1:1f.).

In the New Testament, seeking occurs often in the context of praying: "Ask and you will receive; seek, and you will find" (Luke 9:11). Or more concretely: "Seek first the kingdom of God and his justice" (Matt 6:33). The Rule of Benedict refers to these two texts (58.3f. and 2.35).

Summarizing this regarding 58.7, we can say: Seeking God involves asking, praying, orienting one's entire person toward God, listening, trusting God, obeying God, living according to God's commandments. Looking back to the beginning of the chapter, it is evident that seeking God was already manifest in the persistent knocking on the gate, in insisting on the request, and in the patient bearing of hardship.

This seeking God is given the promise of being heard: "I sought the Lord and he answered me. . . . But those who seek the Lord lack no good thing" (Ps 34:5, 11). "Seek first the kingdom of God . . . and all these things will be given you besides" (Matt 6:33). When we have the courage to seek the one thing necessary, we will find everything in God.

Seeking God becomes concrete in a threefold eagerness for the three "Os"—*opus Dei* (work of God), *oboedientia* (obedience), *obprobria* (trials, hardships).

4. *If he shows eagerness for the opus Dei.* In most cases, we translate *opus Dei* as "worship." Presumably this was the first and the practical meaning for Benedict. Yet the expression also resonates with a broader meaning. *Opus Dei* is God's work in us, God's creation and saving activity, and especially the covenant with God's people (Exod 34:10: *opus Domini*) and the work that is accomplished by Jesus and was given to him by the Father (John 17:4: *opus consumavi*; cf. also John 5:36, 4:34). As a response to this, all our work is *opus Dei*, work which we do for God, our life in faith and good works. Jesus says: "This is the work of God (*opus Dei*) that you believe in the one whom he has sent" (John 6:29). The Rule emphasizes the practice of good works, and the monastic is called worker (Prol 14; 7.49, 70). When Basil establishes that the criterion for a candidate for the monastery is to be whether his desire for the *opus Dei* is sincere and ardent, he means by *opus Dei* the entire monastic striving to live for God (*Reg.* 7). Benedict already limits the meaning of *opus Dei* primarily to the work for God, the Liturgy of the Hours. Yet this is embedded in the prayerful attitude monastics show during the entire day and described in the first step of humility. This attitude prompts us to seek God's face without ceasing and to live under God's watchful eye. The Hour of the Office is "the moment which is singled out and in which this continuous turning to God, which is described in the first step of humility, is being realized."[30] RB 19 begins by mentioning the presence of God who looks down upon human beings everywhere and always. Thus, eagerness for the *opus Dei* is a part of eagerness for all that belongs to God, and is a part of seeking God.

Just as Benedict mentions "meditating" first among the activities of the novices, so here the *opus Dei* comes first. He concedes primacy to prayer (cf. comments on Prol 4; 43.3). If we live accordingly and are open for the work of God, then God can do God's work in us (Prol 30; cf. 7.69ff.), and we will "always [be] fully devoted to the work of the Lord" (1 Cor 15:58; cf. 16:10) which, for Paul, means the work of evangelization.

5. *Eagerness for obedience.* To postpone work and to hasten to the Divine Office (43.1-3) is for Benedict a sign of obedience (5.1-11 describes it in

similar words). Here too he considers the *opus Dei* together with obedience. Obedience is explicitly mentioned in the promise of profession (v. 17, cf. also v. 14). In RB 7 the steps of obedience (two to four) follow the first step of humility. The beginning of the Rule already describes obedience in terms of listening as a return to God. Though obedience requires effort at the beginning, it is still service for Christ. At the end of the Rule, obedience, which is now called a good (*bonum*), is extended to all community members. On this way of obedience we "go to God" (71.2). Obeying God in such openness as well as community members is the way of seeking God in community.

6. *Eagerness for trials.* The Latin word *obprobria* has given rise to many discussions and many abuses. Often it was understood as "eagerness for humiliations" and was interpreted to mean that monastics themselves were to strive for them. This can result in psychological aberrations. Monastery superiors often also deliberately imposed humiliations in order to teach novices humility because they were convinced that only humiliations would lead someone to humility. Did Benedict mean this? He never deliberately imposes humiliations, impossible commands, chicaneries on his monks, although his immediate sources know such practices.[31]

Probably these trials have a very concrete meaning and designate menial tasks, the normal services in a monastery, and for the guests. Basil says that one has to test whether a candidate carries out the orders willingly and accurately, whether he is ready "for all humility," whether he "accepts, without disdain, all the menial and routine tasks he is required to do supposing that there are good reasons that these tasks need to be done." He is given tasks people in the world consider dishonorable (*obprobrium*) and is observed as he carries them out (*Reg.* 6). The Romans considered manual labor as demeaning, as slaves' work. It is easy to imagine that members of noble families who wanted to enter a monastery brought their slaves along in order to be well served in every respect. Yet the monastery—and the candidate discovers this quite early—is not a community where some serve while the others expect to be served. All serve each other just as Christ serves us, and thus they can form a true community without class distinctions. (All also do *lectio* that, in addition to manual labor, represents the other element of social equality and that could be a trial—*obprobrium*—for those candidates who had no education.)

Concretely, these trials probably consisted of weekly kitchen service that included cooking, washing dishes, cleaning the house, laundry, chopping wood, and serving the guests that included making beds, heating water, washing their feet.[32] Thus it is easier to understand why Cassian thinks that monks should learn patience and humility precisely in looking after the guests (*Inst.* IV.7) and why Benedict is at pains to avoid overburdening them with manual labor, on the one hand (48.24; 35.2), and to eliminate causes for grumbling, on the other (35.15). Thus service is probably a matter of serving guests (two months in the guest quarters) and service to the community. It may also at times be work in the fields (48.7). One can imagine that the brothers who are not used to such work may not always do them well, so that at the beginning of the weekly service not only those who serve, but also those who are served, have every reason to pray, "O God, come to my assistance," and afterward to express gratitude, "God you have comforted me" (35.16). Furthermore, it is understandable that someone who has never done such work can legitimately say: "I am a useless worker," or even: "I am the mockery of people" (7.52, here *obprobrium* means mockery; cf. also 7.49).

In serving, one learns to become a servant of Christ and of others, and it shows whether someone "really" seeks God.

Serving in the normal community tasks as a matter of course is today also a necessary part of introducing young people to monastic life. In these trifling service tasks, one can concretely practice the imitation of Christ in devoted service (cf. foot washing, John 13:1-15). Doing so increases love, as Benedict says (35.2), and the young person grows into the community and into the attitude of Christ.

These three criteria, as concrete forms of seeking God, are time and again important for us all, not just as reminiscence, but also as reorientation on our way to God.

7. One must inform the novice beforehand about all the hardships and difficulties through which one goes to God. Perhaps Benedict refers to Christ's word: "How narrow the gate and constricted the road that leads to life" (Matt 7:14). In a similar manner he says in 71.2 that "we go to God through obedience." Thus we can connect hardships and difficulties with obedience and the various community services. Yet at times the *opus Dei* may also be experienced as such.

While in Prol 46 Benedict explicitly states that he does not want to set down anything harsh or burdensome, such things are to be predicted here. It is not something deliberately imposed or commanded, yet Benedict knows that it is usually found on the way and simply happens because we live and serve together as imperfect and weak human beings. Moreover, it is a law of the imitation of Christ whose way also led through hardships and difficulties to the resurrection (cf. fourth step of humility). Nevertheless, Benedict adheres, together with monastic tradition, to the principle that the royal path is gentle and easy even when it feels hard and difficult because it is a matter of carrying the yoke of Christ who carries it with us.[33]

The path to God leads through narrow passages and through darkness so that we participate "in patience in the sufferings of Christ and so become heirs of his kingdom" (Prol 50). Some parts of these hardships and difficulties were experienced by the young person at the very beginning at the gate. Now more of it is predicted so that he or she will really know. *This* way leads to God, and outside of this way there are only detours.

The first goal, admission to the monastery, is now being continued. An endless path opens up that ends only before God. This is the goal to which profession directs us. Just as the call has its origin in God (v. 2), the path also will only end before God (v. 8).

The section from verse 9 to verse 16 is marked by the three readings of the Rule. It begins with the ritual of entering the novitiate and ends with bringing the novice to profession. For this part, only few parallels can be found in old rules, except in RM.

V. 9: If he promises to remain firm and to persevere,
then after two months have passed,
he is to be read this Rule from beginning to end.

V. 10: And he is to be told: "See, this is the law
under which you want to serve.
If you can observe it, enter!
If you cannot do so, leave freely."

V. 11: If he still remains firm,
he is led to the aforementioned novitiate
and is again tested with all patience.

Now the ceremony of entering the novitiate is being described. The young person has already lived monastic life as a guest and has had experiences with his or her own reactions and with the community. Practical experience prevails over theory. The Rule now being read explains monastic life.

This entire process is similar to the preparation for baptism in the early church. We may think of the scrutinies, of the *traditio*, the handing down the important Christian texts; those seeking baptism were called *petentes*, petitioners; and there, too, the right kind of practical experience had great weight as compared with correct doctrine.[34]

1. *If he promises to remain firm and to persevere.* This is the first of three successive promises (vv. 9, 14, 17), and a response to what the Lord himself promised: "No eye has seen and no ear has heard what God has prepared for those who love him" (4.76). The candidate wants to remain firm through the vicissitudes of life, does not want to evade difficulties when they come (cf. commentary to v. 3 [pp. 115–116]). This is not being fixed in

immobility, but rather persevering in moving ahead on the way to God (v. 8). Now the candidate is ready for the second gate.

2. *He is to be read this Rule from beginning to end.* There is a certain discipline of secrecy as one does not simply hand over the Rule of this life to just anyone. Preconditions for productive listening are: being called to this life, living it with others, and ultimately the will to live according to the Rule. In connection with the table reading, RM says: "The rule of the monastery is to be heard by all those who can deservedly follow it" (24.25, cf. 24.20-24). In the development of cenobitic monasticism this practice has evolved only slowly from the preliminary forms of instruction to monastic practices, and all the way to the official readings of the Rule.[35] In RB the reading of the Rule is almost always an acoustical reading; the word enters not only through the eyes, but also through the ears and thus reaches the heart faster. Reading also means to explain the Rule, to learn and repeat it (cf. Hildemar, 535).

This Rule—this must be the Rule of Benedict, in the same or a similar form as it exists today as RB 58 seems to be a chapter that was written relatively late. *Regula* in Latin is a tool to keep something straight, a ruler with which one can draw straight lines. In this manner the Rule as well as the teachings of the Fathers is an aid for walking straight and without detours so that "we can reach our Creator on a straight course" (73.4). Between the Prologue and the chapters of the Rule, many manuscripts have the following sentence: "The Rule is called such because it directs the conduct of the obedient." The Rule is a *magistra*, a master teacher (3.7) drawing from experience and having "authority" so that it can speak for the various groups in the monastery (cf. 73.1). Nonetheless, Benedict never gives his Rule absolute authority (as the Master seems to do at times). Benedict's Rule is only "a small Rule for the beginning" (73.8) that leads to the heights of the Fathers and especially of Sacred Scripture that is the "most reliable"and the "truest" guide (73.3, cf. Prol 21). Benedict never identifies his Rule with the law of God (in contrast to RM 93.15). In the last analysis, *the* Rule is Christ himself. He is the law we follow.

From beginning to end—that probably means nothing is to be left out. There could be the danger to leave out some chapters that do not please or to read only selections of the Rule. The early Fathers had great patience in persevering even with challenging texts that seemed incomprehensible and in listening to their message and what it might mean for them personally.[36]

3. *This is the law (ecce lex).* The expression *ecce* comes from the language of the Bible. This demonstrates again how Benedict's language is shaped by *lectio divina* probably without his being necessarily aware of it.[37]

The law—perhaps we still have an aversion to this word going back to those times when its aspect of obligation was overemphasized and when the law was seen primarily as something limiting. According to Scripture, the law is a gift of God that helps people to live together peacefully. It is a signpost that keeps us from making laborious detours, and it is a railing that, on difficult paths, keeps us from falling into a precipice.

See, this is the law—this certainly is not an invitation to meditate, but to listen and obey. Likewise, we would not look at a signpost in itself, but walk in the direction it indicates. Benedict calls Sacred Scripture in particular "divine law." The abbot is to be learned in it (64.9), and it is read to the guest (53.8). In contrast, he calls the Rule only "law" (vv. 10, 15), while the Master equates it with divine law (93.15: "Accept the law of God, this Rule"). To be sure, a person can make one's own law according to one's own desires as Benedict says the Sarabaites do (1.8). By so doing one becomes a slave, but the law of the Gospel is freeing (cf. Rom 8:2). The highest law is Jesus Christ himself. In this connection, we may recall that the patristic exegesis interpreted the long psalm about the law (Ps 118 [119]) as a psalm of hope for Christ, and of love for Christ, and that it enjoyed great popularity in monastic circles.[38] Christ himself is the way, the truth, the light, justice, the Word, the teaching, the command, and the law of God. From him we can infer how we ought to live. He is, as the Fathers say, the one of whom all the psalms speak and in whom Sacred Scripture has its center.[39]

4. *Under which you want to serve (fight).* The newer editions of the Rule usually translate *militare* with "to serve," older ones with "to fight." Earlier centuries probably had a more positive attitude toward military service. In Benedict's Rule, this word presumably has simply the meaning of "to serve" (cf. Excursus to Prol 3: *Militia* [pp. 24–25]). This service is determined primarily by a personal relationship with Christ in obedience to him. Smaragdus comments on this passage: it does not say "the law under which you will rest or indulge in leisure," but "under which you want to serve."[40]

"You want"—the free will that Benedict esteems highly is taken for granted. The Prologue had issued this invitation: "If you desire true and eternal life . . ." (Prol 17), and later added: "If we want to arrive there . . ." (Prol 22; cf. Prol 42; 7.5). This is not simply liking something, but rather resolutely affirming it with all our strength.

5. *If you can observe it—if you cannot do so.* In the following verses, a style of contrasting expressions is evident: can/cannot, enter/leave freely, accept/cast off. It is a question of an either /or. *"If you can"* is a strong expression. Who can claim this about oneself? When the young Pachomius was told about all the hardships awaiting him, he answered: "I believe in the Lord Jesus Christ who gives me strength and patience" (*Vit. Pach.* 6; cf.

also RM 87.2-3). This shows a being able in the knowledge of being called by God, in trusting that the one who began the good work in us will also bring it to completion (cf. 1 Thess 5:24). Thus in earlier times in our congregation when we were given the Rule we said: "Not out of my own ability, but through the mercies of God I am hoping and desiring to be able to observe everything." According to Prol 29 we are to be convinced that we cannot do the good out of our own power. When all the remedies no longer have an effect on an erring monastic, the abbot prays with all the community members "that the Lord who can do all things may bring healing to the sick brother" (28.5). With Paul we can say: "I have the strength through him who empowers me" (Phil 4:13).

Ability here refers to keeping and observing the Rule; it means being attentive, listening, obeying, carrying it in one's heart so as to follow the teaching of the Rule in every activity and throughout one's life. Today the Rule is complemented by Declarations or Constitutions. Yet Benedict is very clear about the fact that by observing the Rule we have only a "beginning of a good monastic life" (73.1). It does not suffice to cling like a good child to the letter of the Rule and observe it; rather, in accordance with the Rule we are always to strive ahead (cf. commentary on RB 73).

6. *Enter—go freely on your way.* Concretely, "enter" means enter the novitiate and the monastery (while entering in v. 4 designated the entrance into the guest quarters). The radical renunciation of possessions—unlike in the practice of RM—has not yet taken place. While the Master describes leaving as a return to the devil (RM 88.6), Benedict emphasizes that true freedom exists. If God called the candidate to monastic life, leaving would be the freedom to do evil; yet should he or she not be called, leaving would be the better course, the freedom to do good.

In the entire chapter, Benedict attaches great importance to a free and personal decision of the young person and thus provides structures and instructions which favor this. Yet it also becomes clear that it is a serious matter not to follow a true call from God.

7. *If he still remains firm, he is led to the aforementioned novitiate.* After the entire Rule was read and explained to the candidate, and after he or she was given a free choice and has been made aware of the consequences, and if he or she still remains firm, the solemn ceremony of entering into the novitiate can take place. Earlier, the candidate acted; now, he or she is being led. We can go further and say: Here in the monastery, one will now be led like Peter (cf. John 21:18) and will find older monastics who will show the way; the Gospel will lead one, and at the core, it is Christ himself who will ever more take the lead (cf. 5.11; Prol 21; 72.2, 11f.). If God led the candi-

date to this point, God will also guarantee to lead him or her in this place, the monastery, through the given human circumstances to the final goal, to God (v. 8).

And he is again tested in all patience.[41] Testing still continues after the two months; a true decision for life requires long preparation and testing.

To what does patience refer? Certainly the candidate needs patience (cf. v. 3), but here patience probably refers to the community and especially to the novice master. In being patient, one is an image of the patience of God who, according to Prol 37, is waiting for our conversion and wants to lead us to our salvation. Young persons need various lengths of times. "To bear weaknesses with the greatest patience"—this is needed vis-à-vis the candidates.

V. 12: **And after six months have passed,
the Rule is read to him
so that he knows what is at stake when entering.**
V. 13: **And if he still remains firm,
the Rule is read again after four months.**

The three following verses begin with "and" in Latin. This is probably an indication that they describe a continuous development and that everything follows in logical sequence leading to profession.

1. *So that he knows what is at stake when entering.* This "knowing" is not only intellectual knowledge, but a clarity that grows through experience and learning. The verb "to know" occurs several times in this chapter: the novice must "know" that, after profession, he or she is no longer allowed to leave (v. 15); making profession is a consenting to being involved with God, an act with which one must not trifle (v. 18); subsequently, he or she no longer has the right to belong to him- or herself (v. 25). For the priests, Benedict also emphasizes four times what they need to know, in particular, that they have to keep the Rule and monastic discipline (60.2, 5; 62.3, 7). In the monastery the Rule is read frequently so that no one can claim ignorance as an excuse (66.8).

What is the content and the obligation of monastic life? Like others, a priest who enters is asked: "Friend, for what did you come?"[42] These words are relevant again and again, especially in times of crisis. Why did I enter? What did I actually seek? What was my purpose? Such questions can call us to renewed reflection and new orientation.

2. *And if he still remains firm.* Benedict implies that the young person is still free. But one perseveres, remains firm, persists on the way one began. Whoever cannot persevere in a resolution cannot physically remain in the monastery (cf. Hildemar, 541).

V. 14: And if he has duly deliberated with himself
        and promises to keep everything
        and to observe everything with which he is charged,
        then he is to be received into the community.
V. 15: Yet he must know that, from this day on,
        the law of the Rule prohibits him to leave the monastery
V. 16: or to cast off the yoke of the Rule
        which, during a prolonged reflection,
        he was able to refuse or accept.

The third gate now opens for profession. Three preconditions are mentioned in verses 12-14: He knows, stands firm, has thoroughly reflected. Now he can make a promise (v. 14). Verse 15 marks a turn in the chapter: from the many conditional clauses to definite statements. From this day on he is no longer allowed. . .

If he has duly deliberated with himself. Benedict uses the Latin word *deliberatio* only here and even two times in a row. It is connected to the discernment of spirits and the decision.[43] In a similar vein, Gregory the Great says of Benedict that he lived alone with himself (*Dial.* II 3.5). The candidate lives with him- or herself, reflects, deliberates, looks into his or her own depth, honestly confronts him- or herself. As verse 16 says, this deliberation is thorough, painstaking, and long—for Benedict's time. Today we presumably need a longer period for doing this.

2. *If he promises to keep everything and to observe everything with which he is charged.* Twice the word "everything" occurs here. Following Christ is a radical choice and goes all out. Nothing is to be withheld from one's surrender. The Latin word *custodire* means to watch, to keep. As a call to all of us, the Gospel says regarding Mary: "Blessed are they who hear the word of God and observe it" (Luke 11:28). This means attentively accepting [this word], turning it over and over in one's heart, and eventually translating it into action. In the Latin Bible the word occurs often in connection with the commandments. "To serve" in Latin also means to keep, and is used in RB in the context of obedience and of the Rule (62.7; 60.2). The content of this promise is obedience[44] to the Rule as well as to the abbot; these cannot be clearly separated. The cenobites serve "under a rule and under an abbot" (1.2).

3. *Then he is to be received into the community.* This an intensification of "entrance is granted" (v. 4) and "he is led into the novitiate" (v. 11). The reception into the community ends with the words "he is counted as a member of the community (v. 23) and "he is clothed with the things of the monastery" (v. 26). The word *congregatio* occurs for the first time in this

chapter. It designates the monastic community, but also the actual assembly for a liturgical, and especially a eucharistic, celebration (cf. v. 17ff.).

4. *From this day on.* The specifications of time culminate in the expression "from this day on" that is used three times in a solemn manner (vv. 15, 23, 25). All through a rather long period of preparation and testing, there is a dynamic movement toward this day. Then the Rule says: "from this day on." This day divides life into two large periods and opens up the perspective to "the day," that is, the day of the Lord's second coming that for everyone becomes concrete in the day of death. One may also recall the "day of the Lord," the "day the Lord has made," the day of Christ's resurrection that literally divided world history into two epochs. It is certainly evident that this day is important for the candidate because it is an intensification of his or her day of baptism.

5. *He knows that, from this day on, the law of the Rule prohibits.* Benedict is not afraid of negative expressions. The young person is to know his or her obligation clearly. The expression *non licet*, it is prohibited, occurs also when RB speaks about renouncing possessions (33.4, 5; 54.1) and about silence vis-à-vis guests (53.23). These were probably neuralgic points in the time of Benedict!

6. *To leave the monastery.* According to RM, this expression emphasizes stability.[45] Benedict, too, does not like it when monastics "run around outside" because this is "harmful to their souls." Therefore everything is to be inside the monastery walls (66.6-7). Yet already in the following chapter he provides for the possibility to leave the monastery, but in obedience and accompanied by the prayer of the community (67). This shows that "leaving the monastery" in verse 15 means a disobedient departure, a running away from obedience. Benedict uses this expression for a definitive departure, or an apostasy. In verse 28 he says that this occurs upon the insinuation of the devil; in RB 29.1 he calls such a departure a "vice" (*vitium*). For Benedict, it is not simply a question of remaining in a specific place, but of remaining under obedience, and remaining with the community. In his commentary, Hildemar (543) explains that not-leaving is not an absolute precept as there are three reasons to leave the place of the monastery:

(a) to improve the life of a monastic by transferring to a monastery where one can better follow Christ;

(b) for one's own salvation when the Rule is not observed in the place where one lives;

(c) in obedience when a monastic is sent out.

In this promise before profession, obedience and stability are seen together with a life lived according to the Rule.

7. It is prohibited to cast off the yoke of the Rule which he was able to refuse or accept. The expression "the yoke of the Rule" recalls Christ's saying: "Take my yoke upon you and learn from me . . . my yoke is easy and my burden light" (Matt 11:29f.), especially in its monastic interpretation (cf. RM, Th [= theme]13f.). At the end of the Prologue, Benedict tried to reconcile Christ's word about the easy yoke with that about the narrow way (cf. Matt 7:13f.). He found a solution by saying that, while the gate and the way are narrow, the heart widens and does not experience the burden as an oppressive yoke (cf. commentary on Prol 48–49).

According to the Scriptures, there are two yokes: the yoke of sin and of one's own will that each person fashions oneself or accepts to carry (cf. Gal 5:1), and that the Lord can break (cf. Jer 30:8); and the yoke of the Lord who takes us into the Lord's service. Without a yoke, one cannot serve. In a similar way, the fourth step of humility says that the monastic is like a beast of burden before God (7.50). Perhaps we remember the words recited when we received the scapular: "Take the yoke of the Lord upon you and carry his burden which is sweet and light" (cf. also *Vit. Mac.* 2).

In the last analysis, the yoke of the Lord is the Cross of Christ the disciple takes up and that he or she is willing to carry every day (cf. Matt 16:24).[46] During the time of reflection, the candidate had the free choice to accept or refuse this yoke, the Cross of Christ. Yet, once one took it up, one no longer is allowed to cast it off; it is the yoke of the Lord. As Luke 14:23-33 admonishes, one is to reflect *before* building the tower whether or not to begin doing it. Afterward it is necessary to persevere in following Christ who also stays with the one who follows him.

OVERVIEW OF THE SECOND PART

The actual profession ceremony begins with verse 17. Benedict strives to embed the legal elements in a liturgical celebration. If we once more review the historical development, we see more clearly how he assembled individual elements from various traditions that at times were historically far apart into a single liturgical celebration and thus emphasized the importance of this moment. Even the renunciation of ownership is mentioned here although it took place earlier. The sequence is: oral promise, written petition, placing the petition on the altar, prayer with the *Suscipe*, prostration, request for prayers, mention of ownership, and finally, the clothing with the habit. In comparison with RM, it is evident how Benedict simplifies and tightens the ceremony (for example, he omits all the extensive addresses), but is concerned with the juridic elements and with clarity.

V. 17: The one to be received
   promises in the oratory and in the presence of all community members
   stability, fidelity to monastic life and obedience
V. 18: before God and his Saints.
   If he should ever act otherwise, he must know
   that he is condemned by the one whom he mocks.

1. *The one to be received in the oratory.* Now the novice who, hitherto was able to accept or refuse the yoke of the Rule, becomes "the one to be received," the one who is being given the gift of reception.

In this chapter, the movement went from the gate to the guest quarters to the novitiate, and now to the central place of the community. In this place the community is time and again spiritually renewed; here the brothers come together for the *opus Dei*, here the presence of God is especially effective and challenging for them (19.1-2). Thus the Rule says with great emphasis: "in the oratory, in the presence of all community members," and later, "before God and his Saints" (v. 18). The oratory is also the place of contact between the monastery and the world (cf. RB 52 and 53). Guests are brought here (53.8); and in a deeper sense, the encounter with the world happens here for, when someone truly encounters God, he or she is also drawn into God's love for the entire world.

2. *In the presence of all community members.* Presumably the ceremony occurs at the time of worship, more specifically at the time of the Eucharist. The community truly is a *congregatio*, assembled around the altar (cf. comments on v. 20). The expression "in the presence of" occurs again in the following verse ("in the presence of God and his Saints") and indicates how the horizontal and the vertical dimensions interlock in this place and at this hour. All are to be present, no one is to be absent. The community has an important, even a constitutive part (cf. comments on v. 22). The community is witness (cf. RM 89.15), accepts responsibility, acts in praying. Profession fashions an enduring bond between the monastic and the community. For Benedict, the presence of all community members is so important that he emphasizes it even before the presence of God. Moreover, this also corresponds to the title of the chapter. In it Benedict does not want to offer a theology of profession, but rather wants to describe how someone is received into the community.

3. *He promises.* The word "profession" is not used in this chapter; only in RB 5.3 we read: obedience is given "because of the holy service they have professed" (*professi sunt*).[47] Yet implicitly this passage describes the profession as a public promise, a declaration to live monastic life before witnesses, a consenting to be involved with the community and with God.

The content of the promise is described with various expressions in other chapters of the Rule. One promises "to observe the Rule and stability" (60.9) or "holy service" (5.3); the foreign monastic must commit to stability (61.5). The promise in the RM says: "I want to serve God according to the way of life in the Rule which was read to me in this monastery" (89.8). All this allows us to conjecture that verse 17 does not describe a fixed formula, but rather the content of profession.

4. Excursus: Stability

Already earlier the candidate had promised to persevere in his stability (v. 9), then just before profession it is made clear "that he is no longer allowed to leave the monastery" (that is, leave monastic life, v. 15). Entering priests promise stability (60.9) as do foreign monastics who want to remain (61.5). The workshop in which to practice the tools of good works is "stability in community" (4.78). In verse 17, the element of stability, already much emphasized before profession, becomes an explicit promise.

The root of the word "stability" is the Latin verb *stare*, to stand. At the time of the martyrs, it is used for those who remain firm in faith and persevere in it to the end (cf. Matt 10:22; also 1 Cor 16:13; Col 1:23; Eph 6:11-14). The word also means that one knows where one stands and what and who one is. To be at home with oneself is indispensable for finding one's identity.

RB 1.2 says that cenobites serve in the monastery under a rule and an abbot. Stability is connected to all four elements: monastery, community, rule, abbot. This is even more evident in their opposites: hermits live neither in community nor under a rule and an abbot. Gyrovagues are always restless, and this is the external sign that they serve only their own will and live without rule and obedience. The Sarabaites are not tested by any rules, they have no stability, but serve the world, are without a shepherd and outside the Lord's sheepfold (cf. 1.3-12).

It is very difficult to grasp this promise as a vow with a fixed content. The interpretations vary from one commentary to the next. Summarizing we can isolate five main points:

a. *Stability of heart.* On the way to God, it is necessary to persevere; the monastic wants to bind him- or herself firmly to God (cf. RM 88.6), or as Benedict says, wants to persevere to the end (7.36). This is a matter of not leaving the way once it has been chosen (cf. comments on Prol 49–50, pp. 40–44, above). Gregory Of Nyssa says:

> This is the most marvelous thing of all: how the same thing is both a standing still and a moving. . . . I mean by this that the firmer and the more immovable one remains in the Good, the more he progresses in the course of virtues. . . . It is like using the standing still as if it were a wing while the heart flies upward through its stability in the Good.[48]

In this sense stability, remaining in the love of Christ (cf. John 15:9), is a journey to God (cf. v. 8).

b. Stability also includes "*stability of feet*" (RM 64.2) inasmuch as it is an expression of stability of heart. Benedict is aware of the danger of *acedia*, listlessness, when a monastic wants to roam around and seek diversion and no longer can stand remaining in his or her place, work, or *lectio* (cf. 48.18, cf. RB 66–67). In this, Benedict is part of long tradition, especially in Egypt. Antony said: "In whatever place you are sitting, do not easily leave it" (*Apoph*. Antony, 3). In another source we read: "As the tree which is often transplanted, brings no fruit, so the monk who often wanders can bring no fruit" (*Vit. Patr.* V.7.36). "Stay in your cell" says a well-known axiom. This means: face your own shadow, stay with yourself without seeking excuses, accept yourself and trust in God. Learn to love the people around you, see them with the eyes of God, and accept them as God does.

Cultivating local stability thus opposed the bad custom of gyrovagism that was quite common in many monastic circles. Several church councils tried to tie monks to their place.[49] Lérins in particular emphasized stability on the island;[50] yet, stability of place was never understood legalistically. From the beginning there were necessary journeys and thus a departure from cloister. The Master has thirteen chapters discussing this. What is at stake is this: not eluding obedience, the service under a rule, and an abbot.

c. *Stability under obedience.* The monastic no longer has power to dispose either over oneself or over the place. One does not want to evade the labor of obedience, but rather to fight with the weapons of obedience (cf. Prol 2–3). Stability is the fruit of obedience. And when obedience sends someone out of the monastery for some work, then it is part of stability to accept being sent out under obedience.

d. *Stability under a Rule.* Verse 16 says that, after profession, a monastic no longer is allowed to cast off the yoke of the Rule which one accepted as a law of life. He or she does not want to live like the Sarabaites who are not tested by any rule and put together their own laws (cf.

1.8f.). Remaining under a rule, which today is complemented by Declarations and Constitutions, helps to live according to the Gospel.

e. *Stability in community.* For cenobites, this is the core of stability that consists more in a bond to people than in one to a place. From profession on, the monastic wants to run on the way of the Gospel together with these people without separating oneself from them. The bonding with the community occurs at the altar where the community becomes ever more "the Body of Christ" and ever more "the house of God" not built of stone, but of living beings.
To run together—Augustine explains it thus:

> Not so among us. Let all who run the race persevere in their running, for all of them are rewarded. The one who is first at the winning-post waits to be crowned with the late-comer. The reason for this is that the contestants are animated not by greed but by charity. All runners love one another, and the course itself is love (*In Ps.* 39.11).

Stability is bonding with the community. Yet it depends on the structure of the group whether the local community (abbey [monastery, convent]) or the union of houses (priory, congregation) is seen as central.[51]

All this is again a concrete expression of fidelity in following Christ. Stability is a graced answer to God's fidelity: "God, who calls you, is faithful; he will do it" (1 Thess 5:24).

5. *Conversatio morum suorum.* For Benedict's contemporaries, this expression, so puzzling today, was apparently customary and clear. Its meaning can be gathered from passages in the Rule as well as from comparisons with religious texts of his time. The most probable meaning among several possibilities is: virtuous life, monastic life, good ethical way of life, monastic virtues.[52]

Soon the expression *conversatio morum suorum* was no longer understood. Thus *conversio* was substituted both in the profession formula and in the text of the Rule (cf. Hildemar, 541, 532f.). We recall the well-known earlier profession formula: "Stability, conversion of morals, and obedience."

The interpretations of this expression vary considerably. Most Declarations define it as monastic life, as life as it is to be lived in this community, as service in community under a rule and an abbot, as imitation of Christ according to the Rule of Benedict. Monastics place themselves under the living rule of the community in the knowledge that in doing so the imitation of Christ can be realized. (Hermits, gyrovagues, and Sarabaites do not do this.) Yet by living this law of life one acquires only a beginning of *conversatio* as Benedict says in his last chapter (73.1). Perfect *conversatio* is a life according to the Sacred Scriptures and the teachings of the Fathers. The Rule, however, is the basic law of monastic life even though it is "only a little Rule for the beginning" (73.8). Again, it is difficult to grasp *conversatio morum* as a fixed term for the content of profession. The monastic deliberately begins the journey with the community, yet the journey will end only with God whom they want to reach together (72.12).

6. *Obedience.* Obedience was already contained in the two preceding expressions. The monastic wants to persevere, not to evade obedience; he or she affirms the communal striving according to the Rule, he or she obeys a living authority, thus serving under "a rule and an abbot" (1.2). Obedience is the best realization of *conversatio*. Hermits do no practice obedience in this manner, gyrovagues want to evade obedience, and Sarabaites do whatever pleases them at the moment. Cenobites live in community under obedience. Already at the beginning of the Rule, Benedict places obedience in the foreground: return to God in obedience, serve with the weapons of obedience (Prol 2–3). Monastics obey "because of the holy service they have promised" (5.3). Thus monastics renounce individual autonomy and let their activity and being be determined by Christ who acts through intermediaries. Even the oldest commentaries emphasize that obedience here is to be according to the Rule, that is, the abbot cannot command anything that does not correspond to the Rule. Benedict decrees that the abbot must not order anything not in conformity with divine law (2.4). Obedience may be burdensome, but it is a main part of monastic life. Thus Steidle says that the last "and" in the profession formula could simply be translated as "in short: obedience."[53]

A comparison of the three parts of the profession formula with RB 1.2 and the negative counter images of the cenobites can be helpful in explaining this further:

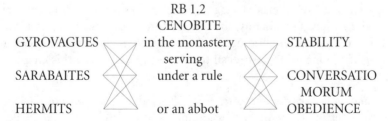

RB 1.2
CENOBITE

GYROVAGUES — in the monastery — STABILITY
serving
SARABAITES — under a rule — CONVERSATIO MORUM
HERMITS — or an abbot — OBEDIENCE

Stability is a particular matter of the monastery, but includes also living according to the Rule and in obedience; it is especially opposed to the gyrovagues, but also the Sarabaites and to some extent the hermits since they, too, left the community. *Conversatio*, in particular, is living according to the Rule, but includes also living in the monastery and in obedience. It is especially opposed to the Sarabaites, but also to the gyrovagues and, inasmuch as it means living in the monastery, to the hermits. Obedience is particularly related to the abbot, but includes also living according to the Rule in the monastery (also obeying each other); in this sense hermits cannot practice obedience nor do gyrovagues and Sarabaites live in obedience.

7. *A formula?* This three-part expression does not provide a literal profession formula, but describes its content according to headings. Benedict eyes the same reality from different points of view. He defines the cenobites as those who serve under a rule and an abbot. In other places he uses different expressions (cf. 5.3 and 60.9). He has no need to be concerned about definitions because their content was known in his surroundings. Only in verse 24 he mentions the renunciation of possessions, and he does not mention celibacy at all. He only names what was especially important in his time. He is not concerned with clearly separated matters of vows, but is concerned with the personal dedication of a person in his or her totality. In this respect, placing the petition on the altar is more important than the oral promise (cf. commentary on v. 20 below).

Later centuries also did not understand these expressions as a formula in a legalistic sense, and soon after Benedict's death very diverse profession formulas circulated not only in the Frankish kingdom, but also in Monte Cassino.[54] Obedience is an important element in all these formulas.

8. *Before God and his saints.* God and his saints are witnesses of the profession. With this expression, our eyes are led from the oratory to the heavenly community of the church triumphant with God at its center. Who is this "God with his angels"? If Benedict follows Cassian, we can assume this means Christ. Similarly, the one making profession in RM addresses Christ.[55]

The image of Christ as ruler, surrounded by his saints, is common in the sixth century. Nonetheless, I suggest that it makes sense to think here of God the Father. Presumably, the celebration of profession takes place within a eucharistic celebration. The "Glory be to the Father" follows after the *Suscipe*. One also must recall the three expressions in this chapter: "from God" (v. 2), "to God" (v. 8), "before God" (v. 18).

9. *Should he ever act otherwise, he is to know that he is condemned by the one whom he mocks.* Before profession the monastic was free to make a decision either way. Benedict respected this freedom. But now, after this life-changing decision that, for those times, was very thoroughly prepared, the only thing that matters is to realize it fully and to deepen it. RM points to

the positive possibility that the monastic will be rewarded for his fidelity, and to the negative one that he will be condemned when not acting according to his promise (89.12-16). Benedict, however, expresses this only negatively. Leaving the monastery is infidelity, mocking God. Of course, this is only true for those who are really called. Hildemar says (542): "The one who promises with words, but does not fulfill them, laughs about God." According to Basil, such a person sins against God (*Reg.* 7). There is a clear realization about how serious this hour is. God's very self is present as a witness and a guarantor. God is faithful. Human beings, however, are apt to break faith. This harsh conclusion sheds light on the significance of the event: fully consenting to being involved with the great God, a definitive engagement, an act of reverence toward God.[56]

V. 19: He writes out his promise in a petition
       in the name of all the Saints whose relics are there,
       and in the name of the abbot who is present.
V. 20: He is to write the petition by his own hand,
       but if he is illiterate,
       another is to write it upon the request of the novice
       who puts his mark to it
       and then with his own hand places the document on the altar.

1. *He writes out his promise in a petition.* One might think that after "making profession" a prayer of gratitude or praise would be suitable. The word *petitio*, "petition," however, indicates that the person stands before God as someone asking for something and thus also receiving something. In RM, the document (*donatio*) contains a list of the possessions the candidate offers "together with his soul" as a donation "to God and to the oratory of the monastery."[57] In contrast, Benedict shows little interest in a candidate's possessions. While for Benedict the petition probably included a document of donation, the promise has precedence over everything else. RB 59.8 states that those who own nothing at all simply write out the petition. The donation of one's person is so important that the petition retains its meaning even when it does not include a document of donation.[58] In this way, the free donation of one's self is also expressed in legal form.

2. *In the name of all the saints whose relics are there and in the name of the abbot who is present.* Mentioning the saints serves to localize the act more precisely: profession was made in this monastery and in this oratory with these saints as patrons. We may also think of the fact that the saints are the masters and patrons of this holy place;[59] they are the ones who entered totally into the sacrifice of Christ. Moreover, the written petition names the present abbot [superior]; thus, the document can be dated legally. Besides,

the abbot [superior] has a particular function in the profession ritual even before the priest who is not even explicitly mentioned. Faith sees the superior as a representative of Christ (2.2). The superior is, however, mentioned in this chapter only after the community has been introduced as witness.

3. *He is to write out this petition by his own hand, but if he is illiterate, another one is to write it out upon the request of the novice who puts his mark on it.* The expression "by his own hand" appears twice in this verse, thus underlining the voluntary nature of the act, but also that the person wants to offer himself with all his abilities: The candidate promises, writes, places on the altar, sings, prostrates himself. By writing it out, the "promise" gains in legal significance, and the candidate participates in the act more fully as a person. If the candidate is illiterate, it is not the superior, but the novice himself who determines who shall write it out. As a realist, Benedict does not expect that someone would have learned to write in one year. The manual sign is probably a cross, as it has been the practice from of old (cf. Hildemar, 546).

This is the first time RB explicitly mentions the writing of something. Otherwise, we find only the expression "it is written" referring to the Sacred Scriptures. Scripture and profession document are two fundamental documents in the monastery: the one is promise and call, the other response to it.

4. *With his own hand he places the document on the altar.* At this point, the candidate proceeds further toward the center. According to the explanations of the Fathers, the altar represents Christ. Ambrose says: "What else is the altar than the form of the body of Christ?"[60] (*De sacr.* V.2.7 and 2.5). Later, the abbot takes the document from the altar (v. 29). In the following chapter Benedict says: "They are to wrap this document (*petitio*) and the hand of the child together with the donation in the altar cloth and are to offer [the boy] in this manner" (59.2). This apparently occurs during the celebration of the Eucharist. Therefore, we can assume with greater justification that profession is made during Eucharist (cf. also 62.2). In this manner, the expression "in the presence of all" gains its full significance: it is the actual assembly of the entire community for the central liturgical act.

In this context, the weight of this gesture becomes clear. The monastic hands over the petition, the expression of his or her personal dedication, with his or her own hand, to the person of Christ, as it were. It is the altar on which the Lord is being sacrificed (Hildemar, 539). In doing this the novice expresses his or her will to enter into Christ's sacrifice, his death, his resurrection, and his surrender for the many. Everything is done for the glory of God the Father (cf. the "Glory be to the Father" that follows later).

This gesture says more than the words of a profession formula. One can call it the heart of the Benedictine profession (cf. Yeo, *Structure*, 330f.). Thus the gesture also resembles an oath that was taken on the altar. And it becomes even clearer that nothing must ever be taken out of this oblation.

V. 21: After he laid it down,
> the novice immediately begins the following verse:
> "Receive me, O Lord, according to your word,
> and I shall live.
> Do not disappoint me in my expectation/hope."

V. 22: This verse is repeated three times by the entire community,
> and the "Glory be to the Father" is to be added.

"Immediately"—against the background of RM (89.18-23), this means: without having the one making profession give long speeches about the significance of this act. This is not the time for many words, but simply for prayer. What the person does here transcends his own strength. Thus the petition is again not followed by a song of gratitude or praise, but, as we may expect, by another humble prayer.

1. *Lord (Domine)*. The Master and Benedict inserted the word "Lord" into verse 116 of Psalm 118 (119). In interpreting the entire psalm, it seems reasonable to see Christ in the word "Lord" (cf. comments on v. 10, p. 127 above). It was the "Lord" who sought workers in the multitude and invited them with the question: "Who is seeking life?" . . . "Before you call me, I will say: 'Here I am.' What, dear brothers, could be more delightful than this inviting voice of the Lord? See in his goodness the Lord shows us the way to life!" (Prol 14–20). What is at stake here is following this Lord.

Ambrose's explanation of Psalm 118:166, which Benedict may have known, is fitting here also:

> If one who is in the bosom of Abraham lives—such as Lazarus, the poor man, how much more so the one who is raised up by Christ? How can he not live for eternity when life eternal has lifted him up, when Christ has assumed him totally to himself, when he belongs totally to the Word and his life is hidden in Jesus? (*In Ps.* 118.15.26).

2. *Receive me (Suscipe me)*. *Suscipere* means to take something very carefully and lifting it up, taking it to oneself, embracing it, cradling it in one's hand, and covering it. The father of the family receives the child after birth, and this means he accepts it. Out of the baptismal font one receives the child. God receives our oblation. The word *suscipere* is also used by Christ: he has accepted human nature, he has taken our sins onto himself.

Suscipere occurs often in the Vulgate. "From my mother's womb you have accepted me" (Ps 138 [139]:13). "I praise you, Lord, for you accepted me" (Ps 29 [30]:2). In particular, we can recall the last word of Stephen: "Lord Jesus, receive my spirit!" (Acts 7:59). Ambrose provides an extensive explanation of the verse in Psalm 118 (119):116:

> Come, then, Lord Jesus, seek your servant, seek your weary sheep. . . . Come, seek the one that has gone astray, come without dogs, come without wicked laborers, come without hirelings . . . come without heralds; for a long time I am awaiting your coming (28) . . . seek me, find me, lift me up, carry me. . . . In kindness lift him up when you have found him . . . and place him on your shoulders (29). . . . Lift me up (*suscipe me*) in that flesh which fell in Adam. . . . Carry me on your cross, which is the salvation of those who go astray. In it alone is rest for the weary, on it alone shall live those who are dying (30) (*In Ps.* 118.22.28-30).

In the course of the old sacrifice of the Mass, the prayer "Receive Holy Trinity" (*Suscipe Sancta Trinitas*) followed, then "May the Lord receive" (*Suscipiat Dominus*). In the Eucharist the priest selects from the gifts bread and wine that he wants to use for the celebration; he removes them from profane use. In the same way, the one making profession becomes an offering. His or her reception occurs through the act of the church who prays with and over him or her.

3. *According to your word.* The Lord's inviting word called a person onto this path. We can also think of all the words of Sacred Scripture, and especially of those that call us to follow Christ and that, at the same time, contain a promise. Hildemar explains: "Lord, it is your word in which you say: 'Whoever leaves everything that he has will receive a hundredfold.' And see, because of this word, because of your command I left the world" (542). Mary's response to the message of the angel is similar: "Behold, I am the handmaid of the Lord. May it be done to me according to your word" (Luke 1:38).

4. *And I shall live.* Hilary says: "For he knows that he has not yet lived, he has yet to live. According to the apostle our life is hidden in Christ (Col 3:3) . . . Receive me (*suscipe me*)" (*In Ps.* 118.15.7). The Lord invited us by asking: "Do you want true and eternal life?" (Prol 14–17, 20). "I shall live," that is, live in the fullest sense: it is a new life that Christ gives to everyone who enters into his sacrifice. The promise of life is again a reference to baptism.[61] After Christ acted in someone, this person can begin to act in Christ and say: " I live, but not I, Christ lives in me" (cf. Gal 2:19).

5. *Do not disappoint me in my expectation/hope.* "To expect" (*expectare*) means to look out, to stretch one's head out. It is a very vital hope. The same

word occurs once again in 49.7: "He is to look forward to holy Easter." What does the young monastic expect? In many expectations, he or she will be disappointed, humiliated, especially when expecting something God does not want to grant. The more we concentrate our expectations on what God promises, the less we will be disappointed, the more we can joyfully hope (cf. Rom 8:19-25).[62] When the monastic is seeking God (v. 7), he or she can be confident: "Before you call, I will say: 'Here I am'" (Prol 18). The Messiah is called "hope/expectation of the peoples." In him we also find the fulfillment of all our expectations and a full life. "No eye has seen and no ear has heard what God has prepared for those who love him" (4.76, 1 Cor 2:9).

The gestures underscore the content of the *Suscipe*: standing with hands raised for the first part, the novice throws him- or herself into the arms of the Father, his or her God;[63] kneeling for the second part, one is available as servant to one's Lord.

It is our custom to sing this verse when a sister or a brother is dying. Here, as in baptism, this verse has its fullest meaning. Yet it can also accompany us during our entire life as an ejaculatory prayer expressing our dedication, hope, and availability.

It is only right that the one who was received by Christ in this way, is now also embraced by the community. This is shown in what follows.

6. *The entire community is to repeat [the verse] three times and to add the "Glory be to the Father."* We might assume that the community changes the verse into "receive him." But all sing three times: "Receive me!" This shows a profound unity with the novice. By singing the verse three times it penetrates the heart more deeply (cf. 35.16-18; 38.3). In RM, only the abbot recites the verse: "Confirm, O God, what you have done in us." RM also does not add a "Glory be to the Father." We may assume that Benedict here wants to underscore the trinitarian dimension that marks the entire ceremony in itself. "Receive me": the dedication of the novice is directed to Christ and is done in the Holy Spirit and toward the Father. When profession is made during a celebration of the Eucharist, the "Glory to the Father" is even more fitting. From this prayer, a trinitarian interpretation of the preceding verse was later developed, for example: "Receive me, Father, according to your Word (Son), and I shall live (in the Holy Spirit).[64]

V. 23: Then the new brother prostrates himself
at the feet of each [community member]
that they are to pray for him,
and from this day he is counted as a member of the community.

1. *The new brother.* For the first time the word "brother" is being used for the candidate, and this is probably done with deliberation. In older rules

we cannot find such an intensification from "the one newly arriving" to "the novice," the "one to be received" and finally to "brother." The Master uses the word "brother" already at the beginning of the entrance (87.1, 4, 25; 88.1, etc.). By handing over the petition and by being received by Christ at the altar the candidate has become a brother or sister. This constitutes the monastic community that receives its new members each time from the altar in the celebration of profession-Eucharist. Brotherhood in Christ is a gift even before it is a task. Here at the altar it is fundamentally and ever newly given. On the other hand, if brotherly or sisterly love is lacking, it is a call that, figuratively speaking, we must go together to the altar. The community lives from the sacrifice of Christ and from the fact that the individual members and all together enter into the surrender of Christ to the Father and for the salvation of the many. Here they find again and again the strength to reconcile with each other and to begin anew.[65]

2. *Then the new brother prostrates himself at the feet of each community member.* In RB, prostration can signify penance, a plea for reconciliation and prayer (cf. 71.8; 67.3f.). One makes a prostration before a guest so as to reverence Christ in the guest (cf. commentary on 53.7, p. 183–184 below). According to the interpretations of the Fathers, this means humbling ourselves before another person and stating that we are the one receiving something. It is an act of dedication, of abandon, even of surrender. Jesus himself knelt before his disciples to wash their feet (John 13:1-15); he even stooped down into the dust of death. Thus, prostrating is also a sign of entering into the emptying of Jesus, the death of Jesus. Smaragdus says the novice is "like a dead person who, having been received, lives eternally" (cf. commentary on this verse).

The path led to the oratory and to its center, the altar, and from the altar it leads to the individual monastics, more concretely to the feet of each individual one. No one is excluded. The altar always directs us back to serving the brothers and sisters.

3. *That they are to pray for him.* This is the first time after having repeated the *Suscipe* that the individual community members are explicitly said to be active. The expression is no longer the passive "one [does]," or "it is done," but "they are to pray." Accepting their responsibility, the individual members support the new member. Profession is a mutual engagement. The new member can count on being carried by the prayer of the community; this will prove its value in difficulties (cf. 27.4; 28.4, to pray for someone; cf. *Vit. Patr.* V.13.13).

This short ritual presumably ended with the kiss of peace as a seal of prayer (cf. commentary on 53.4, p. 179–182 below; also 35.15-17; 38.2-4). Tradition later expanded this "praying." Smaragdus lists: Glory to the Father,

Our Father. Then the abbot says the following prayer: "Receive, O Lord, this your servant so that he, received by you, is saved from the present world and in the coming one may delight in being rewarded by you." Then the new member gives the kiss of peace to all the others (cf. commentary on this verse). Later, additional psalms are added. (Hildemar, 547). At this point, the Mass preface also was inserted.

4. *And from this day on.* The "pure" text (RB [Hanslik] 150) reads: "from this hour on." This points to the importance of this event. Implicitly, Benedict already indicated this when he called the novice "the new brother." This hour marks a change in the life of a person. A new life begins as member of a community through his or her special belonging to Christ.

5. *He is to be counted as a member of the community.* He becomes a full member of the community, officially and legally belonging to it. Presumably this is given a particular emphasis because it is in opposition to RM and Cassian. There, the new brother, if he was a layperson, was tested for yet another year before he definitely became a member.[66] Benedict does not mention the deanery (perhaps a sign that it was disappearing?), but the *congregatio*, the community. Thus, the brother is also under the abbot, although it is not clearly stated that he is assigned to the abbot or a senior member.

Up to verse 23, the unity of the liturgical celebration is impressive. First there is the promise before God, the petition is handed over directly to Christ by placing it on the altar, and furthermore, Christ is petitioned in the *Suscipe* to receive the novice. The one making profession enters into Christ's surrender for the glory of the Father and for the salvation of the many. Logically this leads to the community and to responsibility for the world. The eucharistic event takes a similar course: petition, sacrifice, doxology, Communion, sending out to mission.

V. 24: **If he has possessions,**
   he is to distribute them earlier to the poor
   or to will them to the monastery
   through a legal document without reserving anything for himself.

1. *Earlier.* This is a very vague expression, although Benedict usually is very careful to express himself with precision. This renunciation of possessions may have occurred during the preparatory ritual (vv. 14-16), and the document could have been incorporated into the petition. Presumably, Benedict inserted this remark here because it is to clarify the connection to the clothing with the habit. In doing so, Benedict is in line with Pachomius and Cassian who connect the clothing with the renunciation of possessions.[67]

2. *If he has possessions.* While RM discusses the question of possessions at the very outset in great length,[68] Benedict's brevity is a welcome contrast. He directs more attention to the person of the candidate and his free surrender than to the possessions. In his demands, Benedict is equally radical, but less verbose (cf. 33; 54; 59). In RB 59.6 he also implies that he had many bitter experiences. Having possessions is, however, not a necessary prerequisite for making profession, and renouncing one's possessions is simply part of one's personal surrender.

3. *He is to distribute [them] to the poor.* The first of the two possibilities of relinquishing possessions was practiced in monasticism from its beginnings according to Christ's word: "Go and sell your possessions and give the money to the poor. You will then have treasure in heaven. Afterward, come back and follow me" (Matt 19:21). The *Life* of Antony says that "he pondered how the apostles left everything and followed the savior, how the faithful in Acts sold their property. . . ." With such thoughts he entered the church and heard this very verse from the Gospel. "He immediately left the church and donated his properties, which he had inherited from his ancestors, to the residents of his town. . . . He sold all his remaining possessions and gave [the proceeds] to the poor" (*Vit. Ant.* 2). The possessions of the one entering the community are first to be given to the poor. By renouncing one's possessions, one also renounces the possibilities to help the poor oneself. Taking care of the poor thus is no longer done by an individual, but by the community and in the name of the community (cf. e.g., RB 4.14; 31.9; 53.15).

4. *Or he is to will them to the monastery through a legal document.* Literally, the text says "by a solemn donation," meaning a legally valid donation. Similarly, Benedict says in 59.5 that parents who want to donate possessions to the monastery are to write out a deed of gift (*donatio*).[69] In these lines we can sense that there were some unpleasant incidents. If the candidate should leave later, he should not be able to reclaim his possessions (cf. commentary on the petition).

The possibility to will something to the monastery was not provided everywhere, on the contrary! Cassian states that it is better to accept nothing from someone entering, since this donation might cause pride in the newcomer who might not want to be put on a par with poorer monastics. Cassian, too, speaks of "various experiences" (*Inst.* IV.4). Since, in contrast to this, Benedict provides the possibility of a donation to the monastery, we can assume that material necessity urged him to take this course; his monastery was collectively poor. The following chapter provides the possibility to give "alms" to the monastery (59.4). Alms are given to the poor, and thus the monastery is on the same level as the poor. From this and other indications we can conclude that Benedict did not consider economic poverty as an ideal, but rather as a difficulty he was trying to remedy (cf. on 48.7f.; 33; 2.33-35).

5. *Without reserving anything for himself.* In Latin, the word *nihil* (nothing) recalls the tenor of chapters 33, 54, and 59. Benedict is very strict concerning personal possessions. The monastic is not "to retain anything";[70] positively, this means: the monastic wants to live without anxious care, without distrusting the community, but rather depending upon it. One has no need to procure supplies on which one could live. One now can expect all the necessities from God, from the community, and also from the father or mother of the monastery (33.5). One wants to prefer nothing to the love of Christ (4:21), not one's own possessions, not even oneself. One may recall Philippians 3:7f.: "But whatever gains I had, these I have come to consider a loss because of Christ. More than that, I even consider everything as a loss because of the supreme good of knowing Christ Jesus my Lord. For his sake I have accepted the loss of all things and I consider them so much rubbish that I may gain Christ."

V. 25: He knows that, from this day on,
he does not even have the right to dispose
of his own body.

1. *He knows that from this day on.* This is clear to him in both head and heart. Similarly, verse 12 says: "that he knows what is at stake when entering." He is aware of the significance and the consequences of this day and this hour.

2. *No right to dispose over one's own body.* In RB, the word "own" (*proprium*) occurs several times as contrast to that which is communal. It can designate one's own will that obstructs obedience toward God and the community, or one's own possessions, that which is one's "own," what is excluded and is opposed to the fact that "all things are common to all" (33).

Who has power (*potestas*) over the monastic? It is God, the one who is "powerful" (*potens*), but who exercises this power through intermediaries, the community, the brothers/sisters, the abbot/prioress. In the same way, Cassian says in one breath that the monastic "disposes of all his or her possessions" and realizes that "he or she is no longer his or her own master nor has any power over him- or herself."[71] The Rule of Basil explains the severity of Benedict. Basil answers the questions whether one is allowed to have something of one's own in community by saying that this contradicts the Acts of the Apostles that state all things belong to all. "Thus when someone says that something is his own, he separates himself from the Church of God and also from the love of God who taught through words and deeds that one is to give one's life for one's friends, not simply external possessions."[72]

In 33.3-4, Benedict follows a similar train of thought: The monastics are to own nothing, neither . . . nor . . . nothing. "They do not even have the right to dispose of their bodies and their will." To reserve nothing for oneself, to manage nothing on one's own—Paul uses similar words about marriage: "The wife does not have authority over her body, but rather her husband" (1 Cor 7:4). The union the monastic enters is similarly close. The last free act of disposing was the renunciation of possessions. Now one has no longer any "power" over one's things, body, place, will. This summarizes indirectly the content of all the promises, in particular the promises of celibacy and of poverty, but also that of obedience.

3. *The monastic as servant,* even as slave. In RB 5.3, Benedict summarizes the "holy service which they have promised." Before entering the novitiate, the candidate was asked whether he or she wanted to serve under the law of the Rule (v. 10). At the beginning of the Prologue, one was enjoined to take up weapons in the service of Christ, the true king (Prol 3) and to enter "the school of the Lord's service" (Prol 45). In monastic literature, it is customary to designate profession as the entrance into the service of Christ.[73] This contains the old idea of human bondage. Here it is not simply a question of being dependent in one's actions, but rather of a human being belonging to the Lord with everything one is and has. An old commentary explains the *Suscipe* in this way: "Take me into your service." The monastic begs God to open the door and to receive him or her among his servants.[74]

In the New Testament, all Christians are called *servi* (Greek *douloi*).[75] They are no longer slaves of sin, but belong to Christ and thus, in obeying him, are truly free (cf. Rom 6:16-19; 1 Cor 7:22; 6:19). Paul in particular claims the title "servant" (*doulos*) for himself when, at the beginning of his letters, he introduces himself as "a servant of Jesus Christ." This is a title of honor that has a long tradition (cf. Pss 105 [104]:42; 89 [88]:4; 27 [26]:9) and expresses the fact that, just like the faithful of the Old Testament, someone is totally seized by God, belongs to God, is at God's service, allows God to use one as a tool in God's saving work. The servant's typical attitude is one of listening and obeying.

When called by God, Mary calls herself a "maid servant" of the Lord (*doulè, ancilla*). "Be it done to me!" An attitude similar to the one in the text of the annunciation (Luke 1:26-38) occurs in monastic profession. Upon being called by God, someone responds: "Here I am; I am at your service; let it be done to me; I am yours; you can use me as you see fit; you have all the rights; I am your maid, your servant."

This service is a response to the service Christ did for us. "The Son of Man did not come to be served, but to serve and to give his own life as ransom for the many" (Matt 20:28; cf. foot washing). He serves us first; he is

God's servant who humbles himself in the courage to serve. The response of the monastic is service that, according to Benedict, comprises his or her entire life (Prol 45). The Rule emphasizes obedience in particular (Prol 3, 40; 1.2), but also the *opus Dei* (18.3; 16.2), as well as mutual service (35; 36), and the service for the people outside the monastery (53.13, 18).

With Paul we can summarize this concept in this way: to let the Lord make decisions about me, to listen with full attention and to obey, to become a servant to all (cf. 1 Cor 9:19-21; 2 Cor 4:5). This also sheds light on the three criteria mentioned in verse 7: eagerness for the *opus Dei*, obedience, and service. All this is contained in the concept of being a servant.

4. *The content of the obligations taken on at profession.* Too often the profession "formula" has been separated from the entire profession ceremony. Some saw five vows, others three, and yet others just one. There are significant differences of opinion.[76] Certainly Benedict is not yet familiar with the systematization of the three classical vows that then can be discussed separately according to the material proper to each of them. In addition, the concept of "vow" (*votum*) also had another meaning different from our present one. As we saw above, each part of verse 17 can include the others; they penetrate each other.[77] All three vows are concerned with community, Rule, and abbot, and with following Christ and service to Christ. The "promise" refers mainly to living in community. What we today call the vows is contained more in the petition and in the act of placing the petition on the altar. The person's dedication is not first expressed in words, but in a gesture that is a liturgical act, an act of revering God. The obligation is taken before God and his saints, it will be valid for the person's lifetime and permanently incorporates the person into the community. Through profession, the monastic no longer belongs to oneself; one is now a servant of Christ and of the monastic brothers/sisters.

V. 26: At once, therefore, still in the oratory,
he is stripped of the things he is wearing
and clothed with the things of the monastery.

1. *At once, therefore, still in the oratory.* It matters to Benedict that the clothing be connected with the profession, and he does not want to have the clothing only a year later as is, for example, the case in RM. "Therefore" (*ergo*) shows that the clothing is a result of what precedes it, that is, of renouncing one's possessions or of being counted as a member of the community. Verse 26 is the final act or even the culmination of the ceremony. It still takes place in the oratory. The word "in the oratory" builds a bridge to the beginning of the profession ceremony (v. 17: inclusion!).

2. *He is stripped—clothed*. Benedict composed the two movements as perfect parallels to show that these two steps, which complement each other, are inseparable. The monastic is passive, allowing things to take their course. One no longer wants to claim any right to dispose over oneself. The symbolic significance of such an attitude is less clear for us today. The oldest direction for profession states: "Then they strip him of his worldly clothes and clothe him with the habit of the monks" (Pachomius, *Praec.* 49). And Cassian says: "He is brought to the council of the brothers, stripped of what is his in their midst, and clothed in the garb of the monastery at the hands of the abba" (*Inst.* IV.5). A little later, Cassian says that through this, the one who entered is to understand

> not only that he has been despoiled of all his former things but also that he has put off all worldly pride and has stooped to the poverty and want of Christ—as a monk he should know "that on this day you have died to the world and to its deeds and desires . . . and have been crucified to this world and this world to you" (*Inst.* IV.34).

It is a sort of death that, at the same time, is a passage to a new life. The new habit indicates a new life. From that day on, the monastic has resolutely set out on the path of following Christ; one is wearing the habit of Christ as a sign that one has put on Christ.

3. *His own things—the things of the monastery*. We may be very surprised that Benedict expresses himself in a manner that, to us, seems to lack reverence. Other monastic fathers speak in this connection of the habit, clothes, the holy garment, or the garment of Christ.[78] Benedict does not insinuate that the garments are sacralized nor does he speak theoretically about the significance of the garment. The things the brother or sister owned and wore are contrasted with the things of the monastery. Things (*res*): this is the same word used in verse 24 for the possessions. In verse 26 they designate the clothes that are part of the things one gives up and from which one frees oneself. One is then embedded, as it were, in all the things, the things of the monastery. That is, one is given everything by the monastery, not only the clothes; one now belongs fully to the community. (cf. Cassian, *Inst.* IV.5). It seems that Benedict's first concern is not a sacred garment, but rather the connection to the community and the renunciation of possessions as its prerequisite. Both ideas are linked in a way similar to RB 33: Monastics do not own anything, thus they can live a communal life in which everything belongs to all in common. There they may also expect to receive all necessities from the father/superior of the monastery (33.5).

By briefly reviewing the monastic tradition, we may see more clearly how Benedict views the *monastic habit*.

Seen in human terms, the monastic habit is a covering and a protection against cold and heat.[79] In a dualistic spirituality, for example, that of the Master, it emphasizes the separation from the world (cf. passages mentioned in n. 78). Basil calls it the garment of the Christian (*Reg.* 11); it allows to recognize them as such, and this is a witness.

The monastic habit designates someone as member of a community without any distinctions of class or race. RB 2.20 refers to Paul: "All of you who are baptized in Christ, have put on Christ (as a garment). There are no longer Jews and Greeks, slaves and free, neither man nor woman, for you are all one in Christ" (Gal 3:27f., cf. Augustine, *Praec.* I.3). This garment is a gift; it is given by the abbot/prioress. The monastic lives from the gift and does not get necessary items from somewhere else; he or she wants to depend on the superior and the community.

The garment has a connection to Christ. It indicates that someone has renounced possessions and has "stooped to the poverty and want of Christ" (Cassian, *Inst.* IV.5). Already before the habit had become a distinctive mark for monastics, authors emphasized that their garment should be poor and simple (Basil, *Reg.* 11). The monastic wants to take off his old being with its false dependencies on family, possessions, honor, and one's own will, and above all, he wants to lay down sin. This is a kind of death (cf. also 2 Cor 5:2-7: dying as laying down the garment of one's body). Accordingly, later rituals transformed this stripping into a kind of burial ceremony (complete with pall, funeral dirges, requiem, candles, and so on). At the same time, clothing, however, also signifies putting on the new person. Ambrose says: "Take this garment in order to put on Christ" (*Inst. vg.* 16.102). To become a new person means to walk the way of Christ, to be raised with him. Therefore, the monastic habit is also called "sign of resurrection" (*Vit. Bas.* 4).

Certainly, all this occurs in a foundational manner in baptism upon which profession is founded. The connection between baptism and profession becomes clearer when we reflect about the baptismal practices of the early church. In the *Life* of Basil we read: "He took of his clothes, and with them doubtlessly also his old being; and he descended into the water and was baptized."[80] Those to be baptized are to enter the baptismal waters naked after having taken off all finery. Cyril of Jerusalem reminds them of how Christ was stripped on the cross.[81] Thus it is not surprising that a saying of the Fathers states: "The power which I saw appearing over the baptism, I also saw appearing over the habit of the monk as he was receiving it" (*Vit. Patr.* VI.1.9). Later, great emphasis was placed upon the blessing of the habit. Especially the Eastern Church emphasizes that receiving the habit constitutes a sort of consecration: God accepts the human person and confirms his or her commitment. It is more a gift of God than an act of the human person.[82] Just as in baptism a person is bonded to Christ, so profession is a deepening of this belonging, especially on the subjective side. The person ratifies the baptismal event. In this sense, profession was at times called a "second baptism." This can be misunderstood, but also understood rightly as a an image of taking the baptismal reality seriously.[83]

In RM, tonsure occurs before the clothing with the habit. Benedict seemed to know about tonsure, but does not mention it here (cf. 1.7). Sometimes a new name was given at profession. Already Hildemar mentions that the candidate's head was covered for three days and that he had to remain silent. On the third day the head is uncovered and the candidate may take Communion.[84] These are additional indications of the symbolism of death and resurrection.

The baptismal symbolism of the profession ceremony is obvious. It was already present in the first part of the chapter in the various stages of testing, the reading of the law, and the handing over of the Rule. The "promise" resembles the baptismal promises.[85] The Fathers call baptism also a "pact" or *sacramentum militiae* as in baptism one becomes a "soldier for Christ" (cf. Excursus: *Militia*, p. 23 above). The clothing in particular shows this similarity: one descends naked into the baptismal waters, is buried with Christ, and clothed with a new garment (Christ). According to a ritual book from Monte Cassino, the candidate lying on the pall was told: "Awake, you sleeper and rise from the dead, and Christ will be your light" (Eph 5:14, an old baptismal hymn). Sometimes a candle was given also.

It is striking how sober and terse Benedict's text is. The habit is not sacralized, it only signals renouncing one's own possessions and handing them over to the community and Christ.

V. 27: **The clothes, however, which were taken from him,**
are put into the wardrobe for safekeeping.

V. 28: **For should he ever accede to the devil's prompting**
and leave the monastery—which God forbid—
one is to strip him of the monastery's things
and send him away.

V. 29: **Yet the petition, which the abbot took from the altar,**
is not returned, but will be kept in the monastery.

1. *The clothes, however, which were taken from him, are put into the wardrobe for safekeeping.* This corresponds to tradition. While the Master is primarily concerned that the holy habit is not soiled, Benedict remains silent about this point. Cassian says that, if the monk perseveres, his clothes will later be given to the poor (*Inst.* IV.6).

2. For should he ever accede to the devil's prompting and leave the monastery—which God forbid—one is to strip him of the monastery's things and send him away. After the impressive ceremony, this verse seems almost too realistic. How is it possible, in this moment, to think of the possibility that the monastic may want to leave monastic life after he or she made a life-long commitment! Benedict knows the depths of the human heart even though his dismay is also palpable in this verse.[86] If the monastic agrees to leave, this can only happen because the devil insinuates it and because the monastic goes along with him. According to the teaching of the Rule, he should have "rejected the cunning devil from the sight of his heart, should have destroyed him [the devil] seizing the brood of his thoughts and crushing them on Christ" (Prol 28). This would have helped in temptations (cf. also 4.50; 46.5f.). In the first centuries, people found it difficult to conceive that someone would leave the faith "in good faith" and even more that someone would have good reasons for leaving the monastery after having made profession.

He is "sent away." If he truly makes common cause with the devil, it follows that he can no longer be part of the community and has to part with the "things" of the monastery. Yet one has to consider what preceded this: admonitions, excommunication, the help of elders (*senpectae*), the prayers of all community members, deep concern of the abbot/prioress (cf. RB 27–29). Cassian allows to send away a monastic after profession if he or she is malcontent or disobedient (*Inst.* IV.6). Benedict takes the obligation of the community toward the individual member very seriously.

3. Yet the petition, which the abbot took from the altar, is not returned and will be kept in the monastery. In contrast to the clothes, the petition is kept (and with this word the chapter ends). In this hour, something occurred that cannot be simply erased. The Master is so concerned about the document that the candidate cannot reclaim anything of his possessions (cf. 89.27; 89.31-33; 90.94). Since Benedict requires a petition, even when the candidate has no possessions, preserving it has a deeper meaning. If the monastic becomes unfaithful, the petition remains testifying against him or her. What was placed on the altar cannot be reclaimed. Yet one can also think of all the other community members. At the end of the ceremony, all their petitions were taken from the altar and have been preserved as a written plan for life that needs to be translated into life and whose fulfillment must be the concern of the abbot/prioress as well as of the monastics. In the "lifelong community of the monastery the profession document must be preserved alive. . . . Together with the prostration and the clothing this preservation belongs to the three greatest symbols of reception."[87]

Conclusion

At first sight, the Scriptures do not seem to have an important part in this chapter. Yet, after having interpreted the individual verses, it is evident how the Scriptures are the native soil from which the individual statements grew. The only two explicit Scripture quotes can be used as titles for the two main parts of the chapter. We could entitle the first part, "Test whether the spirits are from God" (1 John 4:1); the second, "Receive me, O Lord" (Ps 118 [119]:116).

We can go through the chapter once more in the light of the various biblical allusions:
insistent knocking: cf. Luke 11:5-10;
seeking God: cf. Ps 14 (15):1-3; Ps 118 (119):2; Wis 1:1ff.;
the hard yet light yoke, the narrow path: cf. Matt 11:28-30; 7:13-14;
the Lord's service: cf. 1 Thess 5:8-9; Eph 6:10-19.

In the second part:
to renounce everything and give it to the poor: cf. Matt 19:21;
not having the right to dispose over oneself: cf. 1 Cor 7:4;
finally stripping of the clothes and clothing connected with baptismal
   symbols: Gal 3:27-29; Rom 6:3-19.

All these texts are connected with the imitation of Christ and with Christian community respectively. The selection of texts with its emphasis on the psalms, the Gospel of Matthew, and the early Christian epistles corresponds to the whole of the Rule.

In reviewing the entire chapter, we can see more clearly how it is placed in the Rule as a whole. In particular, this chapter is related to the Prologue. There, the path to God, the path of life with its narrow beginning, is presented. It is necessary to persevere on this path. Being ready to serve Christ includes and presupposes listening and obeying, and the "prayer" that stands at the beginning of all good works. Although the inviting voice of the Lord in the Prologue seems quite different from the attitude of the monastery toward the new candidate, the basic concern is the same: that those who are truly called are being led to a total commitment.

In the *chapter about receiving guests* (RB 53), the external situation is similar: people who come from the world are being received. Yet there is a striking difference: While the guests are being received as Christ, entrance is not to be easily granted to a new member. While all honor and love are being extended to guests, the newly entering monastic is subjected to insults. While the guests are met immediately and with the eagerness of love, the candidate is left at the gate for several days. Yet the guests are taken only to the oratory (53.8), while the candidate will go all the way to the altar. He or she is to grow into the attitude of Jesus Christ to become capable to serve the guests as Christ did, to wash their feet, to show them humility and reverence and, in particular, to care for the poor.

The first step is the rejection of the "world," meaning concretely, the rejection of possessions, of family, of one's own will, and of ambition. The Fathers called this *xeniteia, peregrinatio*, pilgrimage, traveling through a foreign land. One becomes a stranger like Abraham who left his family, the ancestral home, and his homeland. Because he was a stranger, he was able to be "friendly to strangers," was able to practice *philoxenia* (love of strangers, hospitality). What is described in RB 58 is the prerequisite for serving people (RB 53). We have to be detached from possessions, otherwise we are not able to turn our attention to the poor. We have to be detached from close family ties, otherwise we are not able to direct our attention without exception (and beyond all family ties) to all those who need us. We have to be detached from the desire for power and honor, otherwise we are not able to do true service and to wash the feet of others. In this sense, the "distance from the world" is the prerequisite for a qualified "openness to the world," that is, the distance from the world of having and of pride is the prerequisite for openness to the world that is in need of our service. The spiritual journey in RB 58 leads from an external distance through inner purification to the surrender to Christ, to identifying with him. From there the new member is led into the community and, together with the community, to the service to all those who are in need.

On the surface, the *community* does not appear very often in this chapter. Yet already in the novitiate community is being practiced. The criteria for whether someone has a true calling include the ability of living a communal life as well as eagerness for the *opus Dei*, for obedience (which Benedict extends to include mutual obedience), and for service (cf. RB 35; 36). While the candidate at first faces a vague "one [does, etc.]," this impersonal counterpart changes more and more into a group of individuals. At first, the novice master stands out, then the abbot/prioress is mentioned in the ceremony. During the profession the community ("in the presence of all") begins to be an active partner; the community repeats the *Suscipe*, and the individual monastics pray for the new brother/sister. Renouncing possessions and the right to dispose of oneself make true community possible. The clothing with "the things of the monastery," too, shows the communal aspect. The petition remains irrevocably in the monastery. All the promises (v. 17) refer to the community: stability in community together with which one begins the journey; *conversatio morum* as a communal striving under Rule and abbot/prioress; obedience not only to the abbot/prioress,

but also to the community. We are reminded of the description of cenobites in chapter 1.2. What the candidate practices, including perseverance
in rough and difficult times, purifies his or her love, patience, and stead-
fastness. The brother or sister is led from the altar to the community. "In
Christ we are all one" (2.20).

This chapter brings out the important components of Benedictine life:
liturgy, community, *Christ*. He is not mentioned explicitly, but is present in
the community, in the abbot/prioress, in the altar, in all the signs of his in-
carnation, his sacrifice, his surrender, and his openness to strangers (cf.
chapter on RB 53). The newcomer wants to follow Christ, to become his
servant, to belong to him and thus to share his fate. Thus, he or she patiently bears difficulties, and remains under the yoke that sets him or her
free. With one's petition, one hands oneself over to him, asking him to receive one. One enters into Christ's emptying (expressed symbolically in the
prostration), and is determined, like Christ, not to retain anything. All this
is part of concretizing the expression "to prefer nothing to Christ" (72.11).
And Christ will lead all of them together—together with all human beings—to the Father (cf. 72.12).

Notes

1. Cf. Jerome, *Ep.* 125.20.5; and 71.2.3; Leander, *De Inst.vg.* 21.

2. Cf. Cassian, *Conf.* III.6; Caesarius, *s.* 81.4 in connection with *s.* 81.1-3; Ambrose,
De Abr. II.1.2-3.

3. Cf. the title of *Reg.* 7: to "establish . . . the profession of virginity"; *Ep.* 119.19 requires a clear and explicit *professio* (profession) rather than a tacit one.

4. This document dates from the time when Schenute was abbot; cf. Steidle, *Die
Regel Benedikts*, 287, also for the profession formula, ibid., 286.

5. Cf. *Reg. 4 Patr.* II.18-35: someone who leaves the world must first renounce his
riches. He spends a week outside the gates and is being tested for humility and patience.
The Rule is read to him; he is being instructed about monastic life. *Reg. Mac.* 23 mentions the reading of the Rule and renouncing possessions. Ceasarius's Rule for nuns
(*Reg. vg.* 2.4-5.58) has the following elements: renouncing the world, stability in the
monastery, frequent reading of the Rule, being tested by an older sister for a year, only
then change of clothes as the sign of renouncing possessions.

6. Because of differences in Latin and English, *if/whether* appear eleven times in the
English translation (both RB 80 and the one here) in the first part, and only three times
in the second part as v. 28 uses an inversion rather than a sentence beginning with *if*.

7. The list of chapter titles that can be found in old manuscripts uses the Latin expression *De ordine*, order, manner. Cf. Dürig, *Disciplina*, article "Disciplina," RAC.

8. Cf. Pachomius, *Praec.* 49; Caesarius, *Reg. vg.* 2; *Reg. Mac.* 23; *Reg. 4 Patr.* II.16; RM
90.1; 87.49-52; 90.65, 70.

9. Cf. 7.30 (literally) "He waits for our conversion." Benedict at times also calls the
act of entering conversion, e.g., in 63.7; 2.18. Yet generally he calls monastic life *conver-*

satio, even in passages where RM has *conversio* (compare, e.g., RB 63.1 with RM 11.76; RB 1.3 with RM 1.3). The Master does not use the word *conversatio.*

10. Cf. the title of Pachomius's *Praec.*: "The precepts of our father Pachomius, a man of God, who founded monastic life for cenobites . . . (*conversationem coenobiorum*); *Reg. 4 Patr.* Prol; Caesarius, *Reg. vg.* 58, and *Reg. mon.* 1.

11. Cf. RM 90.1: ". . . let him not be too readily believed."

12. RM 90.71 has only the first part: "Do not trust every spirit, but test them first" (first is inserted by the Master). Cassian uses this quote in connection with the discernment of spirits, *Conf.* I.20.2.

13. Cf. Pachomius, *Praec.* 49; Basil, *Reg.* 6; Augustine, *De op. mon.* XXII.25; RM 87; Fructuosus, *Reg. com.* 18; *Reg. Tarn.* 1; Cassian, *Conf.* I.19. Cf. also Hildemar, 533; Smaragdus's comment on this verse.

14. Cassian, *Inst.* IV.3.1: ten days, and *Conf.* XX.1.3: many days, *Inst.* IV.30. 3: longer; *Reg. 4 Patr.* II.25: a week. The Master is not clear about the length of time.

15. Cf. Vulgate: *Si ille perseveraverit pulsans . . . Petite et dabitur vobis; quaerite et invenietis; pulsate et aperietur vobis.* The closest parallel is *Reg. 4 Patr.* II.27. Cf. also *Vit. Patr.* V.5.15.

16. Cassian, *Inst.* IV.3; Hildemar, 533, speaks of suspicions; in *Vit. Fulg* (Ferrandus) 9 we read that he humbly kissed the hand that rejected him and asked: "Open the door of the monastery for me." And after first scorning him, the elder allowed him to stay with them for a few days.

17. Cf. the rather drastic speeches in RM 90.6-66 and 87.5-24, also *Hist. Laus.* 18.12, 13; *Vit. Pach.* 6.

18. It is possible that Benedict here takes a clue from the ideal of the philosopher who patiently bears injuries, cf. Boethius, *Consolatio* II.7.20 (CC 94.34). Cf. also M. Elizalde, "Nota sobre RB 7, 35 y 58, 3: Tolerar las unjurias," in StMon 11 (1969) 107–114.

19. *Hist. Laus.* 32.5; *Vit. Pach.* 22; Justinian, *Corp. Nov.* 5.2; 123.35; Gregory the Great, *Ep.* 10.24.

20. RM 88.7-9. In Cassian, *Inst.* IV.7, the candidate is entrusted to the porter for a year and helps with taking care of the guests.

EXCURSUS REGARDING THE TWO INTERPRETATIONS of space and time in vv. 4-11:

> *Common interpretation* (most RB commentators)
> 4–5 days at the gate, some days in the guest quarters, then novitiate (v. 5);
> after 2 months of novitiate: first reading of the Rule with ritual "This is the law . . ." (vv. 9ff.), and the candidate is *led back* to the novitiate.

DIFFICULTIES with this interpretation:
- It is surprising that "some days" in the guest quarters is so vague. What is their purpose?
- It is strange that there is no ritual before entering the novitiate and no conditions are mentioned as is the case in the other important steps.
- What does the solemn "Enter . . . leave freely" (v. 10) mean? Where shall he enter if he is simply led back?
- Does the expression "he is to be led" mean led to the novice cell (*ducatur*)? It is only a *leading back.*

Second interpretation (cf. Hildemar, Vogüé, Yeo; I am joining them also):

4–5 days at the gate; some days = two months in the guest quarters (compared with 2–3 years, cf. also RM 88.3).

- Vv. 5-6 are an insert. Benedict does this quite often as if composing by headings. The "guest quarters" induce him to mention the "novice quarters" immediately in the following verse.
- It is striking that vv. 5-6 suddenly speak of novices in the plural while otherwise the novice is mentioned in the singular only. Moreover, these verses describe the two innovations which Benedict did not find in the older sources.
- Thus vv. 9-11 (promise, reading of the Rule, "this is the law. . .") are a good introductory ritual for entering the novitiate. Then the text continues logically: "He is led to the novitiate"; this is a decisive step, an important action.
- In this way the "enter—leave freely" receives its full meaning.
- The further division into 6 and 4 months is psychologically more meaningful. After this solemn ritual, the following period can be longer (6 months).
- Thus, we have three initiations: to the guest quarters, the novitiate, and then into the community when making profession, three gates, as it were, with specific preconditions. This also corresponds to the practice in our monasteries.

21. Unlike RM, Benedict's monastery has several "cells" [quarters]: for the infirm 36.7; for guests 53.21; for the porter 66.2; and here for the novices. A monastic with specific qualifications is assigned to each of them. While the word "novice" occurs in RM only in the singular, Benedict here mentions novices in the plural.

22. Pachomius, *Praec.* 49; RM 50.14, 43; 44.10; also Pachomius, *Praec.* 139f.; Smaragdus in his comment on this verse names psalms, hymns, and rules as the content of "meditating."

23. The Master never uses this word in a qualified sense. Two *apophthegmata* can illustrate its content: *Alph.* Zacharias, 2: "He found abbot Zacharias praying near the pond and saw the Spirit of God resting over him"; Isaac of Kellia, 2: "At present I have nothing to say to him, but if he wants, he can do what he sees me doing." Cf. also Cassian, *Inst.* IV.7: "he is assigned to a senior."

24. Cf. M. Casey, "Intentio cordis," p. 112f.

25. In RB, eagerness, care, keenness (*sollicitudo*) is first directed to human beings: the abbot is to show eagerness and care to the brothers (2.33, 39); the deans (21.2), and seniors must do this also (22.2-3); all are to show eagerness and care in mutual obedience (71.4). In most cases, eagerness and care are expressed in the behavior toward weaker ones—to novices (58.7), to excommunicated monastics (27, title and vv. 1, 5), the sick (36.7), the sick, children, and the poor (31.9), the poor and the strangers (53.15). Yet eagerness and care are also directed to the Liturgy of the Hours (47.1), to thoughts (7.18), to the observance of the Rule (65.17), and finally, to obedience and service (58.7).

26. *s.* 37.9; cf. Sainte-Marie, "Si revera."

27. *s.* 137.8.9.

28. Basil, *Reg.* 14, also *Reg. brev.* 157; cf. *Apophth.* Arsenios, 10: "If we seek God, he will show himself to us, and if we keep him, he will remain close to us."

29. For the following, cf. Turbessi, "*Quaerere Deum.*"

30. Vogüé, "Die drei Kriterien," 46; cf. Hausherr, "*Opus Dei*"; Cassian, *Inst.* IV.33; *Vit. Pach.* 25.

31. Cf. RM 90:5-11; Cassian has an entire list of examples, cf. *Inst.* IV.23-29; IV.3.; in *Inst.* IV.3 he says that, at the gate, the candidate needs to show perseverance in enduring trials.

32. Cf. Smaragdus on this verse, and Hildemar, 534, who list the various tasks. Cassian, *Inst.* IV.30. 4, mentions yard work and all "the tasks which to the brothers seemed quite difficult, menial and demeaning"; and *Reg. 4 Patr.* II.35 shows that the purpose of this was forming a true community: "but if [a noble] wishes to have one of his slaves with him, he should know that he no longer has him as a slave, but as a brother."

33. Cassian, *Conf.* XXIV.25.2; cf. *Reg. 4 Patr.* II.26; RM 90.3; 90.31.

34. Cf. Hippolytus, *Trad. ap.* 16–20 (SC 11.43-45).

35. Cf. Pachomius, *Praec.* 49 who speaks of teaching "practices and customs"; *Reg. Mac.* 23; Caesarius, *Reg. vg.* 58; RM 89.1-2; 87.3.

36. Several times Benedict points out that something is to be read, or said, "to the end": the book for Lenten reading (48.15); the Our Father (13.12), so as not to omit the "Forgive us as we forgive"; and the three psalms of prime (18.5). Otherwise, one might perhaps pray only their beginnings.

37. *Ecce* occurs in important places in the Rule, cf. Prol 18, 20, and at the end of ch. 4 (4.75). Lindermann's and Mohrmann's articles about Benedict's use of Latin have shown again and again to what extent Benedict's language is shaped by Sacred Scripture and the liturgy.

38. Cf. from Origen, Didymus, Eusebius, Athanasius, Theodore up to Ambrose; cf. Fischer, "*Coram Deo*," 147; Harl, "La chaîne," 128–130.

39. Cf. for example, Ambrose, *In Ps.* 36.65 and 1.33; Jerome, *In Mc.* 9.1-7 and *In Ez. Lib.* XIV.46.12-15.

40. Cf. Hildemar, 535: "I want to lay down my arms and serve the almighty God."

41. In RM, it is a mutual testing. The new brother is to test himself in monastic life, and is being tested by the monastery, cf. 88.5, also 90.36, 47. Did perhaps 2 Tim 4:2 influence v. 11? Cf. also Col 1:11; 2 Cor 12:12.

42. The question, "Friend, for what did you come?" is actually the question Jesus directs to Judas at his arrest. Benedict seems to have taken it out of context, yet even so it fits this situation, for everyone is faced with the possibility to betray his or her call and the Lord.

43. Cf. Gelasius, I, *Ep.* 9.21; and Smaragdus's comment on this verse.

44. In RM 90.67 the candidate promises "to obey in every regard and to be always ready to put into practice all his [the abbot's] admonitions and those of the Rule. . . ." This has been compared to the oath of the Roman legionnaires (cf. Herwegen, *Sinn,* 334).

45. RM 90.66; cf. Caesarius *Reg. vg.* 2.

46. Cf. *Reg. 4 Patr.* II.32; Cassian, *Inst.* IV.34.

47. Cf. Cassian, *Conf.* XVII.8.1; XIX.8.4; Augustine, *s.* 355.4.6. In RM, the candidate does not say the word "to promise" (*promittere*).

48. *Life of Moses* II.243-244; cf. McMurry, "On Being 'at Home.'"

49. Cf. Caesarius, *Reg. vg.* 2; *Hist. mon.* 17.439: "Whoever enters here once, stays;" cf. Councils of Chalcedon, 451 C.E., c. 4; Angers, 453 C.E., c. 8; Vannes, 465 C.E., c. 6f.; Orléans, 511 C.E., c. 11 in Hefele, II, 885, 905, 1012.

50. Cf. Pricoco, *L'isola dei Santi* 104, 116; Vogüé, "Persévérer," 349–353; Steidle, "Das Versprechen der 'Beständigkeit,'" 109–111; Eucherius, *H. ad mon* 5 (PL 50.846).

51. In the congregation of the Maurists, profession was made to the congregation, not to the individual house. From the fifteenth century to the French Revolution, a majority of monasteries belonged to such congregations in which the individual monasteries form a body together and are to help each other. Therefore, the individual member has to be ready to move to a different house, cf. Yeo, *Structure*, pp. 223ff. In Cluny, stability was promised to the motherhouse. Abbot Butler as well as Beuron championed local stability.

52. This is a *genetivus inhaerentiae qualitativus*, cf. Steidle, "*De Conversatione norum suorum*" and "Das Versprechen der Beständigkeit," 113f.; Ambrose, *De virginitate* 10.59; Caesarius, *Ep.* 3.4; Cyprian, *Ep.* 4.3; Hoppenbrouwers, "*Conversatio*" (the most thorough study). Explanations for *Conversatio*: (a) as a frequentative word for *conversio*, meaning unceasing conversion, an intensive word for conversion (Linderbauer, Mohrmann, Pascual, Colombas); (b) as derivative of *conversari* and thus synonymous with "communal life" (Lottin); (c) meaning virtuous life, manner of living (Rothenhäusler, Hildemar, Cassian). Benedict uses the word in this sense three times: 58.1; 63.1; 1.3 (in the parallel passages RM uses *conversio*). Perhaps Benedict adopted Cassian's use of term; he calls entrance *conversio* and the practical, ascetical life *conversatio* until the monastic reaches *contemplatio*; cf. *Conf.* XIV.16.3, also *Vit. Pach.* 16; additional passages in note 10, p. 157 above.

53. "Das Versprechen der Beständigkeit," 120. Cf. Hildemar, 542; Steidle, "*Per oboedientiae laborem*," 216; "Versprechen," 117–121; Yeo, *Structure*, 180–182; also, Smaragdus says "obedience according to the Rule."

54. Cf. Herwegen *Geschichte*, 9f. for Monte Cassino, 24 for Flavigny and St. Gall; Smaragdus.

55. Cf. RM 89.18-20; 89.6, 11. Cassian, *Inst.* IV.36.2; IV.37.1. Cf. also Fischer, "*Coram Deo*," 141–143.

56. Cf. Yeo, *Structure*, 328, cf. 259; also Basil, *Reg.* 7, and RM 89.14-16.

57. Cf. RM 89.17-19. Only those candidates who own anything are able to make a *donatio* (RM 87.28).

58. According to Justinian's legislation (*Corp. Nov.* 5.4), the property of a monastic became the possession of the monastery. While this text may not have been available before 537, a Latin translation was probably done soon, although the translation known to us dates from 556. Kay, "Benedict, Justinian and Donations," says that Benedict must have written his Rule before the final defeat of the Ostrogoths, that is, in a time when it was not certain whether Justinian's legislation would prevail because he is still speaking of a "*donatio*" that corresponds to the older legislation (v. 24, 59.5). Thus, Kay dates the final redaction of the Rule in the years between 542–552 while RM would have been written before 535.

59. Herwegen, *Sinn*, 338f.

60. *De sacr.* V.2.7: "You came to the altar; the Lord Jesus calls you . . . and says: 'Kiss me with the kiss of your mouth.' Do you want to conform yourself to Christ?" Cf. Cyril of Alexandria, *De ador. et cult.* IX: "The altar is made out of earth. . . . It is called Emmanuel. First the word was made flesh. The earth is made of earth, the flesh—this is nature. For in Christ everything is surrender." This is also true when the altar is made of stone: "For the stone is the chosen, precious cornerstone, Christ." Cf. Sorci, "Per una teologia dell'altare," 83.

61. Smaragdus comments: "It is the voice of the one who turns himself over to God, who lies, as it were, dead in the tomb of sin and prays that he be accepted and live."

62. Cf. Graduale Romanum (Solesmes, 1974, 17), Offertory for the First Sunday of Advent: "*Universi qui te expectant, non confondentur*" (from Ps 24[25]:1-3; Vulgate has different text).

63. A. Calmet, *Commentaire sur la Règle de S. Benoît* (Paris, 1734) 320.

64. The beginnings of such an interpretation are found in Origen: "Receive me, Father, so that I may totally belong to your Son. After you helped me, I will belong completely to the word, and then I will live the real life" (*Pal. Kat. Ps.* 118 [SC 189] 376; cf. Fischer, "*Coram Deo,*" 149.

65. Cf. Bonhoeffer, *Gemeinsames Leben* (Munich⁴, 1973) 20–22 (*Life Together*. Trans. J. W. Doberstein [New York: Harper and Row, 1954] 21–23).

66. Cassian, *Inst.* IV.7; RM 89.28 together with 90.79-82.

67. Cf. Cassian, *Inst.* IV.5, and Pachomius, *Praec.* 49. In RM, the celebration ends with the kiss of peace (89.26).

68. RM 87, especially vv. 5, 29. Renouncing possessions is a pledge for the loyalty of the candidate. It is important for the Master that the candidate does not hide anything (probably the result of some bitter experiences!) nor steals anything from the monastery. A collectively rich monastery has more reason to look at such possibilities than a collective poor monastery (Benedict). Renouncing possessions is also a sign that the brother offers his soul to God (cf. 87.35, 17). The question of possessions is also important in Pachomius (*Preac.* 49), in *Reg. 4 Patr.* II.17; Caesarius, *Reg. mon.* 1.

69. Cf. *Lib. diurn.* II.2: *decretum sollemniter facientes*, "Bemerkungen zum 4. RB-Kongreß, EA 59 (1983) 69; cf. also RM 87.45; 89.17; Hildemar, 539; Caesarius, *Reg. mon.* 1; *Reg. 4 Patr.* II.34; *Reg. Mac.* 24.

70. Cf. Caesarius, *Reg.mon.* 1.

71. *Inst.* II.3,1; IV.20; *Conf.* XVIII.7.6f.; XXIV.23.1.

72. Basil, *Reg.* 29; 106; cf. *Reg. Mac.* 24.

73. Cf. Cassian, *Inst.* IV.32; IV.38; Basil, *Reg.* 7; RM 90.1; Smaragdus on 58.14; 5.3; Hildemar, 535, 543.

74. J. Mège, *Commentaire sur la Règle de S. Benoît* (Paris, 1687) 689.

75. Cf. Article "Doulos" in ThWNT 2.

76. Cf. Yeo, *Structure*, 349–355. Bernhard of Monte Cassino: *conversio morum* contains celibacy and poverty; Thomas Aquinas: obedience includes poverty and celibacy; Torquemada: *conversio morum* and obedience contain poverty and celibacy; Perez: poverty and celibacy are included in all three Benedictine vows; Haeften: there are actually five vows; Caramuel: stability and *conversio* are actually not vows; Schmier and Steidle: everything can be reduced to obedience.

77. Cf. Art. "Gelübde" in RAC 9 (1976) 1084–1099.

78. Cf. Pachomius, "the habit (*habitus*) of the monks," Cassian, "garments (*vestimenta*) of the monastery"; Caesarius, "the religious habit"; cf. also RM 90.68-70; 95.21; 90.84-86.

79. Cf. Basil, *Reg.* 11. Also Augé, *Abito religioso* and "L'abito monastico."

80. *Vit. Bas.* 4; cf. also Cyprian, *De hab. vg.* 23.

81. *Myst. Kat.* 2.2.

82. Cf. Raffin, "Les rituels orientaux," 169ff.; Déseille, "Les origines," 31; Pseudo Dionysius, *Eccl. Hierarch.* VI.4 (PG 3.535).

83. Cf. Neunheuser, "Mönchsgelübde," 19; cf. also PC 5.

84. Hildemar, 547; for the English Congregation cf. also Yeo, *Structure*, 248 ff.

85. Cf. Herwegen, *Sinn*, 335; *Geschichte*, 15; Yeo, *Structure*, 345–349.

86. "God forbid"—this expression occurs mainly in the passages proper to Benedict. In it one can see what he would like to keep away from his monastery: the temptation of possessions (59.6), opposition of word and deed (4.61), bad choice for an abbot (64.3), pride (28.2), disturbance of the spiritual atmosphere (48.19), prestige of a person (34.2), and finally, getting up too late (11.12).

87. Ch. Happle, "Profeßordnung," 114.

Chapter 53

About the Reception of Guests

Introduction

In recent years, we have come into very close contact with the problem of refugees. We see how thousands of people are fleeing their homes in Africa and Asia and are searching for a new place to live. Yet, regarding refugees, as well as, for example, guest workers, we also experience a growing xenophobia, a hostility toward strangers and foreigners. In industrial nations or in areas where material livelihood is assured there is a growing number of alienated and uprooted people who no longer know where they are truly at home and feel safe.

Could the Rule of Benedict guide us in fulfilling our obligation in the present? In order to recognize how relevant the message of the Rule is today, it is necessary to consider its historical context.

Before doing this, however, we need to reflect about the meaning of the words *philoxenia/hospitalitas* /hospitality.[1] *Xenos* in Greek (in Latin: *peregrinus, hospes, hostis*) means the stranger who may become either a threatening enemy (*hostis*), or a guest through love (*hospes*). Strangers live far from home and are dependent on love and protection. In contrast to the general love for others and to the love of friends, of parents and children, hospitality is the love that extends itself to strangers. Hospitality is the movement in which we move toward strangers, letting them come in so that they, through our love and friendliness, become our friends. This love overcomes the rift created by our natural feelings toward strangers. "Strangers become friends"—this is the very process of hospitality. It is a relationship based not on purchasing and paying, but on free giving and accepting the gift.

H. Nouwen[2] sees in this concept a prototype for all our responsibilities toward human beings and believes that such a concept could open up a new dimension in the way we understand healing relationships. He sees hospitality as a fundamental attitude toward our fellow human beings that can be expressed in very different ways. Hospitality's first gesture does not consist in talking insistently to a person, but rather in inviting this person, to let him or her come in. This requires being open for the unexpected, for some risks, and presupposes that we ourselves are at home with ourselves, having relinquished any strained anxiety for self- preservation. Those who have truly found their own identity are able to be fully present, to share, to serve and to offer help in getting oriented. Hospitality enriches both partners. In the stranger we recognize a mirror image of our own self. The one helping is also on a journey and has an existential need for help. Thus one is quite ready to receive something from the stranger and to open one's hands for the gift the other brings and is.

Excursus: Hospitality in the Sacred Scriptures and in Monasticism before Benedict

RB 53 can be understood only within the framework of Sacred Scripture and of history.

1. Sacred Scripture[3]

Abraham and the patriarchs acknowledged that they were strangers and foreigners (*peregrini*) on earth (Heb 11:13, cf. Gen 23:4). The Israelites were aliens in Egypt, then on their pilgrimage through the desert. This became the symbolic pattern for their lives: all of life is a pilgrimage and a dwelling in alien lands (cf. Ps 38 (39):13; 1 Chr 29:15; Heb 13:14). Thus Christians in the Diaspora are called "strangers and pilgrims" (cf. 1 Pet 2:11) whose "home is in heaven" (Phil 3:20).

God is a God who is friendly toward strangers. The tent of the ark of the covenant, and later the Temple or the Holy City are symbols for this (cf. Ps 60 [61]:5; 26 [27]:4). The image of hospitality, of the banquet, also represents final salvation (Isa 25:6; Matt 8:11). God's *philoxenia*—friendliness to strangers—is a colorful image for God's kindness which is a bending down, and shows, at the same time, God's great plan for salvation: assembling all people for the banquet of peace.

Jesus is the messenger of God's invitation: "Behold, I have prepared my banquet" (Matt 22:4; Luke 14:15-24). Jesus himself acts like God: he accepts the sinners and eats with them (Luke 15:2); like the kind father he has a banquet prepared for the Prodigal Son (cf. Luke

15:23f.); he welcomes the children and calls to himself all those who are weary, burdened (Matt 11:28) and thirsty (John 7:37). As a father of the family he feeds the crowd (Mark 6:31-44). Following the multiplication of the loaves he explains that he himself is the "bread of life" for "the life of the world" (John 6:35, 51). He himself serves the guests (Luke 22:27) and washes their feet (John 13:1-15). He offers himself as their food and even goes so far as to pay with his own life for his friends (Mark 10:45). Or using a metaphor: when the evil one demands that he hand over his table companions (sold into the slavery of sin, cf. Rom 7:14), he goes out himself and suffers death for them. "This action fully shows what hospitality can be and can do and reveals its deepest meaning."[4]

The world that is alienated from God needs not only God's love for strangers that bends down toward us, but someone who is willing to descend into this "strange-ness," who is willing to become a stranger himself (cf. Luke 24:18). Christ has to depend on the hospitality of others (cf. Luke 7:36-50; 19:1-10; 10:38-42); but he is not accepted by those who are his own (John 1:11), has no place to lay his head (Matt 8:20), and eventually dies ostracized "outside the camp" (Heb 13:13), abandoned even by his God. Thus he reconciles the world that is far from God with God (2 Cor 5:19); thus those who were once strangers have come close in Christ Jesus (Eph 2:12, 19). Since then Christ has been present in every stranger, in every person who is ostracized, in every guest: "I was a stranger and you welcomed me" (Matt 25:35).

The coming of Christ is prepared already in the Hebrew Scriptures. Abraham welcomes divine beings.[5] He, a stranger himself, knows how strangers feel at high noon. He "spreads out the net of hospitality," and runs toward them with eagerness. He prostrates himself before them and thus shows that he is the one who is receiving. With his own hand he washes their feet and in joyful haste prepares the meal. The Church Fathers say that Isaac is a fruit of hospitality. The fulfillment of the promises begins here (Gen 18:1-16).

The Christian Scriptures emphasize Christ's presence in the humblest person primarily for the missionaries and for the poor. "Whoever receives you receives me" (Matt 10:40). Matthew 25:31-46 originally focuses on welcoming the poor, those who are hungry and thirsty and naked, the sick and the prisoners.

Several times people invite Jesus, but as soon as he has entered the house, he acts as the host. He breaks the bread (Luke 24:28-32); he brings salvation to Zacchaeus (Luke 19:9); he wants to give every-thing as a gift (Luke 10:38-42) for he comes to serve and not to be served (Martha's misunderstanding). "If anyone opens the door, I will enter his house and dine with him" (Rev 3:20). We practice hos-pitality toward Christ, welcome him, but actually it is Christ who gifts us. The Good News provides an even stronger impulse for Christians to practice hospitality in imitation of God, in imitation of Christ, and as an encounter with the Lord himself.

Yet already the Hebrew Scriptures show great appreciation for hospitality. The models of hospitality such as Abraham (Gen 18:1-16), Lot (Gen 19:1-14), the Shunammite woman (2 Kgs 4:8-17), the widow of Zarephat (1 Kgs 17:8-24), and Job (Job 31:31f.) continue to influence the Bible as well as monasticism. The reason for the com-mand to love the stranger is gratitude to God who freed the Israelites when they were aliens in Egypt (Exod 22:20; Lev 19:34; Exod 23:9). Moreover, it becomes evident that God loves the aliens as well as the poor (Deut 10:18f.).

For the Christian Scriptures, two representative texts are chosen here: "Above all, let your love for one another be intense . . . be mu-tually hospitable to one another without grumbling. As each one has received a gift, use it to serve one another as good stewards of God's varied grace" (1Pet 4:8-10). "Rejoice in hope, endure in affliction, persevere in prayer. Contribute to the needs of the holy ones, exercise hospitality" (Rom 12:12-13). Loving strangers is an important and indispensable element of good works (cf. also Heb 13:2; Rom 16:1f.); it is a test for Christian love, and grants salvation; it is a gift of grace just as is prayer and ardent love. Loving strangers applies especially, as the word indicates, to the strangers and the poor, yet it also char-acterizes the relationships of Christians among themselves.[6]

Bishops have a special obligation to practice hospitality (Titus 1:8; 1 Tim 3:2; Hermas, *Simil.* 9.27.2), as do the widows who must have been "hospitable and washed the feet of the saints" (1 Tim 5:10).

In the early Christian centuries the Good News spreads through the offering of hospitality on which missionaries depended (cf. Acts). The Third Letter of John is of particular importance: "Beloved, you are faithful in all you do for the brothers, especially for strangers. . . . For they have set out for the sake of the Name and are accepting nothing from the pagans. Therefore, we ought to support such per-sons, so that we may be coworkers in the truth" (3 John 5-8). Eagerly practicing hospitality also helps strengthen the faith and the solidarity between the various churches. In the fourth century, Emperor Julian complains that it is mainly "the benevolence toward strangers" that "has favored the bad teachings of Christianity.[7] Scholars name hospitality as the "strongest individual reason for the missionary success of the Church."[8] Hospitality as practiced toward the poor and the hungry becomes one of the most important forms of Christian love.

Looking ahead to chapter 53 in the Rule of Benedict, it becomes evident how deeply it is marked by the spirit of Sacred Scripture. The example of Abraham, perhaps conveyed through the homilies of the Fathers, has been its model, even in the details (as well as the negative example in Luke 7:36-50, cf. also RM 53.43).[9] Just like bishops and widows, monastics have a particular obligation to be hospitable although hospitality is a grace rather than an obligation. It is characteristic for the Bible and for RB that spiritual and social service are seen as one and the same thing. The ones receiving it are the same: strangers, foreigners, pilgrims, brothers in faith, and the poor. Chapter 53 starts from the christological motivation that Christ arrives in the stranger (Matt 25:35).

2. Monasticism before Benedict

Every Christian is obligated to be hospitable. The house of the bishop, however, was seen as a special hostel for strangers. Larger communities at important crossroads had lodging houses for strangers. In the fourth century, Christian hospitality became more institutionalized.[10] Besides bishops and widows, monastics had the duty to provide hospitality. Hospices, homes, and hospitals were set up primarily by monks.[11] As the number of monasteries increased, so did the number of hospices (same root as hospital, hospitality). Monastic communities with their numerous members made extensive care possible. Their love was directed to pilgrims, brothers and sisters in faith, and missionaries, as well as to strangers and to the poor. In the context of increasing social poverty the words "the poor and pilgrims" designated mainly those who were socially poor.[12] Thus, lodging-houses necessarily became poorhouses; and orphanages and hospitals were added. Basil established an entire city of charitable institutions.[13]

It is true that, despite such generally high respect, there also existed a negative attitude toward strangers in monastic circles. Many hermits gave strangers a negative answer and locked their doors or made them wait for a long time. One hermit dug an underground passage so as to get away; another rebuffed strangers harshly. It was said: "If you hear Arsenius is anywhere, do not go there" (*Apoph.* Arsenius, 7); and, "Arsenius said, 'I cannot live with God and with men.'"[14] The Rule of the Master may have been influenced by this negative tradition. He decrees that there be a great distinction between receiving brothers from other monasteries who are to be welcomed with reverence and with prayers and whose feet are to be washed (RM 71–72; 65) and receiving strangers who are met only with distrust (RM 78–79, cf. 95). Negative experiences with gyrovagues (cf. RM 1) probably strengthened such an attitude in the Master. He determines that, after two days, guests must decide whether to work or to leave (RM 78.4f., 10). They are being watched day and night to keep them from stealing (RM 79: the words "observe," "watch" occur nine times; cf. in particular 79.14-17).

Yet in early monasticism it is generally customary to practice generous hospitality that is highly respected as a divine and holy activity. "A virgin who does not practice mercy nor takes care of strangers, is not worthy of this name"[15]—and this is also true for monastics. Typical are two examples from *The Lives of the Desert Fathers (Historia monachorum)* that may have influenced Benedict. "The extent of hospitality with which we were showered, is indescribable. Truly, my coat was torn because each one tried to pull me over to him" (5.5/5.409). "And nowhere have I seen love flourish so greatly, nowhere such quick compassion, such eager hospitality" (20.5-8/21.444).

The motivations for loving strangers vary: we are all pilgrims and strangers (cf. comments on v. 4). Christ welcomed strangers, so we imitate him (cf. comments on v. 13). Above all, it is Christ himself who is welcomed in a stranger (cf. comments on v. 1). Strangers and the poor are the places where God and human beings meet, and thus they are Christ for us, the sacrament of Christ's saving presence. Hence, it is also clear that the one who practices hospitality receives much more than one gives. The poor are our benefactors (cf. comments on v. 14). An additional motivation is the desire to assist people in developing their faith and to lead them to Christ (cf. comments on vv. 8-9).

Soon customs and rituals develop. As illustration we mention an example from the *Lives of the Desert Fathers*: "The brothers came running to meet us. . . . When [Father Apollo] saw us, he first prostrated lying full length on the ground; then getting up he kissed us, and having brought us in, prayed for us; then, after washing our feet with his own hands, he invited us to partake of some refreshment" (8.48-49/7.418).

Yet hospitality creates problems already for the hermits, especially concerning monastic life and the discernment of spirits. One cannot always interrupt prayer or fasting for doing good works even though love of neighbor is generally seen as the higher value (cf. comments on v. 10). Eventually monastic simplicity may suffer, and numerous visitors may keep many monastics from doing their work (cf. comments on v. 16). There is also the fear that the devil comes in disguise (especially in the form of a woman; cf. comments on v. 5). One tries to exclude those who are unwilling to work, criminals, thieves, and also heretics (cf. comments on v. 4). Cenobites must resolve the problem of how to reconcile the service for people with community life and communal prayer. Thus already in the time of Pachomius it is customary to appoint a particular monastic for these services and to specify that guests do not have unlimited access to all rooms and that not all monastics are allowed to talk to them (cf. comments on v. 21ff.).

The Rule of Benedict reflects the biblical as well as the monastic tradition. It is an excellent tool to get to know the treasure of this old tradition which it transmitted to posterity.[16]

In his Rule Benedict first orders the life of his community. In doing this, he provides a healthy basis for the community's openness to outsiders that he introduces in this chapter and continues in the following ones. The first words of the chapter ("all arriving guests") mark a turn within the Rule. This chapter follows chapter 52 about the oratory where we see how the brothers return to their work after prayer. The oratory stands at the threshold between the community and a needy world, and in 53.8 people are again (presumably) brought into the oratory.

OVERVIEW OF THE CHAPTER

The chapter consists of two large parts: verses 1-15 concern the reception of guests, and verses 16-24 concern protective measures for the community. The two parts, however, form a unified whole.[17] The first part in particular is carefully and impressively crafted.[18] This part contains many intensive expressions, a more liturgical and spiritual vocabulary, and thus reflects the liturgical and spiritual chapters of RB to a greater extent.[19] The second part contains more practical instructions and thus reflects the vocabulary of the community chapter to a greater extent.[20] Thus we could ask the following questions: Is love for strangers seen as a spiritual, intense, internal concern, even as liturgy? Is protection of the community a practical necessity?

For the first part, Benedict has taken his inspiration mainly from Sacred Scripture, the *Lives of the Desert Fathers (Historia monachorum)*, from Cassian (regarding fasting), and from the Master (in the way he receives spiritual brothers). The second part, however, reflects toward the end instructions from cenobitic rules about hospitality.[21] Apparently, larger, more established communities have more difficulties regarding hospitality than hermits who live at a greater geographical distance from cities.

Between the first and the second part a development seems to have taken place. In the second part the community seems to have grown; duties and buildings have become more numerous, kitchens are being separated, guests arrive at all times and are never lacking. We can well imagine that the first part was practiced in Subiaco in Benedict's first phase. If from time to time a stranger wanders into this solitary place, the monks can eagerly run to meet him, practice all the welcoming rituals, sit with him, break the fast, and so on. But when considering the situation in Monte Cassino, perhaps at the time of the Gothic Wars, it is understandable that it becomes necessary to have some practical protective measures for the community and to organize the hospitality for strangers. This corresponds to our experience even today. At a great geographical distance from other people, an individual or a small community can generously practice hospitality, but for a larger community, perhaps one located in a city, protection and organization are indispensable.

What might have been Benedict's thoughts (inasmuch as we can even say this) when he added the second part to RB 53 while leaving the first one intact? If the situation of the second part happens (guests arriving at all hours), how is it actually possible that superiors run to meet each guest, practice the entire welcoming ritual, read Scripture with each of them, and so on? Which literary genre is this? These are not spiritual teachings (they seem very concrete), but neither are they practical (or rather impractical!) instructions. The *Lives of the Desert Fathers* and the *Apophthegmata* show a similar style in describing hospitality. There a father even helps a thief take things out of his cell! (*Apoph.* Makarios the Great 18).

What is the purpose when such a story is told? Following Dodd,[22] I would like to call these seemingly concrete instructions "models of action." They are concrete, descriptive instructions meant to indicate the quality (radicality) and direction of our actions. They need to be taken very seriously, but need not be fulfilled literally on the practical level. Rather, they are to inspire our imagination as examples and indicate how we ought to act in other circumstances. All instructions in chapter 53 are obligatory in the sense that from them we can infer the quality, radicality, and direction of our actions; but they are not to be copied, but can rather be expressed in other ways. This is similar to Jesus' instructions about offering the other cheek (Matt 5:39) and tearing out an eye that leads us into sin (Matt 5:29).

OVERVIEW OF THE FIRST PART

Verses 1-15 form a unity in themselves; verse 15 again refers back to words used in verses 1-2 (inclusion).

Verses 1-2 seem to be an explanation of the principle.

Verses 3-7 describe the manner of welcoming the guests, with respect and love, with prayer and kiss of peace, in humility.

Verses 8-14: Those welcomed as guests take part in prayer (liturgy), spiritual dialog and *lectio*, in the meal (this includes an insert regarding fasting), and in a short liturgical ritual for washing their hands and feet.

Verse 15 is both a summary and a culmination: particular care is to be given to strangers and the poor (this includes a short addition).

1. *To which world is hospitality directed?* At first there is strong emphasis on the word "all," and this word is repeated three more times. Yet there are also two clear preferences: for the brothers in faith and the strangers (v. 2), and later for the "poor and the strangers" (v. 15), while the rich are not mentioned in a particularly kind manner.

Interestingly, Benedict at times speaks of guests in the plural, at times of the guest in the singular. All guests are welcomed as Christ (v. 1), they are shown appropriate honor (v. 2) and humility (v. 6); in them the monastics revere Christ (v. 7). Guests are led to prayer (v. 8), and monastics sit with them (v. 8). The hands and feet of all guests are washed (vv. 12-13), and particular care is given to strangers and the poor (v. 15). All these actions can be done to several persons at the same time. In contrast, we find the guest in the singular in the following actions: one approaches the guest (v. 3), prays with him (vv. 4-5), reads Scripture with him, and renders him every human kindness (v. 9). These are all actions in which each guest is addressed as an individual person.

"Deceptions of the devil" may also arrive with guests and need to be repelled. Yet, four times Benedict mentions Christ who, coming from the world, approaches the monastery in the person of the guests, especially the poor (vv. 1, 7, 14, 15).

2. *Who practices hospitality?* First superiors or brothers are mentioned (v. 3). Presumably they are also present at the prayer, the kiss of peace, and the expressions of humility (vv. 4-7). All monastics are mentioned explicitly again only at the time of the foot washing and the accompanying liturgy (v. 13f.). This indicates that all monastics are included when the religious ritual of welcoming the guests takes place (cf. also vv. 23-24).

From verse 3 on, the superior or "whoever is appointed by him" (v. 8) appears most prominently. As a matter of fact, it is the superior who sits with the guest (v. 8) and reads Scripture with him for spiritual edification (v. 9). Probably not all brothers have this skill. The following verses concern the meal (vv. 9-10), the washing of hands (v. 12), and the breaking the fast (v. 10); the abbot has his own kitchen (v. 16). This would, however, not be good for all monastics and, might, in the long run, endanger the discipline of monastic life.

3. *How is hospitality described?* We find the following expressions: appropriate honor, due love, prayer, peace, kiss of peace, humility, adoration, prayer, divine law, human kindness (*humanitas*), washing of hands and feet, greatest care, honor. It is significant that this series of words begins and ends with "honor," the basis for hospitality (cf. 4.8). In addition, these words show an interweaving of the spiritual and human-social dimensions characteristic for Benedict.

4. *The movement of hospitality.* At the outset, the word "to welcome/receive" (*suscipere* which occurs eight times in this chapter) is prevalent, designating a receptive attitude of accepting and receiving, of appreciation and love, not one of of conquering (cf. also 66.1-2: to be present). Following this more receptive attitude we see in verse 3 a "running to meet" as a custom of courtesy that perhaps also has a deeper meaning of anticipating and accommodating the guests in opposition to idle waiting (cf. "with the warmth of love" in 66.4). Subsequently, there are some expressions that emphasize common actions of monastics and guests: they pray together and become "companions in peace" (v. 4); they sit together (v. 8). Yet this external togetherness is not the end, for from there the guests are led to prayer (v. 8). This is the first indication of a goal; and another one follows: that the guest be edified (v. 9). Unlike many of the Desert Fathers, it matters to Benedict whether or not the pilgrims are edified. He wants to help strengthen people's faith.

These four stages (welcoming, running to meet, being together, guiding) also seem important today in all the different kinds of hospitality. First, it is necessary to be present, to accept and welcome, then to approach and accommodate other people. There follows a being with them, companionship, solidarity, yet not simply in order to be with them, but in order to accompany them on their way to find God, to strengthen their faith. Hospitality does not only have a religious motivation and atmosphere, but also has a religious goal.

Title: About Receiving Guests

The title already contains the two distinctive words: This chapter concerns the guests—and thus the eyes are directed to the outside—and the way in which they are being welcomed. In the Rule the word "guest" (*hospes, hospis*) is always used for people who come from outside and for those who need help. In classical Latin, *hospes* (which occurs fourteen times in this chapter) designates a stranger, then also a guest inasmuch as he or she is welcomed. The same word, however, can also be used for the host. In this latter sense, we find it in the Master's satire (RM 1) about the gyrovagues who exploit their benefactors (occurring twenty-three times). It is understandable that the Master has no taste for hospitality.

Suscipere (sus-capere) means to take up, to take upon oneself, to take care, to support. In this chapter the word is connected with Christ, guest, charity, and designates a single movement for which Benedict seems to have used the same word deliberately (seven times when adding *susceptio*). The new community members are also "received" by the community as well as by the abbot (cf. RB 58), and the Lord is asked to "receive me" (58.21). Thus we can say: monastics can receive guests in this manner because they themselves have been received by Christ (RM 88.14: "whom Christ had . . . received as a guest"). Since they themselves are guests and house mates of Christ (cf. "the house of God," v. 22), they can continue to do for others what Christ did for them.

V. 1:   All arriving guests are to be received as Christ,
         for he will say:
         I was a guest (a stranger), and you welcomed me.

1. *All arriving guests.* The word "all" at the very beginning of the chapter is given special emphasis. Perhaps it has become so familiar for us that we no longer sense how astonishing and radical this word is. Extremely different people came to Benedict's monastery: strangers, brothers in faith, foreign monks, the poor, the oppressed, farmers, the rich, clerics, bishops, and kings; yet the majority of them were probably poor. This word "all" is repeated three more times in the course of the chapter (and it may be good to read the passages aloud): "appropriate honor is to be shown to all" (v. 2); "humility is to be shown to all" (v. 6); "all have their feet washed" (v. 13). Hildemar points

out that Benedict emphasizes this word "all" so much because it is hard and difficult, especially when guests are numerous.[23] It is interesting to note that the Master in his chapter about guests uses this word "all" only once: the brother porters "are to keep continuous watch over all the strangers who come" (79.9)[24] as he had good reasons for this. Benedict, too, would have known the same gyrovagues, parasites, idlers, and people unwilling to work. His open attitude is thus all the more astonishing. He wants to receive all persons, be they virtuous or lazy, rich or wretched, of high or low status. There is to be no respect of person. This corresponds to his maxim in 4.8: "to honor all persons," echoing 1 Peter 2:17: "you must esteem everyone." In 4.8 Benedict changed the text of the Master "to honor father and mother" (3.8) and thus already prepared for the practice of hospitality.

In this request, the behavior toward outsiders truly reflects the behavior Benedict desires for the community itself. There, too, very different people are together among whom no distinction is to be made. All brothers are to be honored, respected, and loved (2.16-22); all have their feet washed every week (35.9); all are called to counsel (3.1, 3); all are given help when they need helpers (53.19; 35.4); all hold everything in common (33.6); and the abbot and the cellarer must take care of all (2.38; 31.2, 9).

Monastic tradition often admonishes us to receive all who arrive, without questioning them at length about their motivations or discussing their worth. It is better to welcome an evil person than to exclude a good one.[25]

Benedict uses the word "to come in" (*supervenire*) always in connection with guests (53.16; 42.10; 61.1). By opening the monastery to the world, something uncertain and unexpected approaches the community. Getting involved with people always means getting involved with surprises and to renounce the desire to fix and anticipate every detail. Benedict probably chose the word *supervenire* deliberately as it is used in Scripture for the parousia that surprises us (cf. Luke 21:34f.; also RM 10.92; 90.13).

2. *To receive as Christ.* In such an openness to the unexpected, Christ approaches the monastics. This is the leitmotiv and the theological argument for hospitality. RB 53 repeats this twice almost verbatim (vv. 7, 15). In comparison to other rules, we note that Benedict does not begin the chapter with practical instructions, but emphasizes first its christocentric basis.[26]

The word "as" (*tamquam*) occurs once more in RB 4.2: "love your neighbor as yourself." This does not mean that we make our neighbor transparent for ourselves, but rather that, beginning with the love we naturally have for ourselves, we apply the same love to our neighbor. With strangers (and not only with neighbors) we need a stronger motivation: receiving them "as Christ," that is, our love for Christ is to be the measure of how much we are to love strangers.

For the first time in the Rule, Christ approaches the community from outside the monastery. Until now his presence was emphasized in the abbot, in the sick, in Sacred Scripture, in liturgy, in each brother. But this is, as it were, not the whole Christ. Just like the God of the Hebrew Scriptures, Christ has two aspects: as God who abides in the midst of God's people, in the Temple, and pitches God's tent among them; and as God who appears suddenly and equally suddenly slips away, being unavailable to us. If we emphasized only the first aspect (Christ among us), we would be in danger to think that we could hold on to him and fit him into our system. Yet the approaching Christ "disturbs us," startles us, shatters our established systems; he is always larger than we think and different from our concepts. A community that becomes wrapped up in itself is in danger of missing Christ's coming and thus to close itself to the whole Christ. This seems to be the case for the Master who ends his Rule with the thought that the monastics are inside, enclosed with their God, locking their doors to the outside (95.22f.).

RB 53 celebrates the *adventus domini*, the coming of Christ. The parousia will also arrive unexpectedly; its hour cannot be computed. As in the first coming of Jesus, his last coming will presumably also shatter all our human concepts (cf. comments on vv. 2, 15). Moreover, other words also point to the coming of Christ: "running to meet" (v. 3), honor (v. 2), bowing the head and prostration (v. 7). If we accept the coming of Christ, he will bring mercy and blessings already on earth (cf. comments on vv. 14, 24) and eventually will welcome us into the heavenly home.[27]

3. *For he himself will say.* This "for" (because) is repeated in verse 15 in the same context (for in the poor and the pilgrims Christ is welcomed even more). The following instructions must be well founded and appear reasonable to the monastics. The majority of such arguments in the RB (introduced by "for") refer to the Sacred Scriptures. Sometimes we find such reasoned Scripture quotes at the beginning of a chapter, especially when Benedict teaches a practice that differs from the Master (cf. 27; 36). In 36.2-3 he uses the same Scripture text, but in the past tense ("for he himself said"). In RB 53 the scene of the parousia opens up before our eyes as a future gift. The parable describes how all peoples are brought into the love of God (God's hospitality) and so connects the majesty of Christ with his presence in the least of his brothers and sisters.

4. *I was a stranger, and you welcomed me.* In Matthew 25, the fact of being a stranger is seen together with being hungry, thirsty, and poor. Again and again these verses have aroused hearts and moved preachers.[28] For Benedict, they are the foundation for acting kindly toward the poor and the strangers in contrast to the rules existing in his own world. The

Latin text (*hospes eram et collegistis/collexistis me*) is found neither in the Vulgate nor in the Itala, but in the *Lives of the Desert Fathers*: "We must adore the arriving brothers so that it is certain that in their arrival we have the arrival of our Lord Jesus who says: 'I was a stranger and you welcomed me.'"[29] Then the example of Abraham is mentioned who, by welcoming other human beings, welcomed God. "If you don't want to welcome the stranger as Christ, you better not welcome him at all," says John Chrysostom (*Ecl. elem. hosp.* 23). Many would like to say: "How I would love to have Paul as my guest!" Or: "How I would love to welcome Christ!" Yet the Fathers answer these objections in the following way: We are just as privileged today as were the contemporaries of Jesus; we may welcome him in the stranger and in a poor person. It is only that we do not recognize him straight away, but only by practicing hospitality.[30]

The presence of Christ is mysterious. Christ is no longer in need. Yet, although he as the head is perfect, he is yet poor in his members and dependent on shelter. The stranger and the poor become a sacrament of Christ's saving presence as they are Christ for us.[31] Augustine has Christ say: "I received temporal things. I will return eternal things; I received bread, I will give life. I received hospitality, I will give a home.[32]

V. 2: Proper honor is to be shown to all, especially to the brothers in faith and the strangers (pilgrims).

1. *Proper honor is to be shown to all.* Again the word "all" is repeated echoing RB 4.8: "To honor all people." In principle, honor is due to all persons regardless of their social status. While RB is concerned about *showing* honor (to an elder, the abbot, the weak, and to all, cf. comments on 72.4, p. 59 above), the Master emphasizes rather the honor that someone *receives*. The internal respect of each person is the same and is given to the person. Its external expression (*exhibere*, exhibiting) may vary.[33] Thus Benedict says in verse 15 that the rich exact honor.

To honor all corresponds to Sacred Scripture (cf. 1 Pet 2:17; Rom 12:10; also comments on RB 72.4), and thus this expression can also be interpreted in the sense that all are shown the honor due to them as persons. Yet Scripture also knows that a particular honor is to be shown to weaker members (cf. 1 Cor 12:23f.; 1 Pet 3:7) as well as to leaders (1 Tim 5:17). "Honor everyone who deserves it" (Rom 13:7). Although the same love and respect is due to all, the form of expressing this respect varies toward different people.

2. *Especially to brothers in faith (domesticis fidei).* After having stressed the word "all" twice, Benedict now establishes another hierarchy that is not headed by the rich and the noble, but by brothers in faith and the strangers (cf. v. 15: the poor and the strangers). This is in line with the Gospel and the

Beatitudes (cf. Mark 10:31; Matt 5:3-12) and is a sign for whether or not a community lives according to the Gospel. *Domesticus* designates a person who belongs to the house, to the family; it can be a friend or a family member, but also a farm hand or a servant. Benedict probably alludes to Galatians 6:10. Christians are to do good to all, in particular to those who share the same faith in Christ (thus not especially to pagans or Jews). Ephesians 2:19 calls Christians God's house mates (*domestici Dei*). It is not easy to determine whether Benedict here follows the general Christian use of the word or whether he thinks particularly of monks. The "house of God" (*domus Dei*) can designate the church as well as the monastery (cf. comments on v. 22). Cassian stresses that through profession one becomes a "house mate" (*domesticus*) of the brothers and a brother of Christ (*Inst.* IV.5).

Fides means faith, orthodoxy. Thus the brothers in faith could be seen as orthodox Christians in contrast to Arians. In times of religious wars and heresies these orthodox brothers/sisters in faith probably had to depend particularly on monasteries. Yet *fides* can also mean loyalty, reliability, even vows (cf. RB 1.7) and is used in this sense often by the Master (e.g., in 87-88; cf. especially 87.50, 29; 88.12). "Brothers in faith" can also refer to monks who, through profession, have committed themselves to loyalty to God. If Benedict followed the tradition, the narrow sense of this expression, that is, monks or clerics, seems more likely.[34] The question must remain open. In any case, however, both groups had to depend in a special way on the fraternal help of monasteries.

3. *Especially . . . to strangers.* Here we have another ambiguity: Does *peregrini* mean strangers or pilgrims (the same Latin word is used for both)? In any case, these are first people who are far from their home, presumably strangers, refugees—we think of times of war. The word *peregrini* also occurs in verse 15 in connection with the poor (*pauperes et peregrini*). In Latin, both words have the same meaning, designating persons in need of help (cf. comments on v. 15). Brothers in faith and strangers—Benedict singles out those closest to him as well as those who are farthest away. But certainly pilgrims are not excluded since they are a special kind of these *peregrini*.[35]

V. 3: Therefore, as soon as a guest is announced,
    the superior and/or the brothers
    are to go out to meet him with all the love due to him.

Verses 3-5 describe the first welcome of the stranger: meeting him, prayer, and kiss of peace.

1. *Therefore, as soon as a guest is announced.* With the characteristic word "therefore" (*ergo*) Benedict now begins to draw the first practical consequences from the general biblical principle. As soon as someone is

announced, a reaction can be seen. The same sentence construction occurs in 66.3f. (and in 2.26): "As soon as someone knocks," the porter is to answer immediately, that is, "quickly, with the warmth of love."

2. *The superior and/or the brothers.* The superior is first called prior (perhaps influenced by the *Historia monachorum*?). It is possible that, in a first phase of development, superior and brothers did come out to meet the guest. For a later phase the translation "superiors or brothers" seems to be more realistic (Holzherr, Bihlmeyer). Smaragdus also sensed this difficulty; he translates "superiors or brothers." In addition, he points out that not all, but only certain brothers went to meet the guest.

3. *They are to go out to meet him.* Normally Benedict uses the word *occurrere* (to go to meet) only for the monastics when they are assembling for the liturgy (especially in RB 43), which is also to be done eagerly and promptly since "nothing is to be preferred to the *opus Dei*" (43.3). The Christians of Rome went out to meet Saint Paul after they had received the message of his arrival (Acts 28:15). This is a custom of courtesy. The same word occurs often in the *Historia monachorum*.[36] It indicates that one does not leisurely wait until the guest arrives, but rather anticipates the guest's arrival. Thus the word can also have a deeper meaning. When Christ himself approaches us, we are to run to meet him as some of the Advent antiphons say.[37] In explaining 1 Thessalonians 4:15-17, John Chrysostom says: when the Lord comes down from heaven at the sound of the trumpet, we will run out to meet the Lord. When the king comes into his city, the evil persons in it expect the judgment while the good ones run out to meet him to show him honor (*In Thess. H.* 8.1.17).

4. *With all the love due to him (cum omni officio caritatis). Officium* is what a person is obliged to do, one's task, the appropriate courtesy, the duty, what is proper. Benedict uses this word for duty in general, for work as well as for prayer (cf. e.g., v. 17; Prol 39; title of RB 8; 62.6). This expression again recalls the fervor of love (66.4) with which the porter answers. The love (*caritas*) that is to exist inside the community (cf. comments on RB 72; cf. also RB 35, etc.), becomes equally effective vis-à-vis the persons from outside. Love is a duty that urges us, moves us. Romans 13:8 admonishes: "Owe no debt to anyone except the debt that binds us to love one another."[38] The expression "the duty of love" can designate the internal attitude as well as the external forms of love and politeness.

5. It is obvious that this verse was no longer taken literally in Monte Cassino which had many guests (v. 16). Yet, as a model of action, it points to the radical nature of our attitude, and thus needs to be translated into other forms. Smaragdus explains this passage in the following way: "When

we run after hospitality, we must eagerly seek it and go out to the places where the guests are." Leo the Great admonishes us to find those who are hidden in their modesty and kept back by shame (*s.* 93). Therefore we must not wait until someone knocks on our door. Rather we must try to meet the people where they actually are (literally as well as figuratively), to perceive and anticipate their true needs.

V. 4: **And first they are to pray together**
 and then be joined together with the kiss of peace.
V. 5: **This kiss of peace is to be given only**
 after a preceding prayer
 because of the deceptions of the devil.

1. *And first they are to pray together.* The word "and" shows that this immediately follows showing the love due to them and belongs to this expression of love just as the immediately following kiss of peace (twice a connection with "and"). The Latin word *primitus* (in contrast to *prius*) means first, previously, beforehand. According to the original meaning, praying probably meant a prayer of supplication which, connected with the word "together," was probably a spoken prayer.[39] We recall Prol 4: "Before you begin a good work, pray to him most earnestly that he will bring it to perfection." From the first moment the monastic community shows itself as what it is, a community that totally depends on the grace of God and gives primacy of place to prayer (and especially to liturgy, 43.3). Prayer is an essential element of all human acts that assist someone in need, and thus creates a first basis for hospitality and also indicates the direction of hospitality (cf. comments on vv. 8-9). A spiritual space is to be opened for the one who needs help. Human encounters are to be based on prayer and to reveal the importance of prayer.

Often we have experienced how helpful a prayer for God's blessing can be before a particular discussion, before certain tasks. It makes us mindful, helps us to discern whether, for example, this particular call really comes from God or whether we use it in order to evade our true tasks, whether this act of assistance can also be asked of the community, whether this or that person is really in need of help, or whether we may rather have to encourage someone who is timid. For example, it can be the prayer "O God, come to my assistance" that Benedict deliberately places at the beginning of every fraternal service (35.17). It can be a prayer of praise or supplication that helps us to accept strangers as a gift from God (cf. comments on v. 14). At times we also need the courage to say a prayer with people who are sick or need help. The word "together" normally is used only for the community that Christ leads "together" (which perhaps points to the early

Christian community, cf. comments on 72.12, pp. 71–72 above). In practicing hospitality, the monastic community opens up to people from outside.

2. *And then are to be joined together.* Monastics and guests become companions on the journey, friends and brothers/sisters who share the same destiny and goal. Benedict uses the same word when speaking about joining the monastic community in choir or becoming a member of the monastic community (cf. 43.11; 61.6, 8; 60.8). The monastic and the stranger are living members of the same body.[40] This is in accord with the fact that Benedict here does not borrow from the chapter of RM about welcoming guests (78f.), but from the one about accepting brothers (65; 71f.). The strangers are considered brothers (but not in everything, cf. they "are not associating with each other" in v. 23). This expression also indicates that the monastics do not see themselves only as those who give, but rather as true partners. Augustine said once: "You receive a stranger, whose companion you yourself also are on the road because we are all foreign visitors. Those people are the real Christians who realize that both in their homes and their own country they are foreign visitors."[41] Monastics are also strangers; like Abraham they left house, home and possessions, and together with other brothers/sisters they are on their pilgrimage to God (cf. comments on RB 58.)

Sometimes we resist welcoming a beggar, a stranger, someone who is sick or poor because we have not yet accepted poverty, abandonment, and our own need for help as a reality. Every person is a mirror for what we ourselves are in the depth of our nature. The expression "are to be joined together" (*socientur*) is important for all tasks involving people, tasks that are to be completed in companionship, in mutual giving and receiving.

3. *Through the kiss of peace (in pace).* One could translate this literally with "they become companions in peace." They meet on a deeper level. The word "peace" in RB is not limited to the kiss of peace (which here is the presumed meaning). The Prologue admonished the monastic to "seek and pursue peace" (Prol 17). Jerome interpreted this passage thus: "Pursue peace, that is, pursue hospitality" (*Ep.* 125.4). In RB peace is understood primarily as peace in fraternal love and union (cf. 34.5; 65.11; 4.25). In particular, the word also contains the concrete meaning of reconciliation (4.73 *in pacem redire,* to make peace). This meaning corresponds to that of the Church Fathers. In order to make peace with God, it is necessary to make peace and reconcile with the church as well as with the brother/sister.[42] In peace, vertical and horizontal dimensions are inseparably joined. The foundation of peace is love. Where there is love, there is peace; and peace also brings harmony (*concordia*), meaning that hearts are brought together. For the Church Fathers peace is above all mutual love that yearns for the unity desired by Christ and realizes it.[43]

Certainly we may also think of the biblical concept of peace that designates the integral salvation of individuals and of the community, the salvation that was brought to us through Christ who made peace through his
Cross and who, in his person, is peace (cf. Eph 2:14-16; Rom 15:33; 1 Cor
14:33). Hence, it is clear why peace is so closely connected with hospitality
and became a key concept for our monasteries. The stranger becomes a
companion in peace; and this means not only that one shares in the love
and harmony of the community, but also that, like the monastics, one finds
reconciliation with God and integral salvation through human love (cf.
comments on v. 14).

The kiss of peace is the concrete expression of this will and reality. This
is the meaning of "peace" in its narrow sense and probably its meaning
here. This kiss of peace is the seal of prayer and has found its place at various points in the liturgy, especially—as is the case with Benedict—after the
Lord's Prayer. It is the pledge of goodness and love. Augustine says that,
just as the lips approach each other, so the hearts are to come closer.[44]

The instruction to become companions in peace, or to enter into communion through the kiss of peace, can be a program for the task of our
world: to create reconciliation and understanding, to further harmony and
communion among each other and with God, to seek "what builds up and
promotes peace" (Rom 14:19). This is an answer to the search for peace
today. Within the various efforts to work for peace, it is our task to point to
the foundations and prerequisites for peace.

The meaning of the kiss of peace also sheds new light on the sequence:
prayer is to precede the kiss of peace. The latter is to be a true expression of
fellowship, of the common faith in Christ.[45]

4. *This kiss of peace is to be given only after a preceding prayer because of
the deceptions of the devil.* In a time of religious wars and heresies, it is a risk
for Benedict to welcome a stranger into the community. He does not want
to question these people nor does he require an episcopal reference letter
or a *tessera hospitalis*, as was customary; he also does not demonstrate any
particular rigor to keep certain people away from the beginning,[46] but requires only a prayer at the beginning. In prayer, a person shows how one is
and what one believes, shows concretely whether one is a heretic or even an
apostate. The Master makes a drastic statement in 71.6-8: ". . . for if
prayer is not said first, how will the brother know?—lest a diabolical temptation present itself in human guise. . . . So we may deceive ourselves
with our own sight if we trust human eyes for what we fail to test by means
of divine prayers" (cf. the entire chapter 71 of RM). Therefore, prayer
comes first, and only then they offer each other the gift of peace. It is primarily Christ who approaches the community from the world (this is

emphasized four times in RB 53), but since the world is not yet healed, it also contains dangers which could trip up monastics, especially because they themselves are weak and not sufficiently firm in their faith. Benedict probably would like to exclude apostates and heretics. He is a realist, yet does not see the devil lurking everywhere as does the Master.

Even today the discernment of spirits is relevant (cf. comments on v. 4 above). Benedict envelops our task for the world totally in prayer. This task must be based on prayer and is completed in prayer; thus it is also accompanied by prayer, and it is its goal to lead the guests to prayer (cf. comments on vv. 8-9).

**V. 6: In this greeting, however, all humility is to be shown
to all arriving and departing guests.**

The connection with the greeting indicates that, in concluding, Benedict wants to refer back to the initial greeting while also extending it to the departure for which another ritual is prescribed.[47] Again, this ritual is given to all guests without exception.

Together with honor, humility is the fundamental attitude of hospitality.[48] The entire Rule wants to train monastics in these attitudes, especially RB 7. A similar expression is used for prayer that is to be said "in all humility" (20.1; cf. 20.2; 47.4), for obedience (6.7; 3.4), and for fraternal relationships (31.7, 13). An attitude of humility grows out of faith in Christ's presence in the abbot/prioress, in the brothers/sisters, in the liturgy, and here in the guest. A text later ascribed to Augustine shows the connection between humility and hospitality:

> O truly holy hospitality, the friend of angels, the sister of love, the crown of humility! Whoever possesses you possesses true humility! Whoever possesses humility, practices true hospitality. Brothers, let not only the Fathers teach us to keep hospitality holy, but let us also learn humility from Christ. . . . This is the perfect foundation of hospitality. O truly holy humility, sister and graceful friend of hospitality. Whoever possesses you sees himself in everything as more insignificant than others. Never does he yearn to appear superior to others. He evades the first seats and detests all desire to dominate. Hospitality alone he embraces in love, hospitality alone he desires to practice (*Ad fratres in eremo, s.* 46).

For Benedict, humility is the necessary foundation for all interpersonal relationships toward the inside [the community] and as well as toward the outside [the world].

Smaragdus (on this verse) and Hildemar (503) explain the expression "all humility" as humility of the body (external gestures) and of the heart. Benedict had said that the steps of humility are fitted into our body and soul (7.9). Humility of heart and its external expression in gestures are in harmony. The word *exhibere* (literally: to show outside something that is internal) points to a humility that is being expressed.[49]

V. 7: With head bowed or with a full prostration of the body to the ground Christ is to be adored in them as it is he who is also received.

1. *With head bowed.* The word "to bow" occurs in RB always in connection with humility. In the twelfth step of humility, the monastic also bows the head before God (7.63). Unlike the Master, who has a vast number of different bows, Benedict is rather sober and uses this expression only on important occasions.

2. *Or with a full prostration of the body to the ground.* A living faith in the presence of Christ moves the monastic even to prostrate him- or herself. By prostrating, a person makes oneself as small as possible knowing that, in the presence of the other, this one is the one who receives. In RB a prostration can express a plea for prayer or for reconciliation; in RM it can also express adoration.[50] The Church Fathers describe this in the context of hospitality: Abraham "adored by prostrating himself to the ground; and thus showed in gestures and words his great eagerness, the prominent humility of his soul, the highest degree of hospitality."[51]

Compared with the preceding verses, Benedict here takes a further step by seeing the monastics not only as partners on the same level with the strangers, but as their debtors; they are below them. As a result of humility the monastic "regards himself as the least person" (7.49) and is "convinced of this in the depth of his heart" (7.51). A right, humble, and truthful behavior toward all people presupposes growth in the spiritual life. Growing in the knowledge and love of God, we recognize more and more our sinfulness. More and more we lose the desire to surpass others, more and more we realize that in the presence of others we, too, are the ones who receive. As individuals and as community we are "a useless servant" (7.49; cf. Luke 17:10). Being rooted in humility before God will help us in everyday life to meet the sick, the elderly, the children, and the strangers in this humility and thus to reveal the dignity of each human person.

3. *Christ is to be adored in them as it is he who is also received.* Benedict connects the gesture of prostration with the belief that Christ is present in the guest. It expresses adoration, veneration of Christ. The words "as it is he who is truly received" follow as a confirmation so as to impress this fact on everyone. The word "to adore" (*adorare*) occurs in RB only here. One would expect to find this word in the context of prayer rather than here. It is typical for Benedict that this "adoration" before the stranger and the poor takes place outside, in everyday life. The preceding chapter about the

oratory speaks about praying. True prayer leads to "adoring" Christ in human beings. "The one who says 'this is my body' is the same who also says: 'What you do for the least among you, you did for me.'"[52] Eucharistic adoration should lead us to recognize Christ also in the poor and needy, in fellow brothers and sisters, and to venerate Christ in them. Seeing with Benedict's deep faith we have every reason to prostrate ourselves before each human being, especially before the poor. Christ guarantees the dignity of each human person.

V. 8: But the guests who were received
are to be led to prayer.
After this the superior, or the one whom he has appointed,
is to sit with them.

The words "but the guests who were received" mark the beginning of a second phase that describes the activities in which the guest participates. Verses 8 and 9 have a parallel structure. Both verses first emphasize the spiritual activity (prayer, holy reading), then the human activity (sitting together, meal). Verse 8 speaks of guests; verse 9 of a guest.

1. *But the guests who were received are to be led to prayer.* The expression "led to prayer" points to a first goal of hospitality. Prayer has its place at the beginning of human relationships, and the encounter is to lead to prayer. *Oratio* can generally be translated as prayer (its usual meaning for Benedict), yet it can also mean liturgical prayer. The expression "to be led" suggests a change of place as does the use of the plural "guests"—both indicate a liturgy in the oratory.[53] Moreover, the chapter about the oratory precedes the chapter about the guests.

The community shows its identity as one that gives prayer prime of place. The oratory is a central place for them. Here the presence of God is especially dense (19.1-2), here this divine presence is again and again renewed through the Word of God and the Eucharist, and here the community receives its new members. Thus monastics share their treasured gift with the guest.

"They are to be led to prayer"—this is not a practical instruction simply to be fulfilled on the surface as we, for example, collar a person and force them to go to church or to attend a liturgy. As a model of action, this instruction implies that the spiritual foundations and principles of monastic life are being shared, that we monastics give prayer prime of place in our lives, that we live in the presence of God and thus help to bring others into contact with God and with each other. In addition, it also means that our liturgy is always accessible and radiates beyond the community. If in the oratory we experience time and again the hospitality of our God, we also have the duty to bring others with us into this love of God.

2. *After this the superior, or the one whom he appointed, is to sit with them.* Benedict emphasizes the expression "after this." First the liturgy, the prayer in the oratory is to be experienced, and then one can, perhaps by referring to it, begin a conversation. As so often in the RB, experience precedes instruction (cf. comments on RB 58). Sitting is a posture of listening as well as of teaching. In any case, it indicates that one takes time for another. As old sources indicate, this is probably a spiritual conversation.[54] This requires a great deal of listening, but also of speaking. In this connection, John Chrysostom says that the service of the word often may refresh the needy more than a gift: "A word is better than a gift." And Benedict says: "A good word surpasses the best gift."[55] Benedict does not say much about speaking, but he lays the foundation for a fruitful dialogue: silence as listening, reasonable, and thoughtful speaking (RB 6–7). The old texts are always concerned with helping the guest find salvation and with avoiding talkativeness that is detrimental for both sides.

V. 9: The divine law is to be read to the guest
   so as to edify him;
   and afterwards he is to be shown every human kindness.

1. *The divine law is to be read to the guest.* The abbot is specifically required to be "learned in the divine law in order to have the necessary knowledge from which to draw the old and the new" (64.9). He must be able to use the remedies of Sacred Scripture (28.3). This does not require biblical scholarship, but the art, cultivated by the Fathers, to fathom and explain the Scriptures regarding the situation of an individual person. We may recall the structure of the instructions of the Fathers (*Apophthegmata*): "Give me a word," then a specific instruction from the Sacred Scriptures follows that becomes for the individual "the word" (*sermo*). The expression "the divine law" also points to the fact that Benedict here sees Sacred Scripture as providing assistance for people's actual lives.[56]

"To read" does not only mean a mechanical reading aloud, but also to meditate, repeat, even explain. The word always penetrates us through the ears and from there should reach our heart and then be translated into our lives. "Listen, incline the ear of your heart . . . put it into practice . . . so as to come back" (Prol 1–2). The community lives from the word of God: in the liturgy, in personal Scripture reading, in the table reading, and as taught by the abbot/prioress. Now this is also to be shared with the people coming from outside.

We strive to have Sacred Scripture penetrate our behavior and our lives in community. We are to be living Bibles, that is, not persons whose speech is interlaced with Bible quotes, but rather persons who hear and fulfill the word (cf. Jas 1:22). In general, we try our best to put these instructions of the rule into practice by giving the Scriptures a worthy place in the guest-room, in the hospital, and in our home. Sometimes it is opportune actually to read something from the Scriptures with other people.

2. *So as to edify him.* Today the word "edify" is foreign to us. In the Bible and in the liturgy it is often used in the sense of edifying the community, the church, as well as the faith of individuals. Ephesians 4:29 says, for example: "Never let evil talk pass your lips; say only the good things people need to hear, things that will really help them."[57] Benedict uses this word always in the context of reading (presumably reading Sacred Scripture)[58] and does not follow some of the Desert Fathers who did not care whether or not the guest was edified; rather, it is a real concern for him that the guest is being strengthened in his faith. This is similar to Basil for whom the word "edifi-cation" could be used as thematic concept for all relationships with the out-side world.[59] This goal also further describes the preceding expression: the "reading" is to be done in such a way that it truly edifies the other.

3. *And afterwards he is to be shown every human kindness (humanitas).* For the third time Benedict emphasizes a sequence (vv. 4-5: first/only after; v. 8 after this; v. 9 afterwards): first prayer, then the kiss of peace, first prayer, then dialog/conversation, first reading the Scriptures, then *human-itas*. Monastic tradition has put great emphasis on this sequence. One does not sit down to a meal before having celebrated the liturgy, read the Scrip-tures, or at least, prayed.[60] This clearly shows that the spiritual takes prece-dence. Acting in this manner will also be the best guarantee that everything human is taken seriously and is confirmed in its value.

For us today, this instruction indicates the quality of our acting. It is not always possible to keep the sequence and to fulfill the instruction word by word. People today may need more time before reaching the spiritual level. Most often we begin with the human touches. Yet it is our goal to make Christ known through this very human kindness and thus to lead a person to God.[61]

The word *humanitas* (human kindness) was used frequently in antiq-uity and first meant simply humanity, someone behaving as a human being in a noble and virtuous manner. Here in RB 53 this humanity is ex-plained more by actions than by words.[62] In the entire Rule we find a great appreciation of human nature (in contrast to the many negative tenden-cies of that era and in the Rule of the Master). Benedict devotes much space to what is human. One may recall his empathy, his sense for the human person as such, his reverence before each individual, his positive appreciation of the body. The effort to respect everything that is human is also evident throughout Benedictine history.

In the Latin used by Christians, *humanitas* denotes a comforting, giving love. "The kindness and generous love of God our saviour appeared" (*humanitas*, Titus 3:4). If God is "human," God affirms the human person, and gifts that person with God's full love. For Christians, *humanitas* thus became an important expression of love for the neighbor and for the poor and thus was synonymous with good works. "It is a matter of *humanitas* to help the one who has nothing."[63]

Practiced toward strangers and pilgrims, *humanitas* concretely becomes hospitality and is used synonymously with hospitality. Augustine says: "That person is called human who proves to be a human person, and especially the one who receives another into his home."[64] Within hospitality *humanitas* is given an even more concrete meaning as the meal, especially in monastic literature and presumably also in RB 53. In particular, it is human not to keep the fast stubbornly, but to present the guest with a good meal;[65] yet even then the principle of simplicity and dignity applies (cf. Basil, *Reg. fus.* 20.1-3).

Benedict cultivates humaneness because he lives in Christ. For him there is no dichotomy between care for the body and care for the soul. In today's technological, specialized society there is an increasing desire for spaces where we can be fully human. We may reflect about what we do to cultivate and spread such human values as tact, reverence, attentiveness, courtesy, empathy, politeness, friendship, the furnishing of rooms in simple and good taste, care of our natural environment, and so on.[66] Humaneness, a sense for human persons and their dignity, especially also of weaker ones, is an important task in our world that has become dehumanized in so many respects.

V. 10: The superior is to break his fast on account of the guest
          except on a day of special fast
          which must not be broken.
V. 11: The brothers, however, are to keep the usual fast.

Already the hermits had to deal with the problem of how to reconcile fasting and hospitality. Benedict sets up three principles for his community:

The superior breaks the fast on account of the guest. Here he follows the general solution of the Desert Fathers. Hospitality is a work of Christian love and a divine command; thus, it prevails over one's own ascetic practice and over fasting that is a human command. In the opinion of the Fathers, it is more praiseworthy to show *humanitas*, human kindness, and love to passing brothers than to keep strict abstinence.[67] A monk who has grass growing on his stove, is told: "With this you chased hospitality away" (*Vit. Patr.* V.10.94). This is even true for Lent: one may violate a human command (fasting), but not a divine one (love, ibid. V.13.4). A monk sought help from an elder in Lent and expressed his fear to find his door locked. Yet the Elder said: "It is my rule to welcome you with hospitality" (ibid. V.13.7).

2. *Except on a day of special fast which must not be broken.* Benedict has great appreciation for fasting (cf. 4.13; 49). If the superior would only follow the preceding rule, he would never be able to fast because of the many guests who are never lacking (v. 16). The superior always eats with the guests and strangers as 56.1-2 states. And if there are fewer guests, he can also call brothers to his table. This means that, on ordinary fast days, he eats with the guests prior to the meal of the brothers.[68] Yet on days of special fasting the superior joins the community in fasting.

3. *The brothers, however, are to keep the usual fast.* Community life is to go on without interruption.[69] This regulation is all the more necessary as many guests are present (v. 16). In this concrete situation, Benedict makes an effort to give, on the one hand, the first place to the command of love; yet, on the other hand, to protect the space which the community needs. In doing this the superior is, however, to some extent separated from the brothers. At table, guests are given precedence, and this is probably an indication that love in principle prevails over monastic discipline. Yet at the same time, there is a clear recognition that discipline, asceticism, and daily schedule, the "customs," are necessary for the community as a support for their spiritual life and a safeguard of their love.

V. 12: The abbot is to pour water on the hands of the guests.

Washing people's hands is a service of humility (according to RM 14.74f.). Sulpicius Severus described how Martin of Tours invited him to a meal and how he himself poured water on his hands. He did not dare to prevent the saint from doing this (*Vit. Mart.* 25.3). Perhaps this impressed Benedict. The abbot performs this service himself (here and in the following verse the superior is called "abbot"). This had always been emphasized in the tradition of hospitality. One is not to have servants do this service nor be ashamed to care for the poor oneself, to serve the guests and to wash their feet (cf. comments on v. 13). It is an honor that one's hands may serve human beings in this manner. John Chrysostom says: "Do not be ashamed to take care of the poor. This service will sanctify your hands. And if after this service you stretch out your hands in prayer . . . God will hear you."[70]

V. 13: The abbot as well as the entire community
are to wash the feet of all guests.

As before Benedict repeats that the action—here the foot washing—is offered to all guests. One can well imagine that the monastics recoiled from the feet of many. Yet in this regard, too, there is "no respect of person" (cf. 2.20; 34.2). Not only the abbot, but the entire community wash the feet of all, and in doing so the monastics also participate in this service for others. In this action the two communities, all the guests, and all the monastics meet. This may shed some light on how important this gesture actually is. Hospitality is not only described with words from a liturgical vocabulary, but at the end, a kind of liturgical ritual is celebrated (vv. 13-14). The foot washing has, first, a very practical meaning as people walked barefoot in the heat and on dusty roads. Thus foot washing and love for strangers are inseparably connected.[71] Jesus reproaches the pharisee for not having offered him water to wash his feet (Luke 7:44), and the widows of the early Christian communities must wash the feet of the saints and offer hospitality (1 Tim 5:10).

Later, and especially in cooler climates, this practical meaning of the foot washing is lost. Yet other meanings are present, perhaps already indicated in RB 53 in the very fact that a general foot washing occurs perhaps in the evening, separated from, or after, the meal. Jesus washed the feet of his disciples and performed for them the service of a slave. This was also a sign of his being humbled even to the Cross, a sign of his loving dedication to his disciples and of his forming a true community with them (cf. John 13:8). Hence, the foot washing has come to signal the imitation of Christ among Christians and monastics. They want to serve as Christ served by fully dedicating himself.[72] Other authors emphasize that the foot washing is given to Christ himself who, as it were, holds out his feet to us. It is an honor to serve Christ.[73] As in Christ's gesture, the foot washing is seen as an expression of fraternal love and of unity. Monastics and strangers truly enter a communal bond with each other. The one serving indicates that in Christ he or she becomes one with the brother/sister, that he or she becomes a brother/sister, and that before God the Father they both are equal in human nature, poverty, and grace.[74] According to the Church Fathers, the foot washing has not only the function of an external cleansing, but also cleanses from sin. It is a mystery, a "sacrament." This interpretation was also furthered because the foot washing was often done before or after baptism.

All this shows the importance of the foot washing. Refusing this service is seen as a sign of unbelief. A saying of the Fathers lists three things that must be honored: receiving the sacred mysteries, the table of the brothers, and the basin for the foot washing.[75]

It will probably not happen often that in our service we will actually wash people's feet, yet the meaning of the action is being accomplished in other ways—in unselfish service, in our desire to enter into companionship with others, our courage to perform even menial services as a concrete expression of our imitation of Christ and of our love for him. In our society, with its numerous struggles for power, such a service, with its clear renunciation of dominance, is a true witness for Christ and his Gospel (Luke 22:24-27) as well as a witness for a servant church.

V. 14: After the washing this verse is to be sung:
    "O God, we have received your mercy
    within your temple."

1. *After the washing this verse is to be sung.* The foot washing and the verse form a short liturgy (one manuscript says "a short prayer follows") that may have been done for all the guests in the evening or after the meal. In the Rule of the Master this verse is only sung when foreign brothers are visiting (65.9; 76.3), while at the foot washing for guests the following verse is sung: "You commanded, Lord, that your precepts be diligently kept" (30.6-7). Benedict, however, seems to see the foot washing not so much as a duty, but rather as a grace given by God. Moreover, this is yet another indication that he considers all guests as brothers. The entire psalm from which this verse is taken (Ps 47 [48]) is a song of thanksgiving for God's activity and salvation in God's Holy City. Experiencing God's mercy and kindness awakens gratitude in human beings. Similarly, the porter responds to the call of a stranger or a poor person: "Thanks be to God" (66.3). Augustine explains this expression in this way: "Whoever says 'Thanks be to God' demonstrates his gratitude to God. See whether a brother does not have to thank God when he sees his other brother" (*In Ps.* 132.6). With the same attitude, a monastic, at the end of this chapter, asks the guest for a blessing (53.24).

2. *Within your temple.* Monastics live in God's temple (this word occurs only here), in God's tent (Prol 22–24, 33). The monastery is the house of God (cf. comments on v. 22). God receives them there as guests; they experience God's hospitality. Thus they will pass on this love of God to strangers, taking them also into this divine hospitality. Smaragdus explains this expression thus: they welcome guests within the temple, that is, in their hearts, for our heart is God's temple (cf. comment on this passage). May we go further and interpret "within" in the sense that, in the midst of community, we experience the need of other people as well as the grace that comes from such service? And that all our serving grows from the center of monastic life and, in turn, makes it productive?

3. *We have received, O God, your mercy.* This verse is used in the liturgy for February 2: The Lord comes into his temple, into his own domain. Just like Simeon and Anna, the monastics want to be ready to encounter him; in God they receive mercy and salvation. Most manuscripts have the verb in the past tense, perhaps indicating that the reception of the guests took

place already earlier. The word "receive" is used in this chapter for the guest, for Christ, and for mercy. By welcoming the guest and the stranger, Christ is received and, in Christ, mercy.[76]

Mercy is giving goodness; it means to have a heart for the poor and the needy. In the Rule this kindness is directed above all to the poor and the insignificant and distinguishes especially the abbot (64.9 f.; 34.4; 37.1). It mirrors God's mercy that lasts forever and that the monastic experiences by acknowledging his or her sinfulness. In his experiences with sin, in others and in his community, Benedict must have been deeply impressed by God's mercy (cf. RB 27.8-9); and thus he added as the last instrument of good works, "never lose hope in God's mercy" (4.74 while the Master says "never to despair of God," 3.77).

We have received: At first sight this seems strange since we have the impression that it is the monastics who do everything for other people and practice mercy. Practicing hospitality for strangers and the poor (cf. comments on v. 15) had become synonymous with practicing mercy. Yet in doing this, the monastics are the ones who receive; in giving they are receiving something. The poor and the strangers are not the recipients of alms, but rather benefactors. In this, Benedict follows the Church Fathers who emphasize time and again that in practicing hospitality we are actually the ones who receive something. We receive the blessing of God (v. 24), gain a treasure, the fulfillment of the promises, eternal life, forgiveness of sins, grace and mercy, the eternal hospitality of God. Augustine says: "You only have to offer hospitality to the guest, and then you will certainly ask your guest . . . that he accompany you to the goal . . . I tell you that, when you offer him comfortable hospitality, he will offer you an even more comfortable and grateful hospitality. O how happy you will be when you will be God's guest (Matt 25:35-40) . . . For your hospitality he promised you God's hospitality."[77]

Again we are reminded of exaltation and humiliation, of the revaluation of all values: the poor receive mercy while the rich go away empty. The poor have the ability to receive, to stretch out their hands and to accept gifts. RB 53 shows clearly to what extent humility as being poor in spirit is a fundamental condition for hospitality, for receiving, giving, sharing, and serving. In whatever the monastics do they gratefully acknowledge that it is they themselves who receive God's mercy. This strong belief can impress us and is equally relevant for us today. In all our tasks we are, in a deeper sense, the ones who receive. And the more we acknowledge this fact in gratitude, the more we are again the ones receiving a gift. The Church Fathers are very clear on this point:

> [T]he one receiving is richer than the one handing out. . . . Don't ever say in your heart, "I'm giving, he's receiving; I'm giving him a welcome, he's in

need of shelter." Perhaps what you're in need of is rather more than that. Perhaps the one you are giving a welcome to is a just man; he's in need of bread, you of truth; he's in need of shelter, you of heaven; he's in need of money, you of justice . . . . so let us take care of Christ. He's with us in those who are his . . . By doing this sort of thing, we recognize Christ in good works, with the heart, not the body; not with the eyes of the body, but with the eyes of faith.[78]

V. 15:   Particularly diligent care and concern
        is to be shown in welcoming the poor and the strangers
        because in them Christ is received even more particularly.
        For the imperious behavior of the rich
        exacts special respect all by itself.

At the end of this chapter's first part, it is as if Benedict wanted to emphasize once again that in these actions of hospitality the poor and the strangers are to be preferred. This lends the verse its special weight as it refers back to verses 1-2.

   1. *In particular for the poor and the strangers.* Since the fourth century, the poor and the strangers often designated the same persons, and offering hospitality thus became synonymous with showing compassion to strangers in need.[79] Yet, in contrast to today's concept, the Latin word *pauper* does not mean subhuman poverty, but simply designates someone who has only the bare necessities to live on.[80] RB does not use this word for the monks even if they were truly poor; the word always designates people from outside. Perhaps in view of the social misery of their time, the monks shied away from using the word for themselves; or perhaps they experienced poverty as so oppressing that they no longer used the word for what was associated with voluntary poverty.[81]

   After having emphasized the word "all" four times in RB 53, Benedict now establishes for the second time a hierarchy that differs from that of a bourgeois world: requiring particular care for the poor and the strangers. The reason for such a reversal is not simply human compassion, but the Christian faith that becomes effective in love. One does not inquire whether the poor are clean or in rags, honest or fraudulent; the sole fact that they need help calls for eager care and concern. It is certainly in the line of the Gospel to give preference to the poor, the orphans, and the needy rather than to the rich and the powerful. This corresponds to the values of a God who chooses what is lowly and humbles what is exalted (cf. Luke 1:51-53; Matt 11:25; 1 Cor 1:26-29).

   2. *Particularly diligent care is to be shown.* It is interesting to note that the Latin words *cura* (care) and *sollicitudo/sollicitus* (diligent) occur in RB in

connection with the sick (36.1-7) and the excommunicated brothers (27.1, 5-6), as well as in the chapter about the cellarer (31.19). Diligent, conscientious care is necessary especially for the weak, for those who depend on help, although others are not excluded from such care. This diligence is best described in RB 72. Care for the poor encompasses all this: outdoing one another in showing respect, bearing one another's weaknesses with greatest patience, considering what benefits the poor, and being selfless in showing them fraternal love. We can also think of everything that preceded in RB 53: respect, the love due to guests, prayer, dialog (with a good word), *humanitas*, human kindness, the washing of hands and feet. Care means more than simply giving and helping (categories the Master uses primarily to describe behavior toward the poor). John Chrysostom says: "It is easy to give money, but it requires generosity to become a servant to the poor and to serve them with the joy of love" (*In illud vid.* 15). We may recall what the Good Samaritan did for the man who was robbed on the road to Jericho (Luke 10:34).

The monastery of Monte Cassino probably was poor, but the little they had was shared with the poor as Gregory shows in the *Dialogs* (e.g., II.28). From of old the administration of monastic goods was designed to help the poor. Yet care includes more. RB 4.14-19 says: "to refresh the poor, to clothe the naked, to visit the sick, to bury the dead, to help the troubled and to console the sorrowing." The text continues: "to become a stranger to the ways of the world." Serving the poor contradicts the values of the world. The motivation for this care for the poor is "to prefer nothing to the love of Christ" (4.21).

Care implies that we allow others to enter our own life, our thinking, praying, and working, that we accept our responsibility for them, accompany them on their journey, and try to see how to help them in ways that are effective and lasting. This diligent care was preceded by the fact that the porter responded to the call of the poor "in the fear of God quickly and with the fervor of love" (66.3-4). Care presupposes attentive listening to what the poor say and need. Today the poor call out not only in words, but through their very existence and the extent of their poverty. How do we respond to it? With the fervor of love and in diligent care?

3. *Because in them Christ is received even more particularly.* Benedict shows great courage in saying that in the poor and the strangers Christ is received even more than in others. The reason for diligent care is not human compassion, but rather faith. John Chrysostom says: "By how much the brother may be least, so much more does Christ come to thee through him" (*In Act. H.* 45.3). Thus service to the poor and the needy is in a very special way an encounter with Christ and being gifted with his mercy. This is presumably the reason that this statement follows the psalm

verse, "We have received your mercy," and we receive it especially in the poor. Only when we ourselves are poor and humble, willing to receive, can we help the poor and the strangers. Augustine says:

> God wanted to be needy in the poor. . . . Give of your earthly bread and knock on the door pleading for the heavenly bread; the Lord is the bread. . . . How could he give to you if you do not give to the needy? One [the poor] is needy with regard to you, you are so with regard to another [Christ]; and as you are needy with regard to another, and another one with regard to you, so a poor person is needy with regard to a needy person. Truly, you are needy with regard to him [Christ] who has no need of anything. . . . He does not need anyone for he is the Lord . . . yet he humbled himself to be hungry in his poor . . . so that we can also do something for him.[83]

It is obvious how important this verse with its "preferential option for the poor" is in today's world with its growing poverty. We are reminded of refugees, areas of famine, slums, disasters. Certainly giving and goodwill are not enough. Diligent care includes raising our consciousness, activating the energies of the poor, helping them to help themselves, working toward improving systemic problems, and prophetic admonition of the powerful. All these activities are to be rooted in Christ and lead to him. According to Benedict, spiritual and social dimensions belong together and cannot be separated.

4. *For the imperious behavior of the rich exacts respect all by itself.* Apparently, rich people also come to the monastery. Benedict does not speak of them in a very friendly manner: they spread terror, exact respect that is given voluntarily to others. Terror is always connected with fear and trembling. Benedict's monastery probably suffered under the rich (cf. *Dial.* II.31.1). They are not turned away,[84] but preference is given to the poor.

OVERVIEW OF THE SECOND PART

The first verse takes up the expression "arriving guests"; the last one ends with the word "guest." This part is concerned with a communal organization of hospitality:

Verses 16-20 deal with the kitchen (vv. 19-20 apply the specific case to general situations);

verses 21-22 speak of a guestmaster and the guest quarters;

verses 23-24 could be a postscript: not all brothers speak with a guest.

In the second part of RB 53 the concern for the community is paramount. Twice a purpose is given: "that they [the guests] not disturb the brothers" (v. 16) and "that they [the brothers] may serve without grumbling" (v. 18); both passages concern peace in the community.

The very connection of the two parts in RB 53 constitutes the specific nature of Benedictine hospitality.

V. 16: The abbot and the guests are to have their own kitchen
       so that the guests who arrive at unpredictable hours
       and who are never lacking in a monastery, do not disturb the brothers.

1. *The abbot and the guests are to have their own kitchen.* Verses 10-11 already contain an indirect requirement for a separate kitchen because the guests and the superior do not fast except on very important fasting days. We can sense how the monastery begins to expand. Now there are two kitchens. The reason for this arrangement is probably similar to the one for separating the infirmary (36.7): on the one hand, good care for those who are sick; on the other, protecting the community against pampering. The novices also seem to have their own refectory (58.5).

2. *The guests who arrive at unpredictable hours and are never lacking in a monastery.* This seems to point to the situation in Monte Cassino, but not to the one in Subiaco. The flow of guests has increased; Benedict does not foresee any change in this. We are in the period of the Gothic Wars, and Monte Cassino is located near an important road leading from the south to Rome.

3. *so that . . . the brothers are not disturbed.* Disturbing, disquieting, this is the opposite of order and quiet. Guests may bring disquiet and chaos. It is always Benedict's concern to preserve quiet, prayer, and peace in the community,[85] and to make allowance for the weaknesses of monastics. The community's reserves are not unlimited, yet the community must not lose its ability to give witness to peace and joy.

V. 17: Every year two brothers who can do this service competently
       are to be assigned to this kitchen.

1. *Every year two brothers are to be assigned to this kitchen.* While in RM, two brothers who need not have special qualifications take care of the guests by turns, in RB these monastics are assigned with the purpose to prepare good meals. They work in the kitchen for a year so that they are able to familiarize themselves well with the work.

2. *Brothers who can do this service competently.* Benedict uses the word *officium* for duties in general (Prol 39), for specific duties such as serving at table (35.1), the duty of the cellarer (31.17), and various types of work (48.22); but also for the treasured service of the *opus Dei* (title of RB 8; 16.2; 43.1). This seems to indicate that serving God and serving human beings form a unity, and serving human beings is also worship (cf. the liturgical

vocabulary used in RB 53). Thus this word "service" runs like a red thread through the entire Rule.

The two monastics are to do this service well. This is part of *humanitas* (v. 9). We can imagine that the meals of the community were not always tasty since all monastics (even those who had never done manual work) had to take their turn cooking, and since the cooks changed every week. Certainly service in the guest kitchen is as much a "service in love" (35.6) as that in the monastery kitchen, but a good attitude is not the only thing required. Good will and dedication—as basic as they are—do not suffice, and competence and skill are necessary as well. Today we think of appropriate training.

V. 18: When needed they are to be given helpers
        so that they can serve without grumbling.
        Yet when they have less work,
        they are to go wherever work is assigned to them.
V. 19: This consideration is to apply not only to these brothers,
        but to all services in the monastery:
V. 20: If helpers are needed, they are to be provided,
        yet whenever these helpers are free,
        they obediently do any other task given to them

In verse 18, Benedict is still dealing with the guest kitchen and the cooks. He then adds a general principle (vv. 19-20). Verses 18 and 20 are so similar[86] that they can be interpreted together.

1. *When helpers are needed.* This expression occurs twice in these verses. Benedict is concerned about just distribution of helpers not on the basis of persons or the number of complaints, but on the basis of real need (cf. 34; 55.21). For Benedict, need can designate a weakness, an illness, or some limitation, yet it is never a privilege or a right that can be claimed. Yet external circumstances (a great number of guests) or human limitations of the cooks may result in the need for helpers.

2. *This consideration applies.* The Latin word *consideratio* means considering, reflecting carefully, paying attention to all circumstances, especially taking into account weaknesses and needs (cf. 34.2; 37.3). This consideration is practiced in particular by the abbot who is to have the gift of discretion and who has to consider and discern the actual needs (cf. 48.25; 55.20 f.; 64.17-19).

3. *Helpers are provided.* The Latin word *solacium* means consolation, help, relief. In the same way as in RB 53, helpers are provided for the service in the kitchen and at table so that monastics can serve without sadness

(*sine tristitia* 35.3), or for the cellarer so that he can fulfill his duties with "inner peace" (*aequo animo* 31.17). The porter, too, may need helpers (66.5).[87] While the Master is mainly concerned that things are being done in the right order, Benedict is always concerned with the inner attitude of those who perform the work.[88]

4. *That they can serve without grumbling.* Benedict probably chose the verb "to serve" deliberately. Already in the first part of RB 53 serving was expressed in the foot washing (v. 13); here it is a matter of concrete service regarding the human kindness in which the kitchen servers (and many others in the background!) participate. Benedict particularly likes to use the verb "to serve" for the service in the kitchen (35.1, 6, 13) and the service for the sick (36.1, 4); but the word also refers to liturgical service (19.3; cf. 18.24), and then to all of monastic life (61.10; 5.3) that is a "school for the Lord's service" (Prol 45).

Here as in 41.5 the abbot is to make every effort to avoid any reasons for grumbling. Apparently, there was much grumbling in Benedict's monastery. Often the admonition not to grumble is directed to the monastics, especially concerning food (cf. 40.8f.; 41.5), kitchen service (35.13), distribution of goods (34.6), and obedience (5.14-19).

First Peter 4:9-11 may be a scriptural basis: "Be mutually hospitable without complaining. As generous distributors of God's manifold grace, put your gifts at the service of one another, each with the gift he has received" (The Vulgate text reads: *sine murmuratione . . . administrantes . . . ministrare . . . virtute quam administrat Deus*).

Murmuring can be a lack of faith: someone is jealous and also calculates and compares instead of seeing things from God's vantage point. To be sure, murmuring does not always originate in human malice—and this seems to be Benedict's opinion—it can also happen that someone is burdened with work beyond one's strength so that grumbling is not one's own fault. Therefore the abbot/prioress is admonished to organize all matters in such a manner that "souls may be saved and that the brothers can do the work without reasons from grumbling" (41.5).

It matters to Benedict how the kitchen servers do their work even though they do not have direct contact with the guests. Serving strangers means serving Christ, and this service is holy. God sees our heart (5.18); therefore, all are to do their service without sadness or confusion, without grumbling, or, positively: doing it in peace and joy. Benedict is at pains to make this possible.

5. *When they have less work—when they are free.* It seems that usually a great number of guests is present. Yet is also happens that there is not enough work for two kitchen servers and their helpers respectively. As

Benedict strives on the one hand to avoid overburdening, a mad rush, and thus grumbling and discouragement, so, on the other hand, he also wants to avoid idleness and gossiping (cf. 48.24; 43.8). Thus, when there is not enough work, the helpers go to do a different task (cf. 48.23). The workers are to be distributed in a just manner. Idleness is the enemy of the soul (48.1). The latter was a true danger for Benedict's monks and was probably more real than it is for us today.

6. *They are to go wherever work is assigned to them . . . they obediently do any other task given to them.* After having first shown consideration, Benedict now can also demand that the monastics obey. The superior has the task, even the power (*imperium*) to assign the work and give orders. Obedience guarantees an effective fulfillment of the communal tasks. It is precisely through obedience that all members of the community share in service for the world and bear their part in it, some in one place, others in another.

7. *This consideration is to apply to all services in the monastery.* The word "all" here is emphasized in the same way as in the first part of the chapter ("all guests"). No service is to be exempt from this principle. In Benedict's time, it was apparently possible to respond to all calls from the world and to serve all those who were in need. The monastery had enough members to bring help where it was needed. Nowhere in RB is there an indication that something like a lack of personnel existed.

Yet this is precisely our problem, that the helpers are lacking. The superior may use much consideration and may have much understanding for a situation, yet still is not able to provide effective help. The hard truth is that we are not able to respond to all calls for help "with a quick action" (66.3f.) and to welcome "all guests" in that same manner. In our heart and our prayers we have no limits, yet not in our actual ability to help. In this respect, this second part of RB 53 is today as relevant as the first part: we can accept as many tasks as members of the community can perform without confusion (v. 16), without just grumbling (v. 18; cf. 41.5), in peace of mind (cf. 31.17), without sadness (cf. 35.3), and without discouragement (cf. 48.24, all these passages deal with work!), and as long as true community life is still possible. Yet, if this is no longer guaranteed, we have to make the difficult decision of limiting the work and perhaps even giving up certain tasks. Then we also have to face the pressing question: To whom or what among our tasks do we give precedence? Which tasks do we not relinquish if at all possible? According to RB 53, we, as communities, have a special task toward brothers/sisters in faith, the poor, and the strangers.

V. 21: Furthermore, the guest quarters are to be entrusted to a brother whose soul is filled with the fear of God.

1. *The guest quarters are to be entrusted to a brother.* Benedict uses the word *cella* to designate a certain part of the monastery. Thus, there is the *cella* of the infirmary (36.7), of the novitiate (58.5) where the novices study, eat, and sleep, the *cella* of the porter (66.2), and the *cella* of the dormitory (22.4). While earlier Rules mention only a porter (*ianitor, ostiarius*),[89] RM and RB add guest quarters with brothers responsible for them. Yet in RM they are chosen from the ranks and take their turn doing this work. The growth of the community and the increase in people seeking help were probably the reasons for expanding the monastery buildings. A certain brother is assigned to the guest quarters (the Latin word *adsignare* means to entrust, assign, to place something into someone's hands, cf. also 42.7). Benedict requires that this monastic have certain qualities. He is, like the porter, a representative and an interpreter of the community and shows how the entire community actually wants to be and how it is to fulfill its task in and for the world.[90]

2. *Whose soul is filled with the fear of God.*[91] This is a strong expression: his soul is to be filled, totally penetrated by the fear of God. From RB 53 we can conclude that this monastic is not afraid of the "terror" of the rich, but knows the fear of God. In RB 7 the fear of God, the first step of humility, is said to be identical with living in the presence of God. As in the Scriptures, fear of God is the right attitude before God and human beings during our prayer as well as during our work (cf. 7.10). In fearing God we recognize God's calls, and thus fear of God is especially important for deliberations and discernment (3.11; 64.1; 65.15). For Benedict this virtue has practical consequences. In contrast to the Master, he requires this virtue from the cellarer (31.2), the infirmarian (36.7), the abbot (3.11), the porter (66.4), and the guestmaster (53.21). All of them see every human person from the vantage point of God and are to take special care of those who are insignificant, poor, and weak, in whom Christ can be recognized. A God-fearing brother/sister will make sure that even the lowliest find good care and that everyone finds the care that he or she needs. Such a monastic will be able to listen to the guests with humility. "The fear of God is the beginning of wisdom" (Ps 111:10). It is also characteristic for Benedict that this fear of God is already connected with love (72.9). The porter, for example, responds with the fear of God and the warmth of love (66.4).

V. 22: There a sufficient number of beds is to be provided; and wise persons are to administer wisely the house of God.

1. *There a sufficient number of beds is to be provided.* The Master only said that beds had to be ready (79.1). Yet Benedict is concerned even with small, practical details. Here especially his human kindness (*humanitas*) is clearly

visible. Everyone who has some experience knows that offering hospitality not only means providing strangers with necessities, but that it is equally important to anticipate needs and to make thoughtful preparations as a concrete sign of love.

Here again we clearly see the connection between spirituality and practical details that is a characteristic feature of Benedict's Rule. His piety and faith do not simply remain in his head or even just in his heart, but rather reach all the way into the tip of his fingers. Seeing Christ arriving in a guest leads to the practical consequence that a good bed must already be prepared.

2. *To administer the house of God.* This solemn expression designates not only the monastery, but here the guest quarters in particular. It is not the incense, but rather this individual, thoughtful attention that tells the guests: Yes, this is truly a house of God!

This house belongs to God, and God reigns in it. The brothers/sisters are simply managing it. God received them into God's hospitality, lets them experience God's love; they are God's guests (cf. RM 88.14). John Chrysostom says that the house becomes a church when hospitality is being offered (*In Mt. H.* 48.6). The Vulgate uses the expression *domus Dei* for the church (e.g., 1 Pet 4:17: "in the house of God . . . which is the church of God"). Augustine uses the expression for the monastery, the church building, and the living church.[92] Benedict uses this expression in two other places where, following Augustine, he connects it with peace and a good atmosphere in the community (31.19; 64.5). The monastery is to be a house where God's presence penetrates everything and where everything becomes a vessel of the altar (31.10).[93] Coming back to RB 53.22, we can say that in experiencing human kindness and love the guests are to experience the hospitality of God who allows us to live in God's house as Augustine says at the beginning of his rule (*Praec.* I.2).

3. *Wise persons wisely administer [the house of God].* For many the fear of God already contains wisdom.[94] For others, wisdom is a next step based on fear of God.[95] Benedict mentions wisdom primarily as a quality of those who hold an office. The cellarer's first quality is to be wisdom (31.1). In the same way "virtuous living and wisdom in doctrine" is to be decisive in appointing deans and electing an abbot (64.2; 21.4). The abbot in particular is to be wise and to know how to proceed like a wise physician (27, 2; 28.2). Yet the porter, too, is to be not only mature, but also wise (66.1).[96]

It seems to me that Benedict's use of this expression is guided more by biblical than philosophical models. In the Hebrew Scriptures, wisdom is the necessary quality of a ruler (cf. Wis 7:7; Isa 11:2). His decisions are rooted in personal experience; the wise person knows the world and human beings not simply from studying, but from the heart. A wise person is a realist, knows how to deal with life, is righteous, and has insight (cf. 1 Kgs 3:11; Sir 18:27; Prov 16:16). For Benedict, this probably includes prudent pondering and adjusting on the basis of discernment (cf. 64.16-19). In the Gospel of Matthew, the wise virgins take precautions and stay alert. In wisdom there is a harmony of intellect and life, discernment and virtue (cf. RB 19.4; Basil, *Reg.* 110). Such persons do not easily lose their balance; they see things as they are and as God sees them. They do no act in their first enthusiasm, but rather have a broad perspective and are persistent (Augustine connects this with patience, *Praec.* IV.5). If fear of God is the beginning of wisdom, we can say that such persons are on a spiritual journey.

V. 23: With the guests, however, no one is to associate or speak in any way unless he is commanded to do so.
V. 24: Yet if a brother meets or sees a guest,
he is to greet him humbly, as we have said,
ask for a blessing and continue on his way
saying that he is not allowed to speak with the guest.

These are the concluding verses of the chapter on the guests. At first, they seem quite outdated, and therefore it is especially important to pay attention to what Benedict intends to say in them. The grammatical link ("with the guests, however") indicates that this might be an addition, perhaps a later correction as experience may have made it necessary (v. 22 would have been a beautiful conclusion). The actual formulation of these verses may have been influenced by a reading of the *Rule of the Four Fathers*.

1. *With the guests, however, no one is to associate or speak in any way unless he is commanded to do so.* After Benedict first generously opened the door, he seems to close it again quite vigorously and to isolate the welcomed guest almost in the same manner as he isolates an excommunicated monastic.[97] There are certain brothers/sisters who are charged to associate with the guests and to speak with them—this is the positive expression. Certainly it is first the guestmaster, but there may be others also. For instance, verse 8 says that the superior, "or the one whom he has appointed to do so," is to sit with the guests. The community seems to have grown larger. The superior no longer is able to fulfill these tasks alone, delegating the tasks that are received in obedience. Benedict also may have been influenced by Basil who greatly values the edification of the guest and who, in his later Rules, says that not all monastics have the gift to say the healing words which can serve to strengthen faith (*Reg. fus.* 32.2). Abbot Eugendus of the Jura monastery was above all concerned to assign each brother a task and commission for which he knew gifts from the Holy Spirit had particularly suited the brother. This passage, too, deals with those who seek help (*Vit. Patr. Iur.* 149).

At the same time, Benedict keeps the other monastics away from the guests; they are not to associate or converse with them. Externally, this is in opposition to verse 4 (where they are to meet with guests). Although, in a fundamental way, they are companions on their way to God, they are not companions in every regard. The guests will leave again. Their bond with the community can never be as close as the one between the community members. This is a very real truth: solidarity is first owed to one's own community where the solidarity with those who seek help and are poor has its roots. As monastics, the brothers/sisters cannot be like the poor and the strangers in every respect; rather, they are "unequal allies."[98] Benedict does not say that the brother/sister must not say anything (*loqui*), but rather that he or she is not to begin a conversation (*conloqui*). This direction can be understood when we consider that the number of guests has grown and that their stay is no longer limited to a few days as in the older tradition.[99] Thus Benedict has to protect both the community members and the guests.

He protects the guests from well-meaning monastics who may have differing views of life. They all have only the guests' welfare at heart, but perhaps do not have the gift of discernment, or they may use the guests to satisfy their own needs for affirmation and love. When Pachomius prohibits the guests from walking around in the monastery, he adds that this will keep the guest from being scandalized by the brothers; thus, he is concerned for the welfare of the guest.[100]

Yet Benedict also protects the monastics from talking much and getting worn out. Understandably, there is a clear distinction between welcoming guests and their continued stay in the monastery. The precious gift of the monastery for people from outside is its spiritual space, its atmosphere of quiet and of searching for God. This is to be preserved, and the monastics are to be protected from harm (*destructio*, 67.5) and excessive demands.[101]

2. *Yet if a brother meets or sees a guest.* This shows clearly that the guests were not totally separated and that it was possible for the monastics to meet guests. When there is no external separation, silence creates an internal distance (cf. also RB 67).

3. *He is to greet him humbly, as we have said, to ask for a blessing and to continue on his way.* With these words Benedict himself refers back to verses 6-7 where he had prescribed that monastics show humility that is also expressed in gestures: a bow of the head or a prostration. Here, too, humility, the desire to welcome a guest, is conveyed in a concrete gesture. While we might expect that the guest asks the brother/sister for a blessing, the exact opposite occurs. In the same manner, the porter in 66.3 asks the poor or the guest for a blessing. This is the very same vision of faith that

also illumines verse 14: the monastics are the ones who receive. They receive mercy and blessings[102] from the world (and not only devils as the Master seems to think!). In the deepest sense, the blessing is Christ himself who arrives in the other person. All monastics are to share in this blessing. Yet, since they are still weak to some extent, their faith must not be endangered but shielded from evil.

4. *He is to continue on his way saying that he is not allowed to speak with the guest.* This last sentence presents an obstacle for us today. We would offer a plausible explanation rather than simply say "we are not allowed." Benedict himself often makes an effort to offer reasonable explanations, but sometimes he shows a strong, allergic reaction and counters abuses with a strict "it is not allowed," as, for example, with regard to personal possessions (33.4-5; 54.1). In Benedict's community there were not only intelligent members, but also many who were slow in understanding (cf. 2.12; 30.2), and thus, according to the pedagogy of his time, Benedict simply and categorically says: "It is not allowed."

The old rules give voice to the experience that the brothers desired to associate with the guests for the purpose of gossiping and idle talk which are not conducive to edification. Thus, restrictions existed already from the earliest times.[103]

How can we translate this into our present situation? Each monastic should be mature enough to sense what is helpful to someone else and to know how one is to behave responsibly. In its literal wording this instruction is outdated, but it is rooted in two principles: first, that certain rules are necessary to protect the community and the guests, and that, above all, the value of silence needs to be emphasized. Seen positively, silence is listening: listening for the deepest needs of another and respecting the other who may be searching for one's own way, for one's own God. In silence we come to know others in a deeper manner, and so will not so easily use them for our own affirmation, but rather consider what would be useful to them (72.7). In silence we also see ourselves with all our aggressions and bad feelings and can surrender all our hostilities to God so that God may transform them into kindness and friendliness (cf. hospitality as being friendly to guests).[104] In silence we recognize what unites us with the guest in our depths, and we recognize that, in a deeper way, we are companions on the journey. We all have experienced that true companionship with others grows and deepens in loving silence. Silence must show a loving face.

Today, people seek spaces of silence and humaneness where they can find themselves again. Silence is part of our monastic life as an attitude of being open to God and to human beings; it witnesses to the fact that our loving God speaks to us and that we make room for God.

Conclusion

1. In reviewing the entire chapter on the background of monastic tradition, Benedict's purpose in RB 53 gains greater clarity: he wanted to unite the ideal of the Desert (and Church) Fathers in practicing hospitality that is inspired by the Scriptures and rooted in Christ, with the loving care for a community that was far from ideal.

Most of the instructions in this chapter have models in monastic tradition, especially those in the first part: in Scripture, perhaps mediated through the Church Fathers, in the *Lives of the Desert Fathers (Historia monachorum)*, in the *Lives of the Fathers (Vitae Patrum)*, in RM (its instructions for welcoming spiritual brothers), and in Cassian (with regard to fasting). In the second part, Benedict works quite independently, yet here especially he is in consonance with other chapters of the Rule, particularly chapters 31–41. He shows himself as a manager who finds concrete forms for expressing fraternal love and love for strangers. The final instructions regarding silence may have come from the *Rule of The Four Fathers* while the influence of Basil is evident more in the spirit of the instructions than in direct literal influences.

2. In retrospect, we note once again how the task for the world is enfolded, as it were, in prayer: prayer at the beginning (v. 3) and silence at the end (v. 24). In between we find prayer before the kiss of peace, prayer and "adoration" vis-à-vis the guest, leading the guest to prayer, offering spiritual conversation, the divine law edifying the guest, the foot washing and its liturgy, the plea for a blessing. In the second part, too, words and thoughts point to the unity of work and prayer and to the spiritual atmosphere in the community as shown by the word "service" and "to serve," by the concern that the monastics not be disturbed, by the qualities of the guestmaster, by "fear of God," "wisdom," and by the designation of the monastery as a house of God.

All this is a vivid proclamation of the Gospel. And in this connection we also see how the kiss of peace, the meal and good cooking, the beds that are ready, are part of this proclamation as well as the measures that seem restrictive to us. The foundation and the basic principles for the community are also part of the monastics' duty toward other human beings. Thus the opportunity of leading others to prayer and of edifying them organically grows from their community life. Since the entire community participates in this service to guests, Benedict's special concern is also directed to the community. Community is not just a stepping stone for the individual's particular mission, as it may be at times in some modern congregations (P. Arrupe, s.j., expressed this once). Rather, the communal life and its strengthening are already part of, and witness to, the community's proclamation of the Gospel.

3. Chapter 53 is a mirror of the entire Rule. What is described here as behavior toward outsiders is already present as instruction for the community itself. The behaviors toward outsiders and insiders form a unity. RB 53 is filled with the same spirit as RB 72: the good zeal of fraternal love, the strong connection between the horizontal and the vertical dimensions, Christocentrism, the concern that all together will come into God's presence. With this spirit of reverence, of obedience, of patience, and unselfish love, the entire community can also master its task toward the world. The word "together" (53.4) now applies to all: to the monastics and those entrusted to them. RB 35 and 36 show how fraternal service (including the foot washing) is to be done in love and without grumbling, how all work is to be begun with prayer, and how particular concern is to be shown to the sick in whom Christ is especially present; these chapters show us how we can serve Christ and can serve like Christ. Just as Benedict describes the abbot and the cellarer (cf. 64; 27; 31; 2) in their behavior toward the community, so he also shows them in their tasks toward other people. We recall their concern and their loving zeal, especially for the weak, their humility and mercy, their friendly words and familiarity with Sacred Scripture, their discretion, prudence, and wisdom, as well as their concern for a calm, peaceful, and amiable atmosphere in the community.

Yet RB 53 also shows very clearly how the spiritual basis of the Rule (Prol; chapters 4–7) are an indispensable precondition for the monastics' tasks toward others. In the Prologue we see Christ's hospitality that he offers to the newcomer. Listening is a holistic attitude directing the monastic toward God, Sacred Scripture, the fellow monastic, those in need, and the circumstances of the times. "Seek peace and pursue it" (Prol 17) is the instruction for the tasks toward the world and also means to be hospitable to strangers. In RB 53, the tools of good works that are assembled in RB 4 are being used, especially the love of God and of neighbor, the works of mercy, "preferring nothing to the love of Christ," the same attitudes of love and reverence toward all human beings, but also appreciating *lectio* and prayer, good words and silence. The tasks in the world are the field where we "fulfill God's commands every day" (4.63). Humility in particular is the basis for effective service. Living in the presence of God, in the fear of God, is in RB 53 the precondition for seeing human beings and specific tasks in the light of God. Ready, joyful obedience toward God and Christ's commands coming from the superior and from others help in coping with tasks and guarantee that our work will bring fruit. The eighth step of humility shows how important it is to work together with the community and in the community. The ninth and eleventh steps demonstrate the meaning of reasonable silence and speech also in our service toward others. The sixth and seventh steps of humility, where the monastic sees him- or herself as nothing and accepts it, are the preconditions for meeting others with open hands and in an attitude of receptivity. "To know nothing more dear than Christ" (5.2) is the attitude RB 53 urges as motivation for responding to all persons in need of our help.

4. Commenting on the two parts of the chapter, Vogüé says that here separation from (distance to) the world (in part 2) and openness to the world (in part 1) oppose each other although priority would belong to the separation from the world.[105] In this, Benedict is part of the entire monastic tradition. Like Abraham, someone leaves the world (as expressed in the manner of the first centuries, cf. Gen 12:1), and departs from family and possessions; yet a monastic must also go further and separate the self internally from egotism, vainglory, desire for power, and gossiping; that is, separate the self from the world that is in his or her heart. This is a purification that has as its goal that the person grow ever more and more into Christ. "To become a stranger to the ways of the world, and to prefer nothing to the love of Christ" (4.20). "To renounce oneself to follow Christ" (4.10). This is expressed first negatively, then positively. Christ leading us into the community and through it again to the people outside. Many monastic fathers say that their journey led them from being a stranger to the world (*xeniteia*) to friendliness to strangers (*philoxenia*) and to proclaiming their faith. We see this also in Benedict's life. Yet the world to which we become a "stranger" is the world from which we can gain something, while the world to which we open ourselves as community is a world in need, a world of the poor and the strangers. Persons such as the abbot, the porter, or the guestmaster, who have come to spiritual maturity, are able to serve like Christ and to serve Christ in others; they have grown into Christ in whom the community is also united. In them Benedict shows that his concern is a particular service to the world.[106]

The altar is at the center of chapter 58. It is a sign of the *xeniteia* of Christ, and for the monastic it is the culmination of one's separation from the world, from all that is a hindrance to our following Christ. The monastic enters into Christ's surrender to the Father and his sacrifice for the many. The altar as a symbol of Christ's death is, however, also a symbol for the eucharistic community and for *philoxenia*, hospitality. From the altar, the brother/sister is led into the community and as its member he or she will be enabled to lead others into the *philoxenia*—the hospitality—of God.

Notes

1. Note of the translator: The German word for hospitality is a compound formed of the words *Gast* (guest) and *Freundschaft* (friendship), i.e., offering friendship to guests. This is also true of the Greek word *philoxenia* the author often uses in this chapter. Except in special cases, I am using the English word hospitality for *philoxenia*. The German word *der Fremde* can mean both a stranger (someone we do not know, who is not familiar to us) and a foreigner, an alien (someone from a different country); all three English words are used for *der/die Fremde/n*.

2. *Reaching Out: The Three Movements of the Spiritual Life* (New York: Doubleday, 1975) 46–48, and his article "Hospitality"; also Seasoltz, "Monastic Hospitality," 430–433.

3. Cf. Art. "Xenos," ThWNT, 1–36.

4. Ibid., 25.

5. Cf. the homilies of the Church Fathers: John Chrysostom, *In Gen. H.* 41.3-7; *in Act. H.* 45.3-4; *in Illud, Ne tim.* 4–7; Ambrose, *De Abr.* I.5.33-43.

6. Cf. C. Spicq, *Théologie morale du Nouveau Testament* (Paris, 1965) 814, 809–815; Chadwick, "Justification by Faith," 281; Clemens, *Ep. ad Cor.* 107; 11.1; 12.1.

7. Cf. *Ep.* 49 (84a); Aristides, *Apology* 15.7.

8. Cf. Chadwick, *The Early Church* (Grand Rapids, MI: Eerdmans, 1968) 56f.; Rusche, *Gastfreundschaft*, passim; Art. "Xenos," THWNT, 22; Art. "Gastfreundschaft," RAC, 1105–1109; Greer, "Hospitality," 31–33; Puzicha, *Christus*, 13.

9. Cf. the following elements in RB 53: honor (v. 2), all love due (v. 3), to go out to meet (v. 3), humility (v. 6), to prostrate oneself (v. 7), to adore Christ (v. 7), human kindness (v. 9), meal (v. 9), foot washing with one's own hands (vv. 12, 13), receiving mercy (v. 14), diligent care (v. 15), guest at unpredictable hours (v. 16). Points of contact between RB 53 and Luke 7:36-50: *exhibere* (show), *officium* (love due), *cura, sollicite* (with great care and concern) as well as humility and the kiss of peace. RM 53.43 mentions this text explicitly: "The feet of any visiting outsiders are to be washed because of the account of the woman who washed the Savior's feet while he was at supper and anointed them from the alabaster jar."

10. Cf. Greer, "Hospitality," 34; Gorce, "Gastfreundlichkeit," 91; Kötting, *Peregrinatio religiosa*, 375f.

11. Cf. Severus, *Fremde*, 42–45; Art. "Gastfreundschaft," in RAC, 1115; Art. "Xenodocheion," in PW 9A 2 (1967) 1491. Also c. 75 of the Council of Nicaea, cf. MANSI, II, 1006; Gorce, *Voyages*, 152–167.

12. Cf. Puzicha, *Christus*, 22–24.

13. Cf. Art. "Economia," in DIP, 1015; Giet, *Idées*, 417–423; Art. "Armenpflege," in RAC 1 (1950) 697.

14. *Apoph.* Arsenius, 13; ibid. 28; 1; Makarios, 30; further examples in Gorce, "Gastfreundlichkeit," 66–68; e.g., *Hist. Laus.* 17.10; 35.1; Theodoret, *Hist. Rel.* 15.18.24; *Vit. Patr* III.65; Sulpicius Severus, *Dial.* I.17; II.12.

15. Theodoret, *Hist. Rel.* 30; ibid., 3.10; *Hist. Mon.* 16.437 (14.10*); *Hist. Laus.* 46.5-6; 14.1-4; *Vit. Mel.* 9. *The numbering of paragraphs in the English translation of this work differs from the numbering in the Latin edition of PL which has three-digit page numbers; both numbers will be given. When the translation is quoted, the reference to the translation precedes the one to PL.

16. Cf. Daniélou, "Pour une théologie," 346; Severus, *Fremde*, 56.

17. V. 24 refers back to v. 6 ("greet them humbly as we have said"), and there is an inclusion between "all arriving guests" (v. 1) and the chapter's last word "with the guest" (v. 24).

18. Cf. Borias, "Couches rédactionnelles," 40:

> vv. 1-2 A—all arriving guests . . . are to be welcomed—fact
> B—because . . . you welcomed me (Christ)—reason
> C—proper honor is to be shown—manner
> vv. 6-8 C—all humility is to be shown—manner
> B—Christ is welcomed in them—reason
> A—Having welcomed the guests—fact
> v. 9 C—every human kindness is to be shown to them—manner
> v. 15 A—For the poor and pilgrims—fact
> C—concern is to be shown—manner
> B—because in them . . . Christ is welcomed—reason

19. It seems to me that this part could also be ordered as follows:

> vv. 1-2: all—as Christ—proper honor is to be shown
> vv. 4-5: a kind of liturgy with prayer and kiss of peace
> vv. 6-7: humility is to be shown—prostration
> v. 7: Christ is to be adored and welcome
> v. 9: human kindness is to be shown—vv. 10f.—fasting
> vv. 13-14: a kind of liturgy with foot washing and versicle (prayer)
> v. 15: greatest care is to be shown—Christ is welcomed more particularly.

In comparing how often the important words of the first part occur in other chapters of RB, we count about 192 occurrences in the liturgical and spiritual chapters (Prol to ch. 7; 8–20; 72–73) and 137 in the chapters dealing with community life.

20. For the important words of the second part, we find about 127 occurrences in the community chapters and 56 in the liturgical and spiritual ones.

21. *Reg. 4 Patr.* II.36-42; *Reg. or.* 26.40-41; Pachomius, *Praec.* 50–53; Basil, *Reg. fus.* 32f., 45.

22. *Morale de l'Evangile* (Paris, 1958) 88–93.

23. It is instructive to see how Hildemar in his time interprets this radical word of the Rule. He says it could be understood in the following way: all who actually can be received are to be received as Christ, for the Rule does not command something impossible. For we are unable to serve all as Christ did. Hildemar then quotes Theodulphus: "If St. Benedict were here now, he would certainly have had the door closed to them" (501); cf. Schuler, "Regula nil impossibile dicit."

24. Translator's note: This observation is based on the Latin original that says "all the strangers" (*omnes peregrinos*); since Eberle's English translation says that the porters "are to keep watch at all times over the strangers who come," I have, in consultation with the author, chosen to give my own translation that reflects the use of "all" in the Latin text.

25. So Possidius, *Vit. Aug.* IV.2.4. Cf. Jerome, *Adv. Ruf.* III.17: "Hospitality is dear to us in the monastery: We gladly receive all who come to us. . . . We desire to wash their feet, not to discuss their merits"; also Chrysostom, *In Rom.H.* 21.4; Ambrose, *De offic.* II.107 says that hospitality is to be granted to everyone. Christ himself is hidden in the guest; cf. also *Apoph.* John the Persian, 3, who wanted to wash even the feet of thieves.

26. Cf. Borias, "Hospitalité," 15; Schütz, "Benediktinisches Gemeinschaftsleben," 7; cf. Huerre, "Le moine, l'hôte de Dieu," 50; Leclercq, "The Problem of Social Class and Christology."

27. Cf. *Lives of the Desert Fathers* 8.54/7.418; cf. also the article "Adventus Regis," in LexMA 1 (1977) 170–172.

28. The entire book by M. Puzicha, *Christus*, discusses this. Neither RM nor Pachomius, neither *Reg 4 Patr.* nor Augustine, neither Basil nor Cassian base hospitality on Matt 25. In Matt 25:31-46, Cassian and Basil emphasize those who are hungry and thirsty, but not the strangers.

29. *Lives of the Desert Fathers* 8.48/7.418. Kardong, "To Receive All as Christ," 197, says that the words *suscipe me* and the meaning of *suscipere* here may have influenced the Scripture text. I think it is rather the Scripture text in the version of the *Historia monachorum* that influenced the use of *suscipere* in this chapter. Church Fathers, e.g., Augustine, *s.* 263.3, also have this reading.

30. Cf. Augustine, *s.* 236.6; and *Quaest. Evgl.* II.51.2; Puzicha, 101f.; Augustine, *s.* 103.1.2; Chrysostom, *In Act.H.* 45.3; and *In Gen.H.* 41.4.

31. Puzicha, 133, and passim; Augustine, *s.* 236.3; 239.6; 60.11.

32. Augustine, *s.* 86.4.5; 239.2 and 239.4; Caesarius, *s.* 158.6; cf. comments on vv. 14, 24.

33. Cf. Hildemar, 502. Pachomius, *Praec,* 51f., states that greater honor is due to women and clerics. Vogüé, "Honorer tous les hommes," 138, thinks that additional honor would be seen less as a value, but rather as a source of special neediness which one tries to meet charitably.

34. Pachomius, *Praec.* 51, mentions special honor for clerics or monks; the same is true for *Reg. or.* 40; cf. Isidor, *Reg. mon.* 21; Jerome, *Ep.* 130.14.7. Cf. de Vogüé, "Honorer tous les hommes," 134f.; Linderbauer, *S.Benedicti Regula,* 346f.

35. RB does not provide any further information. In RM the *peregrini* are strangers, pilgrims, or gyrovagues, and life itself is seen as pilgrimage (cf. RM 90.30). In Church Latin, the word can mean pilgrims, and despite wars, this meaning is not excluded for Benedict. In a personal communication to me, de Vogüé expressed his opinion that it meant "stranger." In this case, Benedict would have used two words that are opposed to each other: the nearest and the most distant. Otherwise, we would have to presume that in v. 2 he wanted to emphasize the spiritual component of these guests and in v. 15 their social component. Yet, using the same word with two different meanings in the same chapter is not very logical.

36. *Hist. mon.* 1.403; 5.409; 7.417f.; 21.443. *Reg. Is.* 33; Ambrose, *De offic.* II.104; Chrysostom, *In Gen. H.* 41.4-6; *Vit. Pach.* 22. Additional examples in Gorce, "Gastfreundlichkeit," 76f.

37. *Antiphonale monasticum pro diurnis horibus* (Paris, 1943) 212: "When the Lord comes, go out to meet him" (*Dominus veniet, occurrite illi . . .*); 227: "Blessed are they who are ready to go out to meet him" (*Beati qui parati sunt occurrere illi*).

38. The expression *officium caritatis* occurs in *Hist. mon.* 1.403; similarly in Cassian, *Conf.* XXI.7.2: *humanae caritatis officium.*

39. In RB, *orare pro,* praying for, predominates except in RB 52. Cf. also Gorce, "Gastfreundlichkeit," 85f., *Apoph.* Serapion, 4. Cassian, *Conf.* XVII.3 seems to know a number of psalms that were prayed in such situations; cf. also comments on v. 5.

40. Cf. Augustine, *s.* 236.6. For *societas* as designation of community, cf. Augustine, *Praec.* I.6; IV.9; Basil, *Reg.* 3; Caesarius, *Reg. vg.* 21.

41. *s.* 111.2. Cf. Ambrose, *De Abr.* I.5.34; *De Tob.* 24.91; Gregory of Nazianzen, *Cant. moral.* 34.164/6: "Hospitable (friendly to strangers) is the one who is aware that he himself is a guest (stranger)." RM speaks even more clearly about the life of monks as

pilgrimage, cf. 90.30. Cf. also article on "Peregrinatio" in DIP, on "Stranger" in RAC; Böckmann, "Ouverture au monde," 176–170.

42. C. Pétré, *Caritas*, 302f.; Tertullian, *De or.* 11; Cawly, "Four Themes," 82–91, says that this distinguishes RB from RM.

43. Cf. Pétré, *Caritas*, 306, 301; Cyprian, *De dom. or.* 23; Augustine, *In Joh.* 77.5; 77.4; *In Ep. Joh. Prol.*

44. s. 227; Tertullian, *De or.* 18; cf. Pétré, *Caritas*, 309–311; Art. "Friedenskuss," in RAC, 515–517.

45. For this sequence cf. *Reg. 4 Patr.* II.39; *Lives of the Desert Fathers* 2.7/2.406; 8.48-54/7.417-418.

46. Cf. Basil *Reg.* 87; *Reg. breve.* 155; *Reg. fus.* 20; Gorce, "Gastfreundlichkeit," 74f.; *Vit. Patr.* III.5. Kötting, *Peregrinatio Religiosa*, 378f. has an example of a reference letter; and the *tessera hospitalis* identified its owner as having an orthodox faith. One *tessera* says PYAP (the Greek letters for Father, Son, and Holy Ghost) as proof of orthodox faith, cf. Herwegen, *Sinn*, 307; Severus, *Fremde*, 78. Heretics are also to be welcomed, cf. *Vit. Patr.* V.13.11; *Apoph.* Poemen 78. Generally, it seems that heretics were not given hospitality; cf. Jerome, *Adv. Ruf.* III.17; *Ep.* 58.6.2.

47. Cf. Gorce, "Gastfreundlichkeit," 88; the word *salutatio* (greeting) is used in RM only for spiritual brothers or inside the community.

48. Cf. the sequence in this chapter: *honor-caritas, humilitas-humanitas*. Cf. *Reg. or.* 26; *2 Reg. Patr.* 14; *Lives of the Desert Fathers* 20.6/2.444 also speaks of *humilitas* and *humanitas*.

49. Humility also includes a concrete action. Cf. RB 27.3; Kasch, *Das liturgische Vokabular*, 218. In RB 53 many words occur that designate an external expression, yet their broader meaning includes an internal attitude, e.g., honor, love, join together, peace, humility, humanity, care.

50. Cf. RM 14.32; 19.4; plea for prayer, e.g., RB 67.3f.; 58.23; pleas for reconciliation RB 71.8; 44.1. The same expression "with a full prostration of the body to the ground" also occurs in the *Sacramentarium Gelasianum* XVI.83 and XXXVIII.352.

51. John Chrysostom, *In Gen.H.* 41.4; cf. *Hist. mon.* 7.417-418/8.48ff.

52. John Chrysostom, *In Mt. H.* 50.3; cf. Schütz, "Benediktinisches Gemeinschaftsleben," 8. The Vulgate uses the word "adore" for Abraham's veneration before his guests. Jesus, too, is being adored already before the resurrection; cf. Matt 2:11; 8:2; 9:18, etc., and Peter is venerated in this way by Cornelius, Acts 10:25.

53. *Oratio* used for liturgy, cf. 17.6; this word is not used solely for private prayer, i.e., the silent prayer after the psalms or after a Liturgy of the Hours. The meaning of liturgy in RB 53 is also suggested by early texts: Pachomius, *Praec.* 51; *Lives of the Desert Fathers* 8.49/7.418; 20.6/21.444; cf. Boinot, "L'accueil monastique," 12.

54. *Lives of the Desert Fathers* 2.7/2.406; Augustine, *De op. mon.* XVIII.21; cf. Art. "Gastfreundschaft," in RAC, 1114; Leclercq, "Prière monastique," 387–398; regarding "sitting," cf. Kasch, *Das liturgische Vokabular*, 224f.

55. RB 31.14 (Eccl 18:17); Chrysostom, *In Gen. H.* 41.7; cf. *Reg. 4 Patr.* II.40.

56. Cf. *Reg. 4 Patr.* II.42.

57. Cf. also Eph 4:12, 16; 1 Cor 14:12; Rom 14:19; 15:2; 1 Thess 5:11; Kasch, *Das liturgische Vokabular*, 261f.; Schoenen, "Aedificatio."

58. Cf. RB 38.12; 42.3; 47.3; also, Borias, "Couches rédactionnelles," 44. The Master uses the word rather in connection with speaking, cf. RM 9.30; 8.33; 50.43. Cf. also

Lives of the Desert Fathers 2.7/2.406; 1.55/1.403; *Reg 4 Patr.* II.41f. John Chrysostom, *In Mt.H.* 48.7, has the guest read Scripture aloud; cf. Bouilly, "L'accueil dans la prière," 359. 59. Cf. Basil, *Reg.* 33; 40; 136; 174; *Reg. fus.* 32.2; 45.1-2; 20. This leads to the connection of hospitality and pastoral care as Angerer, "Mönchtum und Seelsorge," 161–163, describes it for the *Lives of the Desert Fathers.* In contrast, there is no interest in edifying the guest, e.g., in A*poph.* Theodor of Pherme, 28; Eulogios, 1.

60. Cf. *Lives of the Desert Fathers* 2.7/2.406; 8.48f./7.418; Gregory the Great, *Dial.* II.1.7. Cf. Gorce, "Gastfreundlichkeit," 87; Pachomius, *Vit. bohar.* 81 (57); *Vit. Patr.* III.5; *Apoph.* Serapion, 4; *Reg. Is.* 33.

61. Cf. Paul VI, *Evangelii Nuntiandi,* 34; 22; 31; John Paul II, *Redemptor Hominis,* 13.

62. Aulinger, "St. Benedict ein Humanist?" 128, and *Das Humanum in der Regel Benedikts.* Cf. also Pignedoli, "Importance," 124; for the concept of *humanitas,* cf. Pétré, *Caritas,* 200–221.

63. Ambrose, *De off.* III.3.20; cf. Hildemar, 503; also Smaragdus.

64. *s.* 174.1; cf. Paulinus of Nola, *Ep.* 13.21; Etheria, *Pereg.* 3.1; Ambrose, *De off.* II.103; Acts 28:1.

65. Examples in RB (Vogüé), 678, with references. Also, *Lives of the Desert Fathers* 17.1f./17.440; Cassian, *Inst.* V.23 and 24, cf. V.26; *Inst.* IV.7; *Conf.* XXI.14; II.2, *Vit. Patr.* V.13.1-10.

66. Cf. Aubert, "Habiter des maisons," 317–319; Winzen, "Conference on the Reception of Guests," 62.

67. Cassian, *Inst.* V.23, V.24; also *Vit. Patr.* V.13.2; cf. Cassian, *Conf.* II.26.2. One monk ate six times on a particular day because guests kept coming, *Vit. Patr.* V.13.3.

68. *Lives of the Desert Fathers* 8.58/7.419; Vogüé, *V,* 1285f. thinks the abbot and the guests ate in the refectory, but at a special table; this is also the case in RM. Benedict makes provision for separate bedrooms for guests (v. 22), but not for a separate dining room.

69. Cf. Basil, *Reg. brev.* 313.

70. *In illud vid.* 15; Cf. *Ecl.elem.hosp. H.* 23; Jerome, *Ep.* 66.11.3-4; 58.6. Puzicha, *Christus,* 57f.; Greer, "Hospitality," 33; *Lives of the Desert Fathers* 2.8/2.406; 8.49/7.418. Yet there is no proof for Tamburrino's thesis that the *Historia monachorum.* influenced Benedict's hand washing, cf. "L'incidenza della correnti spirituali," 138.

71. Cf. for example *Lives of the Desert Fathers* 2.8/2.406; 8.49/7.418; Pachomius, *Praec.* 51; *Vit. Patr.* VI.1.17.

72. Cf. baptismal *ordo* of the *Missale Gothicum,* cf. Schäfer, *Die Fußwaschung,* 10; Augustine, *In Joh.* 58.4; cf. Basil, *Reg. fus.* 20.1. RM 30.4-7 interprets the foot washing as fulfilling God's teaching.

73. Cf. John Chrysostom, *In Gen. H.* 41.4f.; *In illud. vid.* 15, stating that Christ is "not ashamed to hold out his hands to us. He is not ashamed to receive." Perhaps Martin of Tours wants to express this very thing when he makes himself very small as he washes the feet of a guest, cf. Sulpicius Severus, *Vit. Mart.* 25.3.

74. Cf. Severus, *Fremde,* 61; article "Fusswaschung," in RAC, 768; cf. also RB 35.9.

75. *Vit. Patr.* VI.1.17; cf. Jerome, *Adv. Ruf.* III.17; Pachomius, *Preac.* 51; cf. Schäfer, *Fusswaschung,* 27. The Rule of Benedict is the basis for the later development of the foot washing in Western monasticism. On the one hand, it gave rise to the custom of washing the feet of specific guests, that is, the novices, on the eve of their profession (fourteenth and fifteenth centuries). This custom was used in Monte Cassino and came to

Beuron through the brothers Maurus and Placid Wolter who had seen it in St. Paul Outside the Walls. On the other hand, washing the feet of guests developed into the *mandatum pauperum*, washing the feet of the poor, that at times was done daily, e.g., in the circle around Benedict of Aniane. Hildemar locates it after Vespers (508). In the monastery of Hirsau, it was replaced by alms during the winter. In a different cultural environment, especially in colder climates, its meaning as a service of humble love was no longer part of people's actual experience. Yet in the ninth and tenth centuries it became part of the liturgy of the episcopal churches and eventually a part of the official liturgy of Holy Thursday; cf. Schäfer, *Fußwaschung*, especially 99. Also Caesarius, *s.* 83.4, cf. Puzicha, *Christus*, 58–60.

76. Rufinus comments this psalm verse in this sense, cf. *In Ps.* 47(48):10. Mercy can be synonymous with piety, cf. Bartelink, *Umdeutung*, 407; also Puzicha, *Christus*, 132f. Thus, I do not think that one has to identify *Deus* here with Christ as does Borias in "*Dominus et Deus*," 415.

77. Augustine, *De visit. inf.* I.2.; also cf. John Chrysostom, *In illud, Ne tim.* 5; 7; *In Gen. H.* 41.4, 5, 7; *In illud.vid.* 13.; Caesarius, *s.* 25.1; *s.* 158.6.

78. Augustine, *s.* 239.4, 7; *s.* 103.1, 2; *s.* 86.4, 5; Jerome, *Ep.* 66.12.

79. Cf. Puzicha, *Christus*, 16, 21–23; Kötting, *Peregrinatio Religiosa*, 377; cf. also the volume *Carità cristiana*, 111–115, with respect to the work of the deacons in Rome.

80. Cf. Caesarius, *s.* 182.3; cf. J. Dupont, "La povertà religiosa nella luce della Scrittura," in *La povertà religiosa* (Rome, 1975) 8; Puzicha, *Christus*, 24–27.

81. Cf. Böckmann, "Akzentuierungen," 141 (on RB 33).

82. Cf. Paul VI, *Evangelica testificatio*, 17.

83. Cf. *s.* 60.11 in FC 11.271; this sermon was not found in the new translation of Augustine's sermons; the above translation is based on the author's translation with her additions in [ ]; cf. also Isaac of Stella, *s. Fest. omn. sanct.* 1 (PL 194.1693): "Being poor we are to hear the poor one who recommends poverty to the poor."

84. Vogüé, "Honorer tous les hommes," 138, thinks that Benedict saw the wealth of the rich not as a real value, but rather as a source of neediness that called for compassion. In this way he also interprets the "respect due to them" (*congruus honor*). Hildemar, 505, concretizes this idea in the following manner: one tenth of the money is given to the quarters for the rich, double this amount to the hospice for the poor.

85. Cf. RB 48.5; 61.2; 31.18f. *Quies* (silence) does not occur in RB, but Benedict uses the word "peace" to describe the atmosphere in the community, cf., e.g., 34.5; 65.11. He is concerned with preserving a prayerful atmosphere and a climate of fraternal love. Basil uses a similar expression twice in the small *Asceticon, Reg.* 98; 10.

86. The Latin original shows many parallels between v. 18 and v. 20: *ut indigent/ut quando indigent; solacia amministrentur/solacia adcommodentur eis; et iterum/et iterum; quando occupationem minorem habent/quando vacant; exeant ubi eis imperatur in opera/oboediant imperatis.*

87. *Solacium* occurs in 1.4 in its original meaning of consolation; RM uses the word almost always in this sense except in 95.11. In the Vulgate, the word occurs mainly in the Christian Scriptures. Phil 2:1 speaks of the "solace of love" and Col 4:11 of the comfort provided by the presence of brothers.

88. Cf. Vogüé, *Communauté*, 318f.; Engl: *Community and Abbot*, 5/2, 280.

89. Cf. Pachomius, *Praec.* 50: "No one in the monastery has the right to welcome guests to a meal; rather, he sends them to the door of the *xenodochium* (guest quarters)

where they are welcomed by the one who is assigned to this service." This person is called *ianitor* or *ostiarius* (*Praec.* 53, *Reg. or.* 26, 41). Cf. *Lives of the Desert Fathers* 17.1/17.439f., *Hist. Laus.* 7.4; RM 79.1-6: "The guest quarters should be set apart in the monastery, with beds made up. . . . Moreover, for the purpose of precautionary surveillance let two brothers from the same deanery as those who are doing the kitchen service be assigned in turn . . . to keep an eye on strange brothers without their being aware of it. . . ." The significant word here is *custodire*, watch over, keep an eye on.

90. This is in contrast to RM; cf. also Rousselet, "Un modèle," 30f.; Boinot, "L'accueil monastique," 16f.; Gorce, "Gastfreundlichkeit," 75.

91. Cf. *Isaiah, or.* 3.3; Augustine, *Praec.* V.3; Pachomius, *Praec.* 52; cf. Smaragdus on this verse is referring to Ps. 110 (111):10.

92. *In Ps.* 126.3; *s.* 337.3.3. Cf. Mohrmann, "*Domus Dei* chez Augustine," in *Etudes*, II, 73–79. RM's expression *domus divina* shows that the monastery is a church; cf. also Smaragdus on this passage.

93. Cf. Basil, *Reg.* 103–104; Luislampe, "Aspekte," 41–43.

94. E.g., Smaragdus on this verse; cf. Ambrose, *In Ps.* 118.5.37 who says that true wisdom has its origin in the fear of God, and fear of God cannot exist without wisdom.

95. Cf. Ménager, "L'expression *sapientiae doctrinae*"; Jaeger, "The Patristic Conception of Wisdom"; Cawly, "4 Themes," 105–107.

96. Cf. Gorce, "Gastfreundlichkeit," 75; Pachomius, *Vit. boh.* 26.

97. Cf. Vogüé, *VII*, 360f. (*RB-DSC*. 261, 259–265) and *VI*, 1271.

98. Cf. U. Adams, "Radikale Solidarität," in *Ordenskorrespondenz* 20 (1979) 46.

99. Cf. *Hist. Laus.* 7.4; Chrysostom, *In Mt.H.* 48.7; Gorce, "Gastfreundlichkeit," 89f.; RM 78.4-11.

100. Cf. Pachomius, *Vit. boh.* 40; Basil, *Reg. fus.* 45.1; 32.3.

101. Augustine, *s.* 355.1, 2; cf. also Borias, "Hospitalité," 8–11.

102. Cf. Augustine, *s.* 239.2. Regarding *benedictio*/blessing, cf. Kasch, *Das liturgische Vokabular*, 100; for blessings within the monastery cf. 63.15; 71.8; 35.17-18; a blessing to the outside: 66.3.

103. Cf. *Reg. 4 Patr.* II.37-42 listing five things not allowed, nn. 3 and 5 say that only the superior may speak with a guest; cf. also *2 Reg. Patr.* 16; Pachomius, *Praec.* 50; Cassian, *Inst.* IV.16.2; *Reg. Is.* 33.

104. Cf. H. Nouwen, *Clowning in Rome* (New York: Doubleday, 1979) 13–14; Huerre once said: "True hospitality consists in an inner detachment, in emptying out one's ego, in silence which makes it possible to recognize Christ in the guest and to give the guest what he is seeking." (Chapter reflections printed only as a manuscript in German.)

105. Vogüé, *VII*, 363; cf. 360–365 (*RB-DSC* 261; 259–265); cf. also his article "Ospitalità," in DIP, 1014; cf. also Böckmann, "Ouverture."

106. For the connection between monasticism and evangelization, cf., e.g., Seilhac, "Tâches de l'évangelization"; Doppelfeld, *Mönchtum*; Auf der Maur, "Mönche vor St. Benedikt," and "Das alte Mönchtum"; Rudmann, "Mönchtum"; Brechter, "Monastische Lebensform."

Conclusion

Based on the interpretation of the preceding chapters, I will, in conclusion, try to map out the perspectives of the Rule of Benedict with the help of headings and, in doing this, also delineate the profile of its author.

1. The key to the interpretation seems to lie in RB 72.11-12: "To prefer absolutely nothing to Christ who will lead us all together to eternal life."

(a) Just as the Fathers saw Christ as the key to Sacred Scripture, and in particular to the psalms, so Christ has this same function for the interpretation of the Rule of Benedict. It becomes very clear that Christ is the center of the Rule and for Benedict whose enthusiasm for Christ cannot be missed. Love for Christ is the motivation for obedience, for living in community, for being open to the world. Although Benedict is not a theorist, he still instinctively was accurate in bringing out the main points of faith in Christ in a time which had to contend with the heresy of Arianism. Benedict writes from a practical standpoint; he is rooted in monastic practice, in everyday community life, in the experience of liturgy, in the concern for human beings; and from there he always finds, or leads to, the living Christ (though less to the historical Christ). Yet this must be seen within the dynamic journey toward God the Father who is the origin and goal of all our paths and to whom alone honor is due.

(b) Preferring absolutely nothing to Christ will lead us into the community established through Christ, again and again rebuilt, and which, in turn, points to Christ. Christ will lead us all together (*pariter*); each one is responsible for the other and cannot reach the goal without the other.

(c) Preferring nothing to Christ is the reason why the community opens itself to those in need because Christ, too, approaches the monastery from outside. Thus, Benedict's monasticism defines itself not only as a withdrawal from the world. While the individual monastic is asked to renounce the "world" and even the self for the sake of Christ, this renunciation leads into community and, together with it, to the service for other human beings as a means of following Christ.

(d) To prefer nothing to Christ and to allow him to lead us also means to put his word and all of Sacred Scripture above everything else, to recognize them as the highest rule, and to walk "with the Gospel as our guide," as is shown clearly in every chapter of the Rule. In the Rule it is the Word of God that puts everything in its right context.

(e) May Christ lead us all together: Benedict sees himself as being always on the way, never as having arrived; and he wants to bring everyone into this vast, dynamic movement toward the Father. On this very path he wants to persevere, together with us.

2. One of Benedict's special traits is his discernment (*discretio*), his balance and moderation. The Fathers call the middle way the royal way of truth and integrity, avoiding both too much and too little. It is a path on which, time and again, we allow ourselves to be questioned from both sides (cf. Gregory the Great, *Dial.* II.36).

(a) The Rule provides the right teaching about grace and human activity. As much as Benedict emphasizes grace and the importance of prayer as priorities for monastics, he also energetically encourages his monastics to do good and to make every effort to strive continually.

(b) As much as he appreciates the value of community, he still does not ignore the individual person, but rather accords each person loving consideration.

(c) The abbot/superior deserves not just reverence but also love, and is a person of discernment who combines authority with loving intuition.

(d) Benedict protects the individual monastics and the community from bad influences from the world because of their weaknesses and to preserve the spiritual atmosphere in the community, yet in doing so he is open for the needs of the world. He keeps a balance between service to the world and concern for the community.

(e) Benedict himself has deeply experienced God and knows that before God he is a sinner, yet—perhaps for this very reason—he also has a delicate understanding for the human soul and knows well how a newcomer has to be encouraged.

(f) Although Benedict was convinced that his times were decadent (and included himself among the bad monks), he is generally optimistic. With God's grace we can gain a wide heart and true joy already in this life.

(g) Benedict is a practical man and a realist who knows the weaknesses, the difficulties, even the sinfulness of individuals and of the community. Yet his idealism, even his enthusiasm for monastic life, shines through this very knowledge. His hope is rooted in Christ.

(h) Characteristic for Benedict's entire Rule is the fusion of deep spirituality and very practical concrete instructions.

(i) To follow Christ demands a radical stance in our lives. Even Benedict's style reveals an energetic, single-minded person for whom everything is at stake. Yet this is balanced with consideration for the weak and the discouraged. Benedict knows how to meet individuals right where they are.

(k) On the way toward God, Benedict will not just walk, but run. At the end of the Rule he opens the doors wide onto God's infinite space. Yet at the same time he emphasizes persisting in a specific place, and in the stability that includes persevering on the way once begun.

(l) Discernment as distinguishing and deciding requires listening in all directions. Benedict is able to do this because he is firmly rooted, not just in his own native place, his people with their values (the values of the Romans!), but especially also in the church. He strives for the right faith, again and again emphasizes Catholicity though without undue anxiety. He stands in his times with open eyes and open ears and knows what the times need. He takes good things wherever he finds them. We sense that he himself lives from the liturgy and *lectio divina*.

3. This is the way I imagine Benedict:

with both feet firmly planted on the ground,
with open ears listening in all directions,
having penetrating, kind eyes that see through the surface and discover
    Christ in everything and everybody,
with arms stretched out toward the monastics of very different natures
    and toward all people, especially the needy,
but above all with a wide heart where Christ lives,
who spurs him on so that, together with all the monastics, he will reach
    the final goal.

Our interpretation again and again pointed to the fact that despite all the differences in tone and style in the various chapters, we sense the hand of a very vital author in this Rule. He has a message as important today as it was in the sixth century:

"To prefer absolutely nothing to Christ who may lead us all together to eternal life."

Secondary Sources and Studies

In the notes, these works are identified by the author's last name and the first noun or the first few words of the title.

Acción social de la Orden Benedictina. Madrid, 1982.

Adam, A. "Das Mönchtum in der Alten Kirche." In *Kirchengeschichte als Missionsgeschichte*, vol. I, 68–93. Munich, 1974.

Amand, D. *L'ascèse monastique de S. Basile*. Maredsous, 1948.

Angenendt, A. *Monachi Peregrini*. Munich, 1972.

Angerer, J. F. "Mönchtum und Seelsorge, Widerspruch oder Vollendung? Dargestellt an der Historia Monachorum." In: *Studia historico-ecclesiastica* (Festgabe für L. G. Spätling), 147–166. Rome, 1977.

Antonius Magnus Eremita. Ed. B. Steidle (StA 38). Rome, 1956.

Art. "*Apotaxis*." In RAC 1 (1950) 558–564.

Aresu, E. "La vita comune: un obiettivo fondamentale della Regola di S. Benedetto." *S. Benedetto, Benedictina* 617–633.

Art. "Armenfürsorge." In TRE 4 (1979) 16–40.

Art. "Armenpflege." In RAC 1 (1950) 689–698.

Atti del 7° Congresso internazionale di studi sull'Alto Medievo, vols. I and II. Spoleto,1982.

Aubert, D. "Habiter des maisons." CollCist 33 (171) 316–325.

Aubert, R. "La restauration monastique dans l'Europe occidentale du XIX⁰ siècle." RBén 83 (1973) 9–32.

Auer, J. "Militia Christi." GuL 32 (1959) 34–351.

Auf der Mauer, I. "Das alte Mönchtum und die Glaubensverkündigung." *Neue Zeitschrift für Missionswissenschaft* 18 (1962) 275–288.

——. "Mönche vor St. Benedikt als Glaubensboten." EA 39 (1963) 447–463.

Augé, M. "L'abito monastico dalle origini alla regola di S. Benedetto." *Claretianum* 16 (1976) 33–95.

——. *L'abito religioso*. Rome 1977

Augrain, C. "Les sources bibliques du Prologue de la Règle." CollCist 22 (1960) 3–10.

Augusta Maria, Sr. "*Koinonia*: Its Biblical Meaning and Use in Monastic Life." ABR 18 (1967) 189–212.

Aulinger, G. "St. Benedikt ein Humanist?" EA 30 (1954) 120–128.

―――. *Das Humanum in der Regel Benedikts von Nursia.* St. Ottilien, 1950.

Bacht, H. "Antonius und Pachomius: Von der Anachorese zum Coenobitentum." In *Antonius Magnus Eremita* 66–107. Rome, 1956.

―――. "Vom gemeinsamen Leben. Die Bedeutung des pachomianischen Mönchsideals für die Geschichte des christlichen Mönchtums." LuM 11 (1951) 91–110.

―――. *Das Vermächtnis des Ursprungs.* Würzburg, 1972.

―――. *Weltnähe oder Weltdistanz.* Frankfurt, 1962.

Baker, A. "Which came first, the Hermit or the Community?" DR 91 (1973) 290–297.

Balthasar, H. U. von. *Die grossen Ordenregeln.* Einsiedeln, 1961.

Bamberger, J. E. "Good Zeal and the Community." Tj (1974:7) 3–8.

―――. "Chapter 72 of the Rule of S. Benedict." Tj (1974:6) 3–12.

Barros Morães, C. "Plan y contenido de la Regla de S. Benito." Cuad Mon 19 (1984) 1–25.

Barsotti, D. *"Ascolta, o figlio . . .": Commento spirituale al Prologo della Regola di S. Benedetto.* Florence, 1965.

Bartelink, G. J. M. "Umdeutung heidnischer Termini im christlichen Sprachge-brauch." In *Kirchengeschichte als Missionsgeschichte,* vol. I, 397–418. Munich, 1974.

Baus, K. "Das Mönchtum des lateinischen Westens." In: *Handbuch für Kirchengeschichte.* Ed. H. Jedin, vol. II:1, 388–435. Freiburg, 1973.

San Benedetto. Special issue for 1980 of *Benedictina* 28 (1981), fasc. 1 and 2, con-taining many articles; henceforth cited as *S. Benedetto, Benedictina.*

"S. Benedetto agli uomini di oggi." In: *S. Benedetto, Benedictina,* fasc. 1–2.

S. Benedetto e l'oriente cristiano. Novalesa, 1981.

S. Benedict. A Man with an Idea. Ed. J. M. Stanley. Melbourne, 1982.

Benedictus. Der Vater des Abendlandes. Ed. S. Brechter. Munich, 1947.

Benedictus. Studies in Honor of St. Benedict of Nursia. Ed. R. Elder. Kalamazoo: Cistercian, 1981.

Bianchi, E. "Cenobitismo benedettino e monachesimo di Scete." In *S. Benedetto e l'oriente cristiano* 73–84. Novalesa, 1981.

Art. "Bibbia e monachesimo." In DIP 1 (1973) 1448–1458.

La Bible et les Pères. Paris, 1971.

Böckmann, A. "Akzentuierungen der neutestamentlichen Armut nach der Regula Benedicti." RBS 5 (1976) 131–164.

―――. "Vom guten Eifer, den die Mönche haben sollen." EA 60 (1984) 14–40.

―――. "Ouverture au monde et séparation du monde d'après la Règle de S. Benoît." CollCist 46 (1984) 161–176.

Boinot, S. "L'accueil monastique." LL (1972:156) 7–17. (Spanish translation: "La hospitalidad monástica." Cuad Mon 12 [1977] 73–79).

Bonamente, G. "L'ambiente socio-culturale di S. Benedetto: Roma allo scadere del V secolo." In *Benedetto, Benedictina* 23–45.

Bori, P. C. *Chiesa primitiva. L'immagine della comunità delle origini.* Brescia, 1974.

Borias, A. "S. Benoît, maître en patience." LL (1984: 225) 41–51.

————. "S. Benoît, le migrant de Dieu." LL (1981:207) 10–20.

————. "Comment S. Benoît a élaboré et rédigé sa Règle." LL (1976, 175) 5–16.

————. "Le Christ dans la Règle de S. Benoît." RBén 82 (1972) 109–139. ("Christ and the Monk." MSt [1974, 10] 97–129).

————. "Couches rédactionnelles dans la Règle bénédictine." RBén 85 (1975) 38–55.

————. "*Dominus et Deus* dans la Règle de S. Benoît." RBén 79 (1969) 414–423.

————. "Le dynamisme spirituel de S. Benoît." LL (1966, 120) 18–30.

————. "La foi dans la Règle de S. Benoît." RAM 44 (1968) 249–259.

————. "Hospitalitè augustinienne et bénédictine." RHSp 50 (1974) 3–12.

————. "L'influence de S. Cyprien sur la Règle de S. Benoît." RBén 74 (1964) 53–97.

————. "Le moine et sa famille." Coll Cist 40 (1978) 81–110, 195–217.

————. "Nouveaux cas de répétitions." RBén 75 (1965) 312–328.

————. "Quelques exemples d'inclusion dans la Règle bénédictine." RBS 8/9 (1982) 51–57.

————. "La répétition dans la Règle de S. Benoît." RBén 73 (1963) 111–126.

Botz, P. "*Koinonia*: Christian Community." ABR 25 (1974) 485–493.

Bouilly, F. "L'accueil dans la prière de la communauté." CollCist 33 (1971) 358–364.

Braso, G. *Sentier de vie.* (Vie monastique 2) Bellefontaine, 1974.

Brechter, S. "Monastische Lebensform und moderner Missionsauftrag." LuM 43 (1968) 97–106.

————. "Die soziologische Gestalt des Benediktinertums in seinen Anfängen." In: *Benediktus. Der Vater des Abendlandes.* Ed. S. Brechter, 57–76. Munich, 1947.

Burini, C. "La 'comunione' e 'distruzione dei beni' di Atti 2,44 e 4.32.35 nelle regole monastiche di Basilio Magno." In: *S. Benedetto, Benedictina* 151–169.

Butler, C. *Benedictine Monachism.* London/New York: Longmans, ²1924; reprint 1961.

Calati, B. "*Mens biblica* e S. Regola." VitaMon 13 (1959) 39–48.

————. "Pluralismo d'interpretazione della regola benedettina." In: *Figura e Funzione dell' autorità nella comunità religiosa* 404–432. Alba, 1978.

Campenhausen, H. F. von. "Der Kriegsdienst der Christen in der Kirche des Altertums." In: Campenhausen. *Tradition und Leben* 203–215. Tübingen, 1960.

La carità cristiana in Roma. Ed. V. Monachino. Bologna, 1968.

Caron P. G. "Asile et hospitalité dans le droit de l'Eglise primitive." *Revue internationale des droits de l'Antiquité* 10 (1963) 187–197.

Carosi, P. *Il primo monastero benedettino.* StA 39. Rome 1956.

Casey, M. "Community in the Benedictine Rule." RBS 8/9 (1982) 59–65.

————. "Community and Tradition." Tj (1973:4) 45–58.

————. "Discerning the True Values of Monastic Life in a Time of Change." RBS 3/4 (1975) 75–88.

————. "The Hermeneutics of Tradition." Tj (1973:5) 38–50.

————. "*Intentio cordis* (RB 52.4)." RBS 6/7 (1980) 100–120.

————. "RB: Damals und heute. Grundsätze für die Auslegung." MonInf (1984, 38) 19–24.

Cawly, M. "Four Themes in the Rule of St. Benedikt." Wsp 2 (1981) 82–110.

Art. "Cenobio." DIP 2 (1975) 761–764.

Art. "Cénobitisme." DS 2 (1953) 404–416.

Chadwick, J. "Justification by Faith and Hospitality." In: Studia Patristica IV.2 TU 79 (1961) 281–285.

Christophe, P. *Cassien et Césaire, prédicateurs de la morale monastique.* Gembloux, 1969.

Le Coeur: Etudes carmélitaines. Tournai, 1950.

Colombas. G. "El concepto de monje y vida monástica hasta fines de siglo V." StMon 1 (1959) 257–342.

————. *El monacato primitivo.* Vols. I and II. Madrid, 1975.

————. Colombas and Aranguren, I. *La Regla de S. Benito.* Madrid, 1979.

Commandements du Seigneur et libération évangélique. Ed. J. Gribomont (StA 70). Rome, 1977.

Commentaria in S. Regulam. Vol. I. Ed. J. Gribomont (StA 84). Rome, 1982.

Commentationes in Regulam S. Benedicti. Ed. B. Steidle (StA 42). Rome, 1957.

Comunidad cristiana y comunidades monásticas. Ed. C. de la Sterna González (StSil 9). Silos, 1983.

Consider Your Call: A Theology of Monastic Life Today. Ed. D. Rees and others. London: SPCK 1978/Kalamazoo: Cistercian Publications, 1980.

Art. "Contemplation." DS 2 (1953) 1643–2193.

Art. "Conversatio (conversio) morum." DS 2 (1953) 2206–2212.

Art. "Conversio (conversatio) morum." DIP 3 (1976) 106–110.

Art. "Conversio morum." RAC 3 (1957) 422–424.

Coppens, J. "La *koinonia* dans l'Eglise primitive." EThL 47 (1970) 116–121.

Cousin, P. *Précis d'histoire monastique.* Tournai, 1956.

La cultura in Italia fra tardo Antico e alto Medioevo. Vols. I and II. Rome, 1981.

Daniélou, J. "Pour une théologie de l'hospitalité." VS 85 (1951) 339–347.

Dekkers, E. "Les autographes des Pères latins." In: *Colligere fragmenta.* Ed. B. Fischer and V. Fiala (Festschrift for A. Dold) 127–139. Beuron, 1952.

————. "'*Caritatem caste impendant*': Qu'a voulu dire S. Benoît?" *La Ciudad de Dios* 181 (1968) 656–660.

————. "Monastic Life Today: Some Suggestions." MSt (1966:4) 55–60.

Delatte, P. *The Rule of St. Benedict.* London, 1921.

Déseille, P. "Cénobitisme et vie contemplative." CollCist 42 (1962) 264–269.

————. "Les origines de la vie religieuse dans le christianisme." *Lumière et vie* 19 (1970) 25–53.

————. "A propos de l'épilogue du chapitre VII de la Règle." CollCist 21 (1959) 289–301.

————. *Regards sur la tradition monastique.* (Vie monastique 3) Bellefontaine, 1974.

————. "Les sources orientales de la Règle de S. Benoît." (Ms) Spanish translation: "Las fuentes orientales de la Regla de S. Benito." Cuad Mon 11 (1976) 43–75.

Art. "*Disciplina.*" In RAC 3 (1957) 1213–1229.

Doppelfeld, B. *Höre, nimm an, erfülle: St. Benedikts Grundakkord geistlichen Lebens.* Münsterschwarzach, 1981.

―――. "Das Kloster als Familie." EA 50 (1974) 5–20.

―――. *Mönchtum und kirchlicher Heilsdienst: Entstehen und Entwicklung des nordamerikanischen Benediktinertums im 19. Jahrhundert.* Münsterschwarzach, 1974.

―――. *Der Weg zu seinem Zelt.* Münsterschwarzach, 1979

Dürig, W. "*Disciplina.*" *Sacris Erudiri* 4 (1952) 245–279.

Art. "Economia." In DIP 3 (1976) 1011–1049.

Art. "Ecriture Sainte." In DS 4 (1960) 128–278.

Egli, B. *Der vierzehnte Psalm im Prolog der Regel des hl. Benedikt.* Sarnen, 1962.

Emery, P. Y. "Solitude et communion." CollCist 40 (1978) 3–34.

Endress, R. "The Monastery as a Liminal Community." ABR 26 (1975) 142–158.

Enkainia. Ed. E. Edmonds. Düsseldorf, 1956.

Ernetti, P. "La professione monastica secondo S. Pacomio, S. Basilio, S. Cassiano, S. Benedetto." VitaMon 11 (1957) 152–161; 12 (1958) 3–12.

Fattorini, G. "L'ascolto salvifico negli atti degli Apostoli." *Inter Fratres* 30 (1980) 101–110.

―――. "L'immagine biblica della 'corsa' nella Regola di S. Benedetto." In: *S. Benedetto, Benedictina* 457–483.

Faure, M. P. "Partager sa vie avec les autres." CollCist 33 (1971) 365–378.

Fiala, V. "Die besondere Ausprägung des benediktinischen Mönchtums in der Beuroner Kongregation." RBén 83 (1973) 181–228.

Fink, W. "Der Hl. Benedikt und die religiöse Lage auf dem Lande in Italien." SMGBO 61 (1947) 20–39.

Fischer, B. "*Coram Deo = coram Christo.* In: Fischer, B. *Psalmen,* 139–152.

―――. *Die Psalmen als Stimme der Kirche.* Trier, 1982.

―――. "Die Psalmenfrömmigkeit der *Regula S. Benedicti.*" In: Fischer, B. *Psalmen,* 37–71.

Fiske, A. "Cassian and Monastic Friendship." ABR 12 (1961) 190–205.

Art. "Florilegium." In RAC 7 (1966) 1131–1160.

Art. "Florilegium." In TRE 11 (1983) 215–211.

Fontaine, J. "Les chrétiens et le service militaire dans l'Antiquité." *Concilium* 1 (1965) 95–105.

―――. "Le monachisme de S. Benoît au carrefour spirituel de l'orient et de l'occident." *Atti 7° Congresso internazionale,* 21–46.

―――. "La romanité de S. Benoît: vocables et valeurs dans la *Regula Benedicti.*" *Revue des études latines* 58 (1980) 403–427.

Frank, H. "Untersuchungen zur Geschichte der benediktinischen Professliturgie." SMGBO 63 (1951) 93–139.

Frank, K. S. *Basilus von Caesarea: Die Mönchsregeln.* St. Ottilien, 1981.

―――. "Die Erforschung der Anfänge des Mönchtums und die Frage der Hermeneutik." *Franziskanische Studien* 53 (1971) 28–44.

―――. *Frühes Mönchtum im Abendland,* Vols. I and II. Zurich-Munich, 1975.

————. *Grundzüge der Geschichte des christlichen Mönchtums.* Darmstadt, 1975.

————. "Vom Kloster als *scola dominici servitii* zum Kloster als *servitium imperii.*" SMGBO 91 (1980) 80–97.

————. "'Siehe das Gesetz, unter dem du dienen willst.' Der geschichtliche Ort der Benediktusregel." EA 56 (1980) 427–440.

Art. "Fratello." In DIP 4 (1977) 762–794.

Frei, J. "Die Bedeutung der Benediktusregel für das geistliche Leben des Mönchs." EA 55 (1979) 247–256.

Art. "Fremder." In RAC 8 (1972) 306–347.

Art. "Friedenskuss." In RAC 8 (1972) 505–519.

Friedli, R. *Fremdheit als Heimat.* Freiburg (Switzerland), 1974.

Friedrich, F. "*Conversatio morum.* Das zweite Gelübde des Benediktinermönches." SMGBO 59 (1941/42) 200–236.

Art. "Fusswaschung." In RAC 8 (1972) 743–777.

Garrido Bonaño, M. "Fundamentos biblicos de la caridad en las reglas monásticas." *Burgense* 14 (1973) 41–106.

Art. "Gastfreundschaft." In RAC 8 (1972) 1061–1123.

Art. "Gemeinschaft." In RAC 9 (1976) 1100–1145.

Genestout, A. "Unité de composition de la Règle de S. Benoît et de la Règle du Maître d'après leur manière d'introduire les citations de l'Ecriture." *Studia Benedictina* 227–272.

Art. "Gerechtigkeit." In TRE 12 (1984) 404–448.

Gewehr, W. "Zu den Begriffen *anima* und *cor* im frühmittelalterlichen Denken." *Zeitschrift für Religions- und Geistesgeschichte* 27 (1975) 40–55.

Giet, S. *Les idées et l'action sociales de S. Basile.* Paris, 1941.

Gomez, I. "Estabilidad y dinamismo en la Regla de S. Benito." *Yermo* 19 (1981) 61–104.

————. "Los monjes y la acogida." *Yermo* 15 (1977) 143–158.

————. "La vida comunitaria en la *Regula Benedicti.*" *Yermo* 14 (1976) 305–345.

Gorce, D. "Die Gastfreundlichkeit der altchristlichen Einsiedler und Mönche." JAC 15 (1972) 66–91.

————. *Les voyages, l'hospitalité et le port des lettres dans le monde chrétien des IVe et Ve siècles.* Paris, 1925.

Greer, R. "Hospitality in the First Five Centuries of the Church." MSt (1974, 10) 29–54.

Gribomont, J. *S. Basile. Evangile et Eglise.* Mélanges, Vols. I and II. (Spiritualité orientale vols. 36–37). Bellefontaine, 1984.

————. "S. Basilio nella grande tradizione benedettina.In *S. Benedetto e l'oriente cristiano,* 11–36.

————. "Les commentaires d' A. de Vogüé et la grande tradition monastique." *Commentaria in S. Regola,* 109–143.

————. "L'influence de l'orient sur les débuts du monachism latin." In *Oriente cristiano nella storia della civiltà,* 119–128. Rome, 1964.

————. "La Règle et la Bible." In *Atti, 7° Congresso internazionale,* 355–389.

————. "Le monachisme au service de l'Eglise en Syrie et en Cappadoce." StMon 7 (1965) 7–24.

————. "*Sed et regula Patris nostri Basilii.*" *Benedictina* 27 (1980) 27–40.

Grün, A. "Benediktinische Gemeinschaft—Modell für christliches Zusammen-leben." GuL 56 (1983) 243–252.

————. "Die geistliche Botschaft des hl. Benedikt heute." EA 55 (1979) 167–177.

Guillaumont, A. *Aux origines du monachisme chrétien.* (Spiritualité Orientale 30). Bellefontaine, 1979.

————. "Le sens des noms du coeur dans l'"Antiquité." *Coeur. Etudes Carmélites* 41–81.

Guy, J. C. "La place du *contemptus mundi* dans le monachism ancien." RAM 41 (1965) 237–249.

Hacia una relectura de la Regla de S. Benito. (StSil 6) Silos, 1980.

Hagemeyer, O. "Die Entstehung der Regel Benedikts und ihre Geschichte." EA 53 (1977) 271–282.

————. "Gemeinschaft mit Gott und den Menschen. Biblische Aspekte zur Be-gründung und Vertiefung des Leitbildes der Gemeinschaft in der *Regula Bene-dicti* und im frühen Mönchtum." RBS 2 (1973) 49–88.

Hallinger, K. "Benedikt von Monte Cassino. Sein Aufstieg zur Geschichte, zu Kult und Verehrung." RBS 10/11 (1984) 77–89.

————. "Papst Gregor der Grosse und der hl. Benedikt." In *Commentationes in Regulam,* 231–207.

Hanslik, R. "Zur Sprache der *Regula Benedicti* und der *Regula Magistri.*" RBS 1 (1972) 195–207.

Happle, B. "Die Professordnung des 58. Kapitels der Benediktinerregel." EA 31 (1955) 9–22, 101–116.

Harl, M. *La chaîne palestinienne.* (SC 189) Paris, 1972.

Hausherr, I. "Pour comprendre l'orient chrétien. La primauté du spirituel." Or-ChrP 33 (1967) 351–369.

————. "*Opus Dei.*" OrChrP 13 (1947) 195–218. ("*Opus Dei.*" MSt [1975, 11] 181–204).

Henry, A. M. "Mönchtum und Mission." EA 38 (1962) 372–383.

Herausforderung der Mönche. Ed. G. Braulik. Freiburg, 1979.

Herwegen, I. *Geschichte der benediktinischen Professformel.* Münster, 1912.

————. *Sinn und Geist der Benediktinerregel.* Einsiedeln, 1944.

Heufelder, E. *Weite des Herzens. Meditationen über den Geist der Benediktusregel.* Ratisbon, 1971.

Hickey, P. "The Theology of Community in the Rule of S. Benedict." ABR 20 (1969) 431–471.

Hinson Glenn, E. *The Evangelization of the Roman Empire.* Macon (USA), 1981.

Hök, G. "Augustin und die antike Tugendlehre." *Kerygma und Dogma* 6 (1960) 104–130.

Hörger, P. "*Initium conversationis.* Die Professgelübde der *Regula Benedicti.*" In: *Benedictus, Vater,* 213–232.

Hofmeister, P. "Benediktinische Professriten." SMGBO 74 (1963) 241–285.

————. "Mönchtum und Seelsorge bis zum 13. Jahrhundert." SMGBO 65 (1953/54) 209–273.

Holzherr, G. *Die Benediktsregel. Eine Anleitung zu christlichem Leben.* Einsiedeln, 1980.

Art. "Homéliaires." In DS 7 (1969/71) 597–617.

Hoppenbrouwers, H. "*Conversatio.* Une étude sémasiologique." In: *Graecitas et latinitas Christianorum primaeva.* Suppl. fasc. I. 45–95. Nijmwegen, 1964.

Art. "Hospitalité." In DS 7 (1969/71) 808–831.

Hübner, R. "*Rubor confusionis* (RB 73.7). Die bleibende Herausforderung des Basilius von Caesarea für Mönchtum und Kirche." EA 55 (1979) 327–343.

Huerre, D. "Über die Beständigkeit." MonInf (1984, 40) 15–20.

———. "Le moine, l'hôte et Dieu." LL (1971, 149) 10–14 ("The Monk, the Guest and God." MSt [1974, 10] 49–54).

Jaeger, H. "The Patristic Conception of Wisdom in the Light of Biblical and Rabbinical Research." TU 79 (1961) 90–106.

Jaspert, B. "Benedikt von Nursia als Prediger des Evangeliums." EA 55 (1979) 257–270.

———. "Benedikt von Nursia—der Vater des Abendlandes?" EA 49 (1973) 90–104, 190–207.

———. "Die *Regula Benedicti—Regula Magistri*-Kontroverse." SupplRBS 3. Hildesheim, 1975.

———. *Studien zum Mönchtum.* SupplRSB 7. Hildesheim, 1982.

Jean Chrysostome et Augustin. Ed. C. Kannengiesser. (Théologie historique 35) Paris, 1975.

Justice, C. "Evolution of the Teaching on Commitment by Monastic Vow from New Testament Times to the 9th Century." CS 12 (1977) 18–40.

Kardong, T. "Benedict's Peaceable Kingdom." *Benedictines* 37:2 (1982/83) 28–37, 44.

———. "*Iustitia* in the Rule of Benedict." StMon 24 (1982) 43–73.

———. "To Receive All as Christ." CS 19 (1984) 195–207.

Kasch. E. *Das liturgische Vokabular der frühen lateinischen Mönchsregeln.* SupplRBS 2. Hildesheim, 1974.

Kay, R. "Benedict, Justinian and Donationes *mortis causa* in the *Regula Magistri*." RBén 90 (1980) 169–193.

Keating, T. "The Two Streams of Cenobitic Tradition in the Rule of S. Benedict." CS 11 (1976) 257–268.

Kemmer, A. "Christus in der Regel St. Benedikts." *Commentationes in Regulam,* 1–24.

Kinisch, D. "The Vow of Stability." ABR 18 (1963) 5–14, 33–39.

Kirchengeschichte als Missionsgeschichte. Ed. H. Frohnes and others. Vols. I and II. Munich, 1974, 1978.

Kleiner, S. *Dieu premier servi.* Paris, 1974.

Knowles, D. *Christian Monasticism.* St. Leo, FL: Abbey Press 1962; London: 1969.

———. *From Pachomius to Ignatius. A Study on the Constitutional History of the Religious Orders.* Oxford, 1966.

Kötting, B. *Peregrinatio Religiosa. Wallfahrten in der Antike und das Pilgerwesen in der Alten Kirche.* Münster, 1950.

Art. "Koinonia." In DS 8 (1974) 1743–1769.

Kraus, M. "Seht, in seiner Güte zeigt uns der Herr den Weg zum Leben." *Bibel und Liturgie* 57 (1984) 195–199.

Kruse, B. "Nichts der Liebe zu Christus vorziehen." *Cisterzienser Chronik* [Mehrerau] 79 (1962) 39–42, 82–97.

Kuhn, H. *Liebe: Geschichte eines Begriffs.* Munich, 1975.

Lambot, D. "L'influence de S. Augustin sur la Règle de S. Benoît." *Revue liturgique et monastique* 14 (1929) 320–330.

Lecisotti, T. "La venuta di S. Benedetto a Monte Cassino." In *Atti 7° Congresso internazionale,* 685–696.

Leclercq, J. "The Definite Character of Religious Commitment." ABR 23 (1972) 181–205.

———. "Beobachtungen zur Regel des hl. Benediktus: Ein Bericht über Werke von A. de Vogüé." EA 52 (1976) 414–431; 53 (1977) 19–31, 115–122.

———. "Evangile et culture dans la tradition bénédictine." NRTh 104 (1972) 171–182.

———. "La liberté bénédictine." In *Atti 7° Congresso internazionale,* 775–788 ("Benedictine Freedom." CS 16 [1981] 267–279).

———. *Moines et moniales ont-ils un avenir?* Brussels, 1971.

———. "Monachisme chrétien et mission." BullAIM (1979, 26) 9–26 ("Christian Monasticism and Mission." In the AIM Bulletin's English edition [1979, 26] 9–26).

———. "Monastic Profession and the Sacraments." MSt (1968, 5) 59–85.

———. "Prière monastique et accueil." CollCist 33 (1971) 379–400 ("Hospitality and Monastic Prayer." CS 8 [1973] 3–24.)

———. "The Problem of Social Class and Christology in S. Benedict." WSp 2 (1981) 33–51 (Spanish: "El problema de las clases sociales y la cristologia en S. Benito." Cuad Mon 16 [1981] 205–218.)

———. "Profession according to the Rule of S. Benedict." CS 5 (1970) 252–277.

———. "Professione religiosa secondo battesimo." *Vita Religiosa* [Rome] 3 (1967) 3–8.

———. "Le renouveau solesmien et le renouveau religieux du XIXe siècle." StMon 18 (1976) 157–195.

———. *Aux sources de la spiritualité occidentale.* Paris, 1964.

Art. "Lectio divina et lecture spirituelle." In DS 9 (1976) 470–510.

Ledoyen, H. "S. Basile dans la tradition monastique occidentale." *Irénikon* 53 (1980) 30–45.

———. "La Règle de S. Benoît dans la législation monastique." In *Atti 7° Congresso internazionale,* 391–407.

Leloir, L. "La lecture de l'Ecriture selon les anciens Pères." RAM 47 (1971) 183–200.

———. "La prière des Pères d'après les collections arméniennes des Apophtègmes." In *Mélanges liturgiques offerts au R.P.D. Bernard Botte* 311–326. Louvain, 1972.

———. "Témoignage monastique et présence au monde." NRTh 98 (1966) 673–692 ("Monastic Witness and Presence in the World." CS 3 [1968] 56–76).

Lentini, A. *S. Benedetto. La Regola.* Monte Cassino, ²1980.

———. "Il monastero-famiglia, creazione di S. Benedetto." *Monastica* II, 277–282.

———. "Il ritmo prosaico nella Regola di S. Benedetto." (Miscellanea Cassinese 23) Monte Cassino, 1942.

Leroy, J. "Le cénobitisme chez Cassien." RAM 43 (1967) 121–158.

———. "Expérience de Dieu et cénobitisme primitif." In *Expérience de Dieu dans la vie monastique*, 111–130. S. Léger Vauban, 1973. ("Experience of God and Promitive Cenobitism." MSt [1972, 9] 59–82).

Lienhard, J. T. "S. Basil's *Asceticon Parvum* and the RB." StMon 22 (1980) 231–242.

———. "The Study of the Sources of the *Regula Benedicti*: History and Method." ABR 31 (1980) 20–38.

Linage Conde, A. "La *Regula Benedicti*, re-creación *cum amore* de la *Regola Magistri*." In *Hacia una relectura*, 211–229.

Linderbauer, B. *S. Benedicti Regula Monachorum*. Metten, 1922.

Lohse, B. *Askese und Mönchtum in der Antike und in der alten Kirche*. Munich, 1969.

Lorenzi, L. de. "Il Cristo 'Signore' nella vita del monaco." In *S. Benedetto, Benedictina* 363–406.

Lorié, L. Th. A. *Spiritual Terminology in the Latin Translations of the Vita Antonii with Reference to the Fourth and Fifth Century Monastic Literature*. Nijmwegen, 1955.

Lottin, D. "A propos du voeu de *conversatione morum* chez S. Benoît." *Recherches de Théologie ancienne et médiévale* 28 (1961) 154–160.

———. "Le voeu de *conversatione morum* dans la RB." *Recherches de Théologie ancienne et médiévale* 26 (1959) 5–16.

Luiselli, B. "La società dell'Italia romano-gotica." In *Atti 7° Congresso internazionale*, 49–116.

Luislampe, P. "Aspekte einer Theologie der Gemeinschaft in der *Regula Benedicti* im Licht der Basilius-Regeln." RBS 8/9 (1982) 35–50.

Manning, E. "L'*Admonitio S. Basilii ad filium spiritualem* et la Règle de S. Benoît." RAM 42 (1966) 475–479.

———. "Une catéchèse baptismale devient Prologue de la Règle du Maître." *Revue Mabillon* 52 (1962) 61–73.

———. "Le chapitre 73 de la Règle bénédictine est-il de S. Benoît?" *Archivum latinitatis medii aevi* [Brussels] 30 (1960) 129–141.

———. "Correction fraternelle dans la Règle et mentalité contemporaine." LL (1977, 182) 25–30.

———. "L'étude de la *Regula S. Benedicti* dans la perspective du centenaire de 1980." CollCist 41 (1979) 146–154.

———. "L'importance du chapitre 72 de la Règle de S. Benoît." RBS 5 (1976) 285–288.

———. "Observations sur la présence de la Règle du Maître à Subiaco." *Recherches de Théologie ancienne et médiévale* (1966) 338–341.

———. "Problèmes d'exégèse de la Règle de S. Benoît." In *Homenaje a Fray Justo Pérez de Urbel* (StudSil 4), II, 321–330. Silos, 1977.

———. "A propos de la tradition manuscrite de la Règle bénédictine." RBS 10/11 (1984) 47–49.

———. "La signification de *militare—militia—miles* dans la Règle de S. Benoît." RBén 72 (1962) 135–138.

Mara, M. G. "Annuncio evangelico e istanze sociali nel IV secolo." AugR 17 (1977) 7–24.

Margaret, M. "Evolution of the Teaching on Commitment by Monastic Vows." CS 12 (1977) 41–66.

Marrion, M. "Toward a Christology of the Prolog of the Rule of St. Benedict." CS 15 (1980) 256–264; 16 (1981) 3–11, 127–145.

Marrou, H. J. "*Doctrina* et *disciplina* dans la langue des Pères de l'Eglise." *Archivum latinitais medii* aevi 9 (1934) 5–25.

Marsili, S. "L'ultimo capitolo della Regola di S. Benedetto alla luce di Cassiano." In *Pax* (Sorrento) (1934, 11) 17–21; (12) 18–22.

Marty, J. "Sur le devoir de l'hospitalité aux trois premiers siècles." *Revue d'histoire et de philosophie religiueses* 19 (1939) 288–295.

Masai, F. and E. Manning. "Les états du chapitre Ier du Maître et la fin du prologue de la Règle bénédictine." SC 23 (1969) 393–433.

McMurry. J. "On Being 'at home': Reflections on Monastic Stability in the Light of the Philosophy of Gabriel Marcel." MSt (1966, 4) 81–88.

Mélanges bénédictines. S. Wandrille, 1947.

Mélanges offerts à Mlle Mohrmann. Utrecht, 1963.

Ménager, A. "L'expression *sapientiae doctrina* chez S. Benoît." VSSuppl 59 (1939) 80–108, 181–191.

Le mépris du monde: La notion de mépris du monde dans la tradition spirituelle occidentale. Paris, 1965.

Merendino, C. "Persone e comunità nella Regola Benedettina." RiAsc 32 (1963) 125–135.

Metzinger, A. "La comunidad y los ideales comunitários en la Regla de S. Benito." Cuad Mon 4 (1969) 56–85.

Art. "Militia, milito." In TLL 7 (1966) 956–971.

Art. "Milizia." In DIP 5 (1978) 1319–1323.

Miquel, P. "L'oeil et l'oreille." LL (1984, 228) 3–19.

———. "De la stabilité." CollCist 36 (1974) 313–322.

———. *La vie monastique selon S. Benoît.* Paris, 1979.

Miscault. E. de. "Séparation du monde et accueil." CollCist 33 (1971) 329–343 ("Separation from the World and Reception of Guests." CS 8 [1973] 141–156).

Misonne, D. "La restauration monastique du XIXe siècle." RBén 83 (1973) 33–48.

Mohrmann, C. "La langue de S. Benoît." In: Mohrmann, C. *Etudes sur le latin des chrétiens.* Vol. II: *Latin chrétien et médiéval,* 325–345. Rome, 1961.

———. "La latinité de S. Benoît." RBén 62 (1952) 108–139.

Molitor, R. "Von der Mönchsweihe in der lateinischen Kirche." *Theologie und Glaube* [Paderborn] 16 (1924) 584–612.

Art. "Monachisme." In DS 10 (1980) 1524–1617.

Monastica, Vol. II. Miscellanea Cassinese 44. Monte Cassino, 1984.

Le monde latin et la Bible. Ed. J. Fontaine and C. Piétré. Bible de tous les temps 2. Paris, 1985.

Art. "Mondo." In DIP 6 (1980) 53–67.

Moral, T. "La estabilidad benedictina: fuentes, doctrina, proyección actual." In *Hacia una relectura,* 325–358.

Nagel, D. von. "St. Benedikt: Meister des geistlichen Lebens." EA 57 (1981) 28–38.

Nasalli Rocca, E. *Il diritto ospedaliero nei suoi lineamenti storici*. Milan, 1956.

Nash, C. "Conversation of Manners." CS 12 (1977) 109–120.

Neunheuser, B. "Mönchsgelübde als zweite Taufe und unser theologisches Gewissen." LuM 33/34 (1963/64) 63–69.

Nouwen, H.J.M. "Hospitality." MSt (1974, 10) 1–28.

————. "The Poverty of a Host." MSt (1974, 10) 65–70.

————. *Reaching Out: The Three Movements of the Spiritual Life*. New York: Doubleday, 1975.

Ohligslager, M. "De-Hellenization of Monastic Life." ABR 18 (1967) 517–530.

Oppen, D. von. "Der benediktinische Abt und das technische Zeitalter." RBS 2 (1973) 99–115.

Oppenheim, P. *Das Mönchskleid im christlichen Altertum*. Freiburg, 1931.

————. "Mönchsweihe und Taufritus." In Miscellanea Mohlberg, I, 259–282. Rome, 1984.

————. *Symbolik und religiöse Wertung des Mönchskleides im christlichen Altertum*. Münster, 1932.

Art. "Ospitalità." In DIP 6 (1980) 1014–1021.

Otten, R. T. "*Amor, caritas* and *dilectio*: Some Observations on the Vocabulary of Love in the Exegetical Works of S. Ambrose." In *Mélanges Mohrmann* 73–78.

Pantoni, A. *L'acropoli di Monte Cassino e il primitivo monastero di S. Benedetto*. Miscellanea Cassinese 43. Monte Cassino, 1980.

Parys, M. van. "L'accès à l'orient monastique chez S. Benoît." *Irénikon* 47 (1974) 48–58.

Pascher, J. "*Servitus religiosa* seit Augustinus." In *Festschrift E. Eichmann*, 335–352. Paderborn, 1940.

Pascual, A. "La *conversatio morum* benedictina: Sentido y actualidad de este voto." In *Hacia una relectura*, 309–324.

Pawlowski, S. *Die biblischen Grundlagen der Regula Benedicti*. Vienna, 1965.

Penco, G. "*Amore Deum timeant*: Sull'interpunzione di *Regola Benedicti*. chap. 72.9." RBén 64 (1954) 273–277.

————. "La composizione sociale delle comunitá monastiche nei primi secoli." StMon 4 (1962) 257–283.

————. "Il concetto di monaco e di vita monastica in occidente nel secolo VI." StMon 1 (1959) 7–50.

————. "Sul concetto del monastero come *schola*." CollCist 32 (1970) 329–333.

————. "L'ideale monastico nella vita della Chiesa." VitaMon 18 (1964) 6–18, 63–70.

————. "Il monachesimo nel passaggio dal mondo antico a quello medievale." In *S Benedetto. Benedictina*, 46–64.

————. "Sulla professione monastica come secondo battesimo." RiLi 47 (1960) 34–39.

————. "La Regola e le Regole." VitaMon 15 (1960) 81–90.

————. "Ricerche sul capitolo finale della Regola di S. Benedetto." In *Benedictina* 8 (1954) 25–42.

————. *Storia della Chiesa in Italia*. Vol I: *Dalle origini al concilio di Trento*. Milan, 1978.

————. *Storia del monachesimo in Italia.* Rome, 1961.

————. "La vocazione di Abramo nella spiritualità monastica." RiAsc 8 (1963) 148–160.

Pennington, B. "Vocational Discernment in the Rule of St. Benedict." WSp 2 (1981) 52–58.

Art. "Peregrinatio." In DIP 6 (1980) 1424–1436.

Art. "Pères de l'Eglise." In DTC 12 (1933) 1192–1215.

Art. "Perfezione." In DIP 6 (1980) 1438–1518.

Pétré, H. *Caritas: Etude sur le vocabulaire de la charité chrétienne.* Louvain, 1948.

Philoxenia. Ed. A. Kallis. Festschrift für B. Kötting. Münster, 1980.

Picasso, G. "Il rinovamento delle Costituzioni nella storia," A: "Dalle Regole alla Regola nel medievo monastico." *Informationes SCRIS* 9 (1983) 13–27.

Pignedoli, S. "The Importance of Benedictines in the Mission Field." CS 6 (1971) 119–124.

Pricoco, S. *L'isola dei Santi: Il cenobio di Lerino e le origini del monachesimo gallico.* Rome, 1978.

Prinz, F. *Frühes Mönchtum in Frankreich.* Munich, 1965.

————. "Italien, Gallien und das frühe Merowingerreich: Ein Strukturvergleich zweier monastischer Landschaften." In: *Atti del 7⁰ Congresso internazionale,* 113–136.

Art. "Professione." In DIP 7 (1983) 884–971.

Problemi e orientamenti di spiritualità monastica, biblica e liturgica. Ed. C. Vagaggini. Rome, 1961.

Puzicha, M. *Christus peregrinus: Die Fremdenaufnahme (Mt 25:35) als Werk der privaten Wohltätigkeit im Urteil der Alten Kirche.* Münstersche Beiträge zur Theologie 47. Münster, 1979.

————. "Gastfreundschaft: Zum Verständnis von RB 53." EA 58 (1982) 33–46.

Raffin, P. *Les rituels orientaux de la profession monastique.* Spiritualité orientale 4. Bellefontaine, 1969.

Ranke-Heinemann, U. "Die Gottesliebe als ein Motiv für die Entstehung des Mönchtums." *Münchner theologische Zeitschrift* 8 (1957) 289–294.

————. "Zum Motiv der Nachfolge im frühen Mönchtum." EA 36 (1960) 335–347.

————. "Das Verhältnis des frühen Mönchtums zur Welt." *Münchner theologische Zeitschrift* 7 (1956) 289–296.

————. "Zum Vollkommenheitsideal im frühen Mönchtum." EA 35 (1959) 109–121.

Reetz, B. "Das Wort zur Regel: Der Prolog." EA 35 (1959) 131–134, 224–227, 327–330, 387–392, 478–481; 36 (1960) 454–459; 37 (1961) 29–35.

Art. "Regola." In DIP 7 (1983) 1410–1452.

Regula Magistri—Regula S. Benedicti. Ed. B. Steidle. StA 44. Rome, 1959.

Renner, F. "Die Stilformen der Benediktusregel." *Benediktus, Vater,* 375–396.

Resch, P. *La doctrine ascétique des premiers maîtres égyptiens du 4ᵉ siècle.* Paris, 1931.

Riddle, D. W. "Early Christian Hospitality: A Factor in the Gospel-Transmission." JBL 57 (1938) 141–154.

Roberts, A. *Hacia Cristo: La profesión monástica hoy.* Buenos Aires 1978 (*Centered on Christ: An Introduction to Monastic Profession.* St. Bede, 1979).

————. "'Der Liebe Christi nichts vorziehen': Die Keuschheit im monastischen Leben heute." EA 54 (1978) 23–46.

————. "Méthodes spirituelles dans la vie bénédictine hier et aujourd'hui." Coll-Cist 38 (1976) 106–133.

————. "Le sens du voeu de stabilité." CollCist 33 (1971) 257–269 ("The Meaning of the Vow of Stability." CS 7 [1972] 256–269).

Rochais, H. and E. Manning. *La Règle de S. Benoît*. Rochefort, 1980.

Roeltger, G. "Benedictine Missionary Method." *Social Justice Review* 43 (1950) 149–153.

Roth, A. "Ursprung der *Regula Magistri*: Die Kontroverse zwischen M. Masai und A. de Vogüé." EA 60 (1984) 119–127.

Rothenhäusler, M. *Zur Aufnahmeordnung der Regula S. Benedicti*. Münster, 1912.

————. "Der hl. Basilius der Grosse und die hl. Profess." BM 4 (1922) 280–289.

————. "Unter dem Geheimnis des Kreuzes: Die klösterliche Profess bei Cassian." BM 5 (1923) 91–96.

————. "*Honestas morum*: Eine Untersuchung zu cap. 73.3 der *Regula S. Benedicti*." *Studia Benedictina*, 127–156.

————. "Kirche und Kloster: Der Brief des hl. Clemens von Rom und die Regel des hl. Benediktus." BM 25 (1949) 378–380.

Rousseau, O. "The Common Life in the Religious State from Its Beginning to the Twelfth Century." In: *Communal Life*, 15–29. London, 1957.

————. "Le Christ et l'autel: Notes patristiques." LMD (1959, 29) 32–59.

Rousselet, J. "Un modèle, un port?" LL (1972, 156) 30–38.

Roy, O. du. *Moines aujourd'hui: Une expérience de réforme institutionnelle*. Paris, 1972.

————. "Questions posées à la communauté chrétienne aujourd'hui." CollCist 33 (1971) 297–315.

Rudmann, R. *Mönchtum und kirchlicher Dienst in den Schriften Gregors des Grossen*. St. Ottilien, 1956.

Rule and Life. Ed. B. Pennington. Cistercian Publications 12. Spencer, 1971.

Ruppert, F. " *Meditatio–Ruminatio*: Zu einem Grundbegriff christlicher Meditation." EA 53 (1977) 83–93.

————. *Das pachomianische Mönchtum und die Anfänge des klösterlichen Gehorsams*. Münsterschwarzach, 1971.

————, and A. Grün. *Christus im Bruder*. Münsterschwarzach, 1979.

Rusche, H. *Gastfreundschaft in der Verkündigung des Neuen Testamentes und ihr Verhältnis zur Mission*. Münster, 1958.

Russel, R. "The Good Zeal of S. Benedict." DR 79 (1961) 30–45.

Saint Benoît, Sr. "La réception des hôtes dans la Règle de S. Benoît." CollCist 42 (1980) 336–346.

Sainte-Marie, E. de. "*Si revera Deum quaerit. . . .*" VitaMon 10 (1956) 173–177.

————. "Le vocabulaire de la charité dans la Règle de S. Benoît." In: *Mélanges Mohrmann*, 112–120.

Schäfer, T. *Die Fusswaschung im monastischen Brauchtum und in der lateinischen Liturgie*. Beuron, 1956.

Schildenberger, J. "Sankt Benedikt und die Hl. Schrift." EA 56 (1980) 449–457.

Schmeing, C. "Der Mensch zwischen unterwegs und zu Hause: Schöpferische Polaritäten im Sinne Benedikts." EA 56 (1980) 464–476.

Schmidt, M. W. "Christus in den Menschen finden." EA 60 (1984) 456–466.

Schmiedeler, E. "The Benedictine Family Analogy." ABR 2 (1951) 307–334.

Schoenen, A. "*Aedificatio*: Zum Verständnis eines Glaubenswortes in Kult und Schrift." In: *Enkainia*, 14–29.

Schütz, C. "Benediktinisches Gemeinschaftsleben." EA 53 (1977) 5–14.

Schuler, T. "*Regula nil impossibile dicit*: Regeltreue und Regelabweichung bei den karolingischen Benediktinern." RBS 10/11 (1984) 51–67.

Schuster, I. *Storia di S. Benedetto e dei suoi tempi.* Viboldone, 1953.

Seasoltz, K. "Monastic Hospitality." ABR 25 (1974) 427–459.

Seesemann, H. *Der Begriff Koinonia im Neuen Testament.* Giessen, 1933.

Seilhac, L. de. *L'utilisation par S. Césaire d'Arles de la Règle de S. Augustin.* StA 62. Rome, 1974.

———. "Tâches de l'évangélisation et unité de la vie monastique." BullAIM (1978) 24, 7–23 ("The Work of Evangelization and the Unity of Monastic Life." Engl. Edition 1978, 24, 7–21).

La séparation du monde. Paris, 1961.

Serna González, C. de la. "*Honore invicem praevenientes*: La importancia del orden y las relaciones fraternas en la vida cenobítica según RB." In: *Comunidad cristiana*, 131–159.

Severus, E. von. *Fremde beherbergen.* Colmar, n.d.

———. *Gemeinde für die Kirche.* Münster, 1981.

———. "Ein Hörender ruft zum Hören: Elemente benediktinischer Spiritualität." GuL 53 (1980) 244–254.

———. "Eine Mönchsregel als theologische Aussage." EA 59 (1983) 181–191.

———. "Das *Monasterium* als Kirche." In: *Enkainia*, 230–248.

———. "Theologische Elemente der *Regula Benedicti* und theologische Grundtendenzen der Gegenwart." RBS 1 (1972) 233–242.

Sipe, R. "The Psychological Dimensions of the Rule of S. Benedict." ABR 34 (1983) 424–435.

Sorci, P. "Per una teologia dell'altare." In: *Gli Spazi della celebrazione rituale*, 63–87. Milan, 1984.

Spicq, C. *Vie chrétienne et pérégrination selon le Nouveau Testament.* Lectio divina 71. Paris, 1972.

———. *Théologie morale du Nouveau Testament.* Paris, 1965.

Špidlik, T. *La spiritualité de l'orient chrétien.* Orientalia Christiana Analecta 206. Rome, 1978.

Stebler, V. *Die Regel des hl. Benedikt als Norm beschaulichen Lebens.* Olten, 1947.

Steidle, B. "St. Benedikts Kritik am zeitgenössischen Mönchtum." LuM 43 (1966) 20–30.

———. "*De conversatione morum suorum*: Zum philologischen Verständnis von *Regula S. Benedicti*, cap. 58.17." In: *Regula Magistri—RB*, 136–144.

———. "*Dominici schola servitii*: Zum Verständnis des Prologes der Regel St. Benedikts." EA 28 (1952) 397–406.

————. "Der *Genetivus epexegeticus* in der Regel des hl. Benedikt." StMon 2 (1960) 193–203.

————. "Der 'gute Eifer' in der Regel St. Benedikts. (Kap. 72)." EA 37 (1961) 101–115.

————. "*Per oboedientiae laborem . . . per inoboedientiae desidiam*: Zu Prolog 2 der Regel St. Benedikts." EA 53 (1977) 428–435; 54 (1978) 200–216, 280–285.

————. "*Parrhesia–praesumptio* in der Klosterregel St. Benedikts." In: *Zeugnis des Geistes*, 44–61. BM Beiheft, 1947.

————. *Die Regel Benedikts*. Beuron, 2/1952 (*The Rule of St. Benedict: An Introduction, a New Translation and a Commentary*. Trans. U. Schnitzhofer. Canon City, CO, 1967).

————. "Das Versprechen der 'Beständigkeit,' des 'Tugend-Wandels' und des 'Gehorsams' in der Regel St. Benedikts." EA 36 (1960) 105–122.

Stolz, A. *L'ascèse chrétienne*. Chevetogne, 1948.

Studia Benedictina in memoriam gloriosi ante saecula XIV transitus S. P. Benedicti (StA 18/19). Rome, 1947.

Sullivan, K. "A Scripture Scholar Looks at the Rule of St. Benedict." In: *Rule and Life*, 65–76.

Tamburrino, P. "L'incidenza delle correnti spirituali dell'oriente sulla *Regula Benedicti*." In: *S. Benedetto, Benedictina*, 97–150.

————. "*Koinonia*: Die Beziehung 'Monasterium'–'Kirche' im frühen pachomianischen Mönchtum." EA 43 (1967) 5–21.

————. "La *Regula Benedicti* e gli scritti pacomiani." In: *S. Benedetto e l'oriente cristiano*, 37–72.

1500 Jahre St. Benedikt—Patron Europas. Ed. J. Neuhardt. Graz, 1980.

Théologie de la vie monastique. Théologie 49. Aubier, 1961.

Thiry, L. "Individu et societé dans la Règle de S. Benoît." In: *Mélanges bénédictins*, 115–141.

Tillard, J.M.R. "La communauté religieuse." NRTh 104 (1972) 488–519; 105 (1973) 150–187.

Torre, J. M. de la. "El *hapax legomenon 'ausculta'* (Prol) y una relectura teológico-espiritual de la RB." In: *Hacia una relectura*, 69–87.

Tribelli, M. "L'ospitalità benedettina: Punto d'incontro tra il monastero e il mondo." *L'ulivo* 10 (1980) 3, 41–48.

Tunink, W. *Vision of Peace*. New York: Farrar Strauss, 1963.

Turbessi, G. *Ascetismo e monachesimo in S. Benedetto*. Rome, 1965

————. *Cercare Dio nell' ebraismo, nel mondo greco, nella patristica*. Rome, 1980.

————. "*Quaerere Deum*: Il tema della 'ricerca di Dio' nella S. Scrittura." RiBi 10 (1962) 282–296.

————. "La Regola di S. Benedetto nel contesto delle antiche regole monastiche." RBS 1 (1972) 57–90.

Vaccari, A. "La Bibbia nell'ambiente di S. Benedetto." Bibl 29 (1948) 321–344.

Vagaggini, C. "La posizione di S. Benedetto nella questione semipelagiana." In: *Studia Benedictina*, 17–83.

Vandenbroucke, F. "La profession, second baptême." VS 71 (1947) 250–263.

Veilleux, A. "Creativeness and Fidelity to Tradition." CS 3 (1968) 98–103.

———. "De l'interprétation d'une règle monastique." CollCist 31 (1969) 195–209 ("The Interpretation of a Monastic Rule." CS 5 [1970] 48–65).

———. "Le rôle de la sous-culture monastique dans la formation du moine." NRTh 110 (1978) 734–749.

———. "La théologie de l'abbatiat cénobitique et ses implications liturgiques." VSSuppl 21 (1968) 351–393 ("The Abbatial Office in Cenobitic Life." MSt [1968, 6] 1–45).

Verheijen, L. *Nouvelle approche de la Règle de S. Augustin.* Vie Monastique 8. Bellefontaine, 1980.

———. *La Règle de S. Augustin.* 2 vols. Paris, 1967.

———. "Spiritualité et vie monastique chez S. Augustin: L'utilisation monastique des Actes des Apôtres 4:32-35." In: *Jean Chrysostome et Augustin,* 93–123.

Vigolo, G. da. "*Hanc minimam inchoationis*: Note per un commento al cap. 73." *Vita cristiana* 17 (1948) 161–173.

Viller, M. *La spiritualité des premiers siècles chrétiens.* Paris, 1930.

Vir Dei Benedictus. Festgabe zum 1400. Todestag des hl. Benedikt. Münster, 1947.

Vita Comunitaria (Claretianum). Milan, 1979.

Vogüé, A. de. *Autour de S. Benoît.* Vie monastique 4. Bellefontaine, 1975.

———. "Benedikt heute." EA 55 (1979) 81–95 ("S. Benoît aujourd'hui." NRTh 110 [1978] 720–733).

———. "S. Benoît et son temps: Règles italiennes et Règles provençales au VIe siècle." RBS 1 (1972) 169–193.

———. *S. Benoît, sa vie et sa règle: Etudes choisies.* Vie monastique 12. Bellefontaine, 1981.

———. "Cassien, le Maître et S. Benoît." In: *Commandements du Seigneur . . . ,* 223–235.

———. "The Cenobitic Rules of the West." CS 12 (1977) 175–183.

———. *La communauté et l'abbé dans la Règle de S. Benoît.* Bruges, 1961 (*Community and Abbot in the Rule of Saint Benedict.* Cistercian Studies 5/1, 5/2. Kalamazoo, MI: Cistercian, 1978, 1985).

———. "Les deux fonctions de la méditation dans les Règles monastiques anciennes." RHSp 51 (1975) 3–16.

———. "Die drei Kriterien des hl. Benedikt für die Zulassung der Novizen." EA 55 (1979) 42–50 ("Les trois critères de S. Benoît pour l'admission des novices." CollCist 40 [1978] 128–138).

———. "*Per ducatum Evangelii*: La Règle de S. Benoît et l'Evangile." CollCist 35 (1973) 186–198.

———. "L'école du Christ." CollCist 46 (1984) 1–12.

———. "Entre Basile et Benoît: L'*admonitio ad filium spiritualem* du Pseudo-Basile." RBS 10/11 (1984) 19–34.

———. "Les grandes Règles de S. Basile: Un survol." CollCist 41 (1979) 201–226.

———. "'Honorer tous les hommes': Le sens de l'hospitalité bénédictine." RAM 40 (1964) 129–138.

———. "Les mentions des oeuvres de Cassien chez S. Benoît et ses contemporains." StMon 20 (1978) 275–285.

————. "Le monastère: Eglise du Christ." In: *Commenationes in Regulam*, 25–46.

————. "Nouveaux aperçus sur une Règle monastique du VIe siècle." RAM 41 (1965) 19–54.

————. "Die pachomianischen Schriften." EA 58 (1962) 249–264 ("Les écrits pachômiens." CollCist 43 [1981] 20–33).

————. "La paternité du Christ dans la Règle de S. Benoît et la Règle du Maître." VS 110 (1964) 55–67 ("The Fatherhood of Christ in the Rule of S. Benedict and the Rule of the Master." MSt 1968, 5, 45–57).

————. "Persévérer au monastère jusqu'à la mort: La stabilité chez S. Benoît et autour de lui." CollCist 43 (1981) 337–365.

————. "Les recherches de François Masai sur le Maître et S. Benoît." StMon 24 (1982) 7–42, 271–309.

————. (Ed.) *La Règle de S. Benoît*. 2 vols. SC 181–182. Paris, 1972 (cited as RB Vogüé).

————. *La Règle de S. Benoît: Commentaire historique et critique*. 3 vols. SC 184–186. Paris 1971 (cited as Vogüé *IV, V, VI*).

————. *La Règle de S. Benoît: Commentaire doctrinal et spirituel*. Paris 1977 (*The Rule of Saint Benedict: A Doctrinal and Spiritual Commentary*. Trans. J. B. Hasbrouck. Cistercian Studies 54. Kalamazoo, MI: Cistercian 1983, cited as *RB-DSC*)

————. "La Règle de S. Benoît et la vie contemplative." CollCist 27 (1965) 89–107 ("The Rule of Benedict and the Contemplative Life." CS 1 [1966] 385–392).

————. "La Règle d'Eugippe et la fin du Prologue de S. Benoît." CollCist 41 (1979) 265–273.

————. (Ed.) *La Règle du Maître*. 2 vols. SC 105–106. Paris, 1964; cited as RM (Vogüé).

————. "*Sub regula vel abbate*." CollCist 33 (1971) 209–241 ("*Sub regula vel abbate*: The Theological Significance of the Ancient Monastic Rules." In: *Rule and Life*, 21–63).

————. "La rencontre de Benoît et de Scholastique." RHSp 48 (1972) 257–273.

————. "Le rituel monastique chez S. Benoît et chez le Maître." RBén 71 (1961) 236–264.

Volk. P. "Die Schriftzitate der *Regula Benedicti*." In: *Texte und Arbeiten* 15–18 (1930) (1)–(34).

Wathen. A. "*Conversatio* and Stability in the Rule of Benedict." MSt 1975, 11, 1–44.

————. "Fraternity as an Aspect of the Experience of God in the *Cenobium*." MSt (1972, 9) 123–130.

————. "The Exigencies of Benedict's Little Rule for Beginners—RB 72." ABR 29 (1978) 41–46.

————. "Methodological Considerations of the Sources of the *Regula Benedicti* as Instruments of Historical Interpretations." RBS 5 (1976) 101–118.

————. "La *Regula Benedicti* c. 73 e le *Vitae Patrum*." In: *S. Benedetto, Benedictina* 171–197 ("The *Regula Benedicti* c. 73 and the *Vitas Patrum*." CS 19 [1984] 208–231).

————. "Space and Time in the Rule of S. Benedict." CS 17 (1982) 81–98.

Weakland, R. "Community: The Monastic Tradition." ABR 26 (1975) 233–250 ("La comunidad en la tradición monastica." Cuad Mon 11 [1976] 131–143).

———. "Evangelizzazione e vita contemplative." OrLab 29 (1974) 99–108.

Weber, R. "Les chapitres des portiers dans la Règle de S. Benoît et dans celle du Maître." In: *Mélanges bénédictins,* 203–233.

Widhalm, G. M. "Die rhetorischen Elemente in der *Regula Benedicti.*" SupplRBS 2. Hildesheim, 1974.

Winandy, J. "*Conmversatio morum.*" CollCist 22 (1968) 378–386.

———. "La stabilité bénédictine: Un mot et un concept." In: *Atti del 7° Congresso internazionale,* 521–525.

Winzen, D. "Conference on the Reception of Guests." MSt (1974, 10) 55–63.

Art. "Xenos." In ThWNT 5 (1954) 1–36.

Yeo, R. *The Structure and Content of Monastic Profession.* StA 83. Rome, 1982.

Zegveld, A. "*Lectio Divina.*" EA 55 (1979) 178–292 (French translation: CollCist 41 [1979] 291–323).

———. "Que veut dire 'selon la Règle'?" CollCist 41 (1979) 155–176.

Zeiger, I. "*Professio super altare.*" In: *Miscellanea iuridica.* Analecta Greg. 8 161–185. Rome, 1935.

Art. "Zelos." In ThWNT 2 (1935) 879–890.

Zelser, K. "Zur Stellung des *Textus receptus* und des interpolierten Textes in der Textgeschichte der *Regula Benedicti.*" RBén 88 (1978) 205–246.

Zumkeller., A. *Das Mönchtum des hl Augustinus.* Würzburg, ²1968.

Index of Subjects, Authors, and Works

Index of RB References

The chapters and verses of the Prologue which are treated in a chapter of their own are only referenced in places outside this chapter.

When a chapter is mentioned as a whole, the page references appear right after the chapter number.

Index of Hebrew Scriptures: Old Testament

Index of Christian Scriptures: New Testament